COMPUTER BOOK SERIES FROM IDG

Excel For Dummies

Cheat Sheet

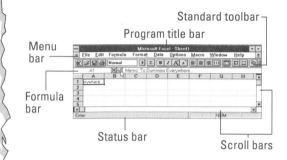

Standard Toolbar

- The Standard toolbar contains the most commonly used tools for performing routine tasks; you can click on the toolbar rather than taking the time to choose the commands on the pull-down menus. Refer to the flip side of this card for a run-down on each tool in this toolbar.

Formula Bar

- You enter and edit information for the current cell in the formula bar. The left side of the bar displays the current cell location by column and row reference. In the middle of the formula bar, the enter box inserts what's in the formula bar into the cell, and the cancel box clears the formula bar. The right side of the formula bar displays the entire cell entry.

- To edit a cell entry, you activate the formula bar by pressing F2 (⌘+U on the Mac). Alternatively, you can click the I-beam pointer exactly where you want to make the change in the text on the formula bar.

Program Title Bar

- The program title bar spells out the title of the application and the name of the active document in a full-size window. You can relocate the entire program window by dragging the program title bar.

- Click on the Control-menu box on the far left to close or resize the window, or to quit or switch programs.

- Click on the Minimize button (the small triangle pointing down) to reduce the window to an icon.

- Click on the Restore button on the far right to shrink a window or bring it back to full size.

Menu Bar

- The menu bar holds the keys to the many features available for your document. Click on one of the menu names or press Alt and then type the underlined letter of the menu you want to open. When the menu is open, you can choose a command by clicking on it or typing its underlined command letter.

Scroll Bars

- The scroll bars enable you to move quickly through a document by clicking on the scroll arrows or dragging the scroll box. Use the vertical scroll bar on the right to move the worksheet up and down. Use the horizontal scroll bar on the bottom to move the worksheet left and right.

Status Bar

- The status bar keeps you informed of the current state of the program or command. The left side of the status bar displays messages; the right side indicates various keyboard modes such as CAPS when Caps Lock is on and NUM when Num Lock is on.

IDG BOOKS

. . . For Dummies: #1 Computer Book Series for Beginners

Excel For Dummies

COMPUTER BOOK SERIES FROM IDG

For those times when you're in a hurry, here is a quick reference of tools on the Standard toolbar and some of the equivalent keyboard shortcuts. Note that some of the tools have no keyboard shortcuts.

The Standard Toolbar

Tool in Question	Tool Name	Windows Shortcut	Macintosh Shortcut
	New Worksheet	Shift + F11	Shift + F11
	Open File	Ctrl + F12	⌘ + O
	Save File	Shift + F12	⌘ + S
	Print	Ctrl + Shift + F12	⌘ + P
Normal	Style Box	Ctrl + S	⌘ + Shift + L
Σ	AutoSum	Alt + =	⌘ + Shift + T
B	Bold	Ctrl + B	⌘ + Shift + B
I	Italic	Ctrl + I	⌘ + Shift +
A	Increase Font Size		
A	Decrease Font Size		
	Left Align		
	Center Align		
	Right Align		
	Center Across Selected Columns		
	AutoFormat		
	Outline Border	Ctrl + Shift + &	⌘ + Option + 0
	Bottom Border		⌘ + Option + ↓
	Copy	Ctrl + C or Ctrl + Insert	⌘ + C
	Paste Formats		
	Chart Wizard		
▶?	Help	Shift + F1	⌘ + /

TM

COMPUTER BOOK SERIES FROM IDG

References for the Rest of Us

Are you intimidated and confused by computers? Do you find that traditional manuals are overloaded with technical details you'll never use? Do your friends and family always call you to fix simple problems on their PCs? Then the *"... For Dummies"* computer book series from IDG™ is for you.

"... For Dummies" books are written for those frustrated computer users who know they aren't really dumb but find that PC hardware, software, and indeed the unique vocabulary of computing make them feel helpless. *"... For Dummies"* books use a lighthearted approach, a down-to-earth style, and even cartoons and humorous icons to diffuse computer novices' fears and build their confidence. Lighthearted but not lightweight, these books are a perfect survival guide for anyone forced to use a computer.

> *"I liked my copy so much I told my friends; now they bought copies."*
>
> **Irene C., Orwell, Ohio**

> *"Quick, concise, nontechnical, and humorous."*
>
> **Jay A., Elburn, IL**

> *"Thanks, I needed this book. Now I can sleep at night."*
>
> **Robin F., British Columbia, Canada**

Already, hundreds of thousands of satisfied readers agree. They have made *"... For Dummies"* books the #1 introductory-level computer book series and have written asking for more. So if you're looking for the most fun and easy way to learn about computers, look to *"... For Dummies"* books to give you a helping hand.

IDG BOOKS

Hundreds of thousands of readers agree, "... For Dummies" computer books are the best:

"Love this book—constant reference piece. Helped me get over the new computer jitters!
— **Charles Ramstack, Waukesha, WI**

"Takes the pain out of DOS (it's the aspirin of computing).... Absolutely superb.... Best book yet on the subject."
— **Jerome Valentine, M.D., Tamarac, FL**

"Clear and concise.... This is a fine book, useful, honest, well produced. I certainly got my money's worth."
— **Howard M. Schott, Boston, MA**

"My new boss stuck me in front of an IBM Compatible and said it was mine now. This is the first book that makes sense."
— **Mary Gallagher, Hartford, CT**

"This is the best, readable book for survival on computers!"
— **Joann Tillberg, Virginia Beach, VA**

"It has been mentioned by [an] experienced computer owner that this book should be given out when any computer is bought.... Understandable, clear and simple wording—distinctive what-to-do and *not to do*.... Thanks many times over."
— **Georgina Strueby, Campbell River, British Columbia**

"It was my most dependable reference book. If I need help, I turn to it first and usually get the answer."
— **D. Huntsberger, Ames, IA**

"Forbidden commands! That alone made it worth the price. This book more than fulfilled its goals. Good going!"
— **Carlos DelRio, Houston, TX**

"This is the only book that I didn't fall asleep reading. All computer companies should give this book away. I thought I was a dummy; now I am only half a one."
— **Richard Cordin, Richmondville, NY**

"It's in English—not in 'computerease.'"
— **William Reimers, Ontario, CA**

"My son is a computer genius and runs his own consulting company. Since he bought me this book, I now understand what I'm doing. I work part-time in his office. You don't know how proud I am of being able to do that."
— **Jo Ann D'Auria, Buffalo Grove, IL**

More Words from the Critics

This "is a light-hearted survey of the operating system everyone loves to hate, with plenty of sugar coating on its information."
— **L.R. Shannon,** *The New York Times*

"*DOS For Dummies* delivers DOS essentials to DOS-phobics in a lively, witty, style.... The book's liberal warnings, helpful tips, reminders, and technical note sidebars greatly enhance the basic instructions."
— *Publishers Weekly* **Magazine**

"How do you become 'computer-literate' if you're not 'literate' to begin with? Answer: You find a computer instruction book that's the equivalent of the Cliff's Notes version of the DOS manual. You're holding that book in your hands."
— **Joe Bob Briggs, Nationally Syndicated Columnist & Drive-in Movie Critic**

And <u>Many Words</u> from the <u>Thousands of Satisfied Readers</u> of DOS For Dummies:

"I loved every page of it. I've been looking for a computer book like this for 6 years."
— **Anita Ramig, Racine, WI**

"First PC-related book I've been able to read cover to cover. Informative and entertaining."
— **Gerard Grenier, Potomac, MD**

"Simple and funny—you're communicating! With the masses!... If you make computers knowledgeable to everyone, then where will the gurus go?"
—**George Akob, Chesapeake, VA**

"Easy, funny book on a horrid subject.... *Great* book—within something like 10 minutes, I am now able to copy disk[s] to [the] hard drive, delete files, use software switches, use directories and other things! Great from a "Mac" point & click user!"
—**Wayne Yoshida, Huntington Beach, CA**

"Dan Gookin cuts the fat and gets to the point.... I really found his approach delightful and helpful. I will recommend it to friends and business acquaintances."
—**Vicki Kendall, Virginia Beach, VA**

TM

by **Greg Harvey**

IDG
BOOKS

IDG Books Worldwide, Inc.
An International Data Group Company
San Mateo, California 94402

Excel For Dummies

Published by
IDG Books Worldwide, Inc.
An International Data Group Company
155 Bovet Road, Suite 610
San Mateo, CA 94402
(415) 312-0650

Library of Congress Catalog Card No.: 92-74310

ISBN 1-878058-63-0

Printed in the United States of America

10 9 8 7 6 5 4 3

Distributed in the United States by IDG Books Worldwide, Inc.

Distributed in Canada by Macmillan of Canada, a Division of Canada Publishing Corporation; by Woodslane Pty. Ltd. in Australia; and by Computer Bookshops in the U.K.

For information on translations and availability in other countries, contact Marc Jeffrey Mikulich, Foreign Rights Manager, at IDG Books Worldwide. FAX (415-358-1260)

For sales inquiries and special prices for bulk quantities, write to the address above or call IDG Books Worldwide at 415-312-0650.

Dedication

In memory of my father who taught me that although there is no shame in being a "dummy," there's also no virtue in remaining one!

Acknowledgments

Let me take this opportunity to thank all of the talented people, both at IDG Books Worldwide and at Harvey & Associates whose dedication and talent combined to make this book so successful.

At IDG Books, I want to thank Terrie and David Solomon (and say hi to Sarah), Mary Bednarek, Diane Steele, Alice Martina Smith, Mary Ann Cordova, Dana Sadoff, and Chuck Hutchinson, as well as the talented designers at University Graphics.

At Harvey & Associates, many thanks to LiLi Micaela and Shane Gearing for their invaluable contributions to both the wit and substance of the book. Thanks guys, for your patience, your humor, and all your help!

(The publisher would like to give special thanks to Patrick J. McGovern, without whom this book would not have been possible.)

Credits

President and Publisher
John J. Kilcullen

Publishing Director
David Solomon

Managing Editor
Mary Bednarek

Production Director
Lana J. Olson

Acquisitions Editor
Terrie Lynn Solomon

Editors
Diane L. Steele
Alice Martina Smith
Sandra Blackthorn

Technical Reviewer
Victor R. Garza

Text Preparation
Mary Ann Cordova
Dana Bryant Sadoff

Proofreader
Charles A. Hutchinson

Indexer
Dick and Anne Bassler

Book Design and Production
Peppy White
Francette M. Ytsma
Tracy Strub
(University Graphics, Palo Alto, California)

About the Author

Greg Harvey, the author of over 30 computer books, has been training business people in the use of IBM PC, DOS, and software application programs such as WordPerfect, Lotus 1-2-3, and dBASE since 1983. He has written numerous training manuals, user guides, and books for business users of software. He currently teaches Lotus 1-2-3 and dBASE courses in the Department of Information Systems at Golden Gate University in San Francisco.

About IDG Books Worldwide

Welcome to the world of IDG Books Worldwide.

IDG Books Worldwide, Inc., is a division of International Data Group (IDG), the world's leading publisher of computer-related information and the leading global provider of information services on information technology. IDG publishes over 181 computer publications in 58 countries. Thirty million people read one or more IDG publications each month.

If you use personal computers, IDG Books is committed to publishing quality books that meet your needs. We rely on our extensive network of publications, including such leading periodicals as *InfoWorld, PC World, Computerworld, Macworld, Lotus, Publish, Network World,* and *SunWorld,* to help us make informed and timely decisions in creating useful computer books that meet your needs.

Every IDG book strives to bring extra value and skill-building instruction to the reader. Our books are written by experts, with the backing of IDG periodicals, and with careful thought devoted to issues such as audience, interior design, use of icons, and illustrations. Our editorial staff is a careful mix of high-tech journalists and experienced book people. Our close contact with the makers of computer products helps ensure accuracy and thorough coverage. Our heavy use of personal computers at every step in production means that we can deliver books in the most timely manner.

We are delivering books of high quality at competitive prices on topics customers want. At IDG, we believe in quality, and we have been delivering quality for over 25 years. You'll find no better book on a subject than an IDG book.

John Kilcullen
President and Publisher
IDG Books Worldwide, Inc.

IDG Books Worldwide, Inc. is a division of International Data Group. The officers are Patrick J. McGovern, Founder and Board Chairman; Walter Boyd, President; Robert A. Farmer, Vice Chairman. International Data Group's publications include: **ARGENTINA's** Computerworld Argentina, InfoWorld Argentina; **ASIA's** Computerworld Hong Kong, PC World Hong Kong, Computerworld Southeast Asia, PC World Singapore, Computerworld Malaysia, PC World Malaysia; **AUSTRALIA's** Computerworld Australia, Australian PC World, Australian Macworld, Profit, Information Decisions, Reseller; **AUSTRIA's** Computerwelt Oesterreich; **BRAZIL's** DataNews, PC Mundo, Mundo IBM, Mundo Unix; **BULGARIA's** Computerworld Bulgaria, Ediworld, PC World Express; **CANADA's** ComputerData, Direct Access, Graduate Computerworld, InfoCanada, Network World Canada; **CHILE's** Computerworld, Informatica; **COLUMBIA's** Computerworld Columbia; **CZECHOSLOVAKIA's** Computerworld Czechoslovakia, PC World Czechoslovakia; **DENMARK's** CAD/CAM WORLD, Communications World, Computerworld Danmark, Computerworld Focus, Computerworld Uddannelse, LAN World, Lotus World, Macintosh Produktkatalog, Macworld Danmark, PC World Danmark, PC World Produktguide, Windows World; **EQUADOR's** PC World; **EGYPT's** PC World Middle East; **FINLAND's** Mikro PC, Tietoviikko, Tietoverkko; **FRANCE's** Computer Direct, Distributique, GOLDEN MAC, InfoPC, Languages & Systems, Le Guide du Monde Informatique, Le Monde Informatique, Telecoms & Reseaux International; **GERMANY's** Computerwoche, Computerwoche Focus, Computerwoche Extra, Computerwoche Karriere, edv aspekte, Information Management, Lotus Welt, Macwelt, Netzwelt, PC Welt, PC Woche, Publish, Unit, Unix Welt; **GREECE's** Infoworld, PC Games, PC World Greece; **HUNGARY's** Computerworld SZT, Mikrovilag Magazin, PC World; **INDIA's** Computers & Communications; **ISRAEL's** Computerworld Israel, PC World Israel; **ITALY's** Computerworld Italia, Macworld Italia, Networking Italia, PC World Italia; **JAPAN's** Computerworld Japan, Macworld Japan, SunWorld Japan; **KOREA's** Computerworld Korea, Macworld Korea, PC World Korea; **MEXICO's** Compu Edicion, Compu Manufactura, Computacion/Punto de Venta, Computerworld Mexico, MacWorld, Mundo Unix, PC World, Windows; **THE NETHERLANDS'** Computer! Totaal, Computerworld Netherlands, LAN Magazine, MacWorld Magazine; **NEW ZEALAND's** Computer Listings, Computerworld New Zealand, New Zealand PC World; **NIGERIA's** PC World Africa; **NORWAY's** Computerworld Norge, C/world, Lotusworld Norge, Macworld Norge, Networld, PC World Ekspress, PC World Norge, PC World's Product Guide, Publish World, Student Guiden, Unix World, Windowsworld, IDG Direct Response; **PERU's** PC World; **PEOPLES REPUBLIC OF CHINA's** China Computerworld, PC World China, Electronics International; **IDG HIGH TECH** Newproductworld, Consumer Electronics New Product World; **PHILLIPPINES'** Computerworld, PC World; **POLAND's** Computerworld Poland, Komputer; **ROMANIA's** InfoClub Magazine; **RUSSIA's** Computerworld-Moscow, Networks, PC World; **SPAIN's** Amiga World, Autoedicion, CIM World, Communicaciones World, Computerworld Espana, Macworld Espana, PC World Espana, Publish; **SWEDEN's** Affarsekonomi Management, Attack, CAD/CAM World, ComputerSweden, Corporate Computing, Digital Varlden, Lokala Natverk/LAN, Lotus World, MAC&PC, Macworld, Mikrodatorn, PC World, Publishing & Design (CAP), Unix/Oppna system, Datalngenjoren, Maxi Data, Windows; **SWITZERLAND's** Computerworld Schweiz, Macworld Schweiz, PC & Workstation; **TAIWAN's** Computerworld Taiwan, PC World Taiwan; **THAILAND's** Thai Computerworld; **TURKEY's** Computerworld Monitor, Macworld Turkiye, PC World Turkiye; **UNITED KINGDOM's** Lotus Magazine, Macworld; **UNITED STATES'** AmigaWorld, Cable in the Classroom, CIO, Computerworld, DOS Resource Guide, Electronic News, Federal Computer Week, GamePro, inCider/A+, IDG Books, InfoWorld, InfoWorld Direct, Lotus, Macworld, MPC World, Network World, NeXTWORLD, PC Games, PC World, PC Letter, Publish, RUN, SunWorld, SWATPro; **VENEZUELA's** Computerworld Venezuela, MicroComputerworld Venezuela; **YUGOSLAVIA's** Moj Mikro.

 The text in this book is printed on recycled paper.

Contents at a Glance

· ·

Introduction 1

Part I: The Absolute Basics 9

Chapter 1: What Have You Gotten Yourself Into? 11
Chapter 2: Concocting Your First Worksheet 45

Part II: The More Things Change 69

Chapter 3: Fancying Up the Figures 71
Chapter 4: How To Make Changes without Messing Up the Entire
Worksheet 109

Part III: Ferreting Out The Information 131

Chapter 5: Keeping on Top of the Information (or How To
Avoid Losing Stuff) 133
Chapter 6: Getting the Information Down on Paper
(or Spreadsheet Printing 101) 155

Part IV: Amazing Things You Can Do with Excel (for Fun and Profit) 175

Chapter 7: A Picture Worth a Thousand Numbers 177
Chapter 8: Facts and Figures at Your Fingertips 197
Chapter 9: Coping with More Than One Document at a Time 219

Part V: Excel — Have It Your Way 237

Chapter 10: Excel Made to Order 239
Chapter 11: Tooling Around 253

Part VI: Excel Function Reference (for Real People) 267

Chapter 12: I Love Everyday Functions 269
Chapter 13: Functions for the More Adventurous 277

Part VII: The Part of Tens 291

Chapter 14: Ten Beginner Basics 293
Chapter 15: Ten Excel Commandments 295
Chapter 16: Ten Printing Pointers 297
Chapter 17: Ten Clever Customizers 299
Chapter 18: Ten Welcome Warnings 301
Chapter 19: Ten Ways To Work Smarter, Faster, and Get
    That Promotion! 303
Chapter 20: Ten Thousand (More or Less) Useful
    Keystroke Shortcuts 305

Glossary **311**

Index **319**

Reader Response Survey .... **End of Book**

Table of Contents

• •

Acknowledgments .... *vii*

Introduction *1*

Part I: The Absolute Basics *9*

Chapter 1: What Have You Gotten Yourself Into? 11
Who Put the "Work" in Worksheet? 12
    So, how big is it? 13
    Meet me at 20th and F streets 13
    Cellmates 15
    What comes after Z? 15
    So, what's this thing good for anyway? 15
Gentlemen, Start Your Spreadsheets! 16
    Bypassing Windows 18
    Opening a document when starting Excel 18
What Happens If I Press This Button 18
    The title bar 19
    The menu bar 20
    The Standard toolbar 20
    The formula bar 21
    The document window 22
    The status bar 25
Making the Mouse Less of a Drag 26
    The many faces of the mouse pointer 27
    Look at that varmint go! 28
    For south paws only! 29
Get Me Out of This Cell! 29
    Scrolling away 30
    Keystrokes for moving the pointer 31
    Moving from block to block 33
    Moving the cell pointer with Goto 34
    Keyboard scrolling without changing the cell pointer's position 34
Menurama: Pull-Down vs. Shortcut 35
    May I take your order, Ma'am? 35
    For 1-2-3 weenies only 36
    Making short work of shortcut menus 37
How To Have an Intelligent Conversation with a Dialog Box 39
Help Is On the Way 43
When It's Quitting Time 44

Chapter 2: Concocting Your First Worksheet 45

Where Do I Begin? 45

The ABCs of Data Entry 47

Is the Data Your Type? 48

    Text (neither fish nor fowl) 48

    Values to the right of me 50

    Number please! 50

    Let's make it a date! 51

    Can you fix my decimal places? 52

    Formulas equal to the task 53

    Following the pecking order 55

    When a formula freaks 56

Correcting Those Nasty Little Typos 57

Home, Home on the Range 59

When You AutoFill It Up 60

    Designer series 61

    Repeat after me 62

Becoming Fully Functional 63

    Paste without waste 63

    I really AutoSum those numbers! 65

Saving the Evidence 67

Part II: The More Things Change **69**

Chapter 3: Fancying Up the Figures **71**

Selectively Yours 72

    Cell selections à la mouse 73

    Cell selections — keyboard style 75

AutoFormat to the Rescue 77

Formats at the Click of a Tool 79

    Shuffling toolbars 80

    Floating toolbars 81

    Docking toolbars 81

    The tools on the Formatting toolbar 83

Formats for Every Value 84

    Money, money, money 86

    Too much to show 86

    Let's all remain comma 87

    Playing the percentages 88

    Decimal wheeling and dealing 88

    What you see is not always what you get 90

Number Formats Made to Order 90

If the Column Fits 92

    Rambling rows 95

    Worksheet hide n' seek 95

Oh, That's Just Fantastic! 98

Line 'Em Up 100

    Up, down, and all around 101

That's a wrap 102
Just point me in the right direction 104
I Think I'm Borderline, or The Patterns of My Cells 105
Going in Style 107

Chapter 4: How To Make Changes without Messing Up the Entire Worksheet 109
Help, My Document's Gone and I Can't Find It! 110
Now, where did I put that darn file? 111
Putting out an A.P.B. for a document 112
Please Do That Old Undo That You Do So Well 114
Redo that old Undo 114
When Undo just won't do 115
Drag Until You Drop 115
You Really AutoFill Those Formulas 119
Everything's relative 121
Dealing in absolutes 121
Pasting the Night Away 124
Copying is much better the second time around 125
Pasting particulars 126
To Clear or Delete, That Is the Question 126
Clearing the air 127
This cell range is condemned 127
Under New Construction 128
Dispelling Your Misspellings 129

Part III: Ferreting Out the Information 131

**Chapter 5: Keeping on Top of the Information
(or How To Avoid Losing Stuff) 133**
Zoom, Zoom, Zoom Went That Window 134
Tapping on My Window Panes 136
Immovable Titles on My Frozen Window Panes 138
We'll Have an Outline in the Old Town Tonight 141
Electronic Post-it Notes 145
Name That Cell 147
Finders Keepers 149
Replacement Costs 151
To Calc or Not To Calc 152
Protect Yourself! 153

**Chapter 6: Getting the Information Down on Paper
(or Spreadsheet Printing 101) 155**
Look Before You Print! 156
The page breaks automatically 159
Printing in a nutshell 159
Printing just the good parts 161
In Pursuit of the Perfect Page 161
Squeezing it all on one page 163

Orienting yourself to the landscape 163
Marginal thinking 164
My header don't know what my footer's doing 165
Entitlements 168
Give Your Page a Break! 170
Printing by Formula 172

Part IV: Amazing Things You Can Do with Excel (For Fun and Profit) 175

Chapter 7: A Picture Worth a Thousand Numbers 177
Charts as if by Magic 178
A Little Change of Chart 184
Accentuate the positive 185
Singularly unattached 188
Getting a new perspective on things 191
A Worksheet without Graphics Is Like 192
Putting one in front of the other 195
Now you see them, now you don't 195
Putting Out the Chart 195

Chapter 8: Facts and Figures at Your Fingertips 197
Data in What Form? 198
The more the merrier: adding new records 200
Finder's keepers: locating, changing, and deleting records 202
Data from A to Z (or "So, Sort Me!") 207
Going for the Record 211
Not just any criteria 212
Using Data Find 214
Excerpts from the database 215

Chapter 9: Coping with More Than One Document at a Time 219
Arranging Documents for Fun and Profit 220
Something borrowed 223
Copy a chart 224
Here Come the Worksheet Clones! 224
Modifications en masse 227
Consolidate your holdings 229
Jot This Down in Your Workbook 231
Documents unbound! 234
By any other name 234
Going to and fro 235

Part V: Excel — Have It Your Way 237

Chapter 10: Excel Made to Order 239
Holy Macros! 239
   A macro a day 241
   Play you back with interest 244
   January, February, June, and July 244
   The relative record 246
The Vision Thing 246
   Putting on a good display 247
   Maintaining your own (Work)space 248
   Colors for every palette 250

Chapter 11: Tooling Around 253
The Right Tool for the Job 253
   Musical toolbars 255
   New tools for old jobs 257
   Spaced-out tools 258
   Toolbar restoration 259
A Toolbar for Every Occasion 260
A Blank Tool Is a Terrible Thing To Waste 263
Just Put on a Happy Toolface 264

Part VI: Excel Function Reference (For Real People) 267

Chapter 12: I Love Everyday Functions 269
To SUM Up 269
I'm Just a PRODUCT of My Times 271
The SUMPRODUCT 271
I'm Just Your AVERAGE Joe 272
COUNT Me In! 273
The MEDIAN Strip 274
How To Get the MAXimum in the MINimum Time 274
Going ROUND About 274
I Want It NOW! 275

Chapter 13: Functions for the More Adventurous 277
High Finance (or I Want My PMT) 277
Just for the Text of It 281
Hey, Look Me Over! 284
Is That Logical? (or IF I Were a Rich Man) 287

Part VII: The Part of Tens *291*

Chapter 14: Ten Beginners Basics 293

Chapter 15 Ten Excel Commandments 295

Chapter 16: Ten Printing Pointers 297

Chapter 17: Ten Clever Customizers 299

Chapter 18: Ten Welcome Warnings 301

Chapter 19: Ten Ways To Work Smarter, Faster, and Get that Promotion 303

Chapter 20: Ten Thousand (More or Less) Useful Keystroke Shortcuts 305

Glossary 311

Index 319

Reader Response Survey .... End of Book

Introduction

· ·

Welcome to *Excel For Dummies*, the definitive work on Excel 4.0 for those of you who have no intention of ever becoming a spreadsheet guru. In this book, you find all the information you need to keep your head above water as you accomplish the everyday tasks that normal people do with Excel. The intention of this book is to keep things simple and not bore you with a lot of technical details you neither need nor care anything about. As much as possible, this book attempts to cut to the chase by telling you in plain terms just what it is you need to do to get a particular thing done with Excel.

Excel For Dummies covers all the fundamental techniques you need to create, edit, format, and print your own worksheets. In addition to learning your way around the worksheet, you are also exposed to the basics of charting and creating databases. Keep in mind that this book just touches on the easiest ways to get a few things done with these features — there is no attempt to cover charting and databases in anything approaching a definitive way. In the main, this book concentrates on the worksheet because this is the part of the program you probably work with most often.

About This Book

This book is not meant to be read from cover to cover. Although its chapters are loosely organized in a logical order (progressing as you might when learning Excel in a classroom situation), each topic covered in a chapter is really meant to stand on its own.

Each discussion of a topic briefly addresses the question of what a particular feature is good for before launching into how to use it. In Excel, as with most other sophisticated programs, there is usually more than one way to get a task done. For the sake of your sanity, I have purposely limited the choices by giving you only the most efficient way to do a particular task. Later on, if you're so tempted, you can experiment with alternative ways of doing a task. For now, just concentrate on learning how to perform the task as described.

As much as possible, I've tried to make it unnecessary to remember anything covered in another section in the book to get something to work in the section you're currently reading. From time to time, however, you come across a cross-reference to another section or chapter in the book. For the most part, such cross-references are meant to help you get more complete information on a subject should you have the time and interest. If you have neither, there's no problem; just ignore the cross-references like they never existed.

How To Use This Book

This book is like a reference where you start out by looking up the topic you need information about (either in the table of contents or the index) and then refer directly to the section of interest. Most topics are explained conversationally (as though you were sitting in the back of a classroom where you can safely nap). Sometimes, however, my regiment-commander mentality takes over, and I list the steps you need to take to get a particular task accomplished in a particular section.

What You Can Safely Ignore

When you come across a section that contains the steps you take to get something done, you can safely ignore all text accompanying the steps (the text that isn't in bold) if you have neither the time nor the inclination to wade through more material.

Whenever possible, I have also tried to separate background or footnote-type information from the essential facts by exiling this kind of junk to a Technical Stuff section flagged with an icon. You can easily disregard text marked this way. Note too, that the information you find flagged with a Tip icon, although designed to help you become more efficient with the program, is also extraneous and can be safely skipped over until you're ready for it.

When you see the bomb that signifies the Warning icon, however, it might be a good idea to linger awhile and take some time to read about what might happen if you do something bad.

Foolish Assumptions

I'm going to make only one assumption about you (let's see how close I get):
You have access to a PC (at least some of the time) that has installed on it some
version of the DOS operating system, Microsoft Windows, and Microsoft Excel.
I'm also assuming that you have no previous experience using Excel.

But wait — maybe there are some things I've overlooked. Some of you may
have upgraded to the latest version of Excel, 4.0, some of you may still be using
Excel 3.0, and still others may be using Excel for the Macintosh.

This book is targeted toward new users of Excel 4.0 for Windows, but there's
still plenty of handy information for users of Excel versions prior to 4.0. To
make sure you know what information is specifically applicable to 4.0, I've
marked the discussion with the special Excel 4.0 icon you see next to this paragraph. This might include stuff like the new toolbars available in 4.0, and other
things you may not have known about.

Don't worry if you don't have much experience with DOS or Windows either, or
if you don't really have a clear idea of what Excel can do for you. If I really feel
that you need some DOS or Windows information that I can't provide within
the framework of this book, I'll let you know that it's time to get out *DOS For
Dummies* or *Windows For Dummies* (both books are published by IDG Books
Worldwide).

For those of you who are using Excel for the Macintosh, be advised that
much of this book's information can apply to you, too. The basic principles
of Excel's operation apply to both platforms. Whenever a procedure is mark-
edly different from the Excel for Windows version, however, you'll see the
paragraph marked by the Mac Track locomotive and the side bracket, just
like this one!

If *Excel For Dummies* piques your interest and you want to learn more, you can
find in-depth information about Excel in two other books published by IDG: The
PC World Excel 4 for Windows Handbook, by John Walkenbach and David
Maguiness, and *Macworld Guide to Microsoft Excel,* by David Maguiness.

How This Book Is Organized

This book is organized in seven parts (you get to see at least seven of those
great cartoons!). Each part contains two or more chapters (to keep the editors
happy) that more or less go together. Each chapter is further divided into
loosely related sections that cover the basics of the topic at hand. You should

not, however, get too hung up about following along with the structure of the book; ultimately, it matters not at all if you learn how to edit the worksheet before you learn how to format it, or learn printing before you learn editing. The important thing is that you find the information — and understand it when you find it — when you need to do any of these things.

Just in case you're interested, a brief synopsis of what you find in each part follows.

Part I: The Absolute Basics

As the name implies, Part I covers such fundamentals as how to start the program, identify the parts of the screen, enter information in the worksheet, save a document, and so on. If you're starting with absolutely no background in using spreadsheets, you for sure want to glance at the information in Chapter 1 to learn what this program is good for before you move on to how to create new worksheets in Chapter 2.

Part II: The More Things Change...

Part II gives you the skinny on how to make worksheets look good as well as how to make major editing changes to them without courting disaster. Refer to Chapter 3 when you need information on changing the way the information appears in the worksheet. Refer to Chapter 4 when you need information on rearranging, deleting, or inserting new information in the worksheet.

Part III: Ferreting Out the Information

Part III lets you know what to do with the information in a worksheet once you're in there. Chapter 5 is full of good ideas on how to keep track of the whereabouts of the information in a worksheet; Chapter 6 gives you the ins and outs of getting the information down on paper.

Part IV: Amazing Things You Can Do with Excel (for Fun and Profit)

Part IV explores some of the other aspects of Excel besides the worksheet. In Chapter 7, you find out just how ridiculously easy it is to create a chart using the data in a worksheet. In Chapter 8, you learn just how useful Excel's database capabilities can be when you have to track and organize a large amount of information. In Chapter 9, you discover how much time and effort you can save by taking information from one worksheet to another (rather than retyping it) and creating similar worksheets from a template.

Part V: Excel — Have It Your Way

Part V gives you ideas about how to customize the way you work with Excel. In Chapter 10, you learn how to change the display options in Excel and how to record and play back macros to automate tasks. In Chapter 11, you learn how to customize the built-in toolbars and create new toolbars of your own.

Part VI: Excel Function Reference (for Real People)

Part VI gives you information on the use of specific Excel functions. Chapter 12 covers everyday functions such as SUM, AVERAGE, and ROUND. Chapter 13 gets more adventurous and covers more sophisticated functions like the financial functions PV and PMT and the text functions PROPER, UPPER, and LOWER.

Part VII: The Part of Tens

As is the tradition in these . . . _For Dummies_ books, the last part contains lists of useful (well, sort of) facts, tips, and suggestions. Don't worry, you won't have to read ten more chapters if you get this far.

Conventions Used in This Book

The following information gives you the lowdown on how things look in this book — publishers call these the book's _conventions_ (no campaigning, flag-waving, name-calling, or finger-pointing is involved, however).

Keyboard and mouse

Excel is a sophisticated program with lots of fancy boxes, plenty of bars, and more menus than you can count. In Chapter 1, I explain all about these features and how to use them. Be sure to review Chapter 1 if you have any questions about how to get around the program.

Although you use the mouse and keyboard shortcut keys to move your way in, out, and around the Excel worksheet, you do have to take some time to enter the data in so that you can eventually mouse around with it. Therefore, this book occasionally encourages you to type something specific into a specific cell in the worksheet. Of course, you can always choose not to follow the instructions, but you should know what they look like anyway. For example, when you are told to enter a specific function, what you are told to type appears like this:

```
=PROPER(this_is_it)
```

When stuff appears on a screened line like this, you type exactly what you see: an equal sign, the word **PROPER**, a left parenthesis, the text **this_is_it** (complete with underscores), and a right parenthesis. You then, of course, have to press Enter to make the entry stick.

When you are asked to type something that's just right there in the paragraph, the word is formatted in **Bold** type.

When Excel isn't talking to you by popping up message boxes, it displays highly informative messages in the status bar at the bottom of the screen. This book renders any messages in a special typeface, like this: Ready. (That's the highly informative status message I mentioned.) This special typeface always identifies any on-screen information or messages.

Special icons

The following icons are strategically placed in the margins to point out stuff you may or may not want to read.

This icon alerts you to nerdy discussions that you well may want to skip (or read when no one else is around).

This icon alerts you to shortcuts or other valuable hints related to the topic at hand.

This icon alerts you to information to keep in mind if you want to meet with a modicum of success.

This icon alerts you to information to keep in mind if you want to avert complete disaster.

This icon alerts you to any significant differences in the workings of Excel for the Macintosh and Excel for Windows.

This icon alerts you to features new with Excel 4.0 for Windows.

Where To Go From Here

If you've never worked with a computer spreadsheet, I suggest you go first to Chapter 1 and find out what you're dealing with. If you're already familiar with the ins and outs of electronic spreadsheets but don't know anything about creating worksheets with Excel, jump into Chapter 2 where you find out how to get started entering data and formulas. Then, as specific needs arise (like "How do I copy a formula?" or "How do I print just a particular section of my worksheet?"), you can go to the table of contents or the index to find the appropriate section and go right to that section for answers.

Part I
The Absolute Basics

YES, MASTER?

The part in which...

You discover that a spreadsheet program is not just a word processor with braces formed by column-and-row gridlines. You find out that Excel exhibits some real smarts that can help you get your work done without involving you in some deep understanding of what's going on — a dummy's dream come true!

You learn how to get in and out of Excel without doing you or your computer any irreparable harm. And you embark on your first solo mission with Excel by getting information into an Excel document and making sure that it stays there so that you don't have to re-create the document all over again the next day!

Chapter 1
What Have You Gotten Yourself Into?

In This Chapter

▶ What makes Excel so special?

▶ How to start Excel

▶ How to open the document you want to work on at the same time you start Excel

▶ How Excel uses the mouse

▶ How to move around the worksheet

▶ How to select commands from the pull-down menus

▶ How to use the shortcut menus

▶ How to make your selections in a dialog box

▶ How to get on-line help anytime you need it

▶ How to exit Excel

As Alice found out in Wonderland, "it's always best to begin at the beginning." Chapter 1, therefore, takes it from the top by acquainting you with the quintessential nature of this spreadsheet beast (actually, Excel is rather more a "beauty" than a "beast"). Then, I'll tell you how to start the darn thing.

Armed with the knowledge of how to get yourself into trouble by starting Excel, it's only fair to then let you know how to bail out of the program when you need to as well as tell you a little about proper etiquette during your stay.

While dispensing this wisdom, I'll protect your inalienable right "to not know," at the same time making sure that you have all of the information you need to keep your head above water.

Listen up, all you Excel Mac users. Instructions that apply specifically to Excel for the Macintosh are marked with this special Mac Tracks icon.

Who Put the "Work" in Worksheet?

In days of yore, mankind crunched numbers not with sophisticated computer spreadsheet programs like Excel but with primitive tools like pencils, papers, and hand-held calculators. Believe it or not, our ancestors actually did financial planning by writing in (by hand, mind you) the numbers they punched up on their calculators onto long green sheets of paper!

These "green" sheets — which, because they were much wider than tall, also became known as *spreadsheets* — used fine gridlines to divide the large sheet into a series of columns and rows. The number cruncher person would then pencil in the calculated figures in the spaces created at the intersection of column and row gridlines. These gridlines helped line up the numbers in the spreadsheet so that other people could tell if the numbers referred to widgets, wodgets, or gadgets.

An electronic spreadsheet program like Excel pays homage to this glorious past by presenting you with a facsimile of the old "green" sheet on your computer screen (see Figure 1-1). In keeping with tradition, the electronic spreadsheet, like its paper spreadsheet counterpart, uses fine gridlines to divide the sheet into a series of columns and rows into which you enter your text and numbers.

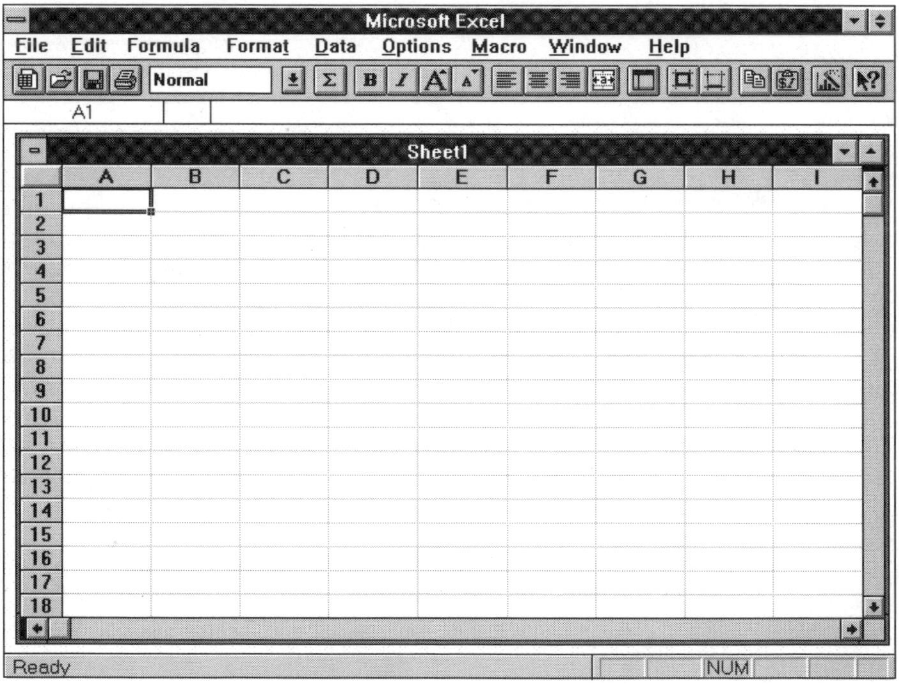

Figure 1-1: Inspired by paper spreadsheets of old, the Excel "electronic" spreadsheet divides the work area into a series of columns and rows.

Note that spreadsheet programs like Excel are more apt to refer to their electronic sheets as *worksheets* rather than *spreadsheets*. You should also note that although it is perfectly acceptable (even preferable) to call one of its electronic spreadsheets a worksheet, you *never, never, never* refer to Excel as a worksheet program — you *always* refer to it as a spreadsheet program (go figure?).

Semantics aside, the electronic worksheet differs from the traditional paper spreadsheet in one other significant way: The worksheet contains a frame used to label the columns and rows. As you can see in Figure 1-1, columns are named for letters of the alphabet, while the rows are numbered.

The columns and rows are labeled because the Excel worksheet is humongous (Figure 1-1 shows only a tiny part of the total worksheet). The column and row labels act like street signs in a city that can help you identify your current location (even when they don't prevent you from becoming lost).

So, how big is it?

The Excel electronic worksheet dwarfs even the largest of paper spreadsheets, consisting as it does of a total of 256 columns and 16,384 rows! This means that if you were to produce the entire worksheet grid on paper, you would need a sheet that was approximately 21 feet wide by 341 feet long!

On a 13-inch monitor screen, you can normally see no more — at the most — than 9 complete columns and 18 complete rows of the entire worksheet. With columns being about 1 inch wide and rows about ¼ inch high, 9 columns represent a scant 4 percent of the total width of the worksheet, while 18 rows are only about ⅒ of one percent of its total length. This should give you some idea of just how little of the total worksheet you can see on the screen as well as just how much area is available.

Meet me at 20th and F streets

I bring up the facts and figures on the worksheet size not to intimidate you but to make you aware of how important it is for the Excel worksheet to have a reference system that keeps you informed at all times of your exact position in the worksheet. Because the worksheet offers you so much room for expansion, if you don't know where you are placing particular information, you can easily lose track of it.

To help you identify the location of entries and find them again, Excel not only displays a frame around the worksheet showing you the column letter and row number, but it also uses these column and row references to keep you constantly informed of your current location.

Figure 1-2 shows you how this works. In this figure, the current location is the intersection of the column F and row 20. This location is indicated in two ways in the worksheet. First, in the worksheet, this area is highlighted with a heavy outline called the *cell pointer*. Second, the column letter and row number appear at the beginning of the bar right above the one containing the column letters (this bar is identified as the *formula bar* in Figure 1-2).

In this example, because the cell pointer is now occupying the space at the intersection of column F and row 20, F20 appears in the formula bar. F20 identifies your location in the worksheet just as if you'd told someone, "I'm at the intersection of 20th and F streets" to pinpoint your location in Kansas City. F20 gives you the current address of the cell pointer relative to a starting point (1st and A streets, called A1 in Excel).

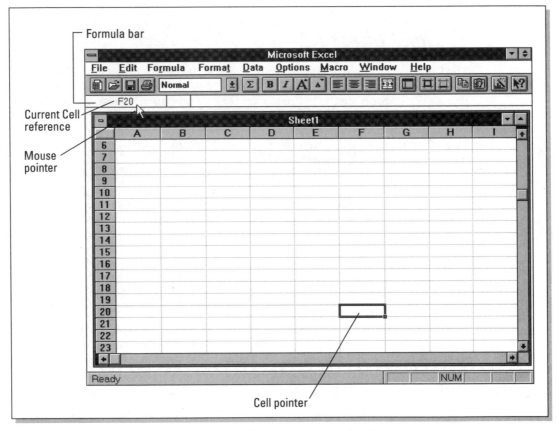

Figure 1-2: Excel tells you exactly where in the worksheet world you are by displaying the current column and row reference on the formula bar.

TECHNICAL STUFF

The R1C1 Reference System

Excel supports an alternate system of cell references called the *R1C1 cell reference system*. In this system, both the columns and rows in the worksheet are numbered, and the row number precedes the column number. For example, in this system, cell A1 is called R1C1 (row 1, column 1), cell A2 is R2C1 (row 2, column 1), and B1 is R1C2 (row 1, column 2). To find out how to switch to this cell reference system, see Chapter 10.

Cellmates

The space identified by the column letter and row number on the formula bar is called a *cell*. The cell pointer actually outlines the borders of the current cell. The worksheet cell works somewhat like a jail cell, at least in the sense that any information you put into the cell of the worksheet remains "imprisoned" there until you — the warden — either clear the information out or move it to another cell. However, unlike the holding tank in the county lockup, a worksheet cell can accommodate only one occupant at a time. So if you try to put new information in a cell that is already occupied, Excel will replace the old occupant with the new one.

What comes after Z?

Our alphabet with its mere 26 letters isn't enough to label the 256 consecutive columns in the Excel worksheet. To make up the difference, Excel doubles up the cell letters in the column reference so that column AA immediately follows column Z. This is followed by column AB, AC, and so on to AZ. After column AZ, you find column BA, then BB, BC, and so on. According to this system for doubling the column letters, the 256th and last column of the worksheet is column IV. This, in turn, gives the very last cell of the worksheet the cell reference IV16384!

So, what's this thing good for anyway?

So far, here's what you know about Excel:

- ✔ Excel uses an electronic worksheet modeled after a paper spreadsheet.

- ✔ The worksheet is divided into columns and rows and contains a frame that labels the columns with letters and rows with numbers.

- ✔ You enter your information in the areas formed by the intersection of each column and row, which is known as a cell.

Put this way, you can easily get the mistaken idea that a spreadsheet program like Excel is little more than a quirky word processor with gridlock that forces you to enter your information in tiny, individual cells instead of offering you the spaciousness of full pages.

Well, I'm here to say that Bill Gates didn't become a billionaire several times over by selling a quirky word processor. The big difference between the cell of a worksheet and the pages of a word processor is that each cell offers computing power along with text editing and formatting capabilities. This computing power takes the form of formulas that you create in various cells of the worksheet.

Quite unlike a paper spreadsheet which contains only values computed somewhere else, an electronic worksheet can store both the formulas and the computed values returned by these formulas. Even better, your formulas can use values stored in other cells of the worksheet, and, as you will see shortly, Excel will automatically update the computed answer returned by such a formula anytime you change these values in the worksheet.

Excel's computational capabilities — combined with its editing and formatting capabilities — make it perfect for generating any kind of document that uses text and numeric entries and makes you perform calculations on the values.

Also, you can make your formulas *dynamic*. This means that their calculations are automatically updated when you change referenced values stored in other cells of the worksheet. Dynamic formulas make it much easier to keep the calculated values in a worksheet document both current and correct.

Gentlemen, Start Your Spreadsheets!

There are several different methods for starting Excel, almost all of which require that you have the Windows program (version 3.0 or higher) running. (Hurry! Get out your copy of *Windows For Dummies*!) In case you've forgotten how to start Windows (or you never knew or cared), you simply turn on your computer, and then type out what you want your favorite team to do:

```
C:\>WIN
```

That is, type **WIN** (after that funny looking C:\>, called the *C prompt),* and press Enter to make the magic happen (you do know where the Enter key is, don't you? — OK, better get out your copy of *DOS For Dummies* as well!).

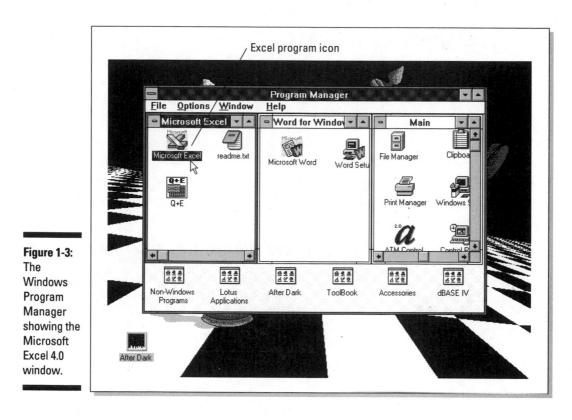

Figure 1-3:
The Windows Program Manager showing the Microsoft Excel 4.0 window.

After what seems like an interminable amount of time (and copyright notices), you will finally be presented with your chess wallpaper (or if you've customized Windows, whatever wallpaper you chose), and, with any luck, the Program Manager window will open just like it did for me in Figure 1-3.

To start Excel, you then need to find the Microsoft Excel 4.0 window. If the window is not visible in the Program Manager, you can open this window by choosing the Microsoft Excel 4.0 command in the Window pull-down menu.

After you locate (and open, if necessary) the Microsoft Excel 4.0 window, you can start the program by positioning the mouse pointer (the arrowhead) on the Microsoft Excel program icon (as identified in Figure 1-3) and double-clicking the left mouse button. If double-clicking doesn't work for you, you can simply click to select the icon (indicated by the highlighting on the icon name) and then press the Enter key.

To start Excel for the Macintosh, open the Excel folder, and then double-click on the Microsoft Excel program icon.

Bypassing Windows

If you don't want to go through all that Windows folderol, you can start Excel from the DOS operating system by combining the Windows and Excel startup commands. This creates what amounts to a Microsoft cheer exhorting the program to thrash its rivals Lotus 1-2-3 and Quattro Pro. To enjoy the cheering, enter the following:

```
C:\>WIN EXCEL
```

That is, type **WIN**, then press the spacebar, then type **EXCEL,** and finally press Enter. Your computer will start Windows and then immediately start Excel.

Opening a document when starting Excel

At times, you may want to get right down to work on a particular worksheet document the moment Excel starts. For these times, you can open the document and start Excel at the same time. The easiest way to do this is to start the File Manager program in Windows, and then use this program to locate the Excel worksheet document you want to work with (Excel documents are pretty easy to spot because their filenames all end in .XLS, which stands for EXceL Sheet).

Once you've found the Excel document that you want to work on in the File Manager, position the mouse pointer on the document name, and then double-click the left mouse button (you can also click on the document name once and then press the Enter key). Because Windows knows that XLS documents are created by Excel, it will start Excel and then Excel will automatically open the document you have selected.

To open an Excel document and start the program from the Finder on the Macintosh, open the folder with the document, and then double-click on the document icon in the folder.

What Happens If I Press This Button

Figure 1-4 identifies the different parts of the Excel program window that appears when you first start the program (assuming that you haven't selected a worksheet document to open as well). As you can see, the Excel window upon opening is full of all kinds of useful, though potentially confusing, stuff.

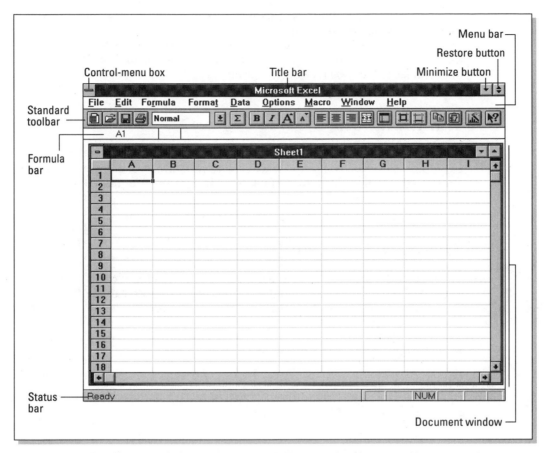

Figure 1-4: The Excel program window contains several different kinds of buttons and bars.

The title bar

The first bar in the Excel window is called the *title bar* because it shows you the name of the program running in the window (Microsoft Excel). The buttons on the title bar of this window should be familiar — they are the Control-menu and sizing buttons common to all Windows applications. You click the Control-menu box to access the Control-menu commands that you use to do things like switch to another Windows application that you have running or run a utility program such as the Control Panel where you can change a number of Windows settings.

You click on the sizing buttons to shrink and expand the Excel window. If you click on the Minimize button, the Excel window shrinks down to a mere program icon on the Windows desktop. If you click the Restore button, the Excel window assumes a somewhat smaller size on the desktop, and the Restore button changes to the Maximize button (used to restore the window to full size).

The menu bar

The second bar in the Excel window is the menu bar. This bar contains the Excel pull-down menus that you use to select various Excel commands (jump ahead to the section "Menurama: Pull-Down vs. Shortcut" for more information on how to select commands).

The Standard toolbar

The Standard toolbar occupies the third bar of the Excel window. Each button in this bar (more commonly called a *tool*) performs a particular function when you click on it with the mouse. For example, you can use the first tool to open a new worksheet document, the second one to open an existing worksheet document, the third one to save the current worksheet document, and the fourth one to print it.

Table 1-1 shows you the name and function of each tool on the Standard toolbar. Rest assured, you will come to know each one intimately as your experience with Excel grows.

Table 1-1:	The Tools on the Standard Toolbar	
Tool	**Tool Name**	**What the Tool Does When You Click It**
	New Worksheet Tool	Opens a new worksheet
	Open File Tool	Lets you open an existing Excel document
	Save File Tool	Saves changes in the active document
	Print Tool	Prints the active document
Normal	Style Box	Applies or defines a cell style
Σ	AutoSum Tool	Sums a list of values with the SUM function
B	Bold Tool	Applies bold formatting to the cell selection
I	Italic Tool	Applies italic formatting to the cell selection
A	Increase Font Size Tool	Increases the font size of the selected text
A	Decrease Font Size Tool	Decreases the font size of the selected text
	Left Align Tool	Left aligns the entries in the cell selection

(continued)

Table 1-1:	The Tools on the Standard Toolbar *(continued)*	
Tool	*Tool Name*	*What the Tool Does When You Click It*
	Center Align Tool	Centers the entries in the cell selection
	Right Align Tool	Right aligns the entries in the cell selection
	Center Across Selected Columns Tool	Centers the entry in the active cell across selected columns
	AutoFormat Tool	Applies the most recently used range format to the table of data that contains the cell pointer
	Outline Border Tool	Adds a border to the outer edges of the cell selection
	Bottom Border Tool	Adds a border to the bottom edge of the cell selection
	Copy Tool	Copies the current selection to the Clipboard
	Paste Formats Tool	Pastes just the formats from the cells copied to the Clipboard
	Chart Wizard Tool	Starts the ChartWizard that steps you through the creation of a new chart in the active document
	Help Tool	Gives you help information on the command or region of the screen that you click with the question mark pointer

The Standard toolbar is so called because it contains the most commonly used tools and is the one that is automatically displayed in the Excel window when you first start the program. Excel does, however, include several other toolbars that you can display as your work requires their special tools. As you soon discover, Excel's toolbars are a real boon to productivity because they make the program's standard routines so much more accessible than the pull-down menus.

The formula bar

The formula bar displays the cell address and the contents of the current cell. This bar is divided into three sections by two vertical lines. If the current cell is empty (as is cell A1 in Figure 1-4), the second and third sections of the formula bar are blank. As soon as you begin typing an entry or building a worksheet formula, these sections of the formula bar come alive.

Although you'll learn more about this in the next chapter, you might want to check out these facts about the sections of the formula bar:

- ✔ An Enter and Cancel box appears in the second section, and each character you type appears in the third section of the bar.

- ✔ The Enter box works like a check mark, and the Cancel box looks like an X.

- ✔ After you complete the entry and enter it in the cell either by clicking on the Enter box or by pressing the Enter key, Excel displays the entire entry or formula in the formula bar and the Cancel and Enter boxes disappear from the center section of the formula bar.

- ✔ The contents of that cell then always appears in the formula bar whenever that cell contains the cell pointer.

The document window

A blank Excel worksheet appears in a new document window right below the formula bar when you first start the program. As you can see in Figure 1-5, this new document window has its own Control-menu box, title bar, and sizing buttons and displays the sheet number as a temporary document name (Sheet1 when you first start Excel, then Sheet2 when you open your next new worksheet document window, and so on).

On the right and bottom sides of the document window, you see scroll bars you can use to bring new parts of the worksheet into view. (Remember, you are only viewing a small percentage of the total worksheet.) At the intersection of these two scroll bars, you'll find a size box that you can use to modify the size and shape of the document window.

As soon as you start Excel, you can immediately begin creating a new worksheet in the blank worksheet document window.

Other types of Excel documents

Worksheets are not the only type of document that Excel uses. In addition to worksheet documents, you can have charts, macro sheets, workbooks, and slide sheets open in the Excel program window. Each of these different types of Excel documents is contained in its own document window.

Sizing and moving document windows

You can use the Control-menu box or the Maximize or Minimize buttons found on the title bar of the document window to automatically change the size of the active document. In addition to these buttons, which are also found on the title bar of the Excel window, each document window contains a size box located in the lower right corner (see Figure 1-5) that you can use to manually control the size of the window.

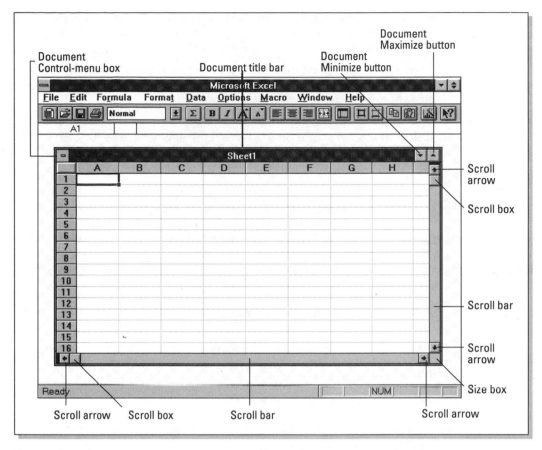

Figure 1-5: Each document window in Excel contains its own Control-menu and sizing buttons.

To change the size of a document window, you simply position the mouse pointer on this button. Then, when the mouse pointer changes shape to a double-headed arrow, you drag the mouse as needed to adjust the size of the side(s) of the window.

Note: The mouse pointer does not change to a two-headed arrow unless it's on the edge of the window. While the pointer is in the button, the pointer remains a single arrow.

✔ If you position the pointer on the bottom side of the window, and then drag the pointer straight up, the window becomes shorter. If you drag straight down, the window becomes longer.

✔ If you position the pointer on the right side of the window, and then drag the pointer straight to the left, the window becomes narrower. If you drag straight to the right, the window becomes wider.

✔ If you position the pointer on the lower-right corner of the window, and then drag the pointer diagonally toward the upper-left corner, the window becomes both shorter and narrower. If you drag diagonally away from the upper-left corner, the window becomes longer and wider.

When the outline of the window reaches the size you want, release the left mouse button; Excel redraws the document window to your new size.

After changing the size of a document window with the size button, you need to use the size button again if you want to restore the window to its original dimensions. Unfortunately, there is no Restore button available that you can click to magically restore the original document window size.

Besides resizing document windows, you can also reposition them in the Excel window.

✔ To move a document window, simply pick it up by the scruff of its neck, which in this case corresponds to the window's title bar.

✔ Once you've got it by the title bar, you can then drag it to the desired position and release the left mouse button.

If you have trouble dragging objects with the mouse, you can also move a document window this way:

✔ Press Ctrl+F7.

✔ Press the arrow keys on the cursor keypad (↑, ↓, →, or ←) until the window is in the position you want.

✔ Finally, press Enter.

If, while doing this, you lose the title bar, just press Alt+- (that's the Alt key and then the hyphen key) and proceed to the next section. Or, you can choose Move and the down arrow.

Maximizing a document window

When you click on the Maximize button in the upper right corner of a document window, Excel enlarges the document window so that it takes up all the space between the formula bar and the last bar in the window. Just like in Figure 1-6, Excel tacks the name of the document window onto the Excel title bar and relocates the document window's Control-menu box and Maximize button at the front and back, respectively, of the Excel menu bar.

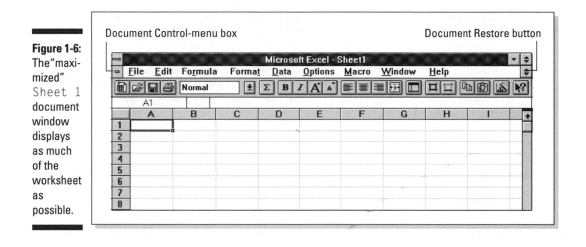

     Document Restore button

Figure 1-6:
The"maxi-
mized"
Sheet 1
document
window
displays
as much
of the
worksheet
as
possible.

In Excel for the Macintosh, the document window has a zoom button in the
upper-right corner. You click on this button when you want to maximize the
window. Click on this button again to restore the document window to its
previous size.

The status bar

The bar at the very bottom of the Excel window is called the *status* bar because
it displays information that keeps you informed of the current state of Excel.
The left part of the status bar displays messages indicating the current activity
you're undertaking or the current command you've selected from the Excel
menu bar. When you first start Excel, the message Ready is displayed in this
area (as shown in Figure 1-4), telling you that the program is ready to accept
your next entry or command.

The right side of the status bar contains six boxes which display different indi-
cators that tell you when you've placed Excel in a particular state that somehow affects how you work with the program.

For example, normally, when you first start Excel, the NUM indicator appears in
this part of the status bar, indicating that you can use the numbers on the numeric keypad to enter values in the worksheet. If you press the Num Lock key,
this NUM indicator disappears. This is your signal that the cursor-movement
functions that are also assigned to this keypad are now in effect. This means,
for instance, that pressing the 6 key will move the cell pointer one cell to the
right instead of entering this value in the formula bar.

Making the Mouse Less of a Drag

Like it or not, the mouse is one of the more challenging computer tools. Let's face it, the little rats demand a level of hand-and-eye coordination that make touch-typing on the keyboard seem like a walk in the park. Mostly, this is because your brain has to learn how to correlate the movement of the mouse pointer across a slightly curved vertical plane (your monitor screen) with smaller movements you make with the mouse on a flat horizontal plane (your desk). Then again, it could also be that most of us are just klutzes!

Whatever the reason, you'll probably find mastering Excel mouse techniques some kind of fun! Keep in mind that the mouse emphasizes a different set of muscles from the keyboard and, therefore, you may experience some initial discomfort in your upper back and shoulder (keep that Ben Gay handy!). But I'm quite sure that with just a modicum of mouse experience under your belt, you too will be double-clicking with the best of them.

Although you can access most of Excel's wonders by using the keyboard, in most cases, the mouse is the most efficient way to select a command or perform a particular procedure. For that reason alone, if you need to use Excel regularly in getting your work done, it's worth your while to master the program's various mouse techniques.

Windows programs such as Excel use three basic mouse techniques to select and manipulate various objects in the program and document windows:

1. Clicking on an object — positioning the pointer on it and then pressing and immediately releasing the left or (more rarely) the right mouse button.

2. Double-clicking on an object — positioning the pointer on it and then pressing and immediately releasing the left mouse button rapidly twice in a row.

3. Dragging an object — positioning the pointer on it and then pressing and holding down the left mouse button as you move the mouse in the direction you wish to drag the object. When you have positioned the object in the desired position on the screen, you then release the left mouse button to place it.

When clicking on an object to select it, make sure that the point of the arrowhead is touching the object you want to select before you click. To avoid moving the pointer slightly before you click, grasp the sides of the mouse between your thumb and your ring and little fingers, and then click the left button with your index finger.

If you run out of room on your desktop for moving the mouse, just pick up the mouse and reposition it on the desk (this does not move the pointer).

Learning the Mouse by Your Lonesome

One of the best (and most fun) ways to master basic mouse techniques is to play the Solitaire card game included in the Windows program (located in the Games group window in the Program Manager). In this computer version of the popular card game, you click on the deck in the upper-left corner when you need to draw cards. You can then drag cards drawn from the deck either to one of the seven row stacks or one of the four suit stacks.

Row stacks are built down in descending order (King to Ace), alternating black and red suits. Suit stacks are built up in ascending order (Ace to King), segregated by suit. To place the next card in the suit in its suit stack, you double-click on the card.

With Solitaire, you can kick back and relax while you master the mouse. And you won't even notice that you just spent another Saturday night alone!

The many faces of the mouse pointer

The shape of the mouse pointer in Excel is anything but static. As you move the mouse pointer to different parts of the Excel screen, the pointer changes shape to indicate a change in function. Table 1-2 shows the various faces of the mouse pointer as well as when each face appears and what you use it for.

Table 1-2:	The Many Mouse Pointer Shapes in Excel
Mouse Pointer Shape	*What It Means*
✛	The shaded thick cross pointer appears as you move the pointer around the cells of the worksheet. Use this pointer to select the cells you want to use.
↖	The arrowhead pointer appears when you position the pointer on the toolbar or the menu bar or on one of the edges of a block of cells you've selected. Use this pointer to select Excel commands or to copy or move a selection of cells with the drag and drop feature.
+	The fill handle (thin black cross) appears when you position the pointer on the lower-right corner of the cell with the cell pointer. Use this pointer to create a sequential series of entries, a block of cells, or to fill a block of cells with the same entry.
I	The I-beam pointer appears when you position the pointer on the formula bar or in a text box in a dialog box. Use this pointer to reposition the insertion point in a text entry or to select text.
↖?	The help pointer appears when you click the Help tool on the Standard toolbar. Use this pointer to get help on a particular Excel command.

Don't confuse the cell pointer with the mouse pointer. The mouse pointer changes shape as you move it around the screen. The cell pointer always maintains the current shape, although it does expand when you select a block of cells. The mouse pointer responds to any movement of your mouse on the desktop and always moves independently of the cell pointer.

Look at that varmint go!

Of these three techniques, double-clicking is sometimes the most troublesome because you need to time the sequence of clicks close enough to each other that Excel interprets them as a double-click rather than two single-clicks. If you find yourself having difficulty mastering the double-click, try slowing down the double-click speed of the mouse.

In addition to the double-click speed, you can also modify the tracking speed (that is, how fast and far the mouse pointer travels across the screen when you move the mouse on the desk) of your mouse. If you keep running out of room on your desk before the pointer reaches the edge of the screen, you want to increase the tracking speed.

To change the double-click or tracking speed for the mouse, start with these steps:

1. **Click on the Control-menu box in the upper-left corner of the Excel window.**

2. **Choose the R̲un command by clicking it or by pressing U̲.**

3. **Select the Control P̲anel option by clicking its button or pressing P̲.**

4. **Open the Windows Control Panel window by clicking the OK button or by pressing Enter.**

5. **Open the Mouse window by double-clicking on the Mouse icon the Control panel or by clicking on it and then pressing the Enter key.**

6. **To change the M̲ouse Tracking Speed, drag its scroll box in either the Slow (left) or Fast (right) direction or click the Slow or Fast scroll arrow.**

   You can also modify the speed by pressing **M**, and then pressing the ← or → key in the Slow or Fast direction.

7. **To change the D̲ouble-Click Speed, drag its scroll box in either the Slow (left) or Fast (right) direction or click the Slow or Fast scroll arrow.**

   You can also modify the speed by pressing **D**, and then pressing the ← or → key in the Slow or Fast direction.

   To test the double-click speed, double-click on the TEST rectangle with the left mouse button. Windows highlights this rectangle as soon as it detects the double-click.

8. **Choose OK or press Enter after making your changes to the mouse tracking and/or double-click speed.**

9. **Double-click on the Control-menu box in the Control Panel window or press Alt+F4 to close this window and return to Excel.**

For south paws only!

Sinister or not, we left handers have to stick together. As a fellow south paw, I feel that I have to let you know that by swapping the left and right mouse buttons, you can save yourself a lot of wear and tear on your left shoulder. After you place the mouse to the left side of the keyboard to have access to it, you are continually forced to twist your hand every time you need to click the left mouse button so that your index finger can reach this button. If you switch the left and right button, you can keep your hand perfectly aligned over the mouse, and your index finger can still reach and click the left button (which is now *physically* the right button).

To switch the left and right buttons, follow the steps outlined for changing the double-click and tracking speed in the previous section. Then add these steps:

1. **While the Mouse window is open, click on the check box in front of Swap Left/Right Buttons to put an X in it.**

   You have to click on this button with the physical left button of the mouse.

2. **Click the OK button.**

   This time, click on it with the physical right button which now functions as the left (simple, yes?) to close the Mouse window.

Thereafter, every time I say "click the left mouse button" or even more commonly just "click the mouse button" in the text, this is your signal to click the physical right button of your mouse. And, on those rare occasions (and there are some in Excel) when I say "click the right mouse button," you know to click the physical left button. Sounds crazy, but I know that you can handle it because you've been making these kinds of left-to-right conversions all of your lives.

Get Me Out of This Cell!

Excel provides several methods for getting around its huge worksheet. One of the easiest ways is to use the scroll bars in the document window to bring new parts of a worksheet into view. Excel also offers a wide range of keystrokes that you can use not only to move a new part of the worksheet into view but also to make a new cell active by placing the cell pointer in it.

Scrolling away

How does scrolling work in Excel? Imagine scrolling the worksheet as if it were a papyrus scroll attached to rollers on the left and right. To bring into view a new section of the papyrus that is hidden on the right, you would crank the left roller until the section with the cells you want to see appears. Likewise, to scroll into view a new section of the worksheet that is hidden on the left, you would crank the right roller until the section of cells appears.

The horizontal scroll bar

To do this type of left/right scrolling to an Excel worksheet, you use the horizontal scroll bar at the bottom of the document window. On the scroll bar, the left and right scroll arrows play the part of the rollers. Now here's the tricky part: The Excel software engineers arranged the scroll arrows just the opposite of the way their roller counterparts function. This means that the left scroll arrow plays the part of the right roller and the right scroll arrow plays the part of the left roller!

- ✔ Clicking on the *left* scroll arrow in the scroll bar is like turning the right roller on the papyrus scroll — the worksheet moves slightly to the right, bringing a new column, previously hidden on the left, into view.

- ✔ Clicking on the *right* scroll arrow is like turning the left roller on the papyrus scroll — the worksheet moves slightly to the left, bringing a new column, previously hidden on the right, into view.

The vertical scroll bar

To visualize scrolling the worksheet up and down with the vertical scroll bar, think of the papyrus worksheet as being suspended vertically between two rollers, with one roller above and the other below. To scroll the papyrus worksheet up to uncover rows that were otherwise hidden at the bottom, you would crank the top roller until the cells you want to see appear. To scroll the papyrus worksheet down so that you can see rows that were otherwise hidden at the top, you crank the bottom roller.

The vertical scroll bar at the right edge of the document window contains up and down scroll arrows. As with the horizontal scroll arrows, you need think of the vertical scroll arrows as having been put on backwards of the rollers on a vertical papyrus scroll.

- ✔ To scroll the worksheet up to bring into view the next hidden row at the bottom, click the down scroll arrow.

- ✔ To scroll the worksheet down to bring into view the next hidden row at the top, click the up scroll arrow.

Scrolling screens

You can also use the scroll bar to scroll larger sections than a column or row at a time.

- ✔ To scroll the worksheet a screenful at a time, click the gray area of the scroll bar between the scroll box and the scroll arrows.

- ✔ To scroll the sheet up or down by a screenful, click the vertical scroll bar (above the scroll box to scroll up and below the scroll box to scroll down).

- ✔ To scroll the sheet left or right by a screenful, click the horizontal scroll bar (left of the scroll box to scroll left and right of the scroll box to scroll right).

After using the scroll bars to move a new part of the worksheet into view, you can quickly redisplay the active cell in the document window by selecting the Show Active Cell command on the Formula menu.

You can drag the scroll box in one direction or the other to scroll larger sections of the worksheet. The position of the scroll box in its scroll bar reflects its relative position in the *active area* of the worksheet (roughly equivalent to the cells in the worksheet that currently have entries — see Technical Stuff if you're just dying to know the precise definition!).

Keystrokes for moving the pointer

The only disadvantage to using the scroll bars to move around is that the scrolls only bring new parts of the worksheet into view — they don't actually change the position of the cell pointer. This means that if you want to start

The Active Area

The last cell in the active area of the worksheet is the one located at the intersection of the last occupied column and row in the worksheet. The active area then encompasses all of the cells between A1 and the last cell in the active area. You can move the pointer to this last active cell by pressing Ctrl+End.

The size of the active area determines how much of the worksheet you scroll when you drag the scroll box to a new position in its scroll bar. For example, if the active area extends to row 100 of the worksheet and you drag the scroll box to the middle of the vertical scroll bar, row 50 will be the first row that appears in the document window. But, if the active area extends to row 200, row 100 will then be the first visible row.

making entries in the cells in a new area of the worksheet, you still have to remember to select the cell or group of cells where you want the data before you begin entering the data.

Excel offers plenty of keystrokes for moving the cell pointer to a new cell. When you use one of these keystrokes, the program automatically scrolls a new part of the worksheet into view if this is required in moving the cell pointer.

Table 1-3 summarizes these keystrokes and how far each moves the cell pointer from its starting position.

Table 1-3:	Keystrokes for Moving the Cell Pointer
Keystroke	*Where the Cell Pointer Moves To*
→ or Tab	Cell to the immediate right
← or Shift+Tab	Cell to the immediate left
↑	Cell up one row
↓	Cell down one row
Home	Cell in column A of the current row
Ctrl+Home	First cell (A1) of the worksheet
Ctrl+End or End, Home	Cell in the lower right corner of the active area in the worksheet
PgUp	Cell one screenful up in the same column
PgDn	Cell one screenful down in the same column
Ctrl+PgUp	Cell one screenful to the left in the same row
Ctrl+PgDn	Cell one screenful to the right in the same row
Ctrl+→ or End, →	First occupied cell to the right in the same row that is either preceded or followed by a blank cell
Ctrl+← or End, ←	First occupied cell to the left in the same row that is either followed or preceded by a blank cell
Ctrl+↑ or End, ↑	First occupied cell above in the same column that is either followed or preceded by a blank cell
Ctrl+↓ or End, ↓	First occupied cell below in the same column that is either preceded or followed by a blank cell

On the Macintosh, instead of pressing Ctrl, you press the ⌘ key when using the keystroke combinations in Table 1-3 to move the cell pointer.

If you have an extended keyboard, be sure that you use ⌘ and not the Control keys.

Moving from block to block

The keystrokes that combine the Ctrl or End key with an arrow key are among the most helpful for moving quickly from one edge to the other in large tables of cell entries or in moving from table to table in a section of the worksheet that contains many blocks of cells.

- ✔ If the cell pointer is positioned on a blank cell somewhere to the left of a table of cell entries that you want to view, pressing Ctrl+→ moves the cell pointer to the first cell entry at the leftmost edge of the table (in the same row, of course).

- ✔ When you press Ctrl+→ a second time, the cell pointer moves to the last cell entry at the rightmost edge (assuming that there are no blank cells in that row of the table).

- ✔ If you then switch direction and press Ctrl+↓, Excel moves right to the last cell entry at the bottom edge of the table (again assuming that there are no blank cells below in that column of the table).

- ✔ If, when the cell pointer is at the bottom of the table, you press Ctrl+↓ again, Excel will move the pointer to the first entry at the top of the next table located below (assuming that there are no other cell entries above this table in the same column).

If you press Ctrl or End and arrow key combinations and there are no more occupied cells in the direction of the arrow key you selected, Excel advances the cell pointer right to the cell at the very edge of the worksheet in that direction.

- ✔ If the cell pointer is located in cell C15 and there are no more occupied cells in row 15, when you press Ctrl+→, Excel will move the cell pointer to cell IV at the rightmost edge of the worksheet.

- ✔ If you are in this cell and there are no more entries below in column C and you press Ctrl+↓, Excel will move the pointer to cell C16384 at the very bottom edge of the worksheet.

When you use Ctrl and an arrow key to move from edge to edge in a table or between tables in a worksheet, you hold down Ctrl while you press one of the four arrow keys (indicated by the + symbol in keystrokes such as Ctrl+→).

When you use End and an arrow key alternative, you must press, and then release the End key *before* you press the arrow key (indicated by the comma in keystrokes such as End,→). Pressing and releasing the End key causes the END indicator to appear on the status bar. This is your sign that Excel is ready for you to press one of the four arrow keys.

Because you can keep the Ctrl key depressed as you press various arrow keys, the Ctrl-plus-arrow key method provides a more fluid method for navigating blocks of cells than the End-then-arrow key method.

Moving the cell pointer with Goto

Excel's Goto feature provides an easy method for moving directly to a distant cell in the worksheet. To do this, you display the Goto dialog box by selecting the <u>G</u>oto command on the For<u>m</u>ula menu or by pressing F5. To move the cell pointer, type the cell reference in the <u>R</u>eference text box that you want to go to, then select the OK button or press the Enter key.

Note*:* When typing the cell reference in the <u>R</u>eference text box, you can type the column letter(s) in upper- or lowercase letters.

When you use the Goto feature to move the cell pointer, Excel remembers the references of the last four cells you visited. These cell references then appear in the <u>G</u>oto list box. You will also notice that the address of the last cell you went to is listed into the <u>R</u>eference box. This makes it possible to quickly move from your present location to your previous location in a worksheet by pressing F5 and the Enter key (provided that you used the Goto feature to move to your present position).

Keyboard scrolling without changing the cell pointer's position

You can use the Scroll Lock key to "freeze" the position of the cell pointer in the worksheet so that you can scroll new areas of the worksheet into view with key-strokes such as PgDn and Ctrl+PgDn without changing the cell pointer's original position (in essence, making these keystrokes work the same way as the scroll bars).

When you press the Scroll Lock key, Excel displays the SCRL mode indicator on the status bar. This is your sign that Scroll Lock is engaged. From then on, when you scroll the worksheet with the keyboard, Excel will not select a new cell as it brings a new section of the worksheet into view.

To "unfreeze" the cell pointer when scrolling the worksheet via the keyboard, just press the Scroll Lock key again so that the SCRL indicator disappears from the status bar.

To display the cell that contains the cell pointer after scrolling with Scroll Lock, choose the S<u>h</u>ow Active Cell command from the For<u>m</u>ula menu.

Menurama: Pull-Down vs. Shortcut

For those occasions when the Excel toolbars don't provide you with a ready-made tool for getting a particular task done, you'll have to turn to Excel's system of menu commands. Excel exhibits a little bit of menu overkill — in addition to the regular pull-down menus found in most all Windows applications, the program also offers a secondary system of *shortcut menus*.

Shortcut menus are so called because they offer faster access to the often used menu commands. Shortcut menus do this because they're attached to a particular screen object (such as a toolbar, document window, or worksheet cell) and contain only the commands that pertain to that object. As a result, shortcut menus often bring together commands otherwise found on several individual pull-down menus on the menu bar.

May I take your order, Ma'am?

As when moving the cell pointer in the worksheet, Excel offers you a choice between using the mouse or the keyboard to select commands from the pull-down menu bars.

- ✔ To open a pull-down menu with the mouse, you simply click on the menu name on the menu bar.

- ✔ To open a pull-down menu with the keyboard, you hold down the Alt key as you type the letter that is underlined in the menu name (also known as the *command letter*). For instance, if you press Alt and then type **R**, Excel will open the Formula menu because the r in Formula is underlined.

- ✔ Alternatively, you can press and release the Alt key or function key F10 to access the menu bar, and then press the → key until you highlight the menu you want to open. Then, to open the menu, you press the ↓ key.

Once you've opened your pull-down menu, you can select any of its commands by clicking on the command with the mouse, typing the underlined letter in the command name, or by pressing the ↓ key until you highlight the command and then pressing the Enter key.

As you learn the Excel commands, you can combine the opening of a menu and selecting one of its menu commands.

- ✔ With the mouse, you click on the menu, and then drag the pointer down the open menu until you highlight the desired command, whereupon you release the mouse button.

- ✔ With the keyboard, you hold down the Alt key as you type both the command letter for the pull-down menu and its command. So to close the active document window by choosing the Close command from the File menu, you simply press Alt, and then type **FC** before releasing the Alt key.

Some commands on the Excel pull-down menus have shortcut keystrokes assigned to them (shown after the command on the pull-down menu). You can use the shortcut keystrokes to select the desired command instead of having to access the pull-down menus.

For example, to save the active document, you can press the shortcut keys Shift+F12 instead of selecting the Save option on the File menu.

Many commands on the pull-down menus lead to the display of a dialog box, containing further commands and options (see "How To Have an Intelligent Conversation with a Dialog Box"). You can tell which commands on a pull-down menu lead to dialog boxes because the command name is followed by three periods (known as an *ellipsis*).

For example, you know that selecting the Save As command on the File menu opens a dialog box because the command is listed as Save As... on the File menu.

Also, note that pull-down menu commands are not always available to you. You can tell when a command is not currently available because the command name appears in light gray (or *dimmed*) on the pull-down menu. A command on a pull-down menu remains dimmed until the conditions under which it operates exist in your document.

For example, the Paste command on the Edit menu remains dimmed as long as the Clipboard is empty. But, as soon as you move or copy some information into the Clipboard with the Cut or Copy commands on the Edit menu, the Paste option is no longer dimmed and appears in normal bold type when you open the Edit menu, indicating, of course, that this command is now available for your use.

For 1-2-3 weenies only

If you ever used (or tried to use) Lotus 1-2-3 for DOS, you may remember that you press the slash key (/ — the key that does double duty with the ?) to activate the 1-2-3 menus. In deference to the millions of 1-2-3 users, Excel also recognizes and responds appropriately (that is, it activates the menu bar) when you press the / key. It is only right that Excel borrows this keystroke from Lotus 1-2-3 since 1-2-3 borrowed it from its predecessor, VisiCalc, which actually originated its usage.

Because the slash key activates the menus, you can use it instead of the Alt key with the command letters when you want to select Excel commands with the keyboard. For example, instead of pressing Alt+FS to save changes to the active document, you can just as well press /FS (almost takes you home, doesn't it?).

The Old Favorites

Actually, Excel has it all worked out so that 1-2-3 converts like yourself can have almost all of your old favorite navigation keys back the way "Lotus intended them." For example, you know how the Tab and Shift+Tab in Excel only move the cell pointer one cell left and right, instead of scrolling the worksheet left and right by a screenful as they do in 1-2-3. Well, you can restore the so-called Big Right and Big Left scrolling function (as well as moving to the first cell with Home key instead of the beginning of the row) by activating the Alternate Navigation Keys option. To find out how to do this, see Chapter 10.

Making short work of shortcut menus

Unlike the pull-down menus which you can access either with the mouse or the keyboard, you *must* use the mouse to open shortcut menus and select their commands. Because shortcut menus are attached to particular objects on the screen like a document window, toolbar, or worksheet cell, Excel uses the *right* mouse button to open shortcut menus (clicking on a screen object such as a cell with the *left* mouse button simply selects that object).

To display a shortcut menu on the Macintosh, hold down the ⌘+option keys as you click the object such as the cell or toolbar.

Figure 1-7 shows you the shortcut menu attached to the Excel toolbars. To open this menu, you position the mouse pointer somewhere on the toolbar and click on the right mouse button. Be sure that you don't click on the left button or you'll end up activating the tool that the pointer is on!

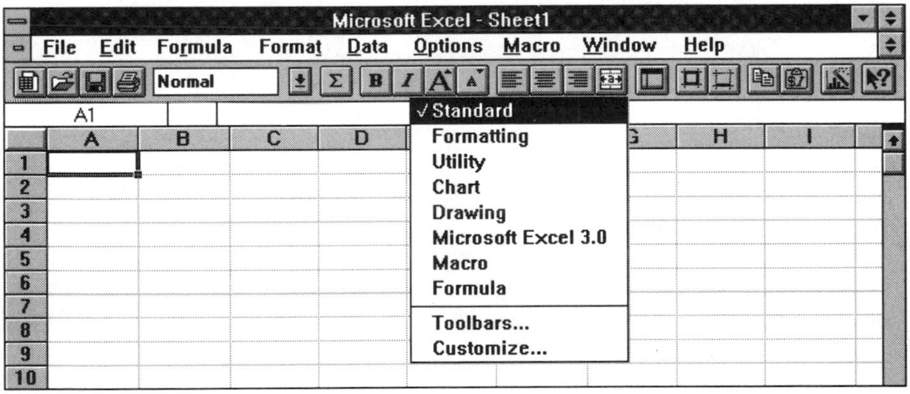

Figure 1-7:
The Toolbar shortcut menu.

Microsoft Excel - Sheet1

File Edit Formula Format Data Options Macro Window Help

| | | | | | | | | | | | | | |

A1

	A	B	C	D	√ Standard		G	H	I
1					**Formatting**				
2					**Utility**				
3					**Chart**				
4					**Drawing**				
5					**Microsoft Excel 3.0**				
6					**Macro**				
7					**Formula**				
8					**Toolbars...**				
9					**Customize...**				
10									

Once you open the Toolbar shortcut menu, you can use its commands to display or hide any of the built-in toolbars or to customize the toolbars (see Chapter 11 for details).

Figure 1-8 shows you the shortcut menu attached to any of the cells in the worksheet. To open this shortcut menu, you position the pointer on any one of the cells and click the right mouse button. Note that you can also open this shortcut menu and apply its commands to the group of cells that you have selected (you'll learn how to make cell selections in Chapter 2).

Because the commands on shortcut menus do not contain command letters (although some of them do display shortcut keystrokes), to select one of their commands, you must either click the command with the mouse or press ↑ or ↓ until you highlight the command and press Enter.

Now here's the trick if you use the mouse: You have to remember to switch gears and click the shortcut menu command with the *left* mouse button!

Click *right* to open the shortcut menu, and then click *left* to select a shortcut command.

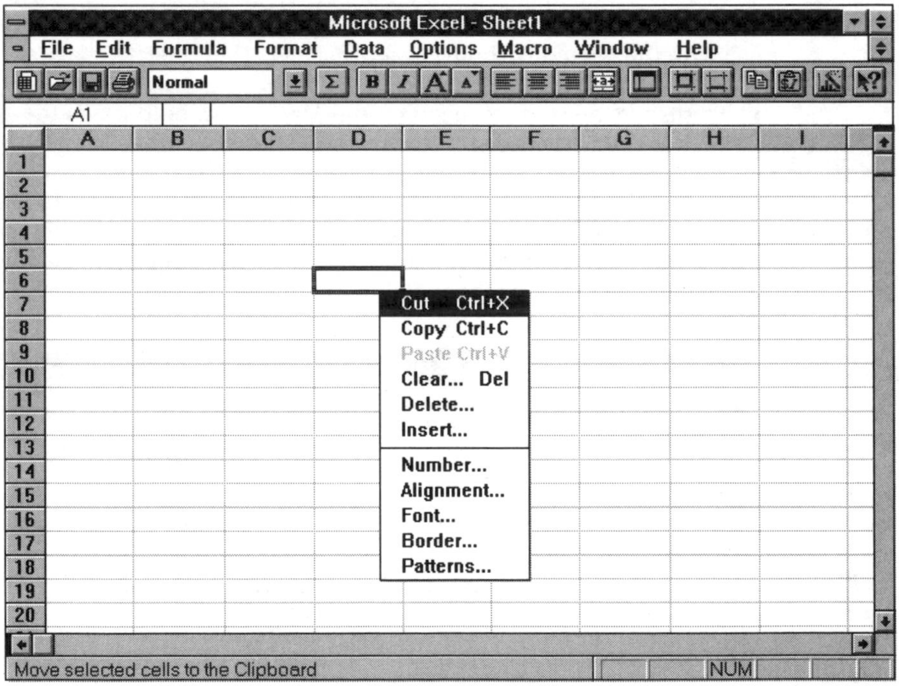

Microsoft Excel - Sheet1

| File | Edit | Formula | Format | Data | Options | Macro | Window | Help |

Normal

A1

	A	B	C	D	E	F	G	H	I
1									
2									
3									
4									
5									
6									
7				Cut Ctrl+X					
8				Copy Ctrl+C					
9				Paste Ctrl+V					
10				Clear... Del					
11				Delete...					
12				Insert...					
13									
14				Number...					
15				Alignment...					
16				Font...					
17				Border...					
18				Patterns...					
19									
20									

Move selected cells to the Clipboard   NUM

Figure 1-8:
The worksheet cell shortcut menu.

If you want, you can avoid this kind of right/left switching altogether by clicking on the right mouse button to open the shortcut menu. Then, *without releasing the right mouse button*, drag the pointer down to the command you want to select. Once the desired command is highlighted, you then release the right mouse button and voilà, Excel either performs the called-for action or opens the attached dialog box!

There is one shortcut menu that you can open with the keyboard — the shortcut menu attached to the worksheet document window. To open this shortcut menu right below the document window's Control-menu box, press Shift+F10.

Note: This keystroke works for any type of Excel document window except a Chart.

How To Have an Intelligent Conversation with a Dialog Box

Many an Excel command is attached to a dialog box that presents you with a variety of options you can apply to the command. Figures 1-9 and 1-10 show you the Save As and Display Options dialog boxes. Between these two dialog boxes, you will find all of the different types of buttons and boxes used by Excel in Table 1-4.

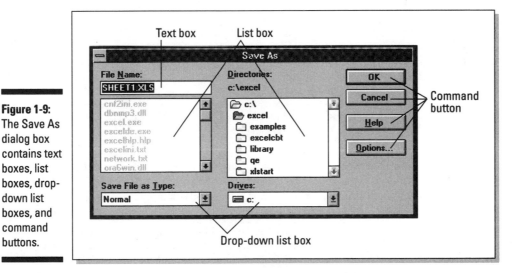

Figure 1-9: The Save As dialog box contains text boxes, list boxes, drop-down list boxes, and command buttons.

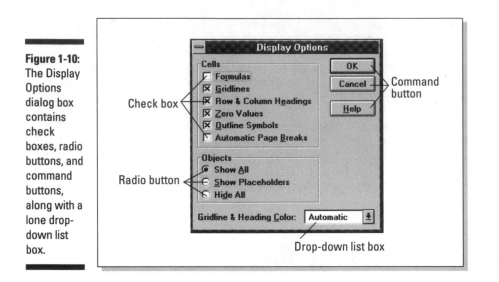

Figure 1-10:
The Display Options dialog box contains check boxes, radio buttons, and command buttons, along with a lone drop-down list box.

Excel dialog boxes have Control-menu boxes in the upper-left corner that you can use to move or close the dialog box. You can move a dialog box within the active document window by dragging its title bar.

Note: Although you can move a dialog box out of the way of some data in your worksheet, you can't change the box's size or shape — these dimensions are permanently fixed by the program.

Table 1-4:	The Parts of a Dialog Box
Button or Box	***What It's Good For***
Text Box	Provides a place for typing a new entry. Many text boxes contain default entries you can edit or replace.
List Box	Provides a list of options from which you choose. If the list box contains more options that can be displayed in its box, the list box contains a scroll bar which you can use to bring new options into view. Some list boxes are attached to a text box, allowing you to make a new entry in the text box either by typing it or by selecting it in the related list box.
Drop-Down List Box	Provides a condensed version of a standard list box that, instead of displaying several options in its list, shows only the current option (which originally is also the default option). To open the list box and display the other options, you click the drop-down button that accompanies the box. Once the list is displayed, you can select a new option from it as you would in any standard list box.

(continued)

Table 1-4:	The Parts of a Dialog Box *(continued)*
Button or Box	*What It's Good For*
Check Box	Presents a dialog box option that you can turn on or off. When the check box contains an X, you know that its option is selected. When a check box is blank, you know that its option is not selected.
Radio (Option) Button	Presents items that have mutually exclusive options. The option button consists of a circle followed by the name option. Option buttons are always arranged in groups and only one of the options in the group can be selected at one time. Excel lets you know which option is currently selected by placing a dot in the middle of its circle (when an option button is selected it looks like a knob on an old-fashioned radio, thus the name *radio button*).
Command Button	Initiates an action. The command button is rectangular in shape and the name of the command is displayed within the button. If a name in a command button is followed by an ellipsis (...), Excel displays another dialog box containing even more options when you select the button.

Many dialog boxes contain default options or entries that are automatically selected unless you make new choices before you close the dialog box.

- ✔ To close a dialog box and put your selections in effect, choose the OK button or the Close button (some boxes lack an OK button).

- ✔ If the OK button is surrounded by a dark border, which is very often the case, you can also press the Enter key to put your selections into effect.

- ✔ To close a dialog box without putting your selections into effect, you can either double-click the Control-menu box in the box's upper-left corner, select the Cancel or Close button in the dialog box, or, more simply, press the Esc key.

Most dialog boxes group related options together as an item (often, this is done by placing a box around the options). When making selections in a dialog box with the mouse, you simply click on the selection you want to use or, in the case of text entries, modify.

When making selections with the keyboard, however, you must sometimes first activate the item before you can select any of its options.

- ✔ Press the Tab key until you activate one of the options in the item (Shift+Tab activates the previous item).
- ✔ When you press Tab (or Shift+Tab), Excel indicates which option is activated either by highlighting the default entry or placing a dotted line around the name of the option.
- ✔ After activating an option, you can change its setting either by pressing ↑ or ↓ (this works with sets of radio buttons or options in a list or drop-down list boxes), pressing the spacebar (this works to select and deselect check boxes), or by typing a new entry (used in text boxes).

You can also select an option by pressing the Alt key and then typing the underlined (command) letter in the option or item name.

- ✔ By pressing Alt and typing the command letter of a text box option, you select the entry in that text box (which you can then replace by typing the new entry).
- ✔ By pressing Alt and typing the command letter of a check box option, you can turn the option on and off (by adding or removing its X).
- ✔ By pressing Alt and typing the command letter of a radio button, you can select the option while at the same time deselecting whatever radio button was previously current.
- ✔ By pressing Alt and typing the command letter of a command button, you initiate its command or display another dialog box.

The Mac, of course, does not have an Alt key. If you are keyboard-minded, however, you can activate the menu bar and have Excel display the command letters on the pull-down menus by typing the / (forward slash) located on the same key as the question mark.

You can also select a list box option by typing the first few characters of its name — as soon as you begin typing, Excel will open a text box to contain your characters and jump to the first option in the list box whose name begins with the characters you enter.

In addition to the more elaborate dialog boxes shown in Figures 1-9 and 1-10, you will also encounter a simpler type of dialog box used to display messages and warnings (these dialog boxes are appropriately known as *alert boxes*). Many dialog boxes of this type contain just an OK button that you must select to close the dialog box after reading the message.

Help Is on the Way

You can get on-line help with Excel at anytime you need it while using the program. The only problem with the Help system is that it's really only truly helpful when you're familiar with the Excel jargon. If you don't know what Excel calls a particular feature, you'll have trouble locating it in the help topics (just like trying to look up a word you have no idea how to spell in a dictionary).

The easiest way to avoid this dilemma is to use the Help tool on the Standard toolbar to get help information specific to the particular command you want to use. When you click on the Help tool, Excel changes the mouse pointer shape by adding a question mark to it. To get help on a particular command or a part of the Excel window, you use this question mark pointer to select it.

For example, say that you want to refresh your memory on how you use the AutoSum tool on the Standard toolbar to total a column of numbers. You simply click the Help tool, and then click the AutoSum tool with the question mark pointer. When you do this, the program displays the Microsoft Excel Help window displaying a brief paragraph of information on using the AutoSum tool.

You can also use the Help tool to get information on any of the commands on the pull-down menus. Suppose that you are curious about the function of the Border command on the Format pull-down. To obtain information on what this command does and how you use it, you click the Help tool; then click on the Format menu with the question mark pointer. Once this menu is open, click on the Border command. Doing this will open the Microsoft Excel Help window with several screenfuls of information on adding borders to cells in a worksheet.

When reading a help topic in the Microsoft Help system, you may notice that certain terms are underlined (and in a different color on a color monitor).

- ✔ A term underlined with a solid underline is called a *jump term* because when you click on it, the Help system immediately "jumps" you to a related help topic.

- ✔ A term underlined with a dotted line is a *glossary term*, meaning that it is attached to a brief definition. When you click a glossary term, the Help system displays the definition in a small pop-up dialog box as long as you hold down the mouse button.

If you are running Excel for the Macintosh under System 7, the Help commands are located on the pull-down menu attached to the question mark icon located on the far right of the menu bar. In addition to standard help commands, Excel 4.0 offers balloon help so that you can identify the names of the different parts of the Excel screen. Note that balloon help is especially good for identifying the different tools on an unfamiliar toolbar.

If you come upon a help topic that you would like to print out, you can do this by selecting the Print Topic command from the File menu (be sure that your printer is turned on first and that you select the File menu in the Microsoft Excel Help window on the right — not the Excel window beneath).

You can also copy information from an Excel help topic to your word processor or even to an Excel document. To copy help information, choose the Copy command from the Edit menu (in the Microsoft Excel Help window). The Help system will display a Copy dialog box where you can select as much of the text as you want to copy. Drag the I-beam cursor through the text you want to copy (or hold down the Shift key as you press the arrow keys), and then select the Copy command button.

Once you've copied the selected information in this manner, you can copy the help information into a word processing document or worksheet by starting the program and opening the document (if necessary), and then choosing the Paste command on the program's Edit menu.

If you are experiencing problems with the software or some sort of software/ hardware incompatibilities that are driving you nuts, select the Product Support command on the Help pull-down menu (in the Excel window, not the Microsoft Excel Help window), and then click on the `Microsoft Product Support Services in the United States` jump term. This takes you to a help topic explaining the product support policies and containing the on-line support telephone number.

When It's Quitting Time

When you're ready to call it a day and quit Excel, you have several choices for shutting the program down. One way to exit Excel is by choosing the Exit command on the File menu. You can accomplish the same thing by double-clicking on the Control-menu box on the Excel window or by pressing Alt+F4.

If you try to exit Excel after working on a document and you haven't saved your latest changes, the program will beep at you and display an alert box asking if you want to save your changes. To save your changes before exiting, choose the Yes command button (for detailed information on saving documents, see Chapter 2). If you've just been playing around in the worksheet and don't want to save your changes, you can abandon the document by choosing the No button.

Chapter 2
Concocting Your First Worksheet

● ●

In This Chapter

▶ How to start a new worksheet document

▶ How to enter different types of information in the document

▶ How to create simple formulas

▶ How to correct mistakes you make when entering information

▶ How to enter information in a group of cells

▶ How to repeat an entry in a group of cells

▶ How to use the AutoFill feature to extend a series of entries

▶ How to enter and use built-in functions in formulas

▶ How to save a worksheet document

● ●

*N*ow that you know how to get into Excel and display that great big blank worksheet on the screen, it's high time you learned what to do with it. To that point, this chapter focuses on the ins and outs of getting information into the worksheet.

After you learn how to fill up a worksheet with the requisite raw data and formulas, you learn what has to be the most important lesson of all: how to save all the information on disk so that you don't ever have to enter the stuff again!

Where Do I Begin?

When you start Excel without specifying a document to open, you see a blank worksheet in a new document window (temporarily named Sheet1). To begin a new worksheet, you simply start entering information in the Sheet1 document window.

Here are a few simple guidelines to keep in mind when you start working in the sheet:

- ✔ Whenever you can, organize your information in tables of data that use adjacent (neighboring) columns and rows. Start the tables in the upper-left corner of the worksheet and work your way down the sheet, rather than across the sheet, whenever possible. When it's practical, separate each table by no more than a single column or row.

- ✔ When you set up these tables, don't skip columns and rows just to "space out" the information. In Chapter 3, you learn how to place as much white space as you want between information in adjacent columns and rows by widening columns, heightening rows, and changing the alignment.

- ✔ Reserve a single column at the left edge of the table for the table's row headings.

- ✔ Reserve a single row at the top of the table for the table's column headings.

- ✔ If your table requires a title, put the title in the row above the column headings. Put the title in the same column as the row headings. You learn how to center this title across the columns of the entire table in Chapter 3.

You may wonder why, after the big deal about the size of the Excel worksheet in Chapter 1, the emphasis in these guidelines is on keeping information as close together as possible in the worksheet. After all, given the vast amount of wide-open space in an Excel worksheet, it seems natural that space conservation would be one of your lowest priorities when setting out your information.

You would be right, except that space conservation in the worksheet equals memory conservation. You see, as the table grows and expands into new areas of the worksheet, Excel decides on a certain amount of computer memory to hold open for the cell entries. If you skip columns and rows that you really don't need to skip, you waste computer memory that could otherwise be used to store more information in the worksheet.

Keep in mind that it's the amount of computer memory available to Excel that determines the ultimate size of the worksheet, not the total number of cells in the blank worksheet. When you run out of memory, you've effectively run out of space — no matter how many columns and rows are still left to fill. To maximize the information you can get into a worksheet, always adopt the "covered wagon" approach to worksheet design.

To check out how much computer memory is available to Excel at any given time, choose the About Microsoft Excel command from the Help menu. The About Microsoft Excel dialog box appears, displaying the serial number of your copy of Excel, the available memory in *kilobytes* (thousands of bytes), and whether a math co-processor chip is present (this chip can speed up worksheet calculations quite a bit). When you finish viewing this information, choose OK or press Esc to close the dialog box.

The ABCs of Data Entry

To enter information in a new worksheet, simply select the cell where you want the information to appear and begin typing. As soon as you type the first character of the entry, Excel activates the formula bar, displaying the current cell address on the left; the cancel and enter boxes in the center section; and the characters you typed, followed by the insertion point (the flashing vertical bar) on the right. As you continue to type, Excel displays your progress both on the formula bar and in the active cell in the worksheet (see Figure 2-1).

After you finish typing an entry, you still have to enter it in the active cell by clicking on the enter box (the one with the check mark in it) on the formula bar, pressing Enter, or pressing one of the direction keys like ↓ or →.

If you click on the enter box or press Enter, Excel does not move the cell pointer after completing the cell entry. If you press an arrow key, Excel completes the cell entry and selects the next cell in the direction of the arrow.

On the Macintosh, you can complete an entry by pressing either the Return key or the Enter key (located on the numeric keypad on the extended keyboard). If you press the Return key, Excel enters the information and moves the cell pointer down one row. If you press the Enter key, Excel enters the information without moving the cell pointer.

As soon as you complete your entry in the active cell, Excel deactivates the formula bar by removing the cancel and enter boxes. The information you entered continues to appear in the cell in the worksheet. Every time you put the cell pointer into that particular cell, the cell entry will reappear on the formula bar.

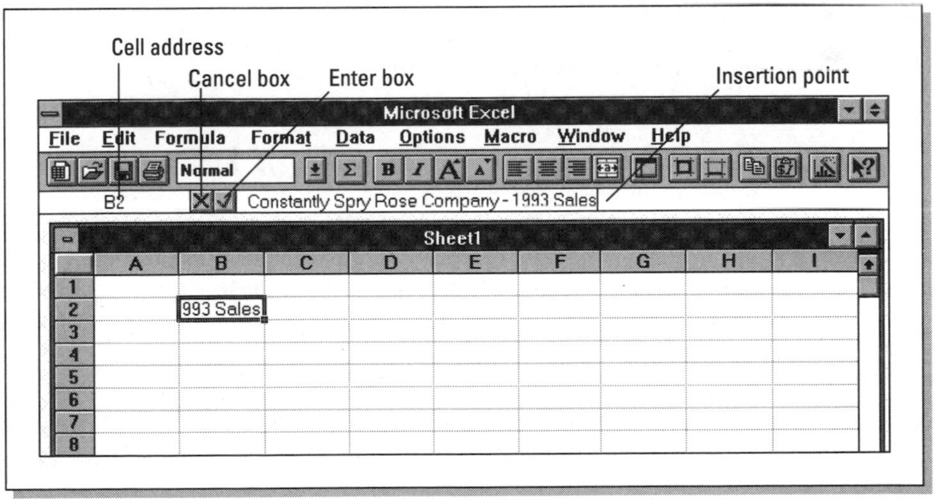

Figure 2-1:
Entering information in a blank worksheet cell.

If you realize you're just about to put information in the wrong cell, you can clear and deactivate the formula bar before you complete the entry by clicking on the cancel box (the one with the X in it) or by pressing Esc.

Excel can automatically advance the cell pointer to the next cell down in the column every time you press Enter to complete an entry. If you want to customize Excel this way, choose the Workspace command from the Options menu and activate the Move Selection after Enter check box option in the Workspace Options dialog box.

Is the Data Your Type?

Excel checks each entry you make to see whether you've entered a formula that should be calculated. Excel performs the check to classify the entry as one of three different types of data: *text,* a *value,* or a *formula.*

If Excel finds that the entry is a formula, the program calculates the formula and displays the computed result in the worksheet cell (you continue to see the formula itself, however, on the formula bar). If Excel is satisfied that the entry does not qualify as a formula (I'll give you the qualifications for a *bona fide* formula later in this chapter), the program then determines whether the entry should be classified as text or as a value.

Note: Excel must make this determination because it aligns text entries in cells differently than values. Also, most formulas work properly only when they are fed values. You can foul up formulas if you enter text in a cell where a value ought to be.

In contrast to formulas, text and values are considered *constants.* They are constants because they only change when you edit or replace them in their cells. Formulas, on the other hand, update their computed values as soon as you modify any of the values they use.

Text (neither fish nor fowl)

Excel reads any entry that doesn't shake out as either a formula or a value as text — making text the catchall category of Excel entries. Most text entries (also known as *labels*) consist of a combination of letters and punctuation or letters and numbers used for titles and headings in the worksheet.

You can tell right away that Excel has accepted a cell entry as text because text entries are automatically aligned at the left edge of their cells. If the text entry is wider than the cell can display, the display of the entry spills over into the neighboring cell or cells on the right, provided that the next cell is blank (see Figure 2-2).

If, sometime later, you enter information in the cell next door, Excel cuts off the spill-over of the long text entry (see Figure 2-3). Not to worry: Excel doesn't actually lop these characters off the cell entry — it simply shaves the display to make room for the new entry. If you feel separation anxiety for your "missing" text, just widen the column for the cell that contains the missing characters (to learn how to do this, skip ahead to Chapter 3).

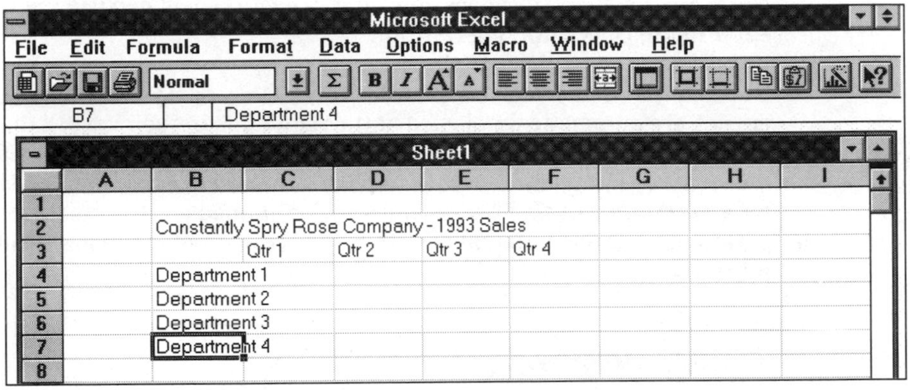

Figure 2-2:
Long text
entries
appear in
neighboring
blank cells.

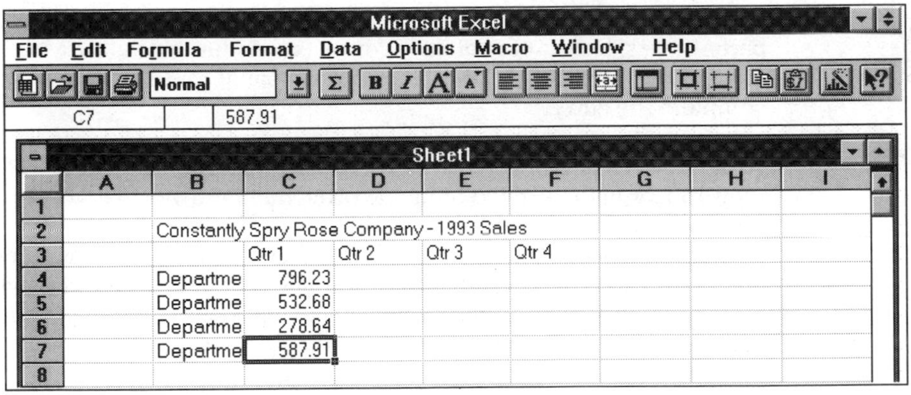

Figure 2-3:
Cell entries
cut off the
display of
spill-over
text.

A space, although undetectable to the eye, is considered as much a text character as the letter A or Z. If you introduce a space into an otherwise completely numeric entry, Excel categorizes the entry as text (indicated by its alignment at the left edge of the cell). If you feed that entry into a formula, the text classification completely throws off the answer because text entries are treated like zeros (0) in a formula.

Values to the right of me

Values in Excel can be of two kinds: numbers that represent quantities (such as 10 departments or 100 dollars) and numbers that represent dates (such as January 11, 1993) or times (such as 11:59 AM).

Note: Almost all the formulas you enter in a worksheet can use the values you enter in the cells without any problem.

You can tell when Excel has accepted a cell entry as a value because numeric entries are automatically aligned at the right edge of their cells. If the value is wider than the cell can display, Excel automatically converts the value to *scientific notation* (for example, 6E+08 indicates that the 6 is followed by eight zeros for a grand total of six hundred million). To change a value that's been converted to scientific notation back to a normal number, simply widen the column for that cell.

Number please!

To enter a numeric value, select a cell and type the number. To enter negative values in a cell, begin the number with the minus sign or hyphen (–), for example, **–175**. Alternatively, enclose the number in parentheses: **(175)**. If you use parentheses, Excel automatically converts the numeric value to one with a minus sign; if you enter **(5.75)** in a cell, Excel changes it to -5.75 as soon as you complete the entry.

With numeric values, you can include dollar signs ($) and commas (,) just as they appear in the printed or handwritten numbers you are working from. Just be aware that when you enter a number with commas, Excel assigns a number format to the value that matches your use of commas (for more information on number formats and how they are used, see Chapter 3). Likewise, when you preface a financial figure with a dollar sign, Excel assigns an appropriate dollar number format to the value (one that automatically inserts commas between the thousands).

When a numeric value uses decimal places, use the period as the decimal point. When you enter decimal values, the program automatically adds a zero before the decimal point (Excel inserts 0.34 in a cell when you enter **.34**) and drops trailing zeros entered after the decimal point (Excel inserts 12.5 in a cell when you enter **12.50**).

If you don't know the decimal equivalent for a value, you can enter the value as a fraction. For example, enter **2 3/16** (with a space between the 2 and 3) instead of **2.1875**. When you enter the fractional form of a decimal number, Excel inputs the decimal equivalent in the cell, although it displays the fraction in the cell by assigning it a special fractional number format. When you enter simple fractions such as 3/4 or 5/8, you must enter them as a mixed number preceded by zero; for example, enter **0 3/4** or **0 5/8** (be sure to include a space between the zero and the fraction).

When entering a numeric value in a cell that represents a percentage, you have a choice. You can either divide the number by 100 and enter the decimal equivalent (for example, enter **.12** for 12 percent) or you can enter the number with the percent sign (for example, enter **12%**). Either way, Excel stores the decimal value in the cell (0.12 in this example). If you use the percent sign, Excel assigns a percentage number format to the value in the worksheet so that it appears as 12%.

Let's make it a date!

It may strike you as odd that dates and times are entered in the cells of a worksheet as values rather than as text. The only reason dates and times are entered as values is so that they can be used in formulas.

Although you can enter dates as text without anything bad happening to you or the worksheet, you won't be able to use such dates in calculations performed by formulas. For example, if you enter two dates as values, you can then set up a formula that subtracts the more recent date from the older date and returns the number of days between them. If you enter the two dates as text entries, Excel cannot calculate the difference between them with a formula.

Dates are stored as serial numbers that indicate how many days have elapsed from a starting date; times are stored as decimal fractions indicating the elapsed part of the 24-hour period. Excel supports two date systems: the 1900 date system used by Excel for Windows where January 1, 1900, is the starting date (serial number 1) and the 1904 system used by Excel for the Macintosh where January 2, 1904, is the starting date.

Excel determines whether the date or time you type is entered as a value or as text by the format you follow. If you follow one of Excel's built-in date and time formats, the program recognizes the date or time as a value. If you don't follow one of the built-in formats, the program enters the date or time as a text entry — it's as simple as that.

Excel recognizes the following time formats:

> 3:21 PM
>
> 3:21:04 PM
>
> 15:21
>
> 15:21:04

Excel knows the following date formats:

> 10/25/93 or 10-25-93
>
> 25-Oct-93
>
> 10-Oct
>
> Oct-93

Notice that one of the most commonly used date formats (the one that spells out the full name of the month, follows the day of the month with a comma, and uses four digits for the year) is not on this list. For example, if you enter **October 25, 1993** in a cell, Excel accepts the date as a text entry.

To get around this problem, enter the date using one of the formats Excel knows (for example, **10/25/93** or **10-25-93**), and then create a date format of your own to display the date in the form October 25, 1993 (see Chapter 3 for details on how to do this).

Can you fix my decimal places?

If you find that you need to enter a whole slew of numbers that use the same number of decimal places, you can turn on Excel's Fixed Decimal setting and have the program enter the decimals for you. This feature really comes in handy when you have to enter hundreds of financial figures that all use two decimal places for the number of cents.

To *fix* the number of decimal places in a numeric entry, follow these steps:

1. Choose the <u>W</u>orkspace command from the <u>O</u>ptions menu.

The Workspace Options dialog box appears.

2. **Click on the Fixed Decimal check box.**

   By default, Excel fixes the decimal place two places to the left of the last number you type.

3. **To change the default setting, type a new number in the Places text box.**

   For example, type **3** in the Places text box to enter numbers with the following decimal placement: 00.000.

4. **Choose OK or press Enter.**

   Excel displays the FIX status indicator on the status bar to let you know that the Fixed Decimal feature is active.

After fixing the decimal place in numeric values, Excel automatically adds the decimal point to any numeric value you enter — all you do is type the digits and complete the entry in the cell. For example, to enter the numeric value 100.99 in a cell after fixing the decimal point at 2 places, type the digits **10099**. When you click on the enter box, press Enter, or press an arrow key to complete the cell entry, Excel inputs the value 100.99 in the cell.

Remember that while the Fixed Decimal setting is turned on, Excel adds a decimal point to all the numeric values you enter. If you want to enter a number without a decimal point or one with a decimal point in a position different from the one called for by this feature, type the decimal point (the period) yourself. For example, to enter the number 1099 instead of 10.99 when the decimal point is fixed at 2 places, type **1099.** in the cell.

When you're ready to return to normal data entry for numerical values (where you enter any decimal points yourself), open the Workspace Options dialog box again and deselect the Fixed Decimal check box. Excel removes the FIX indicator from the status bar.

To make the Fixed Decimal feature work even more efficiently, select the block of the cells where the numbers are to be entered (see "Home, Home on the Range," later in this chapter), press Num Lock, and then enter the values from the numeric keypad. This approach enables you to do true 10-key data entry: all you have to do to enter a value in a cell is type its digits and press Enter on the numeric keypad — Excel inserts the decimal point in the proper place.

Formulas equal to the task

As entries go in Excel, formulas are the real workhorses of the worksheet. If you set up a formula properly, it computes the right answer when you first enter it into a cell, and from then on, it keeps itself up to date, recalculating the results whenever you change any of the values the formula uses.

You inform Excel that you are entering a formula in the current cell, rather than some text or a value, by starting the formula with the equal sign (=). Most simple formulas follow the equal sign with a built-in function such as SUM or AVERAGE (see "Becoming Fully Functional," later in this chapter, for more information on using functions in formulas). Other simple formulas use a series of values or cell references (that contain values) separated by one or more of the following mathematical operators:

+ (plus sign) for addition

– (minus sign or hyphen) for subtraction

* (asterisk) for multiplication

/ (slash) for division

^ (caret) for raising a number to a power

For example, to create a formula in cell C5 that multiplies a value entered in cell A5 by a value in cell B5, enter the following formula in cell C5:

```
=A5*B5
```

To enter this formula in cell C5, follow these steps:

1. **Select cell C5.**

2. **Type the entire formula =A5*B5 in the formula bar and press Enter.**

   OR

1. **Type = (equal sign).**

2. **Select cell A5 in the worksheet by using the mouse or the keyboard.**

   This action places the cell reference A5 in the formula bar.

3. **Type *.**

   The asterisk is used for multiplication rather than the *x* you used in school. (Do not type the period, however.)

4. **Select cell B5 in the worksheet.**

   This action places the cell reference B5 in the formula.

5. **Click on the enter box or press Enter.**

The method of selecting the cells you use in a formula, rather than typing their cell references, is known as *pointing*. Pointing is not only quicker than typing cell references, it also reduces the risk that you might type the wrong cell reference. When you type a cell reference, you can easily type the wrong column letter or row number and not realize your mistake just by looking at the calculated result returned in the cell.

If you select the cell you want to use in a formula either by clicking on it or moving the cell pointer to it, there is less chance that you'll enter the wrong cell reference.

When you finish entering the formula =**A5*B5** in cell C5 of the worksheet, Excel displays the calculated result depending on the values currently entered in cells A5 and B5. Here are some examples:

- ✔ If cell A5 contains the value 20, and cell B5 contains 100, the program displays the result 2000 in cell C5 of the worksheet.

- ✔ If you change the value in cell A5 to **10**, the calculated value in cell C5 immediately changes to 1000.

- ✔ If you clear cell B5 of its entry without replacing it with a new one, the calculated value in cell C5 changes to 0.

Note: Empty cells carry a zero value; the formula A5*B5 is equivalent to 20*0 when you clear cell B5.

The major strength of the electronic spreadsheet is the capability of formulas to automatically change their calculated results to match changes in the cells referenced by the formulas.

Following the pecking order

Many formulas you create perform more than one mathematical operation. Excel performs each operation in the left-to-right direction, according to a pecking order (order of operations) that says multiplication and division pull more weight than addition and subtraction and are, therefore, performed first.

Consider the series of operations in the following formula:

```
=A2+B2*C2
```

If cell A2 contains the number 5, B2 contains the number 10, and C2 contains the number 2, Excel evaluates the following formula:

```
=5+10*2
```

In this formula, Excel multiplies 10 times 2 to equal 20 and then adds this result to 5 to produce the result, 25.

If you want Excel to perform the addition between the values in cells A2 and B2 before the program multiplies the result by the value in cell C2, enclose the addition operation in parentheses as follows:

```
=(A2+B2)*C2
```

The parentheses around the addition tell Excel you want this operation performed before the multiplication. If cell A2 contains the value 5, B2 contains the value 10, and C2 contains 2, Excel adds 5 and 10 to equal 15 and then multiplies this result by 2 to produce the result, 30.

In fancier formulas, you may need to add more than one set of parentheses, one within another (like the wooden Russian dolls that nest within each other) to indicate the order in which you want the calculations to take place. When nesting parentheses, Excel first performs the calculation contained in the most inside pair of parentheses, and then uses that result in further calculations as the program works its way outward. For example, consider the following formula:

```
=(A4+(B4-C4))*D4
```

Excel first subtracts the value in cell C4 from the value in cell B4, adds the difference to the value in cell A4, and, finally, multiplies that sum by the value in D4.

Without the additions of the two sets of nested parentheses, left to its own devices Excel would first multiply the value in cell C4 by that in D4, add the value in A4 to that in B4, and then perform the subtraction.

When nesting parentheses in a formula, pair them properly so that you have a right parenthesis for every left parenthesis in the formula. If you do not include a right parenthesis for every left one, Excel displays an alert dialog box with the message Parentheses do not match when you try to enter the formula. After you close this dialog box, Excel goes right back to the formula bar, where you can insert the missing parenthesis and press Enter to correct the unbalanced condition. By the way, Excel always highlights matched parentheses.

When a formula freaks

Under certain circumstances, even the best formulas can freak out in a worksheet. You can tell right away that a formula's gone haywire because instead of the nice calculated value you expect when you enter the formula, you get a strange, incomprehensible message in all uppercase letters beginning with the number sign (#) and ending with an exclamation point or, in one case, a question mark. This weirdness is known, in the parlance of spreadsheets, as an *error value*. Its purpose is to let you know that some element — either in the formula itself or in a cell referred to by the formula — is preventing Excel from returning the anticipated calculated value.

The worst thing about error values is that they can contaminate other formulas in the worksheet. If a formula returns an error value to a cell, and a second formula in another cell refers to the value calculated by the first formula, the second formula returns the same error value.

Once an error value shows up in a cell, you have to discover what caused the error and edit the worksheet. Table 2-1 lists the error values you might run into in a worksheet and explains the most common causes.

Table 2-1:	Error Values That Can Be Returned by Formulas
What Shows Up in the Cell	*What's Going On Here?*
#DIV/0!	Appears when the formula calls for division by a cell that either contains the value 0 or, as is more often the case, is empty. Division by zero is a no-no according to our math.
#NAME?	Appears when the formula refers to a *range name* (see Chapter 5 for info on naming ranges) that doesn't exist in the worksheet. This error value appears when you type the wrong range name or fail to enclose in quotation marks some text used in the formula, causing Excel to think that the text refers to a range name (see Chapter 13 for info on quotation marks).
#NULL!	Appears most often when you insert a space, where you should have used a comma, to separate cell references used as arguments for functions (see "Becoming Fully Functional," later in this chapter).
#NUM!	Appears when Excel encounters a problem with a number in the formula, such as the wrong type of argument in an Excel function or a calculation that produces a number too large or too small to be represented in the worksheet.
#REF!	Appears when Excel encounters an invalid cell reference, such as when you delete a cell referred to in a formula or paste cells over cells referred to in a formula.
#VALUE!	Appears when you use the wrong type of argument in a function, the wrong type of operator, or when you call for a mathematical operation that refers to cells that contain text entries.

Correcting Those Nasty Little Typos

When you enter information in a cell, it's quite easy to make a mistake (but the only time a mistake matters is when you don't catch it!). You both make and notice your mistakes at different times in the process of entering information in cells. Use the following list to apply the appropriate first aid:

✔ If you catch the mistake before you complete the entry, you can delete it by pressing Backspace (the key immediately above the Enter key) until you remove all the incorrect characters from the formula bar. Then you can retype the rest of the entry or the formula before you insert it into the current cell.

✔ If you don't discover the mistake until after you've completed the cell entry, you can either replace the entry in its entirety or just edit the incorrect parts. To replace a cell entry, select the cell and type the replacement.

✔ You have the opportunity to restore the current entry if you discover you are about to replace the wrong cell. Although Excel appears to wipe out the current cell entry from the formula bar the moment you begin typing, the program doesn't actually replace the current information with the new entry until you complete the entry by clicking on the enter box, pressing Enter, or pressing one of the arrow keys. To clear the formula bar of what you've just typed and restore the current entry, click on the cancel box (the one with the *X*) or press Esc.

✔ If the error in an entry is relatively easy to fix and the entry is long, you probably want to edit the cell entry rather than replace it. To edit the cell entry, select its cell and then reactivate the formula bar so that you can make editing corrections. Excel does not let you edit the contents of a cell within the worksheet itself (this takes some getting used to, especially if your background is in word processing).

✔ To reactivate the formula bar with the mouse, position the mouse pointer on the formula bar at the first character in the entry that needs editing and click the mouse button to place the insertion point in front of that character. When you position the mouse pointer in the formula-bar area, the pointer changes from the arrowhead to an I-beam. Place the I-beam between two characters on the formula bar and click the mouse button to place the insertion point between the characters.

✔ To reactivate the formula with the keyboard, press F2 to locate the insertion point at the end of the cell entry in the formula bar. You can then use the arrow keys to move to the place in the entry that needs editing.

To activate the formula bar in Excel for the Macintosh so that you can move the insertion point with the arrow keys, press ⌘+U.

Table 2-2 lists the keystrokes you can use to reposition the insertion point in the cell entry and delete unwanted characters. If you want to insert new characters at the insertion point, simply start typing. If you want to delete existing characters at the insertion point as you type new ones, press Ins to switch from the normal insert mode to overtype mode. Excel lets you know that you have switched to overtype mode by displaying the OVR mode indicator on the status bar. To return to normal insert mode, press Ins a second time. When you finish making corrections to the cell entry, you must reenter the edited entry before Excel updates the contents of the cell.

You can reenter the edited cell contents by clicking on the enter box or pressing Enter, but you can't use the arrow keys. When you are editing a cell entry, the arrow keys only move the insertion point through the entry.

Table 2-2:	Keystrokes for Editing Cell Entries on the Formula Bar
Keystroke	*What the Keystroke Does*
Del	Deletes the character following the insertion point
Backspace	Deletes the character in front of the insertion point
→	Positions the insertion point one character to the right
←	Positions the insertion point one character to the left
↑	Positions the insertion point, when it is at the end of the cell entry, to its preceding position to the left
Home	Moves the insertion point in front of the first character of the cell entry
End or ↓	Moves the insertion point after the last character in the cell entry
Ctrl+→	Positions the insertion point in front of the next word in the cell entry
Ctrl+←	Positions the insertion in front of the preceding word in the cell entry
Ins	Switches between insert and overtype mode (indicated by the OVR indicator on the status bar)

Home, Home on the Range

When you want to enter a table of information in a new worksheet, you can simplify the job of entering the data if you select all the empty cells in which you want to make entries before you begin entering any information. Just position the cell pointer in the first cell of what is to become the data table and then select all the cells in the subsequent columns and rows (for information on the ways to select a range of cells, see Chapter 3). After you select the block of cells, you can begin entering the first entry.

When you select a block of cells (also known as a *range*) before you start entering information, Excel restricts data entry to that range as follows:

✔ The program automatically advances the cell pointer to the next cell in the range when you click on the enter box or press Enter to complete each cell entry.

✔ In a cell range that contains several different rows and columns, Excel advances the cell pointer down each row of the column as you make your entries. When the cell pointer reaches the cell in the last row of the column, the cell pointer advances to the first selected row in the next column to the right. If the cell range uses only one row, Excel advances the cell pointer from left to right across the row.

✔ When you finish entering information in the last cell in the selected range, Excel positions the cell pointer in the first cell of the now-completed data table. To deselect the cell range, click the mouse pointer on one of the cells in the worksheet (inside or outside the selected range — it doesn't matter) or press one of the arrow keys.

Be sure that you don't press one of the arrow keys to complete a cell entry within a preselected cell range instead of clicking on the enter box or pressing Enter. Pressing an arrow key deselects the range of cells when Excel moves the cell pointer. To move the cell pointer around a cell range without deselecting the range, try these methods:

✔ Press Tab or Enter to advance to the next cell across the rows of the range.

✔ Press Shift+Tab or Shift+Enter to move back to the previous cell.

✔ Press Tab or Enter to move to the next cell down the columns of the range.

✔ Press Shift+Tab or Shift+Enter to move up the columns.

✔ Press Ctrl+. (period) to move from one corner of the range to another.

When You AutoFill It Up

Many of the worksheets you create with Excel require the entry of a series of sequential dates or numbers. For example, a worksheet may require you to title the columns with the 12 months from January through December or to number the rows from 1 to 100.

Excel's AutoFill feature makes short work of this kind of repetitive task. All you have to enter is the starting values for the series. In most cases, AutoFill is smart enough to figure out how to extend the series for you when you drag the fill handle to the right (to take the series across columns to the right) or down (to extend the series to the rows below).

When creating a series with the fill handle, you can drag in only one direction. For example, you can extend the series or fill the range to the left or right of the cell range that contains the initial values, or you can extend the series or fill the range above or below the cell range that contains the initial values. You can't, however, extend the series or fill the range in two directions at the same time (such as down and to the right by dragging the fill handle diagonally).

When you release the mouse button after extending the range with the fill handle, Excel either creates a series in all of the cells you selected or fills the entire range with the initial value. Table 2-3 shows some of the different initial values that AutoFill can use and the types of series that Excel can create from them.

Table 2-3: Samples of Series You Can Create with AutoFill	
Value Entered in First Cell	*Extended Series Created by AutoFill in the Next Three Cells*
June	July, August, September
Jun	Jul, Aug, Sep
Tuesday	Wednesday, Thursday, Friday
Tue	Wed, Thu, Fri
4/1/93	4/2/93, 4/3/93, 4/4/93
Jan-93	Feb-93, Mar-93, Apr-93
15-Feb	16-Feb, 17-Feb, 18-Feb
10:00 PM	11:00 PM, 12:00 AM, 1:00 AM
8:01	9:01, 10:01, 11:01
Quarter 1	Quarter 2, Quarter 3, Quarter 4
Qtr2	Qtr3, Qtr4, Qtr1
Q3	Q4, Q1, Q2
Product 1	Product 2, Product 3, Product 4
1st Product	2nd Product, 3rd Product, 4th Product

Designer series

AutoFill uses the initial value you select (date, time, day, year, and so on) to "design" the series. All of the sample series shown in Table 2-3 change by a factor of 1 (one day, one month, or one number). You can tell AutoFill to create a series changed by some other value: Enter in neighboring cells two sample values that describe the amount of change you want between each value in the series. Make these two values the initial selection that you extend with the fill handle.

For example, to start a series with Saturday and enter every other day across a row, enter **Saturday** in the first cell and **Monday** in the cell next door. After selecting both cells, drag the fill handle across the cells to the right as far you need to extend the series. When you release the mouse button, Excel follows the example set in the first two cells by entering every other day (Wednesday to the right of Monday, Friday to the right of Wednesday, and so on).

You can fill a cell range with AutoFill (rather than create a series) by copying one entry to all the cells of the range. To fill a cell range, hold the Ctrl key before you click the thin-black cross pointer on the lower-right corner of the cell and drag the fill handle. When you hold the Ctrl key, a plus sign appears to the right of the black cross — your sign that AutoFill will *copy* the value in the active cell instead of create a series using it.

Repeat after me

You can save a lot of time and energy when you want the same entry (text, value, or formula) to appear in many cells of the worksheet; you can enter the information in all the cells in one operation. You first select the cell ranges to hold the information (Excel lets you select more than one cell range for this kind of thing — see Chapter 3 for details). Then you construct the entry on the formula bar and press Ctrl+Enter to get the entry into all the selected ranges.

The key to making this operation a success is to hold the Ctrl key as you press Enter so that Excel inserts the entry on the formula bar into all the selected cells. If you forget to hold Ctrl, and you just press Enter, Excel only places the entry in the first cell of the selected cell range.

Figure 2-4 illustrates a sample worksheet in which you want to enter *Total* as the column heading in cell G3 and as the row heading in cell B8. To make this entry in both cells in one operation, select both cells before you enter **Total** on the formula bar. When you press Ctrl+Enter, Excel inserts the entry in both cells G3 and B8.

If you are fortunate enough to have the extended keyboard with Control keys for the Macintosh, you can repeat an entry by pressing Control+Return (not the Enter key).

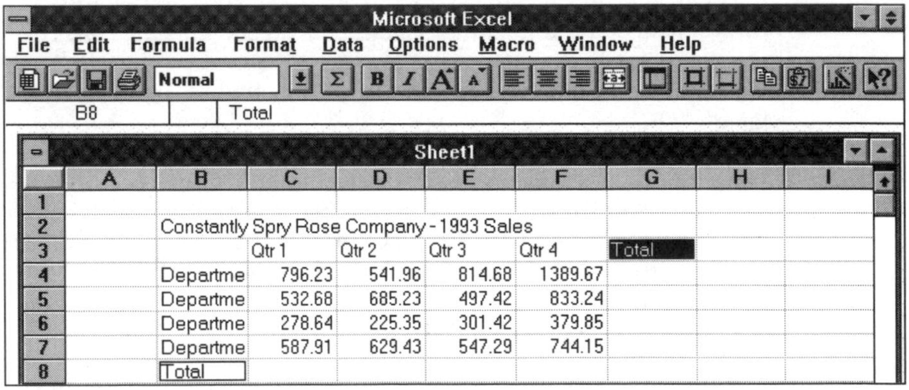

Figure 2-4:
Entering the
same value
in more than
one cell.

	A	B	C	D	E	F	G	H	I
1									
2		Constantly Spry Rose Company - 1993 Sales							
3			Qtr 1	Qtr 2	Qtr 3	Qtr 4	Total		
4		Departme	796.23	541.96	814.68	1389.67			
5		Departme	532.68	685.23	497.42	833.24			
6		Departme	278.64	225.35	301.42	379.85			
7		Departme	587.91	629.43	547.29	744.15			
8		Total							

Becoming Fully Functional

Earlier in this chapter, you learned how to create formulas that perform a series of simple mathematical operations such as addition, subtraction, multiplication, and division. Instead of creating more complex formulas from scratch out of an intricate combination of these operations, you can find an Excel function to get the job done.

A *function* is a predefined formula that performs a particular type of computation. All you have to do to use a function is supply the values that the function uses when performing its calculations (such values are known as the *arguments* of the function). As with simple formulas, you can enter the arguments for most functions either as a numerical value (for example, **22** or **-4.56**) or, as is more common, as a cell reference (for example, **B10**) or as a cell range (for example, **C3:F3**).

Just as with a formula you build yourself, each function you use must start with an equal sign (=) so that Excel knows to enter the function as a formula instead of as text. Following the equal sign, you enter the name of the function (in uppercase or lowercase, it doesn't matter as long as you don't misspell the name). Following the name of the function, you enter the arguments required to perform the calculations. All function arguments are enclosed in a pair of parentheses.

If you type the function on the formula bar, remember not to insert spaces between the equal sign, function name, and the arguments enclosed in parentheses. Some functions use more than one value when performing their designated calculations. When this is the case, you separate each function with a comma (not a space).

After you type the equal sign, function name, and the left parenthesis that marks the beginning of the arguments for the function, you can point to any cell or cell range you want to use as the first argument instead of typing the cell references. When the function uses more than one argument, you can point to the cells or cell ranges you want to use for the second argument right after you type the , (comma) to complete the first argument.

After you finish entering the last argument, type a right parenthesis to mark the end of the argument list, and then click on the enter box or press Enter to insert the function in the cell and have Excel calculate the answer.

Paste without waste

Although you can enter a function by typing it on the formula bar, you are usually better off inserting it with the Paste Function command on the Formula menu. When you choose this command, Excel opens the Paste Function dialog box shown in Figure 2-5.

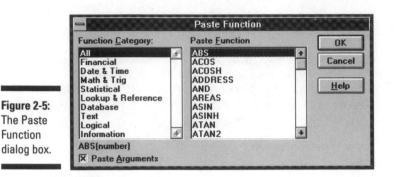

Figure 2-5:
The Paste
Function
dialog box.

This dialog box contains the Paste Function list box: an alphabetical list of all the built-in functions in Excel. To narrow the list of functions to those in a particular category, select the category in the Function Category list box.

To insert a function onto the formula bar, double-click on the desired function in the Paste Function list box or select it and then choose OK. Excel inserts the function along with the required equal sign and a description of the arguments it requires. (If you don't want the argument description included, deselect the Paste Arguments check box before you paste the function.)

For example, if you double-click on the ROUND function (used to round off numbers) in the Paste Function list box with the Paste Arguments check box selected, Excel inserts the following function on the formula bar, with the description of the first argument, *number,* selected:

```
=ROUND(number,num_digits)
```

Follow these steps to complete the function:

1. **Click on the cell that contains the number or type the number or cell reference.**

   This operation replaces the *number* argument with the actual number you want to round off.

2. **Select the *num_digits* argument description in the formula bar by dragging the insertion point through this text; then type the number of decimal places.**

   This operation specifies how many decimal places to use in rounding the number.

3. **After replacing the descriptions of the arguments with the real McCoys, enter the ROUND function in the cell as you would enter any other formula.**

I really AutoSum those numbers!

Before leaving this fascinating discussion on entering functions, I want you to be aware of the AutoSum tool on the Standard toolbar (the one with the Greek letter sigma that looks like a sorority pin). This little tool is worth its weight in gold — check out the following tasks:

✔ Use the AutoSum tool to insert the SUM function in the formula bar (for more information on using SUM and other prominent functions, jump to Chapters 12 and 13).

✔ Use the AutoSum tool to tell Excel to select the cell range containing the values you want totaled. Nine times out of ten, Excel highlights the correct cell range. For that tenth case, you can correct the range by simply dragging the cell pointer through the correct range of cells.

✔ Use the AutoSum tool to total a list of numbers: select the cell in which you want the sum to appear and click on the tool.

✔ Use the AutoSum tool to sum a list of values entered in a column.

Figure 2-6 shows how to use the AutoSum tool to total the sales for Department 1 in row 4. To total the sales in this row, position the cell pointer in cell G4 where the four-quarter total is to appear and click on the AutoSum tool. Excel inserts the SUM function (equal sign and all) onto the formula bar, places a *marquee* (the moving dotted line) around the cells C4, D4, E4, and F4, and uses the cell range C4:F4 as the argument of the SUM function.

Figure 2-7 shows the worksheet after you insert the function in cell G4. The calculated total appears in cell G5 while the following SUM formula appears in the formula bar:

```
=SUM(C4:F4)
```

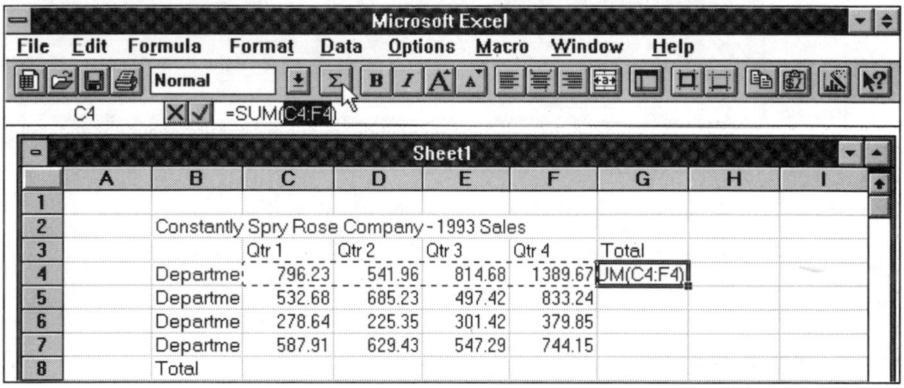

Figure 2-6:
Using
AutoSum
to total the
Department 1
sales figures
in row 4.

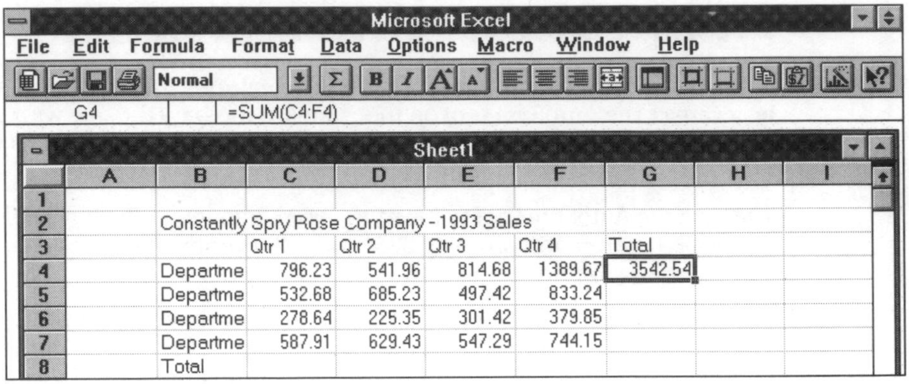

Figure 2-7:
The worksheet after entering the SUM function.

After entering the function to total the sales for Department 1, you can copy this formula to total sales for Departments 2, 3, and 4 by dragging the fill handle down column G until the cell range G4:G7 is highlighted.

Figure 2-8 illustrates how you can use the AutoSum tool to total the first-quarter sales in column C. Position the cell pointer in cell C8 where you want the total to appear. When you click on the AutoSum tool, Excel places the marquee around cells C4, C5, C6, and C7 and correctly enters the cell range C4:C7 as the argument of the SUM function.

Figure 2-9 shows the worksheet after inserting the function in cell C8 and using the AutoFill feature to copy the formula to cells D8, E8, F8, and G8 to the right. (To use AutoFill, drag the fill handle through the cells to the right until you reach cell G8 before you release the mouse button.)

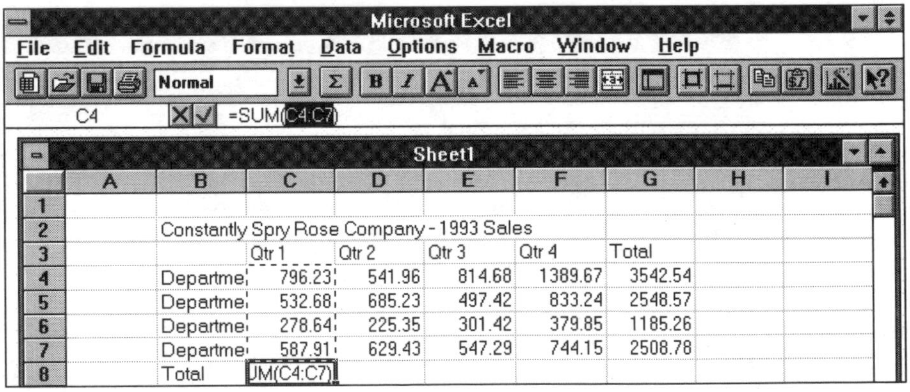

Figure 2-8:
Using AutoSum to total the Qtr 1 sales figures in column C.

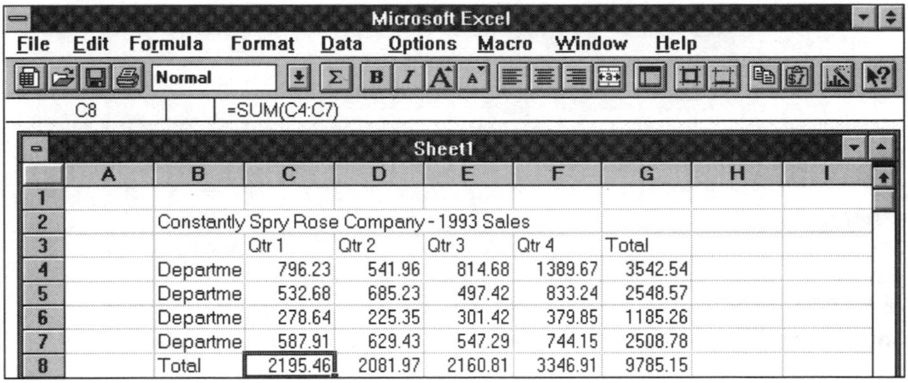

Figure 2-9:
The
worksheet
after
copying
the SUM
formula.

	A	B	C	D	E	F	G	H	I
1									
2		Constantly Spry Rose Company - 1993 Sales							
3			Qtr 1	Qtr 2	Qtr 3	Qtr 4	Total		
4		Departme	796.23	541.96	814.68	1389.67	3542.54		
5		Departme	532.68	685.23	497.42	833.24	2548.57		
6		Departme	278.64	225.35	301.42	379.85	1185.26		
7		Departme	587.91	629.43	547.29	744.15	2508.78		
8		Total	2195.46	2081.97	2160.81	3346.91	9785.15		

Saving the Evidence

All the work you do in a worksheet is at risk until you save the document onto disk. Should you lose power or should your computer crash for any reason before you save the document, you're out of luck. You have to re-create each and every keystroke — a painful task, made all the worse because it's so unnecessary. To avoid this unpleasantness altogether, adopt this rule of thumb: save your worksheet any time you've entered more information than you could possibly bear to lose.

To encourage frequent saving on your part, Excel even provides you with a Save File tool on the Standard toolbar (the one with the picture of the disk, third from the left). You don't even have to take the time and trouble to choose the Save command from the File menu; you can simply click on this tool whenever you want to save new work on disk.

The first time you click on the File Save tool, Excel displays the File Save As dialog box (similar to the one shown in Figure 2-10). You can use this dialog box to replace the temporary document name (Sheet1, Sheet2, and the like) with a more descriptive filename and to select a new drive and directory before you save it to the file. It's just this easy:

- ✔ To change the drive where the file is to be saved, click on the Drives drop-down list button and select the appropriate drive letter in the list box.

- ✔ To change the directory where you want the document stored, click on the appropriate folder in the Directories list box.

- ✔ To rename the document, type the filename in the File Name text box. When you first open the Save As dialog box, the suggested filename is selected; you can just start typing the new filename to replace it.

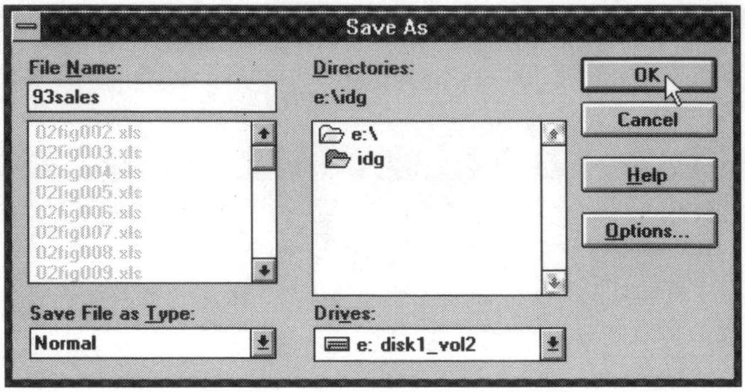

Figure 2-10:
The File
Save As
dialog box.

Save As		
File Name:	**Directories:**	OK
93sales	e:\idg	Cancel
02fig002.xls	📁 e:\	Help
02fig003.xls	📁 idg	
02fig004.xls		Options...
02fig005.xls		
02fig006.xls		
02fig007.xls		
02fig008.xls		
02fig009.xls		
Save File as Type:	**Drives:**	
Normal	💾 e: disk1_vol2	

WARNING!

Remember that you can have NO SPACES in filenames and that filenames can have no more than eight characters. Excel automatically adds the file extension XLS to the main file name you assign to your document, indicating that the file contains an Excel worksheet. When you edit a filename (as opposed to replacing it), be careful that you leave the XLS extension intact.

MAC TRACKS

Of course, all this nonsense about no spaces, no more than eight characters, and weird-looking XLS filename extensions appended to worksheet filenames does not pertain at all to the Macintosh. You can give worksheet files descriptive names up to 32 characters long, adding spaces as necessary to separate the words.

When you finish making changes in the Save As dialog box, choose OK or press Enter to save the document. Excel displays the filename you assigned in the document title bar. You can save all subsequent changes to the worksheet by clicking on the File Save tool.

You don't have to fool with the Save As dialog box again unless you want to rename the worksheet or save a copy of it in a different directory. If you want to do either of these things, you must choose the Save As command from the File menu rather than click on the File Save tool.

Part II
The More Things Change . . .

The 5th Wave   By Rich Tennant

"For further thoughts on that subject, I'm going to down-load Leviticus and go through the menu to Job, chapter 2, verse 6, file 'J', it reads..."

The part in which...

You learn how to put some sizzle in your worksheet by dressing up the lackluster facts and figures that you've entered. Here, you learn how to outfit your worksheet data in new fonts and font styles at the click of a tool. You also learn how to "accentuate the positive" by rearranging the entries in their cells, changing the width of columns and rows, and adding pizzazz with new borders, colors, and patterns.

After learning how to show off your information to its best advantage, you learn how to cope with those inevitable — and seemingly unending — changes that need to be made to a worksheet. After you get through this part, you can undo your boo-boos and copy and move information to new places in the worksheet. You learn how to add new sections to the worksheet and how to remove those that you now want to abandon — all without hopelessly messing up the structure of the original document!

Chapter 3
Fancying Up the Figures

. . . .

In This Chapter

▶ How to select ranges of cells with the mouse and the keyboard

▶ How to use the AutoFormat feature to spruce up a table of figures

▶ How to apply built-in number formats to a cell selection

▶ How to create custom formats

▶ How to change the widths of certain columns in the worksheet

▶ How to adjust the height of certain rows in the worksheet

▶ How to hide columns and rows in the worksheet

▶ How to assign a new font and font size to a cell selection

▶ How to change the alignment of the entries in a cell selection

▶ How to change the way entries are justified in a cell selection

▶ How to apply borders, shading, or colors to a cell selection

▶ How to use styles to format a cell selection

. . . .

*N*ow that you know how to get information into a worksheet and how to get it to stay there, you're ready to learn about all the ways you can pretty it up. In spreadsheet programs like Excel, you normally don't worry about formatting the information until after you enter all the data in the worksheet.

After you decide on the formatting you want to apply to a portion of the worksheet, you select all the cells to be beautified and then click on the appropriate tool or choose the menu command to apply that formatting. This means that before you learn about all the fabulous formatting features you can use to dress up cells, you first need to know how to pick out the group of cells you want to apply the formatting to.

Entering information into a cell and formatting that information are two distinct procedures in a spreadsheet program like Excel. So when you change the entry in a formatted cell, the new entry assumes the cell's formatting. This means that you can format blank cells in a worksheet; when you make entries in those cells, the entries are displayed with that formatting.

Selectively Yours

Given the extremely rectangular nature of the worksheet and its components, it shouldn't come as a surprise to find that all the cell selections you make in the worksheet have the same kind of Mondrian-like feel: they are all basically just cell blocks made up of different numbers and arrangements of cells.

A *cell selection* (also known as a *cell range*) is whatever collection of neighboring cells you pick out for formatting or editing in some way. The smallest possible cell selection in the worksheet is just one cell (the so-called *active cell;* the cell with the cell pointer is really just a single cell selection). The largest possible cell selection in the worksheet is all of the cells in the worksheet (the whole enchilada, so to speak). Most of the cell selections you need for formatting a worksheet will probably be somewhere in between, consisting of cells in several adjacent columns and rows.

Excel shows a cell selection in the worksheet by highlighting the block (Figure 3-1 shows several cell selections of different sizes and shapes).

In Excel, you can select more than one cell range at a time (a phenomenon somewhat ingloriously called a *discontinuous* or *nonadjacent selection*). In fact, although I billed Figure 3-1 as having several cell selections, it is really just one, big, discontinuous selection.

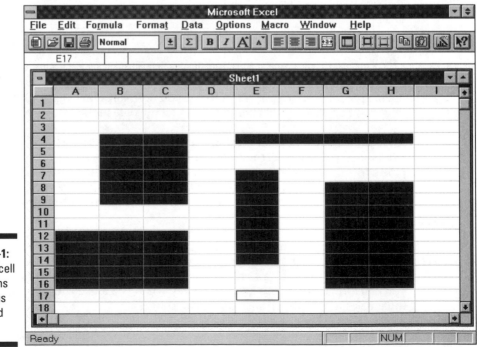

Figure 3-1:
Several cell selections of various sizes and shapes.

Cell selections à la mouse

The mouse is a natural for selecting a range of cells. Just position the mouse pointer (in its thick-shaded cross form) on the first cell and drag in the direction you want to extend the selection.

✔ To extend the cell selection to columns to the right, drag right, highlighting neighboring cells as you go.

✔ To extend the selection to rows to the bottom, drag down.

✔ To extend the selection down and to the right at the same time, drag diagonally towards the cell in the lower-right corner of the block you are highlighting.

To speed up the selection procedure, you can use the old Shift-click method: click on the first cell in the selection to establish the cell pointer, position the mouse pointer in the last cell catercorner from the first cell, press the Shift key, and click the mouse button again. When you click the mouse button the second time, Excel selects all the cells in the columns and rows between the first cell and second cell.

The Shift key works with the mouse like an *extend* key to extend a selection from the first object you select all the way through to and including the second object. Shift enables you to select the first and last cell as well as all the intervening cells in a worksheet or all the document names in a dialog list box.

If, when making a cell selection with the mouse, you notice that you have included the wrong cells before you release the mouse button, you can deselect the cells and resize the selection by moving the pointer in the opposite direction. If you've already released the mouse button, click on the first cell in the highlighted range to select just that cell (and deselect all the others) and then start the whole selection process again.

Making a discontinuous selection

To select more than one range (group of cells) at the same time, highlight the first cell range, and then hold down the Ctrl key as you click on the first cell of the second range and drag the pointer through the cells in this range. As long as you hold down Ctrl as you select the subsequent ranges, Excel doesn't deselect the first range.

The Ctrl key works with the mouse like an *add* key to include nonneighboring objects in Excel. With Ctrl, you can add to the selection of cells in a worksheet or to the document names in a dialog list box without having to deselect those already selected.

Selecting entire columns and rows

You can use the worksheet frame to select entire columns and rows.

- ✔ To select every single cell in a particular column, click on its column letter on the frame at the top of the worksheet document window.

- ✔ To select every cell in a particular row, click on its row number on the frame at the left edge of the document window.

- ✔ To select more than one whole column or row at the same time, press and hold down the Ctrl key while you click on the column letters or row numbers of the columns and rows you want to add to the selection.

- ✔ To select each and every cell in the worksheet, click on the button in the upper-left corner of the frame (to the left of the row of column letters and above the column of row numbers).

You really AutoSelect me

Excel provides a really quick way (called AutoSelect) to select all the cells in a table of data entered as a block (don't try this when you need to select empty cells). To use AutoSelect, click on one of the cells in any of the four corners of the table, hold down the Shift key, and then double-click on the edge of the cell in the direction in which you want to expand the selection.

- ✔ Double-click on the top of the active cell to select cells in rows above.

- ✔ Double-click on the right edge of the cell to select cells in columns to the right.

- ✔ Double-click on the bottom edge of the cell to select cells in rows below.

- ✔ Double-click on the left edge of the cell to select cells in columns to the left.

Before you double-click on the edge of the cell, be sure that the mouse pointer changes from the thick-shaded cross shape to its arrowhead guise.

After expanding the cell selection by double-clicking on one edge of the first cell, you can expand that cell selection in a second direction by double-clicking on one of its edges with the arrowhead pointer.

For example, to select a large table of data with AutoSelect, click on the first cell in the table (the cell in the upper-left corner), hold down the Shift key, and double-click on the right edge of that cell to expand the selection to the last column of the table. Then double-click on the bottom edge of the selection to extend the selection down to the last row of the table.

Note: You can just as easily extend the cell selection down first by holding down the Shift key and double-clicking on the bottom of the first cell before you extend to the right by double-clicking on the right edge of the selection.

Cell selections — keyboard style

If you're not really keen on using the mouse, you can use the keyboard to select the cells you want to use. In keeping with the Shift-click method of selecting cells, the easiest way to select cells with the keyboard is to combine the Shift key with other keystrokes that move the cell pointer (Chapter 1 lists these keystrokes).

Start by positioning the cell pointer in the first cell of the selection and then hold down the Shift key as you press the appropriate cell-pointer movement keys. When you hold the Shift key as you press direction keys such as the arrow keys ($\uparrow$, $\leftarrow$, $\downarrow$, $\rightarrow$), PgUp, PgDn, Ctrl+PgUp, or Ctrl+PgDn, Excel anchors the selection on the current cell and not only moves the cell pointer as usual but also highlights cells as it goes.

When making a cell selection this way, you can continue to alter the size and shape of the cell range with the cell-pointer movement keys as long as you don't release the Shift key. Once you let up on the Shift key, pressing any of the cell-pointer movement keys immediately collapses the selection, reducing it to just the cell with cell pointer.

If holding down the Shift key as you move the cell pointer is too tiring, you can place Excel in extend mode by pressing (and promptly releasing) F8 before you press any cell-pointer movement key. Excel displays the EXT (for extend) indicator on the status bar — your sign that the program will select all the cells that you move the cell pointer through. When you've highlighted all the cells you want in the cell range, press F8 again to turn off extend mode.

The keyboard equivalent of AutoSelect

When you're in a hurry to select a block of cell entries in the worksheet, combine F8 (or the Shift key) with the Ctrl-arrow keys or End-arrow keys to zip the cell pointer from one end of a block to the other. *Voilà*, you have the keyboard equivalent of AutoSelect.

To select an entire table of data, follow these steps:

1. **First position the cell pointer in the first cell (the cell in the upper-left corner of the table).**

2. **Press F8 (or hold down the Shift key), and then press Ctrl+$\rightarrow$ (or End, $\rightarrow$ if you prefer) to extend the cell selection to the cells in the columns on the right.**

3. **Then press Ctrl+$\downarrow$ (or End, $\downarrow$ if you prefer) to extend the selection to the cells in the rows below.**

Again the directions are arbitrary — you can just as well press Ctrl+↓ (or End, ↓) before you press Ctrl+→ (or End, →). Just be sure (if you're using the Shift key instead of F8) that you don't let up on the Shift key until after you finish performing these two directional maneuvers.

Discontinuous keyboard selections

Selecting more than one cell range is a little more complicated with the keyboard than it is with the mouse. When using the keyboard, you alternate between anchoring the cell pointer and moving the cell pointer to select the cell range, unanchoring the cell pointer, and repositioning it at the beginning of the next range. To unanchor the cell pointer so that you can move it into position for selecting another range, press Shift+F8. This puts you in add mode, in which you move to the first cell of the next range without selecting any more cells. Excel lets you know that the cell pointer is unanchored by displaying the ADD indicator on the status bar.

To select more than one cell range with the keyboard, follow these steps:

1. **Move the cell pointer to the first cell of the first cell range you want to select.**

2. **Press F8 to get into extend mode.**

   Move the cell pointer to select all the cells in the first cell range. Alternatively, hold down the Shift key as you move the cell pointer.

3. **Press Shift+F8 to switch to add mode.**

   The ADD indicator appears in the status bar. Move the cell pointer to the first cell of the next range you want to select.

4. **Repeat steps 2 and 3 until you have selected all the cell ranges you want to use.**

Selecting cells with the Goto feature

If you want to select a really big cell range that would take a long time to select by pressing various cell-pointer movement keys, use the Goto feature to extend the range to a far distant cell. Follow these steps.

1. **Start by positioning the cell pointer in the first cell of the range; then press F8 to anchor the cell pointer.**

2. **Press F5 to open the Goto dialog box, type the address of the last cell in the range (the cell catercorner from the first cell), and then press Enter.**

   Because Excel is in extend mode, the program not only moves the cell pointer to the designated cell address but selects all the intervening cells as well.

AutoFormat to the Rescue

Now that you know all about selecting the cells you want to format, I'm going to teach you a formatting technique that doesn't require any kind of cell selection. (Kinda figures, doesn't it?) In fact, the AutoFormat feature is so automatic that to use it, you only need to have the cell pointer somewhere within the table of data you want to format when you choose the AutoFormat command from the Format menu.

As soon as you open the AutoFormat dialog box, Excel automatically selects all the cells in the table (you get a rude message in an alert box if you choose the command when the cell pointer isn't within the confines of the table or in one of the cells directly bordering the table).

Once you open the AutoFormat dialog box, you can make short work of formatting the selected table by choosing one of the 14 built-in table formats. Here's how:

1. **First click on a format in the Table Format list box.**

   This should give you an idea of what kind of formatting is included in a particular table format and how it makes the table look. Excel applies the formatting to a sample table of data in the Sample area of the AutoFormat dialog box (unfortunately, Excel can't display a miniature of your table in the Sample area).

2. **Continue selecting formats from the list box in this manner to preview other table formats to find the one you want to use.**

3. **Once you find the table format you want to go with, close the AutoFormat dialog box and apply the selected format to the table in the worksheet by clicking on the OK button.**

4. **Once you're familiar enough with the table formats to know which one you want to use, you can save time by double-clicking on the desired format in the Table Format list box both to close the dialog box and apply the formatting to the selected table.**

If you ever goof up and select a table format that you just absolutely hate once you see it in the worksheet, choose the Undo AutoFormat command from the Edit menu (or press Ctrl+Z) before you do anything else; Excel restores the table to its previous state (for more on getting yourself out of a jam with the Undo feature, see Chapter 4).

Each of the 14 built-in table formats offered by AutoFormat is nothing more than a particular combination of various kinds of cell and data formatting that Excel applies to the cell selection in a single operation. (Boy, does this ever save time!) Each one enhances the headings and values in the table in a slightly different way.

Figure 3-2 shows the yearly sales table introduced in Chapter 2 just before the Classic 1 table format was selected from the AutoFormat dialog box. Figure 3-3 shows the sales table after the Classic 1 format is applied to it.

Notice that not only did Excel add italics and bold attributes to some of the headings and draw borderlines to separate the headings from the rest of the data, the program also increased the width of column B so that you can see all of the Department row headings (all of the table formats resize the columns to fit their longest data entry — a feature known as *adjusting the column to best fit*). Figure 3-4 shows the table after the Colorful 2 table format is applied.

If your table is laid out like the sample sales table shown in Figures 3-2, 3-3, and 3-4, with its title in the row right above the one with the column headings, limit your table-format selections to Classic 1 or 2, Colorful 1 or 2, or List 3. With all the other table formats, Excel widens the first column to best fit the table title — in the sample sales table, Excel would widen the first column so that all of the title *Constantly Spry Rose Company—1993 Sales* appears in column B without any spillover. To prevent this from happening when you use other table formats, leave a blank row between the title of the table and the column headings.

Figure 3-2:
Using
AutoFormat
to select
and apply
formatting
to a table of
data.

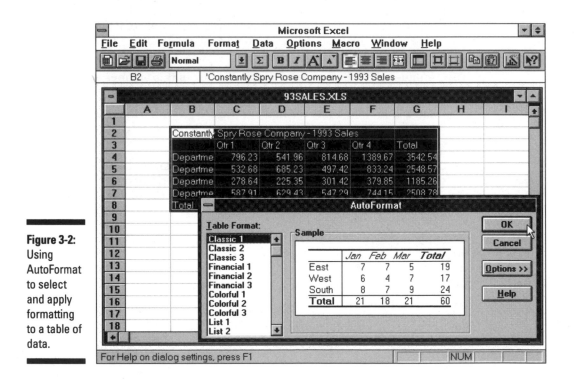

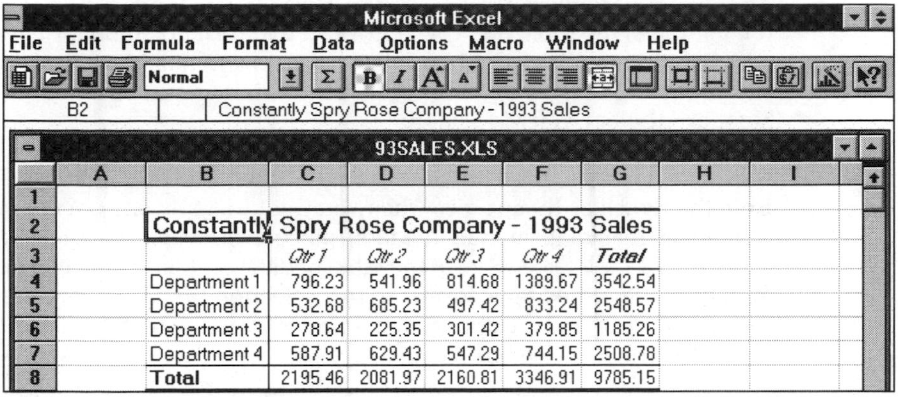

Figure 3-3:
Sample
sales table
after the
Classic 1
table format
is applied.

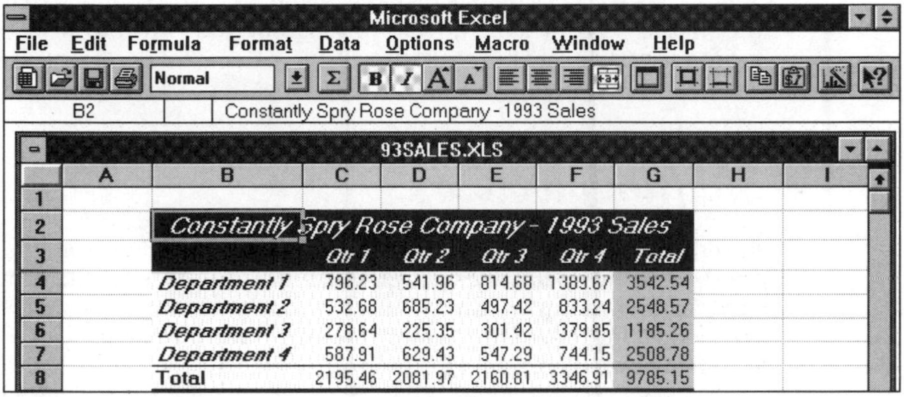

Figure 3-4:
Sample
sales table
after the
Colorful 2
table format
is applied.

Formats at the Click of a Tool

Some worksheets require a lighter touch than what is offered by the Auto Format feature. For example, you may have a table where the only emphasis you want to add is to make bold the column headings at the top of the table and to underline the row of totals at the bottom (done by drawing a borderline along the bottom of the cells).

With the formatting tools on the Standard and Formatting toolbars, you can accomplish most data and cell formatting without ever venturing into the shortcut menus, let alone (heaven forbid) opening up the pull-down menus.

Although the Standard toolbar offers a mixed bag of tools, the group of tools in the middle of the toolbar is geared toward the most common formatting tasks: adding bold or italics to certain cell entries or switching the alignment of data to left, center, or right (for a refresher on the names and uses of the tools in the Standard toolbar, refer to Chapter 1).

Don't overlook the AutoFormat tool on the Standard toolbar (the one seventh from the right) for those times when you want to apply one of the built-in table formats instead of formatting the table piecemeal. When you click on the AutoFormat tool, Excel selects the table of data containing the cell pointer and applies the last-used table format to this selection (if you haven't used any table formats in the current work session, Excel applies the first format in the list in the AutoFormat dialog box to the table).

If you don't get the table format you want the first time you click on the AutoFormat tool, apply the next table format in the list by holding down the Shift key as you click on this tool a second time. If you continue to hold down the Shift key and click on the AutoFormat tool, you cycle through the 14 built-in formats (it takes a while to get through all of them, however, because Excel is very pokey in applying each new table format to the cell selection).

Shuffling toolbars

In addition to the formatting tools on the Standard toolbar, you have access to another toolbar created just for making formatting changes (its name is, cleverly, the Formatting toolbar). To display the Formatting toolbar, use the shortcut menu attached to the Standard toolbar. Open this menu by clicking on the Standard toolbar with the right mouse button. Then click on the name Formatting (listed right below Standard — the check mark in front of the toolbar name means that that toolbar is already displayed).

Figure 3-5 shows the Formatting toolbar. Notice that when you first display the Formatting toolbar, it appears in its own window in the worksheet document window.

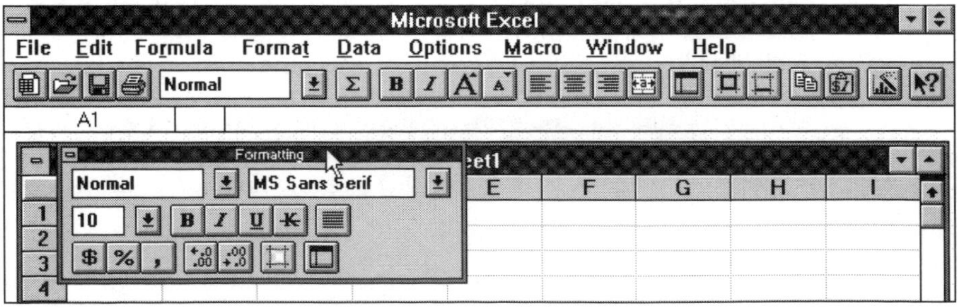

Figure 3-5:
The Formatting toolbar.

To open the toolbar shortcut menu on the Macintosh, press the ⌘+Option keys as you click on the toolbar.

Floating toolbars

Most Excel toolbars appear in their own little windows somewhere within the worksheet document window the first time you display them. These toolbars are referred to as *floating toolbars* because they have no permanent home in the Excel window.

- ✔ You can move a floating toolbar around the worksheet document by dragging it by its little title bar.

- ✔ You can resize a floating toolbar by dragging any one of its sides (wait until the mouse pointer changes to a double-headed arrow before you start dragging).

- ✔ As you drag a side, the outline of the toolbar assumes a new shape to accommodate the tools in a prescribed tool arrangement. When the toolbar outline assumes the shape you want, release the mouse button; Excel redraws the toolbar.

- ✔ To close a floating toolbar when you no longer want it in the document window, click on the close box (the small box in the upper-left corner of the toolbar window).

Docking toolbars

Three of the built-in toolbars, the Standard, Chart, and Excel 3.0 toolbars, do not automatically appear as floating toolbars in the active worksheet document window. Instead, they assume a stationary position in the Excel window — the Standard and Excel 3.0 toolbars appear at the top of the screen between the menu bar and the formula bar, and the Chart toolbar appears at the bottom right of the screen above the status bar. Toolbars like the Standard, Excel 3.0, and Chart toolbars that assume a stationary position don't have a close box. These toolbars are known as *docked toolbars* (*beached* is more like it).

Although the other toolbars first appear as floating toolbars, you can dock them as well. There are four docking stations, corresponding to the four sides of the document window (above, below, left, and right). To dock a floating toolbar in one of these areas, drag it by the title bar as far to the side of the window as possible and release the mouse button. Toolbars you dock on the left or right of the document window reorient their tools so that they run vertically down the toolbar.

Because of this change in orientation, Excel won't let you dock on the left or right side of the screen a toolbar like the Standard, Excel 3.0, or Formatting toolbar that contains a Style or Font Name box. You can dock these toolbars only at the top or bottom. This restriction exists because these toolbars have drop-down list boxes, and the program can't reorient a drop-down list box so that it pops out rather than drops up or down.

You can dock more than one toolbar in the same area of the screen. For example, you can dock the Formatting toolbar right underneath the Standard toolbar at the top of the screen. However, because these toolbars contain some of the same tools, you may find this arrangement confusing until you really get to know the tools on each toolbar. Instead, try docking the Formatting toolbar at the bottom of the screen like it is in Figure 3-6.

It's a cinch to "undock" a toolbar. Just double-click on it. The toolbar will be redisplayed in its own "undocked" document window. Of course, you can also undock a toolbar simply by dragging it to some place in the document window.

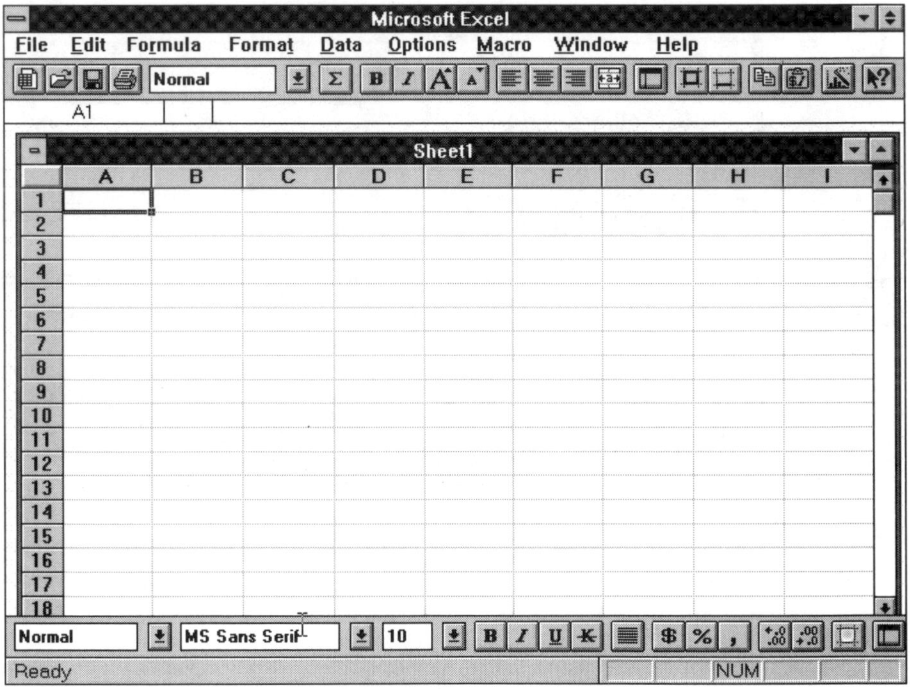

Figure 3-6:
The
Formatting
toolbar
docked
above the
status bar at
the bottom
of the
worksheet
document
window.

Sometimes after docking a toolbar, the active document window loses one or the other of the scroll bars. To get the missing scroll bar back, click on the document Maximize button to max out the current document. If you're working with an empty worksheet (like Sheet1), you can properly size the document window and restore the scroll bars by closing the worksheet with the Close command on the File menu and then opening a new worksheet in its place by clicking on the New Worksheet tool on the Standard toolbar (the very first tool). When Excel opens the new worksheet (Sheet2), the document window fits nicely (with all the scroll bars intact) and your current toolbar-docking arrangement.

The tools on the Formatting toolbar

The Formatting toolbar contains several duplicate tools also found on the Standard toolbar (the Style box, Bold tool, Italic tool, and AutoFormat tool — described in Chapter 1) as well as quite a few useful and unique formatting tools. (Jump ahead to Chapter 11 to find out how to replace the cloned tools on the Formatting toolbar with other unused tools.)

Table 3-1 identifies all the tools on the Formatting toolbar that aren't repeated from the Standard toolbar, and gives you a brief description of how to use them.

Table 3-1:	Unique Tools on the Formatting Toolbar	
Tool	*Tool Name*	*What the Tool Does When You Click on It*
MS Sans Serif	Font Name box	Applies a new font to the entries in the cell selection.
10	Font Size box	Applies a new font size to the entries in the cell selection.
U	Underline tool	Underlines the *entries* in the cell selection (not the cells). If the entries are already underlined, clicking on this tool removes the underlining.
*	Strikeout tool	Applies the ~~strikeout~~ style (a line through the middle) to entries in the cell selection. If the entry already appears in strikeout, clicking on this tool removes the strikeout style.
▦	Justify Align tool	Justifies a long text entry in the active cell so that all the text appears evenly distributed on several lines in that cell.
$	Currency Style tool	Applies a Currency number format to the cell selection to display all values with a dollar sign, with commas between thousands, and two decimal places.
%	Percent Style tool	Applies a Percentage number format to the cell selection: the values are multiplied by 100 and displayed with a percent sign and no decimal places.

(continued)

Table 3-1:	Unique Tools on the Formatting Toolbar *(continued)*	
Tool	*Tool Name*	*What the Tool Does When You Click on It*
	Comma Style tool	Applies a Comma number format to the cell selection to display commas separating thousands and two decimal places.
	Increase Decimal tool	Adds one decimal place to the number format in the cell selection each time you click on the tool. Reverses direction and reduces the number of decimal places when you hold down the Shift key as you click on this tool.
	Decrease Decimal tool	Reduces one decimal place from the number format in the cell selection each time you click on the tool. Reverses direction and adds one decimal place when you hold the Shift key as you click on this tool.
	Light Shading tool	Applies a light gray color to the cells in the current selection.

Formats for Every Value

As you learned in Chapter 2, how you enter values into a worksheet determines the type of number format they get. Here are some examples:

- ✔ If you enter a financial value complete with the dollar sign and two decimal places, Excel assigns a Currency number format to the cell along with the entry.

- ✔ If you enter a value representing a percentage as a whole number followed by the percent sign without any decimal places, Excel assigns to the cell the Percentage number format that follows this pattern along with the entry.

- ✔ If you enter a date (remember that dates are values too) that follows one of the built-in Excel number formats like 02/19/93 or 19-Feb-93, the program assigns a Date number format that follows the pattern of the date along with a special value representing the date.

Although it's fine to format values as you go in this manner (and even necessary in the case of dates), you don't have to do it this way. You can always assign a number format to a group of values after you enter them. In fact, formatting numbers after the fact is often the most efficient way to go because it's just a two-step procedure:

1. Select all the cells containing the values that need dressing up.

2. Select the number format you want to use.

Many times, you can use one of the tools on the Formatting toolbar — if not, you can select a format number from the Number Format dialog box.

Even if you're a crack typist and prefer (thank you very much) to enter each value exactly as you want it to appear in the worksheet, you have to resort to using number formats when you want the values you enter to match those calculated by Excel.

You see, Excel applies a comprehensive number format to all the values it calculates (as well as any you enter that don't exactly follow one of the other Excel formats). As luck would have it, the numbers Excel puts into this format usually don't match those you've formatted yourself, which can really mess up the look of the worksheet.

Excel formats all calculated values and values that don't follow the pattern of a predefined number format with a general-purpose format called, appropriately enough, the General format. The problem with the General format is that it has the nasty habit of dropping all leading and trailing zeros from the entries. This makes it very hard to line up numbers in a column on their decimal points. That's why Excel also has number formats.

Figure 3-7 shows this sad state of affairs. The figure shows a sample worksheet with the first-quarter sales figures before any of the values have been formatted. Notice how the columns of monthly sales figures zig and zag. This is the fault of Excel's General number format; the only cure is to format the values with another more uniform number format.

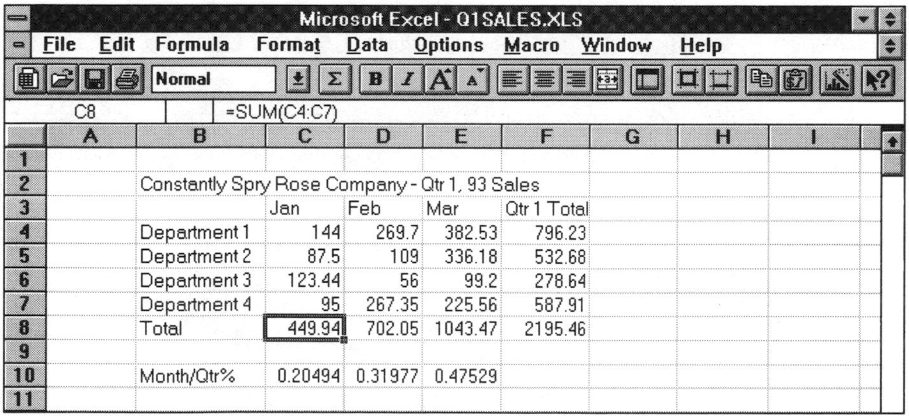

Figure 3-7:
First-quarter
sales figures
before
formatting.

Money, money, money

Given the financial nature of most worksheets, you probably use the Currency format more than any other. This is a really easy format to apply because the Formatting toolbar contains a Currency Style tool which adds a dollar sign, commas between thousands of dollars, and two decimal places to any values in a selected range. If any of the values in the cell selection are negative, this Currency format displays them in parentheses (the way accountants like them) and displays them in red on a color monitor (the way governments like them).

Figure 3-8 shows the sample worksheet after only the cells that contain the totals are selected. To format these selected cells with the Currency format, click on the Currency Style tool on the Formatting toolbar (the one with the $, Ace). Although you could put all the figures in the table into the Currency format to line up the decimal points, this would result in a superabundance of dollar signs in a fairly small table. In this example, only the totals are formatted.

Too much to show

Figure 3-9 shows the totals in the first-quarter sales worksheet after they have been zapped with the Currency Style tool. As you can see, something must have gone wrong because cell E8 contains ######## instead of the March sales total. In fact, this string of pound signs where a dollar amount should be merely indicates that the Currency format added so much to the display of the value that Excel can no longer display it in the current column width.

To get rid of the pound signs and bring back the value, widen column E (to find out how to do this, jump ahead to "If the Column Fits..." later in this chapter).

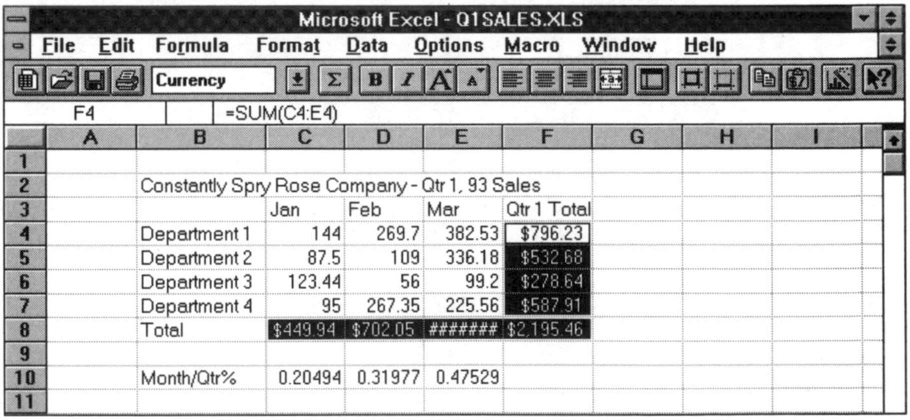

Figure 3-8:
First-quarter sales totals before formatting.

	A	B	C	D	E	F	G	H	I
1									
2		Constantly Spry Rose Company - Qtr 1, 93 Sales							
3			Jan	Feb	Mar	Qtr 1 Total			
4		Department 1	144	269.7	382.53	$796.23			
5		Department 2	87.5	109	336.18	$532.68			
6		Department 3	123.44	56	99.2	$278.64			
7		Department 4	95	267.35	225.56	$587.91			
8		Total	$449.94	$702.05	######	$2,195.46			
9									
10		Month/Qtr%	0.20494	0.31977	0.47529				
11									

Microsoft Excel - Q1SALES.XLS

File Edit Formula Format Data Options Macro Window Help

Currency

F4   =SUM(C4:E4)

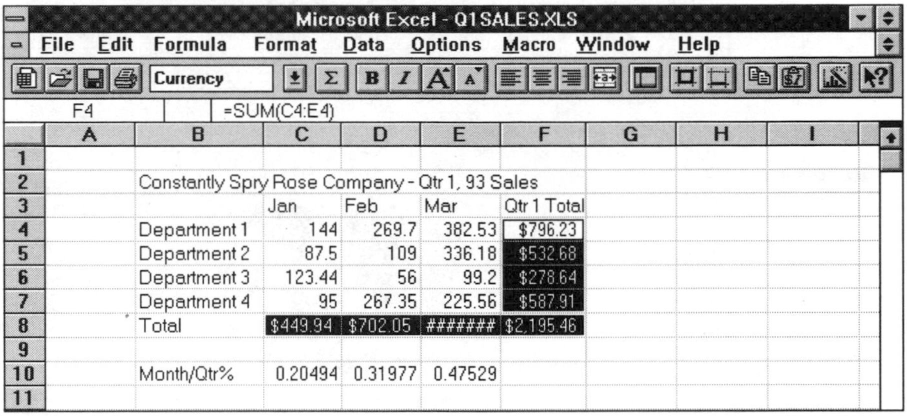

Figure 3-9:
First-
quarter
sales totals
with the
Currency
format.

Let's all remain comma

The Comma format offers a good alternative to the Currency format. Like Currency, the Comma format inserts commas in larger numbers to separate thousands, hundred thousands, millions, and, well, you get the idea.

This format also displays two decimal places and puts negative values in parentheses and in red (on a color monitor). What it doesn't display is dollar signs. This makes it perfect for formatting tables where it's obvious that you're dealing with dollars and cents or for larger values that have nothing to do with money.

The Comma format also works well for the bulk of the values in the sample first-quarter sales worksheet. Figure 3-10 shows this table after the 12 cells were formatted with the Currency format. To do this, select the cell range C4:E7 and click on the Comma Style tool on the Formatting toolbar. (Would it be too obvious to point out that this tool is the one with the tiny little comma right next to the tool with the %?)

Figure 3-10 shows how the Comma format takes care of the earlier alignment problem in the quarterly sales figures. Moreover, notice how the Comma-formatted monthly sales figures align perfectly with the Currency-formatted monthly totals in row 8. If you look real close (you might need a magnifying glass for this one), you see that these formatted values no longer abut the right edges of their cells; they've moved slightly to the left. The gap on the right between the last digit and the cell border is there to accommodate the right parenthesis in negative values, ensuring that they too align precisely on the decimal point.

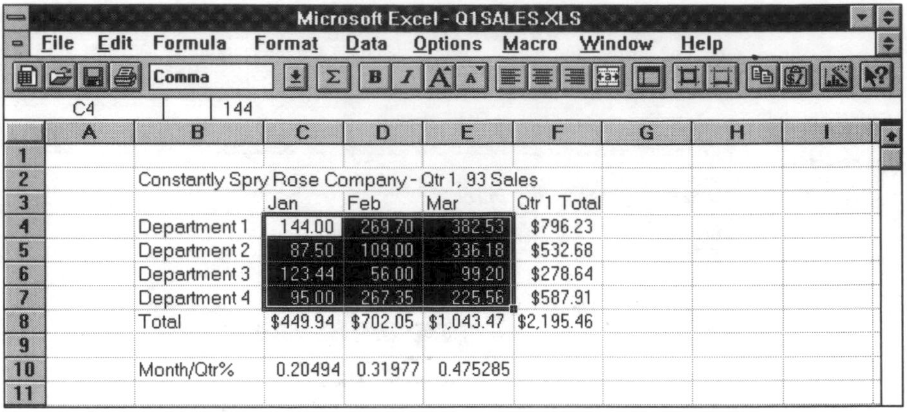

Figure 3-10:
First-quarter sales figures with the Comma format.

	A	B	C	D	E	F	G	H	I
1									
2		Constantly Spry Rose Company - Qtr 1, 93 Sales							
3			Jan	Feb	Mar	Qtr 1 Total			
4		Department 1	144.00	269.70	382.53	$796.23			
5		Department 2	87.50	109.00	336.18	$532.68			
6		Department 3	123.44	56.00	99.20	$278.64			
7		Department 4	95.00	267.35	225.56	$587.91			
8		Total	$449.94	$702.05	$1,043.47	$2,195.46			
9									
10		Month/Qtr%	0.20494	0.31977	0.475285				
11									

Playing the percentages

Many worksheets use percentages in the form of interest rates, growth rates, inflation rates, and so on. To insert a percentage in a cell, place the percent sign (%) after the number. To indicate an interest rate of 12 percent, for example, you enter **12%** in the cell. When you do this, Excel assigns a Percent number format and at the same time divides the value by 100 (that's what makes it a percentage) and places the result in the cell (0.12 in this example).

Not all percentages in a worksheet are entered by hand in this manner. Some may be calculated by a formula and returned to their cells as raw decimal values. In such cases, you should add a Percent format to convert the calculated decimal values to percentages (done by multiplying the decimal value by 100 and adding a percent sign).

The sample first-quarter sales worksheet just happens to have some percentages calculated by formulas in row 10 that need formatting (these formulas indicate what percentage each monthly total is of the first-quarter total). Figure 3-11 shows these values after they have been formatted with a Percent format. To accomplish this feat, you simply select the cells and click on the Percent Style tool on the Formatting toolbar. (Need I point out that it's the tool with the % sign?)

Decimal wheeling and dealing

You can increase or decrease the number of decimal places used in a number entered with the Currency Style, Comma, or Percent Style tool on the Formatting toolbar simply by clicking on the Increase Decimal tool or the Decrease Decimal tool also located on this toolbar (remember to click on these tools while the cell range you just formatted is still selected).

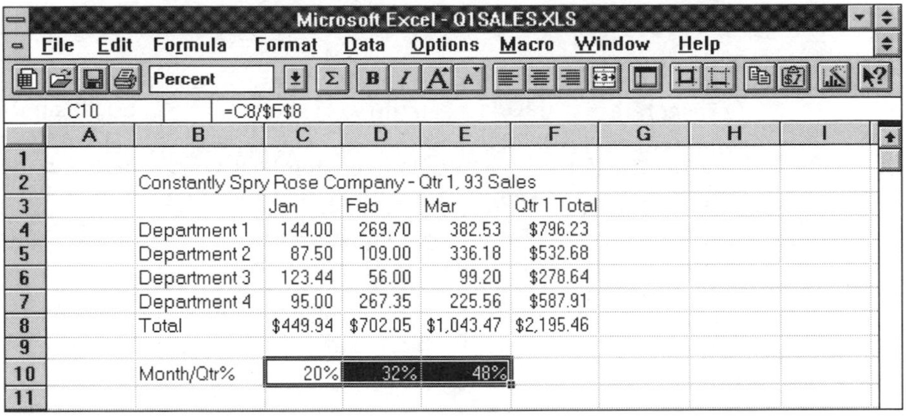

Figure 3-11:
Monthly-to-quarterly sales percentages formatted with the Percent format.

Each time you click on the Increase Decimal tool, Excel adds another decimal place to the number format you applied. Figure 3-12 shows percentages in the cell range C10:E10 after the number of decimal places in the Percent format were increased from none to two (the Percent Style doesn't use any decimal places). This was accomplished by clicking on the Increase Decimal tool twice in a row.

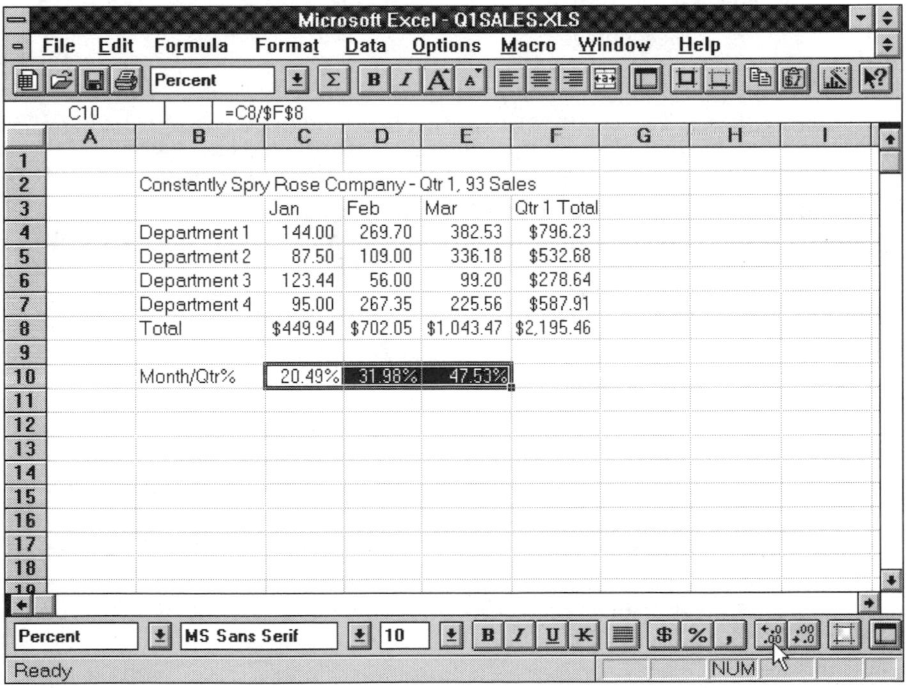

Figure 3-12:
Monthly-to-quarterly sales percentages after two decimal places were added.

What you see is not always what you get

Make no mistake about it, all that these fancy number formats do is spiff up the presentation of the values in the worksheet. Like a good illusionist, a particular number format sometimes appears to magically transform some entries, but in reality, the entries are the same old numbers you started with. For example, suppose that a formula returns the following value:

```
25.6456
```

Now suppose that you format the cell containing this value with the Currency Style tool. The value now appears as follows:

```
$25.65
```

This change may lead you to believe that Excel rounded the value up to two decimal places. In fact, the program has rounded up only the *display* of the calculated value — the cell still contains the same old value of 25.6456. If you use this cell in another worksheet formula, keep in mind that Excel uses the behind-the-scenes value in its calculation, not the spiffed-up one shown in the cell.

But what if you want the values to match their formatted appearance in the worksheet? Well, Excel can do that in a single step. Be aware, however, that this is a one-way trip. You can convert all underlying values to the way they are displayed by selecting a single check box, but you can't return them to their previous state by deselecting the check box.

Before you convert the precision of all values in the worksheet to their displayed form, be sure that they're all formatted with the right number of decimal places. Then choose the Calculation command from the Options menu. In the dialog box, click on the Precision as Displayed check box, and then click on the OK button or press Enter. Excel displays an alert dialog box telling you that your data will permanently lose accuracy. When you click on the OK button or press Enter, the program converts all values to match their display.

Number Formats Made to Order

Excel supports a whole bunch more number formats (that you will seldom, if ever, use) than just the Currency, Comma, and Percent formats. To use them, select the cell range (or ranges) to be formatted and select the Number command on the cell shortcut menu (click the right mouse button somewhere in the cell selection) or the Number command on the Format menu to open the Number Format dialog box. Then choose the desired format from the Format Codes list box.

TECHNICAL STUFF

Number Formats for the Overly Curious

If you just have to know what some of these Number format codes mean, here goes. Each number format can control how positive numbers, negative numbers, and everything else looks. These parts are divided by semicolons (any format not so divided covers all the other types of entries). The 0 is a placeholder for a digit and is filled by a zero if the value lacks a digit in that place. The # sign is a placeholder for a digit not to be filled if the value lacks a digit for that place. *M*s are used for months in dates or minutes in time, *D*s for days, *Y*s for years, *H*s for hours, and *S*s for seconds.

There's only one problem with doing this: Excel wasn't lying when it called them *format* ***codes.*** All you see in the Format Codes list box is a bunch of weird-looking codes composed of lots of #s, *0*s, *?*s, *D*s, *M*s, and *Y*s. Rather than work yourself into a lather (or, heaven forbid, do something nerdy like trying to decipher this gibberish), make life easier and focus your attention on the Sample area at the very bottom of the Number Format dialog box as you select various formats from the Format Codes list box. There, Excel shows how the value in the active cell of the selected range will look in the selected format. As soon as you see what you like, go for it by clicking on the OK button or pressing Enter.

In addition to choosing built-in formats from the Number Format dialog box, you can also build number formats of your own there. Although you do have to use codes (ugh), you really don't have to be a rocket scientist to figure out how to do it. (Not that being a rocket scientist would hurt!)

Rather than bore you with a lot of examples of custom formats that would only prove how smart (nerdy?) I am, I just want to introduce you to two custom formats you might actually find quite handy in your worksheets — one to format dates in full (as in *February 15, 1993*) and the other to hide entries in their cells. These formats aren't that complex (and besides, they work even if you don't understand their codes).

To build a custom number format, click on the Codes text box in the Number Format dialog box and replace whatever is currently in the box with (guess what?) the codes for your made-up format. For the full-month codes, enter the following in this box:

```
mmmm dd, yyyy
```

The *mmmm* tells Excel to spell out the full name of the month, the *dd* says to display the date (including a leading zero, as in 03), the comma after the *dd* says to insert a comma after the date, the space after says to insert a space after the comma, and the *yyyy* says to use all four digits of the year.

The second custom format is even easier to enter in the Codes text box (although it is stranger looking). To create a format that blanks out the display of any cell entry, just enter three semicolons in a row in the Codes text box, with no spaces or no nothing in between, just like this:

```
;;;
```

This says to display nothing for positive values, nothing for negative values, and, while you're at it, nothing for anything else in the cell.

When you apply this hidden format to cells, the cell display disappears in the worksheet (the contents still show up on the formula bar when you select the cell). This format is most useful when you want to remove certain information from a printed report without deleting it from the worksheet. To make hidden entries reappear, simply apply one of the visible number formats (the General format, for example) to cells.

After entering the codes in the Codes text box, click on the OK button to apply the custom format to the current cell selection. Custom formats are saved as part of the worksheet the next time you save the document. (Remember, don't neglect that Save File tool on the Standard toolbar!)

To use a custom format on a cell selection, select the custom format from the Format Codes list box in the Number Format dialog box. Because Excel always puts custom number formats at the very bottom of the list, they can be a pain to use. To get directly to the bottom of the Format Codes list box, press Ctrl+PgDn — until you reach the last format in the list box — as soon as you open the Number Format dialog box. To make custom formats directly accessible, create a style that uses them — see "Going in Style" near the end of this chapter to find out how.

If the Column Fits...

Adjusting column widths is one of those never-ending worksheet chores on a par with housekeeping chores like doing dishes or dusting. It seems that no sooner do you finish putting all the columns in order than you make a change to the worksheet (like formatting a table of figures) that requires new column-width adjustments.

Fortunately, Excel makes changing the column widths a breeze. The easiest way to adjust a column is with the so-called *best-fit method.* With this method, Excel automatically determines how much to widen or narrow the column to fit the longest entry currently in the column.

Here's how to do a best-fit:

1. **Position the mouse pointer on the column frame, on the right border of the column that needs adjusting.**

2. **When the mouse pointer changes to a double-headed arrow pointing left and right, double-click the mouse button.**

   Excel widens or narrows the column width to suit the longest entry.

You can do a best-fit for more than one column at a time. Simply select all the columns that need adjusting (if the columns neighbor one another, drag through their column letters on the frame; if they don't, hold Ctrl as you click on the individual column letters). Once the columns are selected, double-click on any of the right borders on the frame.

Best-fit doesn't always produce the expected results. All you have to do is best-fit a column with a table title to become acquainted with this fact. A long title that spills into several columns to the right produces an awfully wide column when you use best-fit (just look at what happened to the size of column B in Figure 3-13 after best-fit was used).

When best-fit won't do, drag the right border of the column (on the frame) until it's the size you need (as shown in Figures 3-13 and 3-14) rather than double-clicking on it. This manual technique also works when more than one column is selected. Just be aware that all selected columns assume whatever size you make the one that you're actually dragging.

You can also set the widths of columns from the Column Width dialog box. When you use the dialog box, you enter the number of characters you want for the column width. To open this dialog box, choose the Column Width command from the column shortcut menu (opened by clicking on any selected column or column letter with the right mouse button) or the Column Width command from the Format menu.

The Standard Width text box in the Column Width dialog box shows how many characters are in the standard column width in the worksheet. To change the widths of all columns in the worksheet (except those already adjusted manually or with best-fit), enter a new value in the Standard Width text box and click on the OK button (make sure that the Use Standard Width check box is still selected).

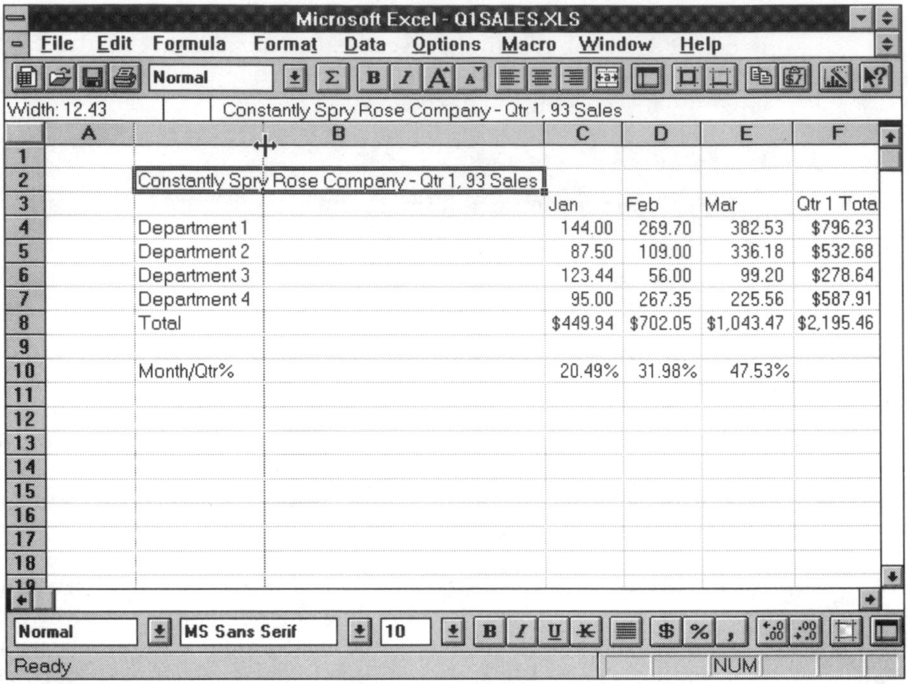

Figure 3-13:
Column B is
wide enough
to hold the
lengthy table
title.

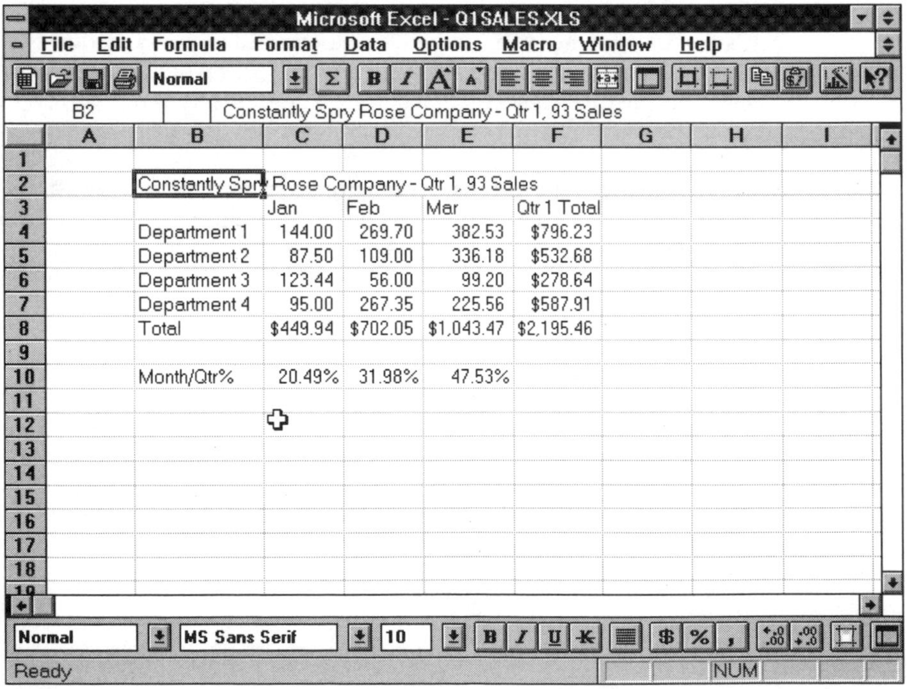

Figure 3-14:
Column B
after
resizing.

To set a new width for just the selected column (or columns), enter a new value in the Column Width text box and click on the OK button. When you enter a new value in this text box, Excel automatically deselects the Use Standard Width check box. To have the program return the selected column to the standard column width, select this check box again before you click on OK.

If you want to have Excel size the column with best-fit, click on the Best Fit button instead of OK.

Rambling rows

The story with adjusting the heights of rows is pretty much the same as that for adjusting columns, except that you do a lot less row adjusting than you do column adjusting. That's because Excel automatically changes the height of the rows to accommodate changes to their entries (such as selecting a larger font size or wrapping text in a cell — both of these techniques are coming right up). Most row-height adjustments come about when you want to increase the amount of space between a table title and the table or between a row of column headings and the table of information without actually adding a blank row (see "Line 'Em Up" later in this chapter for details).

To increase the height of a row, drag the bottom border of the row frame down until the row is high enough and then release the mouse button. To shorten a row, reverse this process and drag the bottom border of the row frame. To use best-fit, double-click on the bottom row frame border.

As with columns, you can also adjust the height of selected rows with a dialog box. To open the Row Height dialog box, choose the Row Height command from the row shortcut menu (opened by clicking on any selected row or row number with the right mouse button) or the Row Height command from the Format menu. To set a new row height for the selected row (or rows), enter the number of characters in the Row Height text box and click on OK. To return to the standard row height (which you can't change), select the Use Standard Height check box instead.

Worksheet hide n' seek

If you get carried away and make a column too narrow or a row too short, it actually disappears from the worksheet. You may wonder why in the world you would spend all that time entering and formatting information only to go and hide it.

Actually, you play hide and seek with worksheet information mostly when setting up printed reports. For example, you may have a worksheet that contains a column listing employee salaries required in calculating the departmental budget figures but that you would prefer to leave off most printed reports. Rather than waste time moving the column of salary figures outside the area to be printed, you can just hide the column until after you print the report.

I won't lie to you — hiding and redisplaying columns with the mouse can be tricky. It requires a degree of precision that you may not possess (especially if you've just recently started using the rodent). For that reason, I want you to know how to hide and unhide columns and rows with dialog boxes.

Suppose that you need to hide column B in the worksheet because it contains some irrelevant or sensitive information you don't want printed. To hide this column, follow these steps:

1. **Click on the letter *B* on the frame to select the column.**

2. **Click on the letter *B* again, this time with the *right* mouse button.**

   The column shortcut menu appears.

3. **Click on the Column Width command.**

   The Column Width dialog box appears.

4. **Click on the H̲ide button.**

   That's all there is to it — column B goes *poof!* All the information in the column disappears from the worksheet.

Note: When you hide column B, notice that the row of column letters in the frame now reads A, C, D, E, F, and so forth.

So now, suppose that you've printed the worksheet and need to make a change to one of the entries in column B. To unhide the column, follow these steps:

1. **Position the mouse pointer on column letter A in the frame and drag the pointer right to select both columns A and C.**

   You must drag from A to C to include hidden column B as part of the column selection — don't click with the Ctrl key or you won't get B.

2. **Click somewhere in the selected columns with the right mouse button.**

   The column shortcut menu appears.

3. **Select the Column Width command.**

   The Column Width dialog box appears.

4. **Click on the U̲nhide button.**

   Excel brings back the hidden B column and all three columns (A, B, and C) are selected. Click the mouse pointer on any cell in the worksheet to deselect the columns.

If you consider yourself a real mouse master, you can hide and unhide columns solely by dragging the mouse pointer.

- ✔ To hide a column with the mouse, drag the column's right edge to the left until it's on top of the left edge and then release the mouse button.

- ✔ To hide a row with the mouse, drag the row's bottom border up until it's on top of the upper border.

As you drag a border, Excel replaces the cell address on the formula bar with the current column width or row height measurement. When the Width or Height indicator reaches 0.00, you know it's time to release the mouse button.

Figure 3-15 shows the first-quarter sales worksheet during the process of hiding row 10. In this figure, the bottom border of row 10 is on top of the upper border of this row (see the Height 0.00 on the formula bar). As soon as you release the mouse button, this row is gone.

Unhiding a column or row with the mouse is a reversal of the hiding process. This time, you drag the column or row border in between the nonsequential columns or rows in the opposite direction (right for columns and down for rows). The only trick to this is that you must position the mouse pointer just right on the column or row border so that the pointer doesn't just change to a double-header arrow but changes to a double-headed arrow split in the middle (contrast the shape of the pointer in Figure 3-15 with that in Figure 3-16).

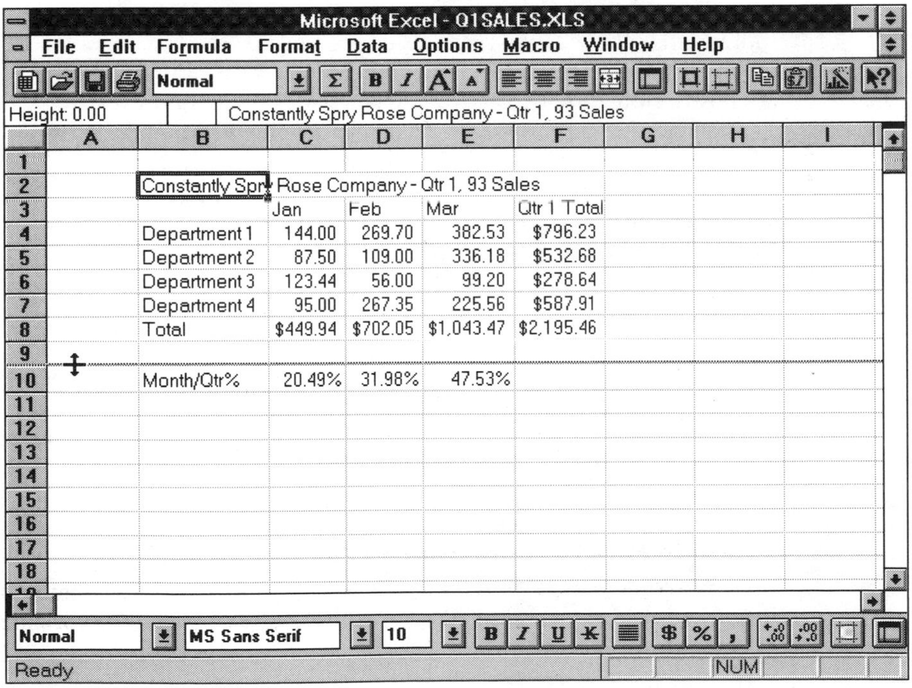

Figure 3-15: Hiding row 10 with the mouse.

—	Microsoft Excel - Q1SALES.XLS	▼ ▲

File   Edit   Formula   Format   Data   Options   Macro   Window   Help

Height: 12.75 | Constantly Spry Rose Company - Qtr 1, 93 Sales

	A	B	C	D	E	F	G	H	I
1									
2		Constantly Spr Rose Company - Qtr 1, 93 Sales							
3			Jan	Feb	Mar	Qtr 1 Total			
4		Department 1	144.00	269.70	382.53	$796.23			
5		Department 2	87.50	109.00	336.18	$532.68			
6		Department 3	123.44	56.00	99.20	$278.64			
7		Department 4	95.00	267.35	225.56	$587.91			
8		Total	$449.94	$702.05	$1,043.47	$2,195.46			
9									
11									
12	÷								
13									
14									
15									
16									
17									
18									
19									
20									

Normal | MS Sans Serif | 10 | B I U K | ▦ $ % , ⁘⁙ | ▢ ▢

Ready | NUM

Figure 3-16:
Unhiding
row 10 with
the mouse.

Figure 3-16 shows the first-quarter sales worksheet the moment before row 10 is unhidden with the mouse. In this figure, you see the mouse pointer (with the split in the middle of the double-headed arrow) after dragging the border of row 10 down. Note the Height: 12.75 indicator, the standard row height for this worksheet. As soon as you release the mouse button, Excel redisplays row 10.

Oh, That's Just Fontastic!

When you start a new worksheet, Excel assigns a uniform font and type size to all the cell entries you make. This font varies according to the printer you use — for a laser printer like the HP LaserJet or Apple LaserWriter, Excel uses a font called MS Sans Serif (for Microsoft Sans Serif) in a 10-point size. Although this font is fine for normal entries, you may want to use something with a little more zing for titles and headings in the worksheet.

If you don't especially care for the standard font that Excel uses, modify it by re-defining the font for the Normal style (the style assigned to all empty cells in a new worksheet) as described in "Going in Style," later in this chapter.

With the tools on the Standard and Formatting toolbars, you can make most font changes (including selecting a new font style or new font size) without having to resort to the Font command on the cell shortcut menu or the Font command on the Format pull-down menu.

✔ To select a new font for a cell selection, click on the drop-down button next to the Font Name box on the Formatting toolbar; then select the name of the font you want to use from the list box.

✔ If you want to change the font size, click on the drop-down button next to the Font Size box on the Formatting toolbar; then select the new font size. Alternatively, click on the Increase Font Size or Decrease Font Size tool on the Standard toolbar until the font is the size you want.

You can also add the attributes of bold, italics, underlining, or strikeout to the font you're using. The Formatting toolbar contains the Bold, Italic, Underline, and Strikeout tools. The Standard toolbar also contains the Bold and Italic tools. Remember that you use these tools not only to add attributes to a cell selection but to remove them as well.

After you click on one of these attribute tools, notice that the tool changes by losing the shading around its right and bottom edge and becoming a lighter shade of gray. This is done to make it appear as though a tool button is pushed in. When you click on a "pushed-in" tool to remove an attribute, Excel changes the tool back to its original form so that it no longer appears pushed in.

Although you probably make most font changes with the toolbars, on rare occasions you may find it more convenient to use the Font dialog box. As you can see in Figure 3-17, this dialog box brings together under one roof fonts, font styles such as bold and italics, effects like underlining and strikeout, as well as color changes. When you want to make a lot of font-related changes to a cell selection, the Font dialog box may be your best bet. One of the nice things about using this dialog box is that it contains a Sample box that shows you how your font changes appear (on-screen at least).

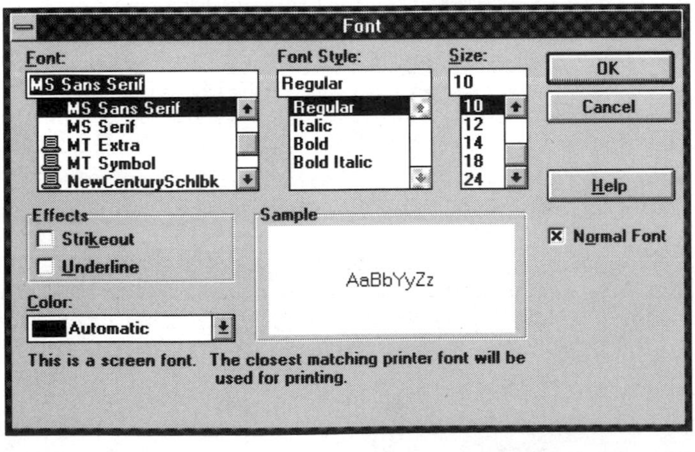

Figure 3-17:
The Font
dialog box.

If you change font colors and then print the worksheet with a black-and-white printer, Excel renders the colors as shades of gray. The Automatic choice in the Font dialog box Color drop-down list box picks up the color assigned in Windows as the window text color (this color is black unless you changed it in the Windows Control Panel).

Line 'Em Up

You already know that the alignment assigned to cell entries when you first make them is simply a function of the type of entry it is: all text entries are left-aligned and all values are right-aligned. You can, however, alter this standard arrangement any time it suits you.

The Standard toolbar contains three alignment tools: the Left Align, Center Align, and Right Align tools. These tools align the current cell selection exactly as you expect them to. Next door to the Right Align tool, you find the Center Across Selected Columns tool.

Despite its horrible name, you'll want to get to know this tool. You can use it to center a worksheet title across the entire width in seconds. Figures 3-18 and 3-19 show how you can use this tool. In Figure 3-18, notice that the title for the sales table is entered in cell B2. Because it's a long text entry, it spills over to the empty cells to the right. To center this title over the table, select the cell range B2:G2 (the width of the table) as shown in Figure 3-18 and then click on the Center Across Selected Columns tool on the Standard toolbar. Figure 3-19 shows the result. Now the title is properly centered over the table.

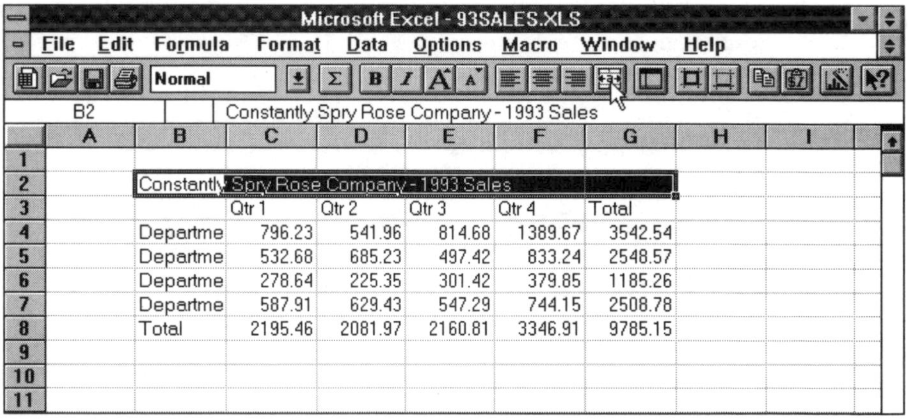

Figure 3-18: Centering a title over a table with the Center Across Selected Columns tool.

Microsoft Excel - 93SALES.XLS

| | File | Edit | Formula | Format | Data | Options | Macro | Window | Help |

Normal

B2   Constantly Spry Rose Company - 1993 Sales

	A	B	C	D	E	F	G	H	I
1									
2		Constantly Spry Rose Company - 1993 Sales							
3			Qtr 1	Qtr 2	Qtr 3	Qtr 4	Total		
4		Departme	796.23	541.96	814.68	1389.67	3542.54		
5		Departme	532.68	685.23	497.42	833.24	2548.57		
6		Departme	278.64	225.35	301.42	379.85	1185.26		
7		Departme	587.91	629.43	547.29	744.15	2508.78		
8		Total	2195.46	2081.97	2160.81	3346.91	9785.15		
9									
10									
11									

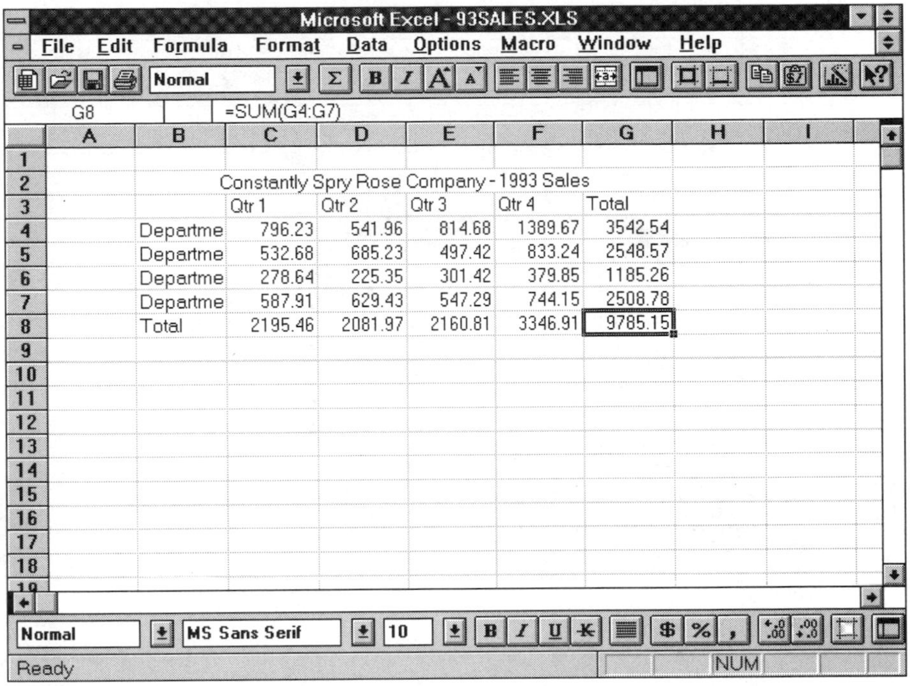

Figure 3-19:
The worksheet title after it is centered over the table.

Up, down, and all around

Left, right, and *center alignment* all refer to the placement of a text entry in relation to the left and right cell borders. You can also align entries in relation to the top and bottom borders of their cells. Normally, all entries are vertically aligned with the bottom of the cells. You can also vertically center an entry in its cell or align it with the top of its cell.

To change the vertical alignment of a cell selection, open the Alignment dialog box (shown in Figure 3-20) and click on the Top, Center, or Bottom radio button. To open the Alignment dialog box, select the Alignment command from the cell shortcut menu or choose the Alignment command from the Format menu.

Figure 3-21 shows the title for the 1993 sales table after it was centered vertically in its cell (this text entry was previously centered across the cell range B2:G2; the height of row B was increased from the normal 12.75 characters to 22.50 characters).

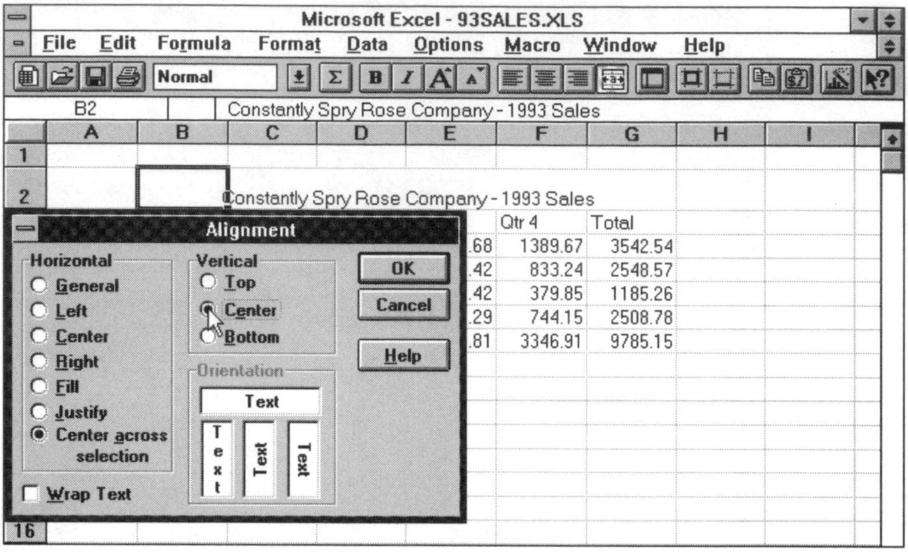

Figure 3-20:
The Alignment dialog box.

Figure 3-20 shows the Microsoft Excel - 93SALES.XLS window with the Alignment dialog box. Menu bar: File, Edit, Formula, Format, Data, Options, Macro, Window, Help. Cell B2 contains "Constantly Spry Rose Company - 1993 Sales".

The Alignment dialog box shows:
- **Horizontal**: General, Left, Center, Right, Fill, Justify, Center across selection (selected)
- **Vertical**: Top, Center (selected), Bottom
- **Orientation**: Text
- Wrap Text (unchecked)
- OK, Cancel, Help buttons

Partially visible data in the worksheet:
Qtr 4	Total
1389.67	3542.54
833.24	2548.57
379.85	1185.26
744.15	2508.78
3346.91	9785.15

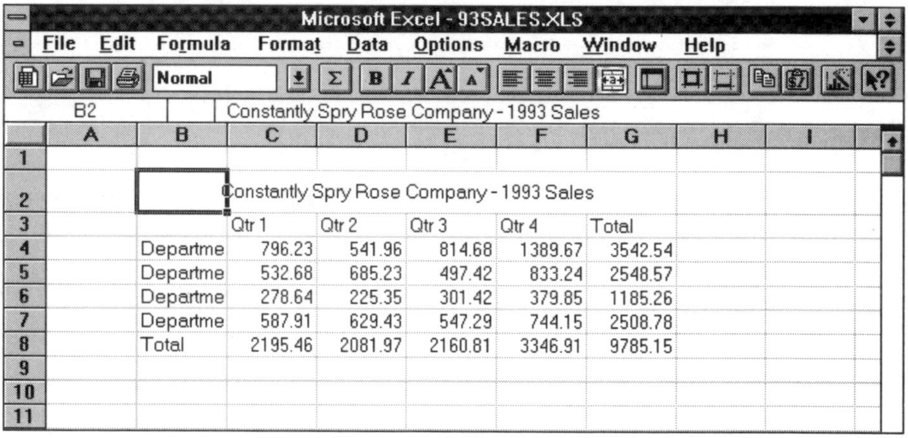

Figure 3-21:
The table title after centering it vertically in its cell.

Figure 3-21 shows the Microsoft Excel - 93SALES.XLS window. Cell B2 contains "Constantly Spry Rose Company - 1993 Sales".

		Qtr 1	Qtr 2	Qtr 3	Qtr 4	Total
Departme		796.23	541.96	814.68	1389.67	3542.54
Departme		532.68	685.23	497.42	833.24	2548.57
Departme		278.64	225.35	301.42	379.85	1185.26
Departme		587.91	629.43	547.29	744.15	2508.78
Total		2195.46	2081.97	2160.81	3346.91	9785.15

That's a wrap

Traditionally, column headings in worksheet tables have been a problem because you either had to keep them really short or abbreviate them if you wanted to avoid widening all the columns more than the data warranted. You can get around this problem in Excel by using the text-wrap feature (see Figure 3-22). This figure shows an invoice in which the column headings use text-wrap to avoid widening the columns more than invoice entries require.

To create the effect shown in Figure 3-22, select the cells with the column head-ings (row 6) and then click on the Wrap Text check box in the Alignment dialog box to turn on text wrap.

When you turn on text wrap, Excel breaks up the long text entries in the selec-tion (that either spill over or are cut off) into separate lines. To accommodate more than one line in a cell, the program automatically expands the row height so that the entire wrapped-text entry is visible.

When you turn on text wrap, Excel continues to use the horizontal and vertical alignment you specified for the cell. Note that you can use any of the Horizontal alignment options including Left, Center, Right, Justify, or Center across selec-tion. You can't, however, use the Fill option. Select the Fill radio button only when you want Excel to repeat the entry across the entire width of the cell.

If you want to wrap a text entry in its cell and have Excel justify the text with both the left and right border of the cell, do this by selecting the cell and click-ing on the Justify Align tool on the Formatting toolbar (the one between the Strikeout and Currency Style tool) instead of selecting the Justify radio button in the Alignment dialog box.

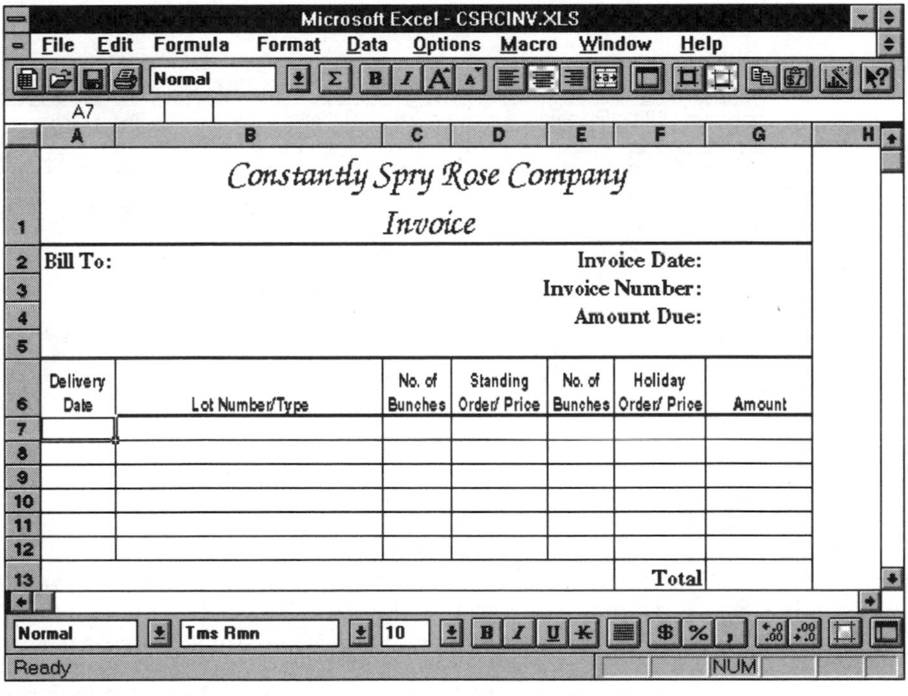

Figure 3-22:
An invoice form with the column heading using text wrap.

You can break a long text entry into separate lines by positioning the insertion point in the formula bar at the place where you want the new line to start and pressing Alt+Enter. Excel expands the formula bar and starts a new line. When you enter the text in the cell by pressing Enter, Excel marks the line break with the | character. You must still select the <u>W</u>rap Text check box in the Alignment dialog box to display the text on separate lines; your work in specifying where the lines are to break pays off then.

Just point me in the right direction

Instead of wrapping text entries in cells, you may find it more beneficial to change the orientation of the text. Figure 3-23 shows a situation where changing the orientation of the column headings works much better than wrapping them in their cells.

This example shows an order form that uses skinny columns to form the boxes in the printed form where the florist fills in the number of bunches of the types of flowers ordered according to color and length. To avoid widening the columns as much as it would take to accommodate the column headings (even when wrapped on several lines), the orientation was changed for the cell selection (C3:N3) from normal left-to-right to rotated up.

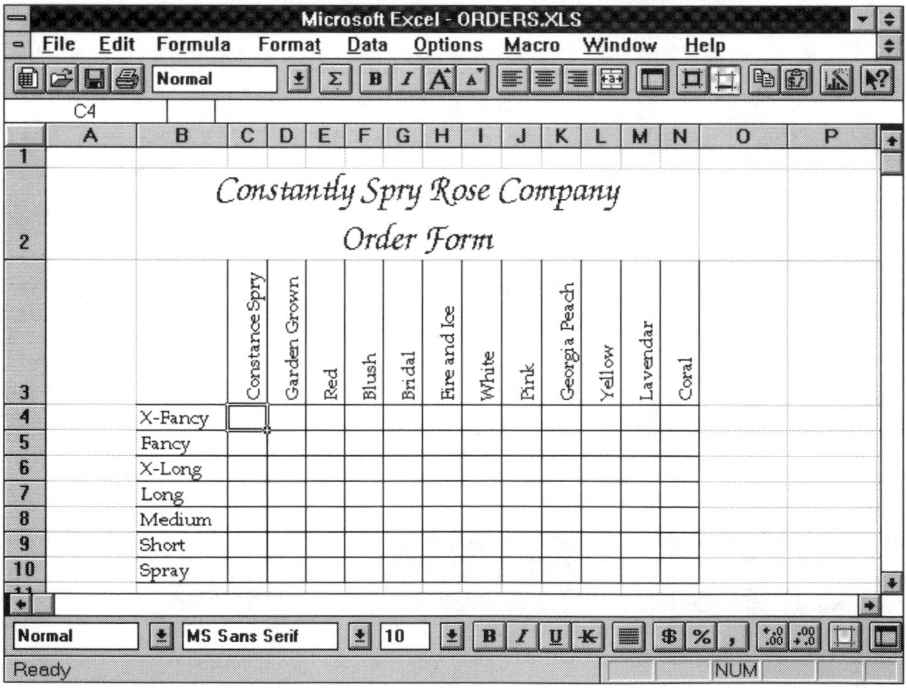

Figure 3-23:
An order form with column headings that use the rotated-up text orientation.

To change the text orientation, open the Alignment dialog box by choosing the Alignment command from the cell shortcut menu or by choosing Alignment from the Format menu. Then click on the Text box in the Orientation area that you want to use. Note that Orientation options are not available when the Wrap Text box is selected (Excel can't rotate *and* wrap at the same time), nor are these options available when you select the Fill, Justify, or Center across selection radio button.

I Think I'm Borderline, or The Patterns of My Cells

The gridlines displayed in the worksheet are just guidelines to help you keep your place as you work in the document. You can choose to print them with your data or not. To emphasize sections of the worksheet or parts of a particular table, you can add borderlines or shading to certain cells. Don't confuse the *borderlines* you add to accent a particular cell selection with the *gridlines* used to define cell borders in the worksheet — borders you add are printed whether or not you print the worksheet gridlines.

To better see the borders you add to the cells in a worksheet, remove the gridlines normally displayed in the worksheet.

> ✔ To do this, choose the Display command from the Options menu and then deselect the Gridlines check box. Note that this affects only the worksheet display.

> ✔ To remove the gridlines from a printed version of the worksheet, choose the Page Setup command from the File menu and deselect the Cell Gridlines check box.

To add borders to a cell selection, open the Border dialog box (shown in Figure 3-24) by choosing the Border command from the cell shortcut menu or by choosing Border from the Format menu. Select the type of line you want to use in the Style area of the dialog box, and then select from the Border section of the dialog box the edge or edges you want this line applied to.

> ✔ To make Excel draw borders around only the outside edges of the entire selection, choose the Outline check box in the Border section.

> ✔ If you want borderlines to appear around all four edges of each cell in the selection, select the Left, Right, Top, and Bottom check boxes instead.

> ✔ When you want to add a borderline to a single cell or around the outer edge of a cell selection, you don't even have to open the Border dialog box; you can simply select the cell or cell range and click on the Outline Border tool on the Standard toolbar (the one right next to AutoFormat).

Figure 3-24:
The Border
dialog box.

> ✔ If you want to add borderlines to the bottom edge of a cell or cell selection,
> click on the Bottom Border tool located right next door to the Outline Bor-
> der tool.

The only problem you ever have with borderlines is when you remove them
from the worksheet. To get rid of borders, you must select the cell or cells that
presently contain them, open the Border dialog box, and remove the currently
used border style from each and every edge option (Outline, Left, Right, Top,
and Bottom).

To remove a border style from an edge, you can either press the underlined
command letter, click on the box in front of the border option, or click on the
blank border style (the one in the lower-right corner of the Style area).

Of course, the problem you often have is figuring out which cells contain the
borders you want to remove; what appears at first glance as a row of cells with
borders on their bottom edges could really be a border on the top edges of the
cells in the row below. If you ever try to remove borders from a cell selection
only to find that they're still there, select the cells in the neighboring ranges and
try deleting the borders from there as well.

You can also add emphasis to particular sections of the worksheet or one of its
tables by shading these areas. To apply a light-gray color to a cell selection,
click on the Light Shading tool on the Formatting toolbar (the one second from
the right).

Because most printers produce the light-gray color as a light shading pattern,
you can use this tool to shade cells in most cases. Should you actually want to
assign a specific shading pattern, however, select one from the Patterns dialog
box (shown in Figure 3-25). To open the Patterns dialog box, choose the Patterns command from the cell shortcut menu or choose Patterns from the Format menu.

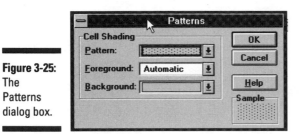

Figure 3-25:
The
Patterns
dialog box.

To choose a new pattern, click on the button next to the Pattern drop-down list box and choose the desired shading pattern. If you want, you can also fool around with the foreground and background colors used in the pattern by choosing options from the Foreground and Background drop-down list boxes. Excel shows what your creation looks like in the Sample area of the Patterns dialog box.

You can assign the first available shading pattern to the cell selection you're adding borders to by clicking on the Shade check box in the Border dialog box when you're specifying which borders to apply.

To remove a shading pattern from cells, select the cell range, open the Patterns dialog box, choose the None option from the Pattern drop-down list box, and then click on OK. If the Formatting toolbar is displayed, you can remove the shading pattern by clicking on the Light Shade tool twice in a row. The first time you click on this tool, Excel replaces the current shading pattern with the light-gray color. The second time you click on this tool, the program removes the light-gray color from the selection.

Going in Style

Cell styles are Excel's way of bringing together under one roof a whole lot of different kinds of formatting (including the number format, font, font size, font attributes, alignment, and cell borders and patterns). Excel includes six built-in cell styles you can use in any worksheet: Comma, Comma (0), Currency, Currency (0), Normal, and Percent.

The most common of these styles is the Normal style. This is the one automatically used in formatting all cells in a new worksheet. The other five styles are used to format cell selections with different number formats.

To apply any of these built-in cell styles (or any others you create on your own) to the current cell selection, simply click on the Style box drop-down button and choose the desired style from the list box. (Remember that the Style box appears on both the Standard and Formatting toolbars.)

To change the font used in the Normal style, follow these steps:

1. **Select the Style command from the Format pull-down menu.**

   The Style dialog box appears.

2. **Make sure that Normal is shown in the Style Name drop-down list box.**

3. **Click on the Define command button.**

   Excel expands the Style dialog box to show the elements included in the selected style and the buttons you can select to change it.

4. **Click on the Font command button at the bottom of the expanded Style dialog box.**

5. **Make any desired changes.**

   Select the font, font style, font size, as well as any effects or color changes you want to make in the Font dialog box.

6. **Click on the OK button in the Style dialog box or press Enter.**

   Excel changes all text formatted with the Normal style as well as the column letters and row numbers on the frame to the new font.

Creating new cell styles for a worksheet is as simple as falling off a log. All you do is format one of the cell entries in the worksheet to use all the formatting you want to include in the new style. Then, with the cell pointer located in the sample formatted cell, click on the Style box and replace the current style name with a new name (do this by pressing Ctrl+S and then typing the new name). When you finish naming the style, apply it to the current cell by pressing Enter. The next time you save the worksheet, Excel saves the new style as part of the worksheet. To apply the new style to other cells in the worksheet, select the cells and then select the style name from the Style drop-down list box.

As mentioned previously, styles are a great way to make custom number formats a lot easier to use in a worksheet. For example, you can create a Hidden style to use a custom number format that hides all types of entries; you can create a Full Month style to convert dates entered with a more abbreviated date format to a date format that displays the whole shebang. All you do is create these custom number formats (refer to "Number Formats Made to Order," earlier in this chapter, for details on how to go about doing this), apply them to a sample cell in the worksheet, and create a style named *Hidden* and one named *Full Month*. After saving the worksheet with these new styles, you can apply them to other cells in the worksheet directly from the Style box on either the Standard or the Formatting toolbar.

Chapter 4
How To Make Changes without Messing Up the Entire Worksheet

● ●

In This Chapter

▶ How to open a document that needs editing

▶ How to use the Undo feature to recover from a mistake

▶ How to use the drag-and-drop feature to move or copy entries in the document

▶ How to use the Cut, Copy, and Paste commands to move and copy information

▶ How to copy formulas

▶ How to delete entries from a cell selection

▶ How to delete rows and columns from the worksheet

▶ How to insert new rows and columns in the worksheet

▶ How to use the Speller to catch and eliminate spelling errors

● ●

*P*icture this: you've just finished creating, formatting, and printing a major project with Excel — a worksheet with your department's budget for the next fiscal year. Because you finally understand a little bit about how this thing works, you got the job done in crack time. You're actually ahead of schedule.

You turned the document over to your boss so that she can check the numbers. There's plenty of time for making those inevitable last-minute corrections — you're feeling on top of this situation.

Then comes the reality check — your boss brings the document back, and she's plainly agitated. "We forgot to include the estimates for the temps and our overtime hours. They've got to go right here. While you're adding them, can you move these rows of figures up and those columns over?"

As she continues to suggest improvements to go along with the one major addition you have to make, your heart begins to sink. These modifications are in a different league from "let's change these column headings from bold to italics and add shading to that row of totals." Clearly, you're looking at a lot more work on this baby than you had contemplated. Even worse, you're looking at making structural changes that threaten to unravel the very fabric of your beautiful worksheet.

As this fable points out, editing a worksheet can occur on two different levels: You can make changes that affect the contents of the cells, such as copying a row of column headings or moving a table to a new area in the worksheet. You can make changes that affect the structure of the worksheet itself, such as inserting new columns or rows (so that you can enter new data originally left out) or deleting unnecessary columns or rows from an existing table without leaving any gaps.

In this chapter, you learn how to safely make both types of changes to a worksheet. As you see, the mechanics of copying and moving data or inserting and deleting rows are simple to master. It's the impact that such actions have on the worksheet that takes a little more effort to understand. Not to worry! You always have the Undo feature to fall back on for those (rare?) times when you make a little tiny change that throws the entire worksheet into complete and utter chaos.

Help, My Document's Gone and I Can't Find It!

Before you can do any damage (I mean, make any changes) to a worksheet document, you have to open it up in Excel. To open a worksheet document, you can click on the Open File tool on the Standard toolbar (the one second from the left with the picture of a file folder opening up), you can choose Open from the File menu, or you can even press the keystroke shortcut Ctrl+F12.

Any way you do it, Excel displays the Open dialog box shown in Figure 4-1. Use this dialog box to select the document you want to work on from the File Name list box and then open it by choosing OK or pressing Enter. If you're real handy with the mouse, double-click on the document name to open it.

As alternatives to these file-opening methods, try the following:

  ✔ At the bottom of the File menu, Excel lists the last four documents you opened. If the worksheet you want to work with is one of these four, you can open it by selecting its filename from the menu.

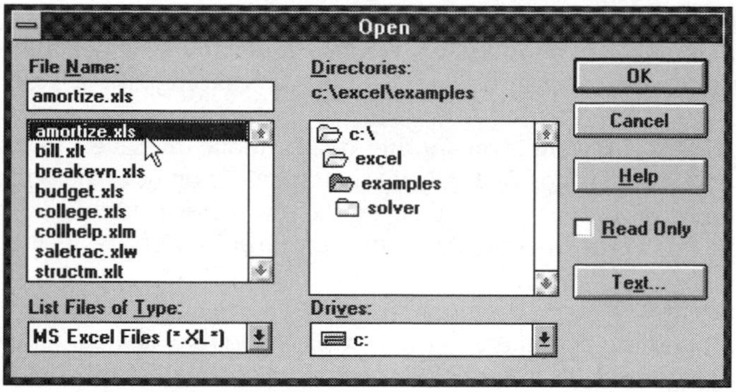

Figure 4-1:
The Open
dialog box.

> ✔ If you know you're going to edit more than one of the worksheets listed in
> the File Name list box of the Open dialog box, select multiple files from the
> list box and Excel opens all of them (in the order they're listed) when you
> choose OK. After the files are open, you can switch documents by selecting
> their filenames from the Window pull-down menu.

Now, where did I put that darn file?

The only problem you can encounter opening a document in the Open dialog
box is locating the filename. Everything's hunky-dory as long you can find the
document in the File Name list box.

But what about those times when a file seems to have mysteriously migrated
and is now nowhere to be found in the list? (These times seem to happen quite
frequently to my students.) I hate to tell you this, but you're going to have to roll
up your shirt sleeves and just go out and search for it, even though this means
getting involved with the — dare I say it— *DOS file structure.* Actually, with Windows, that's not as bad as it sounds.

The first thing to do before you begin actively searching for the missing document is to find out where in the world you are — what's the current disk drive
and directory? Excel lists this information in the Open dialog box right below the
Directories title. For example, the first time you display the Open dialog box, you
may see the following listed after the Directories title:

```
c:\excel
```

This tells you that you are looking at the list of Excel documents in the EXCEL
directory on drive C (the hard disk you never get to see). Chances are good that
when you first saved and named a worksheet, you didn't save it in this directory

because this directory is meant to hold only the Excel program files. If you did save documents here, get out your *Windows For Dummies* book and look up how to move them to another directory that you've created just for Excel documents.

If the document you want is on another disk, choose its drive letter from the Dri̱ves drop-down list box (actually, in the Open dialog box, the box pops up rather than drops down). After you select a new drive from this list box, Excel lists all the Excel-type documents in the root directory of the newly selected drive.

If you don't find the document in this new list, you may also have to change the directory. To do this, double-click on the name of the desired directory in the D̲irectories list box or select the folder and press Enter. Excel updates the list in the File N̲ame list box to show all Excel documents in the newly selected directory.

If you liken the computer's storage system to a traditional file cabinet, the disk drives (A, B, C, and down the line) compare to the file drawers; the file folders within each drawer compare to the directories on a disk; the paper documents in the folders compare to electronic files. Using this analogy, files in the root directory of a disk are like paper documents stuffed in at the very front of a file drawer without being placed in any of the file folders that follow.

Putting out an A.P.B. for a document

But what about those times when you haven't the foggiest idea where you saved the worksheet? That's when you need to turn to the Windows File Manager and use its search facility to find the missing document. With the Search command, the File Manager can look for a file in all the directories on a particular disk. When it finds the file, you can open the worksheet document right from the File Manager.

Be aware that if you open a document from the File Manager, the File Manager reappears when you finally exit Excel. To close the File Manager window and return to the Program Manager, choose E̲xit from the File Manager File menu.

To find a missing Excel document with the Windows File Manager, follow these steps:

1. **Press Alt+Tab until the words *Program Manager* pop up**.

   Release these keys to open the Program Manager window in front of the Excel window.

2. Find the Main window in the Program Manager window.

In the Main window, locate the File Manager icon (the one with the picture of the file cabinet).

3. Double-click on the File Manager icon.

Alternatively, select the icon and press Enter. The File Manager window opens.

4. Choose Search from the File menu.

The Search dialog box appears.

5. Enter the name of the worksheet document you want to find in the Search For text box.

If you're not sure of the filename, *edit* (don't replace) the funny * . * currently displayed in this text box. Press the Home key to move the insertion point in front of the first asterisk (*), type the first character or few characters of the filename (if you know them). Then press the End key, press the Backspace key to delete the second asterisk and replace it with **xls** (make sure that you don't fool with that period in front of the *xls*).

6. Press the Tab key to advance to the Start From text box.

Type the letter of the drive you suspect has your document; follow the drive letter with a colon, as in **A:** or **D:** (make sure that you press Shift with the colon key; a semicolon won't cut it).

7. Choose OK or press Enter.

The File Manager searches the specified drive for the file. If it doesn't find the file, an alert box appears, indicating that no matching files were found. Choose OK and repeat steps 4 through 7 to search another drive or use another search pattern.

If the File Manager locates the document, it selects the file in a Search Results window. To open that file and return to Excel, simply press the Enter key.

If you're using System 7 on the Mac, you can use the Find command on the Finder's File menu to locate a misplaced Excel document. To return to the Finder from Excel, click on the Excel icon on the far right of the menu bar, and then drag down until you choose the Finder command. To search for the missing Excel document, choose the Find command on the File menu (right next to the Apple menu) or press ⌘+F. Enter the name of the file you are searching for and then choose the Find button or press Return. When the Finder locates the Excel document, it opens the folder that contains it and selects the document. To open the document and reactivate Excel, simply double-click on the selected icon.

Please Do That Old Undo That You Do So Well

Before you start fooling with your work of art, you should know how to get to the Undo feature should you somehow manage to do something that messes up the document. The Undo command on the Edit menu is a regular chameleon command. If you delete the contents of a cell selection with the Clear command on this same menu, Undo changes to Undo Clear. If you move some entries to a new part of the worksheet with the Cut and Paste commands (again, found on the Edit menu), the Undo command changes to Undo Paste.

The Undo command on the Edit menu changes in response to whatever action you just took. Because it keeps changing after each action, you've got to re-member to strike when the iron is hot, so to speak, by using the Undo feature to restore the worksheet to its previous state *before* you choose another com-mand. It's imperative that you don't get going so fast that you make several changes in a row without stopping to check how each one affects the worksheet. For example, if you delete a value from a cell, and then change the font in another cell and widen its column before you realize that you deleted the wrong value, you can't use the Undo feature to restore the deleted value. All you can use Undo for in this case is to restore the column to its previous width (because this was the last action you completed).

In addition to choosing Undo (in whatever guise it appears in) from the Edit menu, you can also choose this command by pressing Ctrl+Z (perhaps for *unZap*). If the Utility toolbar is displayed, you can click on the Undo tool (the very first tool on the toolbar, with the picture of a pencil with an eraser and diagonal lines running through it).

Redo that old Undo

After choosing the Undo command (by whatever means you find most conve-nient), the command changes yet again — this time to a Redo command. If you delete an entry from a cell with Clear from the Edit menu and then choose Undo Clear from the Edit menu (or press Ctrl+Z or click on the Undo tool on the Utility toolbar), the next time you open the Edit menu, you see the following command at the top where Undo normally appears:

```
Redo (u) Clear Ctrl+Z
```

The (u) appears after Redo to remind you that **U** remains the command letter even though *Redo* doesn't have a *u* in it. When you choose the Redo command, Excel redoes the thing you just undid. Actually, this sounds more complicated than it is. It simply means that you use Undo to switch back and forth between the result of an action and the state of the worksheet just before that action until you decide how you want the worksheet (or they turn off the lights and lock up the building).

When Undo just won't do

Just when you think it is safe to begin gutting the company's most important worksheet, I really feel I've got to inform you that Undo doesn't work in all situations. Although you can undo your latest erroneous cell deletion, bad move, or unwise copy, you can't undo your latest inaccurate file deletion or imprudent save (when you meant to choose Save As from the File menu to save the edited worksheet under a different document name but instead chose Save and ended up saving the changes as part of the current document).

Unfortunately, Excel doesn't let you know when you are about to take a step from which there is no return until it's too late. After you've gone and done the undoable and you open the Edit menu right where you expect the Undo *blah, blah* command to be, it now says

```
Can't Undo
```

To add insult to injury, this extremely unhelpful command appears dimmed to indicate that you can't choose it — as though being able to choose it would change anything!

There is one exception to this rule — a time when the program gives you advance warning (which you should heed). When you choose a command that is normally undoable but currently — because you're low on memory, or the change will affect so much of the worksheet, or both — Excel knows it can't undo the change if it goes through with it. The program then displays an alert box telling you there isn't enough memory to undo this action and asking whether you want to go ahead anyway. If you click on the Yes button and complete the edit, just realize that you do so without any possibility of pardon. If you find out, too late, that you deleted a row of essential formulas (that you forgot about because you couldn't see them), you can't bring them back with Undo.

Drag Until You Drop

The first editing technique you learn is called *drag-and-drop*. As the name implies, it's a mouse technique you can use to pick up a cell selection and drop it into a new place on the worksheet. Although drag-and-drop is primarily a technique for moving cell entries around a worksheet, you can adapt it to copy a cell selection as well.

To use drag-and-drop to move a range of cell entries (you can only move one cell range at a time), follow these steps:

1. Select the range as you normally would.

2. Position the mouse pointer on one of the edges of the selected range.

Your signal that you can start dragging the cell range to its new position in the worksheet is when the pointer changes to the arrowhead.

3. Drag.

As you drag, you actually move only the outline of the cell range. Drag the outline until it's positioned around the new cells in the worksheet where you want the entries to appear.

4. Release the mouse button.

The cell entries within that range reappear in the new location as soon as you release the mouse button.

Figures 4-2 and 4-3 show how you can drag-and-drop to move a cell range. In Figure 4-2, the cell range B8:G8 (containing the quarterly totals) is selected and is about to be moved to row 10 to make room for sales figures for Departments 5 and 6, which weren't compiled when this worksheet was first created. In Figure 4-3, you see the worksheet after you complete this move. The selection is just cell C10.

Notice in Figure 4-3 that the argument for the SUM function in cell C10 has not kept pace with the change — it continues to sum only the range C4:C7. Eventually, this range must be expanded to include cells C8 and C9, the first-quarter sales figures for Departments 5 and 6 (you'll do this in the upcoming section, "You Really AutoFill Those Formulas").

Figure 4-2:
Dragging a selection to its new position in a worksheet.

Microsoft Excel - 93SALES.XLS

File Edit Formula Format Data Options Macro Window Help

Normal

B8 | Total

	A	B	C	D	E	F	G	H	I
1									
2		Constantly Spry Rose Company - 1993 Sales							
3			Qtr 1	Qtr 2	Qtr 3	Qtr 4	Total		
4		Department 1	796.23	541.96	814.68	1389.67	3542.54		
5		Department 2	532.68	685.23	497.42	833.24	2548.57		
6		Department 3	278.64	225.35	301.42	379.85	1185.26		
7		Department 4	587.91	629.43	547.29	744.15	2508.78		
8		Total	2195.46	2081.97	2160.81	3346.91	9785.15		
9									
10									
11									

Figure 4-3:
The
worksheet
after the
drag-and-
drop
operation.

	Microsoft Excel - 93SALES.XLS							

File Edit Formula Format Data Options Macro Window Help

	Normal		Σ	B	I	A	A								

C10   =SUM(C4:C7)

	A	B	C	D	E	F	G	H	I
1									
2			Constantly Spry Rose Company - 1993 Sales						
3			Qtr 1	Qtr 2	Qtr 3	Qtr 4	Total		
4		Department 1	796.23	541.96	814.68	1389.67	3542.54		
5		Department 2	532.68	685.23	497.42	833.24	2548.57		
6		Department 3	278.64	225.35	301.42	379.85	1185.26		
7		Department 4	587.91	629.43	547.29	744.15	2508.78		
8									
9									
10		Total	2195.46	2081.97	2160.81	3346.91	9785.15		
11									

Okay, so that's moving a cell range with drag-and-drop. But what if you want to copy a cell range instead? For example, you need to start a new table in rows farther down the worksheet, and you want to copy the cell range with the for-matted title and column headings for the new table. To copy the formatted title range in the sample worksheet, follow these steps:

1. **Select the cell range B3:G3.**

2. **Hold the Ctrl key as you position the mouse pointer on an edge of the selection.**

   The pointer changes from a thick-shaded cross to an arrowhead with a + (plus) sign to the right of it. This is your sign that drag-and-drop will *copy* the selection rather than *move* it.

3. **Drag the cell-selection outline to the place where you want the copy to appear and release the mouse button.**

To copy with drag-and-drop on the Mac, hold the Control key (not the ⌘ key that normally does the job of Ctrl in Excel for Macintosh) as you drag the selection. The Control key is found only on the extended keyboard. If you have a regular keyboard, you have to use Copy and Paste — see "Pasting the Night Away," later in this chapter, for details.

If, when using drag-and-drop, you position the outline of the selection so that it overlaps any part of cells that already contain entries, Excel displays an alert box with the following question:

    Overwrite non blank cells in destination?

To avoid replacing existing entries, choose Cancel in this alert box. To go ahead and exterminate the little darlings, choose OK or press Enter.

Like the Klingons of Star Trek fame, spreadsheets such as Excel never take prisoners. When you place or move a new entry into an occupied cell, the new entry completely replaces the old as though the old entry never existed in that cell.

To insert the cell range you're moving or copying within a populated region of the worksheet without wiping out existing entries, hold the Shift key as you drag the selection (if you're copying, hold both the Shift and Ctrl keys). This time, instead of dragging a rectangular outline of the cell range, you drag an I-beam shape that shows where the selection will be inserted when you release the mouse button. As you move the I-beam shape, notice that it gloms on to the column and row borders as you move it. When you position the I-beam shape at the column or row border where you want the cell range to be inserted, release the mouse button. Excel inserts the cell range and repatriates the existing entries to neighboring blank cells (out of harm's way).

When using drag-and-drop in insert mode, think of the I-beam shape as a pry bar that pulls apart the columns or rows along the axis of the I. Figures 4-4 and 4-5 show how to use the I-beam to move the departmental totals in column F of the 1993 Quarter 1 sales worksheet to column C. When you drag the cell range F3:F8 to the cell range C3:C8, you can be sure that Excel will insert these totals while moving the existing columns of sales entries to the right.

Figure 4-4 shows the worksheet after I selected the cell range of totals (F3:F8), held the Shift key, and dragged the I-beam shape until it rested on the border between columns B and C (between the column of row headings and the January sales figures).

Figure 4-4:
Dragging the departmental totals from column F to column C, replacing no existing entries.

	Microsoft Excel - Q1SALES.XLS							
File	Edit	Formula	Format	Data	Options	Macro	Window	Help

	Normal	Σ	B	I	A	A'						

F3			Qtr 1 Total					
	A	**B**	**C**	**D**	**E**	**F**	**G**	**H**
1								
2		Constantly Spry Rose Company - Qtr 1, 93 Sales						
3			Jan	Feb	Mar	Qtr 1 Total		
4		Department 1	144.00	269.70	382.53	$796.23		
5		Department 2	87.50	109.00	336.18	$532.68		
6		Department 3	123.44	56.00	99.20	$278.64		
7		Department 4	95.00	267.35	225.56	$587.91		
8		Total	$449.94	$702.05	$1,043.47	$2,195.46		
9								
10								
11								

But I did just what you said...

Drag-and-drop in insert mode is one of Excel's most finicky features. Sometimes, you do everything just right and you still get the alert box indicating that Excel is about to replace existing entries instead of pushing them aside (always choose the Cancel button). Fortunately, you can insert things with the Cut and Insert Paste commands (see "Pasting the Night Away," later in this chapter) without worrying about which way the I-beam selection goes.

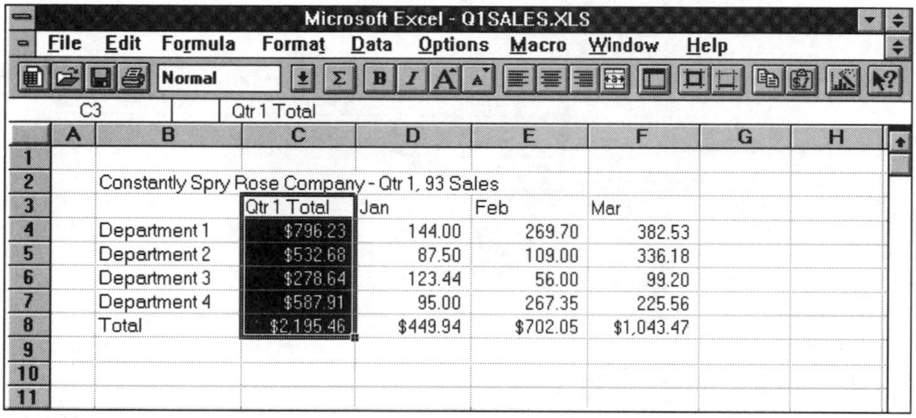

Figure 4-5: The worksheet after the department total cell range was inserted in column C.

	Microsoft Excel - Q1SALES.XLS						
File Edit Formula Format Data Options Macro Window Help							

C3 — Qtr 1 Total

	A	B	C	D	E	F	G	H
1								
2		Constantly Spry Rose Company - Qtr 1, 93 Sales						
3			Qtr 1 Total	Jan	Feb	Mar		
4		Department 1	$796.23	144.00	269.70	382.53		
5		Department 2	$532.68	87.50	109.00	336.18		
6		Department 3	$278.64	123.44	56.00	99.20		
7		Department 4	$587.91	95.00	267.35	225.56		
8		Total	$2,195.46	$449.94	$702.05	$1,043.47		
9								
10								
11								

Notice the orientation of the I-beam shape in Figure 4-4, how the long part of the I runs with the column border. Getting the I-beam selection indicator to assume this orientation can be tricky. To prepare to drag the cell selection, position the mouse pointer on one of the long edges (either the left or right) of the selection. When you drag the selection, position the mouse pointer slightly in front of the column border (not on it).

You Really AutoFill Those Formulas

Copying with drag-and-drop (by holding the Ctrl key) is useful when you need to copy a bunch of neighboring cells to a new part of the worksheet. Frequently, you need to copy the formula you've just created to a bunch of neighboring cells that need to perform the same type of calculation (such as totaling columns of figures). This type of copy, although quite common, can't be done with drag-and-drop. Instead, use the AutoFill feature (introduced in Chapter 2) or the Copy and Paste commands (see "Pasting the Night Away," coming right up).

Figures 4-6 and 4-7 show how you can use AutoFill to copy one formula to a range of cells. Figure 4-6 shows the 1993 sales worksheet after the yearly sales figures for Departments 5 and 6 were added. Remember that these figures were missing from the original worksheet, so I made room for them by moving the totals down to row 10 (you can see this back in Figure 4-3).

Unfortunately, Excel doesn't update the sum formulas to include the new rows (the SUM function still uses C4:C7 when it should be extended to include rows 8 and 9). To make the SUM function include all the rows, position the cell pointer in cell C10 and click on the AutoSum tool on the Standard toolbar. Excel suggests the new range C4:C9 for the SUM function.

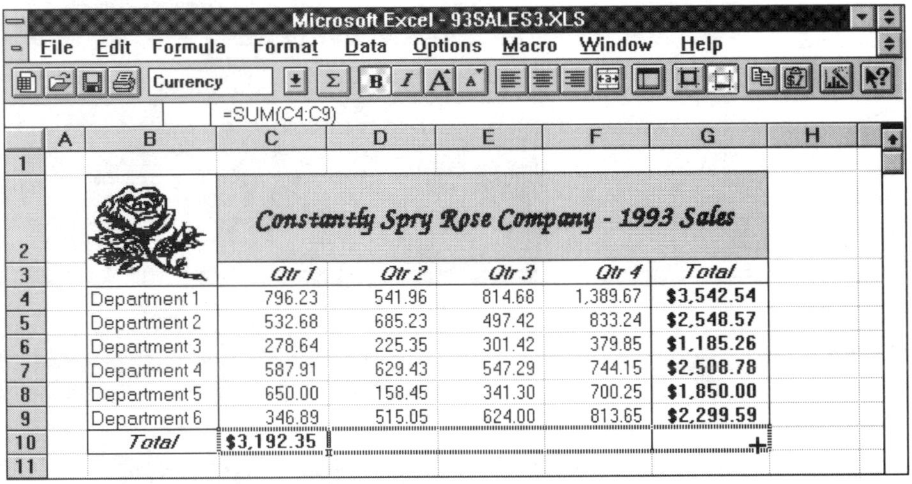

Figure 4-6:
Copying a formula to a cell range with AutoFill.

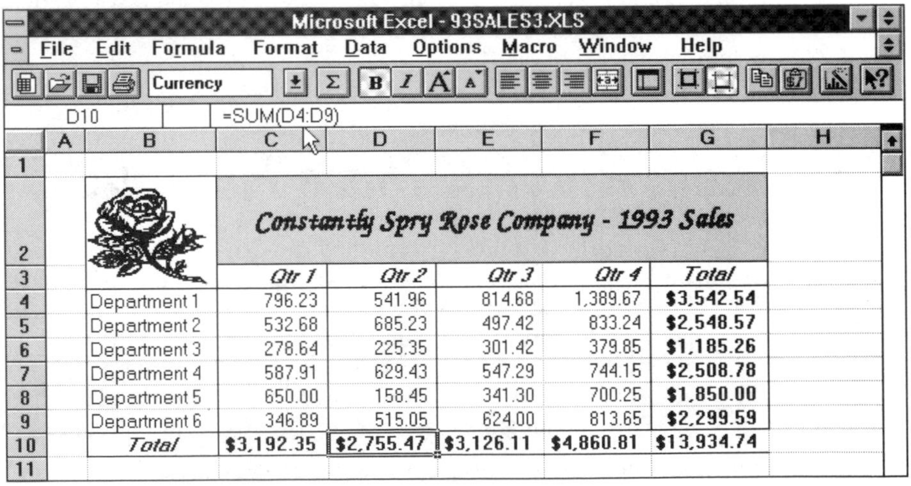

		Qtr 1	Qtr 2	Qtr 3	Qtr 4	Total
4	Department 1	796.23	541.96	814.68	1,389.67	**$3,542.54**
5	Department 2	532.68	685.23	497.42	833.24	**$2,548.57**
6	Department 3	278.64	225.35	301.42	379.85	**$1,185.26**
7	Department 4	587.91	629.43	547.29	744.15	**$2,508.78**
8	Department 5	650.00	158.45	341.30	700.25	**$1,850.00**
9	Department 6	346.89	515.05	624.00	813.65	**$2,299.59**
10	Total	$3,192.35				

Microsoft Excel - 93SALES3.XLS — =SUM(C4:C9) — Constantly Spry Rose Company - 1993 Sales

Figure 4-7:
The worksheet after the formula for totaling quarterly sales figures was copied.

		Qtr 1	Qtr 2	Qtr 3	Qtr 4	Total
4	Department 1	796.23	541.96	814.68	1,389.67	**$3,542.54**
5	Department 2	532.68	685.23	497.42	833.24	**$2,548.57**
6	Department 3	278.64	225.35	301.42	379.85	**$1,185.26**
7	Department 4	587.91	629.43	547.29	744.15	**$2,508.78**
8	Department 5	650.00	158.45	341.30	700.25	**$1,850.00**
9	Department 6	346.89	515.05	624.00	813.65	**$2,299.59**
10	Total	$3,192.35	$2,755.47	$3,126.11	$4,860.81	$13,934.74

Microsoft Excel - 93SALES3.XLS — D10 =SUM(D4:D9) — Constantly Spry Rose Company - 1993 Sales

Figure 4-6 shows the worksheet after I re-created the SUM formula in cell C10 with the AutoSum tool to include the expanded range. I dragged the fill handle to select the cell range D10:G10 (where this formula should be copied). Notice that I deleted the original formulas from the cell range D10:G10 in this figure to make it easier to see what's going on; normally, you just copy over the original outdated formulas and replace them with new correct copies.

Everything's relative

Refer to Figure 4-7 to see the worksheet after the formula in cell C10 is copied to the cell range D10:G10 and cell D10 is active. Notice how Excel handles the copying of formulas. The original formula in cell C10 is as follows:

```
=SUM(C4:C9)
```

When the original formula is copied next door to cell D10, Excel changes the formula slightly so that it looks like this:

```
=SUM(D4:D9)
```

Excel adjusts the column reference, changing it from *C* to *D,* because you copied from left to right across the rows.

When you copy a formula to a cell range that extends down the rows, Excel adjusts the row numbers in the copies rather than column letters to suit the position of each copy. For example, cell G4 in the sample 1993 sales worksheet contains the following formula:

```
=SUM(C4:F4)
```

When you copy this formula down to cell G5, Excel changes the copy of the formula to the following:

```
=SUM(C5:F5)
```

Excel adjusts the row reference to keep current with the new row 5 position. Because Excel adjusts the cell references in copies of a formula relative to the direction of the copying, the cell references are known as *relative cell references*.

Dealing in absolutes

All new formulas you create naturally contain relative cell references unless you say otherwise. Because most copies you make of formulas require adjustments of their cell references, you rarely have to give this arrangement a second thought. Then, every once in a while, you come across an exception that calls for limiting when and how cell references are adjusted in copies.

One of the most common of these exceptions is when you want to compare a range of different values to a single value. This happens most often when you want to compute what percentage each part is to the total. For example, in the 1993 sales worksheet, you encounter this situation in creating and copying a formula that calculates what percentage each quarterly total (in the cell range C10:F10) is of the yearly total in cell G10.

Suppose that you want to enter these formulas in row 12 of the 1993 worksheet, starting in cell C12. The formula in cell C12 for calculating the percentage of the first-quarter total in cell C10 is very straightforward:

```
=C10/G10
```

This formula divides the first-quarter total in cell C10 by the yearly total in G10 (what could be easier?). Look, however, at what would happen if you dragged the fill handle one cell to the right to copy this formula to cell D12:

```
=D10/H10
```

The adjustment of the first cell reference from C10 to D10 is just what the doctor ordered. However, the adjustment of the second cell reference from G10 to H10 is disaster. You not only don't calculate what percentage the second-quarter sales are of the yearly sales, you also end up with one of those horrible #DIV/0! error things in cell D12.

To stop Excel from adjusting a cell reference in a formula in any copies you make, convert the cell reference from relative to absolute. You can do this by pressing F4 or by choosing <u>R</u>eference from the Fo<u>r</u>mula menu at the same time you select the cell (with the mouse or keyboard).

On the Mac, ⌘+T (for *absoluTe?*) is the keystroke shortcut for changing a cell reference in a formula from relative to absolute. F4 on the extended keyboard won't cut it — this is the keystroke shortcut for pasting information.

Excel indicates that you've made the cell reference absolute by placing dollar signs in front of the column letter and row number. For example, look at Figure 4-8. Cell C12 in this figure contains the correct formula to copy to the cell range D12:F12:

```
=C10/$G$10
```

Figure 4-9 shows the worksheet after this formula is copied to the range D12:F12 with the fill handle and cell D12 is selected. Notice that the formula bar shows that this cell contains the following formula:

```
=D10/$G$10
```

Because G10 was changed to $G$10 in the original formula, all the copies have this same absolute reference.

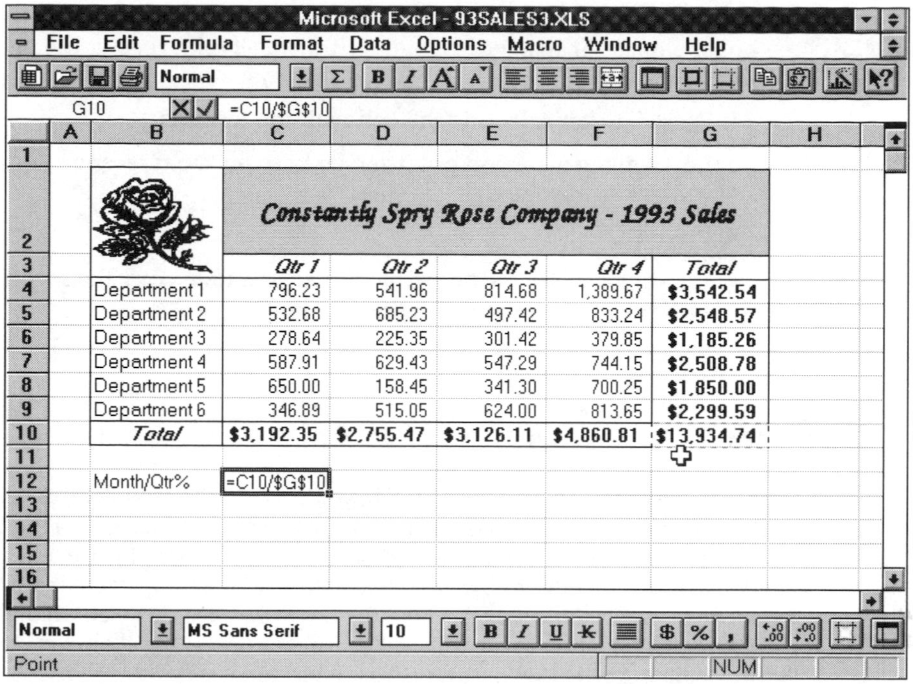

Figure 4-8: A
formula for
computing
the
percentage
each
quarterly
total is of the
yearly total.

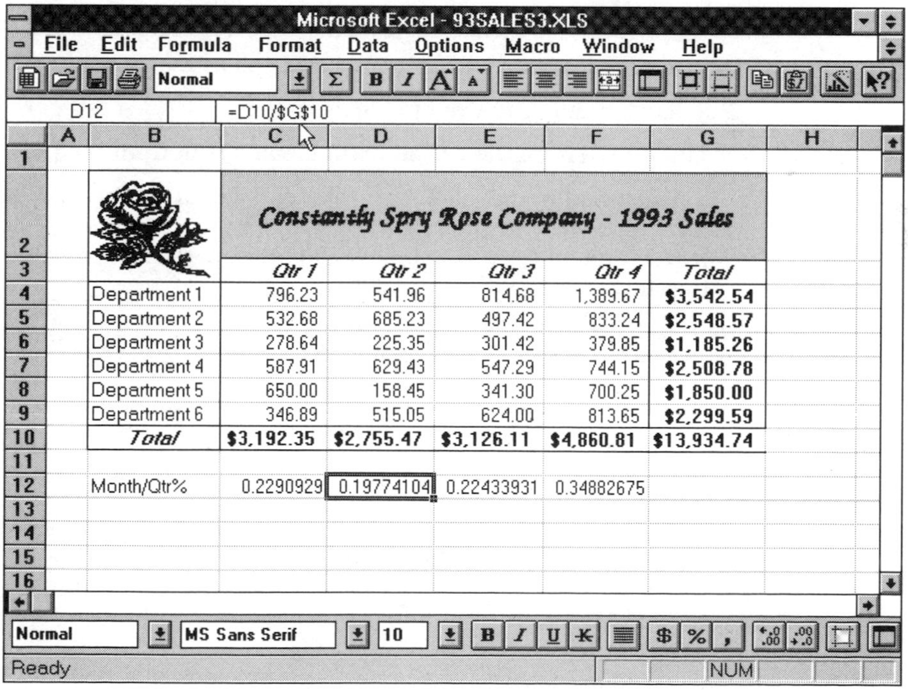

Figure 4-9:
The
worksheet
after the
formula is
copied.

If you goof up and copy a formula where one or more of the cell references should have been absolute, but you left them all relative, edit the original formula as follows:

1. **Press F2 after selecting the cell with the formula.**

2. **Position the insertion point somewhere on the reference you want to convert to absolute.**

3. **Press F4.**

4. **When you finish editing, press Enter and then copy the formula to the messed-up cell range with the fill handle.**

Pasting the Night Away

Instead of drag-and-drop or AutoFill, you can use the standby Cut, Copy, and Paste commands to move or copy information in a worksheet. These commands use the Clipboard as a kind of electronic halfway house where the information you cut or copy remains until you decide to paste it somewhere. Because of this Clipboard arrangement, you can use these commands to move or copy information to any other worksheet open in Excel or even to other programs running in Windows (like a Word for Windows document). This kind of moving or copying across documents is not possible with drag-and-drop or AutoFill.

To move a cell selection with Cut and Paste, follow these steps:

1. **Select the cells you want to move.**

2. **Choose Cut from the cell shortcut menu or Cut from the Edit menu.**

   You can cut through all these menus and just press Ctrl+X. When you do, Excel surrounds the cell selection with a *marquee* (a dotted line that travels around the cells' outline) and displays the following message on the status bar:

   ```
   Select destination and press Enter or choose Paste
   ```

3. **Move the cell pointer to, or select, the cell in the upper-left corner of the new range to which you want the information moved.**

4. **Press the Enter key to complete the move operation.**

   Alternatively, if you're feeling really ambitious, choose Paste from the cell shortcut menu, Paste from the Edit menu, or press Ctrl+V.

Notice that when you indicate the destination range, you don't have to select a range of blank cells that matches the shape and size of the cell selection you're moving. Excel only needs to know the location of the cell in the upper-left corner of the destination range to figure out where to put the rest of the cells.

In fact, you can mess yourself up if you select more than the first cell of the destination range and the selected range doesn't exactly match the size and shape of the selection you're moving. When you press Enter, Excel displays an alert box with the following message:

```
Cut and paste areas are different shapes
```

If you choose OK to get rid of this dialog box, you have to correct the size of the destination range to successfully complete the move operation.

Copying a cell selection with the Copy and Paste commands follows an identical procedure to the one you use with the Cut and Paste commands. After selecting the range to copy, you have even more choices about how to get the information into the Clipboard. Instead of choosing Copy from the cell shortcut menu or Copy from the Edit menu, you can press Ctrl+C or click on the Copy tool on the Standard toolbar (the one fourth from the right with the picture of the duplicate clipboards).

Copying is much better the second time around

When copying a selection with the Copy and Paste commands and the Clipboard, you can copy the information multiple times. Just make sure that, instead of pressing Enter to complete the first copy operation, you choose the Paste command (from the cell shortcut menu or the Edit menu) or press Ctrl+V.

When you use the Paste command to complete a copy operation, Excel copies the selection to the range you designated without removing the marquee from the original selection. This is your signal that you can select another destination range (either in the same or a different document).

After selecting the first cell of the next range where you want the selection copied, choose the Paste command again. You can continue in this manner, pasting the same selection to your heart's content. When you make the last copy, press Enter instead of choosing the Paste command. If you forget and choose Paste, get rid of the marquee around the original cell range by pressing the Esc key.

Pasting particulars

Normally, Excel copies all the information in the range of cells you selected: formatting as well as the formulas, text, and other values you entered. If you want, you can specify that only the entries be copied (without the formatting) or that just the formatting be copied (without the entries). You can even have Excel copy only values in a cell selection, which means that Excel copies all text entries and values entered in a cell selection but does *not* include formulas or formatting. When you paste values, all formulas in the cell selection are discarded and only the calculated values are retained — these values appear in the new cell range just as though you entered them manually. You may find occasions to use any of the following operations:

✔ To chuck the formulas and copy only text and values from a cell selection without their formatting, copy the cells to the Clipboard with the Copy command or the Copy tool on the Standard toolbar.

✔ To paste only the text and values, click on the Paste Values tool on the Utility toolbar (the fourth tool from the left, with the plain *12* on a picture of the clipboard). If the Utility toolbar is not displayed, choose Paste Special from the Edit menu, click on the Values radio button, and press Enter.

✔ If your intention is to copy all types of entries in the cell selection (formulas, text, and values) but leave behind the formatting, click on the Formulas radio button instead of the Values button (Excel doesn't provide a tool that does this). Only use the Values option when you don't want to copy the formulas, just their current values.

✔ To copy the formatting from a cell selection and leave the cell entries in the dust, click on the Paste Formats tool found on both the Standard and Utility toolbars (this tool has the formatted *$1* on the picture of the Clipboard — third from the right on the Standard toolbar and fifth from the left on the Utility toolbar). You can also do this copy operation by clicking on the Formats radio button in the Paste Special dialog box.

To Clear or Delete, That Is the Question

You can perform the following two kinds of deletions in a worksheet:

✔ The first type is rightfully referred to as *clearing a cell*: it deletes or empties the cell's contents without removing the cell from the worksheet, which would alter the layout of the surrounding cells.

✔ The second type of deletion, correctly referred to as *deleting a cell,* gets rid of the whole kit and caboodle — the cell structure along with all its contents and formatting. When you delete a cell, Excel has to shuffle the position of entries in the surrounding cells to plug up any gaps made by its demise.

Clearing the air

To clear a selection rather than delete it, select the range of cells to be cleared and press Del or choose Clear from the cell shortcut menu or Clear from the Edit menu. Any way you choose it, Excel displays a Clear dialog box that lets you decide what elements you want to remove. In the Clear dialog box you can do the following:

✔ By default, the Formulas radio button is selected in the Clear dialog box, meaning that if you choose OK or press Enter, Excel deletes all the entries (formulas, text, and values) in the selection but leaves behind all formatting and notes assigned to the cells (for information on how to add notes to cells, see Chapter 5).

✔ If you want to get rid of all formatting and notes as well as entries, click on the All radio button before you choose OK or press Enter.

✔ To delete only the formatting without touching anything else, click on the Formats button.

✔ If you want to remove only the notes in the cell range, click on the Notes radio button.

This cell range is condemned

To delete a cell selection rather than clear out its contents, select the cell range and choose Delete from the cell shortcut menu or Delete from the Edit menu. Excel displays a Delete dialog box that you use to indicate how Excel should shift the cells left behind to fill in the gaps made by the deletion. Use the Delete dialog box for these options:

✔ By default, the Shift Cells Left radio button is selected, meaning that Excel moves entries from neighboring columns on the right to the left to fill in gaps created when you delete the cell selection by choosing OK or pressing Enter.

✔ If you want Excel to move entries up from neighboring rows below, click on the Shift Cells Up radio button.

✔ If you decide to remove all the rows selected in the cell range (instead of restricting the deletion to just those few columns selected), click on the Entire Row radio button in the Delete dialog box.

✔ If you decide to delete all the columns highlighted in the cell range (instead of restricting the deletion to just those few rows selected), click on the Entire Column radio button.

✔ If you know ahead of time that you want to delete an entire column or row from the worksheet, you can select the column or row on the window frame and then choose Delete from the shortcut menu or Delete from the Edit menu. You can remove more than one column or row at a time provided that they all neighbor one another and that you select them by dragging through their column letters or row numbers (Excel can't delete nonadjacent selections).

Deleting entire columns and rows from a worksheet is risky business unless you are sure that the columns and rows in question contain nothing of value. Remember, when you delete an entire row from the worksheet, you delete *all information from column A through IV* in that row (and you can see only a very few columns in this row). Likewise, when you delete an entire column from the worksheet, you delete *all information from row 1 through 16384* in that column.

Under New Construction

For those inevitable times when you need to squeeze new entries into an already populated region of the worksheet, you can insert new cells in the area rather than go through all the trouble of moving and rearranging several individual cell ranges. To insert a new cell range, select the cells (many of which are already occupied) where you want the new cells to appear and then choose Insert from the cell shortcut menu or Insert from the Edit menu to display the Insert dialog box with the following options:

✔ When you insert new cells, you can decide how Excel should shift existing entries to make room for you. By default, Excel shifts cells to the right (the Shift Cells Right radio button is selected).

✔ To instruct the program to shift existing entries down instead, click on the Shift Cells Down radio button before choosing OK or pressing Enter.

✔ As when you delete cells, when you insert cells with the Insert dialog box, you can insert complete rows or columns in the cell range by clicking on either the Entire Row or the Entire Column radio button. You can also select the row number or column letter on the frame before you choose the Insert command.

Keep in mind that, just as when you delete whole columns and rows, inserting entire columns and rows affects the entire worksheet, not just the part you see. If you don't know what's out in the hinterlands of the worksheet, you can't be sure how the insertion will impact (perhaps, sabotage) entries in the other unseen areas.

Dispelling Your Misspellings

You'll be happy to know that Excel has a spelling checker that can catch and eliminate all those embarrassing little spelling errors. There's no longer any excuse for putting out worksheets with typos in the titles or headings.

To check the spelling in a worksheet, choose the Spelling command from the Options menu or click on the Check Spelling tool (the one with a check mark under *ABC*) on the Utility toolbar. Excel begins checking the spelling of all text entries in the worksheet. When the program comes across an unknown word, it displays the Spelling dialog box, similar to the one shown in Figure 4-10.

Excel suggests replacements for the unknown word, with the most likely replacement appearing in the Change To list box in the Spelling dialog box. Use the Spelling dialog box options as follows:

✔ To replace the word listed after the Not in Dictionary prompt with the word listed in the Change To list box, click on the Change button.

✔ To change all occurrences of this misspelled word in the worksheet, click on the Change All button.

✔ If you want to add the unknown word to a custom dictionary so that it won't be flagged when you check the spelling in the worksheet later on, click on the Add button.

Notice that the Excel spelling checker not only flags words not found in its built-in or custom dictionary but also flags occurrences of double words in a cell entry (such as *total total*) or words with unusual capitalization (such as *NEw York* instead of *New York*).

Keep in mind that you can check the spelling of just a particular group of entries by selecting the cell range before you choose Spelling from the Options menu or click on the Check Spelling tool in the Utility toolbar.

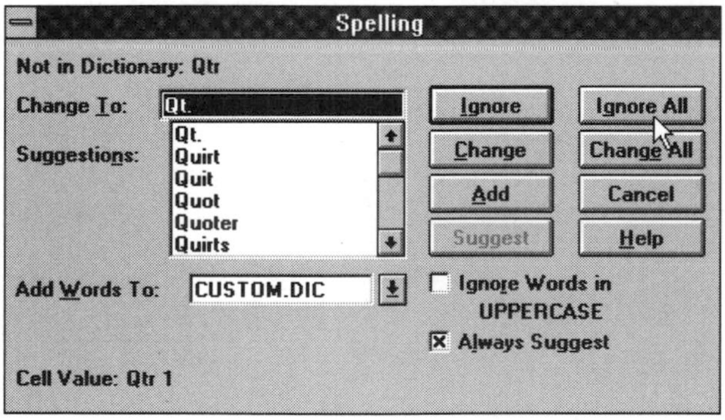

Figure 4-10:
The Spelling
dialog box.

Spelling
Not in Dictionary: Qtr
Change To: Qt.
Suggestions: Qt. / Quirt / Quit / Quot / Quoter / Quirts
Ignore / Ignore All
Change / Change All
Add / Cancel
Suggest / Help
Add Words To: CUSTOM.DIC
☐ Ignore Words in UPPERCASE
☒ Always Suggest
Cell Value: Qtr 1

Part III
Ferreting Out
The Information

The 5th Wave — By Rich Tennant

"HOLD ON, THAT'S NOT A SYNTAX ERROR, IT'S JUST A DONUT CRUMB ON THE SCREEN."

The part in which...

You learn all kinds of neat tricks for overseeing the information you've got in your worksheet and for getting it down on paper. First, you learn how to unearth stuff that you thought was lost and gone forever by using a series of stratagems like zooming in and out on the worksheet, splitting the document window into panes, marking your place with electronic post-it notes, assigning English-like names to worksheet cells, and, last but not least, using the Find command to hunt down specific text or values.

After learning how to stay on top of the info, you're ready to print it. You learn how to print all or just part of your worksheet, get the whole thing to fit on a single page, and print reports with headers and footers. You can print certain rows and columns with worksheet headings on each page, insert your own page breaks, and print a copy of your worksheet showing the formulas in each cell and the worksheet row and column frame. Wow!

Chapter 5
Keeping on Top of the Information (or How To Avoid Losing Stuff)

In This Chapter

▶ How to use the Zoom feature to enlarge or reduce the worksheet display

▶ How to split a document window into two or four panes

▶ How to freeze information on-screen as worksheet titles

▶ How to use worksheet outlining to display more or fewer levels of detail

▶ How to add notes to cells

▶ How to use descriptive names for cell ranges

▶ How to use the Find feature to locate information in the worksheet

▶ How to use the Replace feature to replace existing entries with new ones

▶ How to switch to manual recalculation to control when a worksheet is recalculated

▶ How to protect a worksheet from further changes

You already know that the Excel worksheet offers an awfully big place in which to store information. Because your computer monitor only lets you see a tiny parcel of the total worksheet real estate at any one time, the issue of keeping on top of information is not a small one.

Although the Excel worksheet employs a coherent cell-coordinate system you can use to get anywhere in the great big worksheet, you've got to admit that this A1, B2 stuff, although highly logical, remains fairly alien to human thinking. (I mean, saying, "go to cell IV88" just doesn't have anywhere near the same impact as saying "go to the corner of Hollywood and Vine.") Consider for a moment how hard it is to come up with a meaningful association between the 1992 depreciation schedule and its location in the cell range AC50:AN75 so that you can remember where to find it.

In this chapter, you learn some of the more effective techniques for keeping on top of information. First, you learn how to change the perspective on a work-sheet by zooming in and out on the information, how to split the document window into separate panes, and how to keep particular rows and columns on the screen at all times. You also learn how to use Excel's outline feature to quickly expand and contract how much table information appears on-screen.

And as if that weren't enough, you also learn how to add reminders to cells with notes, assign descriptive, English-type names to cell ranges (like Hollywood and Vine!), and use the Find and Replace commands to locate and, if necessary, replace entries anywhere in the worksheet. Finally, you learn how to control when Excel recalculates the worksheet and how to limit where changes can be made.

Zoom, Zoom, Zoom Went That Window

So what are you going to do now that the boss won't spring for that 19-inch monitor for your computer? All day long, it seems that you're either straining your eyes to read all the information in those little tiny cells or you're scrolling like mad trying to locate a table you can't seem to find today. Never fear, the Zoom feature is here. You can use Zoom like a magnifying glass to blow up part of the worksheet or shrink it down to size.

Figure 5-1 shows a blowup of an employee-roster worksheet after increasing it to 200% magnification (twice normal size). To blow up a worksheet like this, choose Zoom from the Window menu and click on the 200% radio button in the Zoom dialog box. You sure don't need your reading glasses to read the names in those cells! The only problem with 200% magnification is that you can see so few cells at one time.

Figure 5-2 shows the same employee worksheet, this time at 25% magnification (roughly one-quarter normal size). To reduce the display to this magnification, open the Zoom dialog box and click on the 25% radio button. Whew! At this size, the only thing you can be sure of is that you can't read a thing! However, notice that with this bird's-eye view, you can see at a glance how far down the employee roster extends.

The Zoom command has five precise magnification settings (200%, 100%, 75%, 50%, and 25%). To use other settings than those Excel offers, you can use the following options:

✔ If you want settings in between these (such as 150% or 85%) or settings greater or less than the highest or lowest (such as 400% or 15%), you can click on the Custom radio button and enter the magnification percentage in its text box.

✔ If you don't know what percentage to enter to display a particular cell range on the screen, select the range, open the Zoom dialog box, and click on the Fit Selection radio button. Excel figures out the percentage necessary to fit that range on the screen when you choose OK or press Enter.

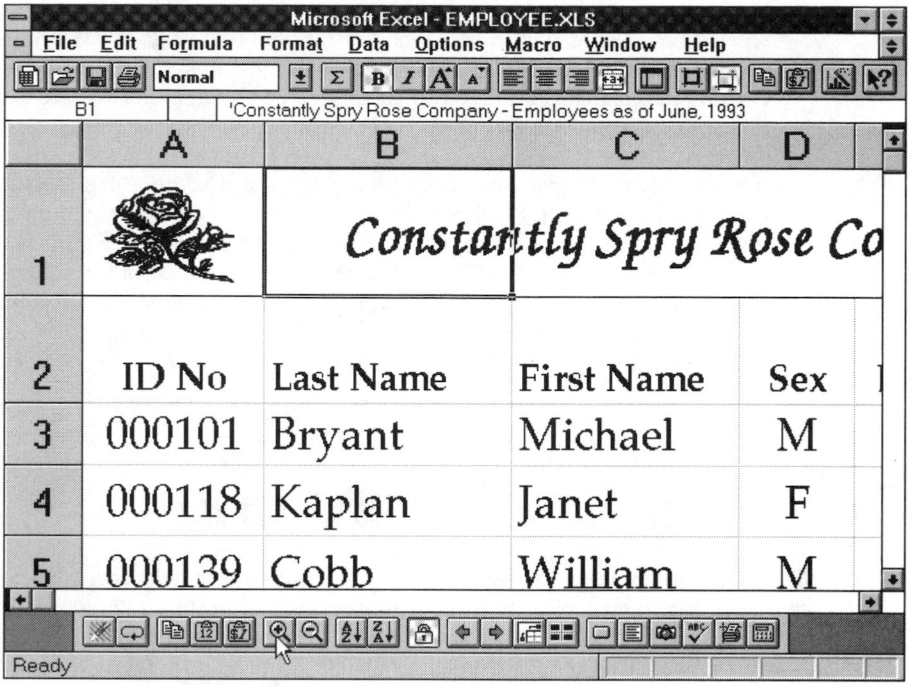

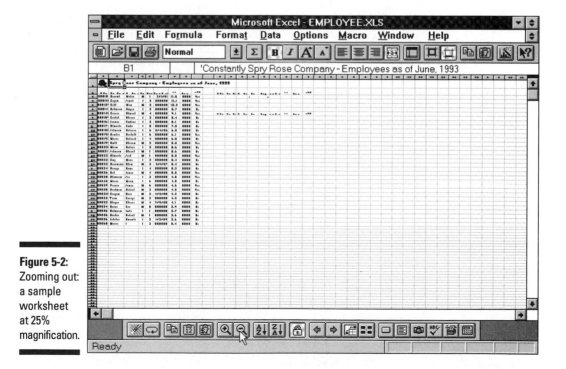

Figure 5-1:
Zooming in:
a sample
worksheet at
200%
magnification.

Figure 5-2:
Zooming out:
a sample
worksheet
at 25%
magnification.

You can use the Zoom command to locate and move to a new cell range in the worksheet. First, select a small magnification, such as 25%. Then locate the cell range you want to move to and select one of its cells. Finally, choose the Zoom command again and choose the 100% setting. When Excel returns the display to normal size, the cell you selected and its surrounding range appear on-screen.

If the Utility toolbar is on-screen (you can see it docked at the bottom of the document window in Figures 5-1 and 5-2), you can change the magnification by clicking on the Zoom In tool (the one with the picture of the magnifying glass and a +) or the Zoom Out tool (the one with the picture of the magnifying glass and a –). Clicking on these tools either increases or decreases the magnification using the five built-in settings (25%, 50%, 75%, 100%, and 200%). You can reverse the effect of these tools by holding the Shift key as you click (the + changes to a –).

Tapping on My Window Panes

Although zooming in and out on the worksheet can help you get your bearings, it can't bring together two separate sections so that you can compare their data on the screen (at least not at a normal size where you can actually read the information). To manage this kind of trick, split the document window into separate panes and then scroll the worksheet in each pane so that they display the parts you want to compare.

Splitting the window is easy. Figure 5-3 shows a sample income statement after I split its worksheet window horizontally into two panes and scrolled up to rows 13 through 17 in the second pane. Each pane has its own vertical scroll bar, which enables you to scroll different parts of the worksheet into view.

To split a worksheet into two horizontal panes, you can drag the *split bar,* located right above the scroll arrow at the very top of the vertical scroll bar, down until the window is divided as you want it. Use the following steps:

1. **Click on the split bar.**

   The mouse pointer changes to a double-headed arrow with a split in its middle (like the one used to display hidden rows).

2. **Drag.**

   A gray bar appears in the document window, showing you the row at which the window will split.

3. **Release the mouse button.**

   Excel divides the window into horizontal panes at the pointer's location and adds a vertical scroll bar to the new pane.

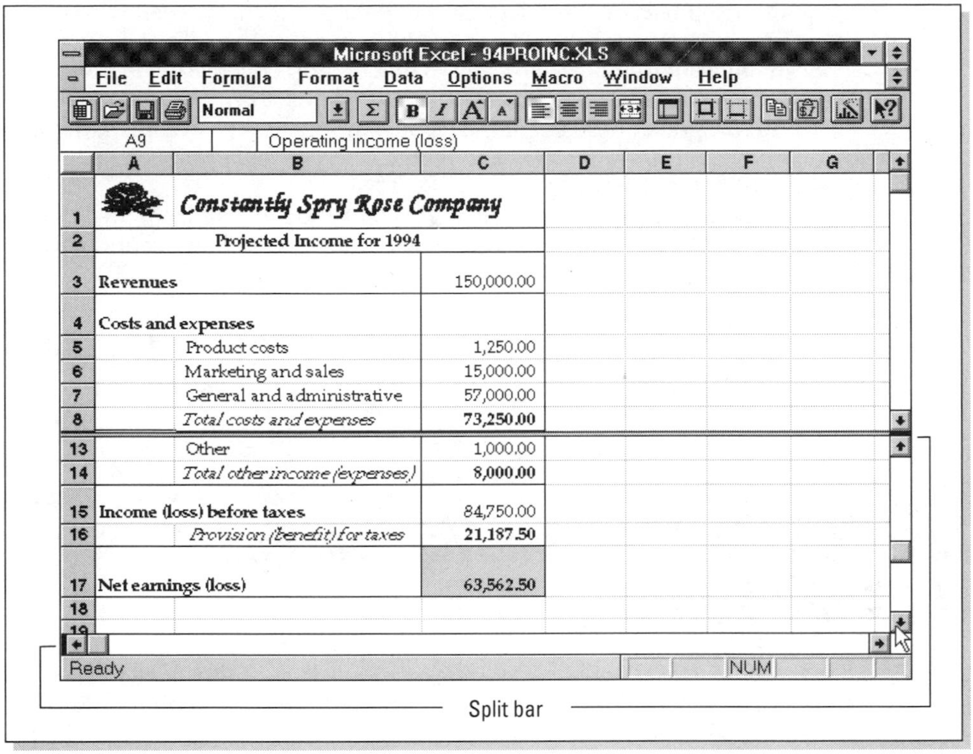

Figure 5-3: The worksheet in a split document window after scrolling up the income statement in the lower pane.

You can also split the document window into vertical panes. Follow these steps:

1. **Click on the split bar located at the left edge of the horizontal scroll bar.**

2. **Drag to the right until you reach the column at which you want the window divided.**

3. **Release the mouse button.**

    Excel splits the window at that column and adds a second horizontal scroll bar to the new pane.

Instead of dragging split bars, you can divide a document window with the Split command on the Window menu. When you choose this command, Excel uses the position of the cell pointer to determine where to split the window into panes. The program splits the window vertically at the left edge of the pointer and horizontally along the top edge. If you want the window split into only two panes, position the cell pointer either in the first column of the desired row (for two horizontal panes at that row) or in the first row of the desired column (for two vertical panes at that column).

When the left edge of the cell pointer is right up against the left edge of the document window (as it is when the pointer is in column A), the program doesn't split the window vertically. When the top edge of the pointer is right up against the top edge of the document window (as it is when the pointer is in cell C1), the program doesn't split the window horizontally — it splits the window vertically along the left edge of column C.

If you position the cell pointer in cell D6 and choose Split from the Window menu, the window splits into four panes: a horizontal split occurs between rows 5 and 6, and a vertical split occurs between columns C and D.

After the window is split into panes, you can move the cell pointer into a particular pane either by clicking on one of its cells or by pressing Shift+F6. To remove the panes from a window, choose the Remove Split from the Window menu.

Immovable Titles on My Frozen Window Panes

Window panes are great for viewing different parts of the same worksheet that normally can't be seen together. They can also be used to freeze headings in the top rows and first columns so that the headings stay in view at all times no matter how you scroll through the worksheet. Frozen headings are especially helpful when you work with a table which contains information that extends beyond the rows and columns shown on-screen.

Figure 5-4 shows just such a table. The employee-roster worksheet contains many more rows than you can see at one time (unless you decrease the magnification to 25% with Zoom, which makes the data too small to read). As a matter of fact, this worksheet continues down to row 33.

By splitting the document window into two horizontal panes between rows 2 and 3 and then freezing the top pane, you can keep in row 2 the column headings that identify each column of information on the screen as you scroll the worksheet up and down to review information on different employees. If you further split the window into vertical panes between columns B and C, you can keep the identification numbers and last names on the screen as you scroll the worksheet left and right.

Figure 5-4 shows the employee roster after splitting the window into four panes and freezing them. To create and freeze these panes, follow these steps:

1. **Position the cell pointer in cell C3.**

2. **Choose Split from the Window menu.**

3. **Choose Freeze Panes.**

   Alternatively, you can create the panes by dragging the split bars.

   Excel freezes the top and left window pane above row 3 and left of column C.

Because the upper and left panes are frozen, the program does not add a second horizontal and vertical scroll bar to the new panes. Notice that the borders of frozen panes are represented by a single line rather than a thin bar as is the case with unfrozen panes. (To help you see the frozen panes in the Figures 5-4 through 5-6, I removed the worksheet gridlines — see Chapter 10 for information about how you can change or remove gridlines.)

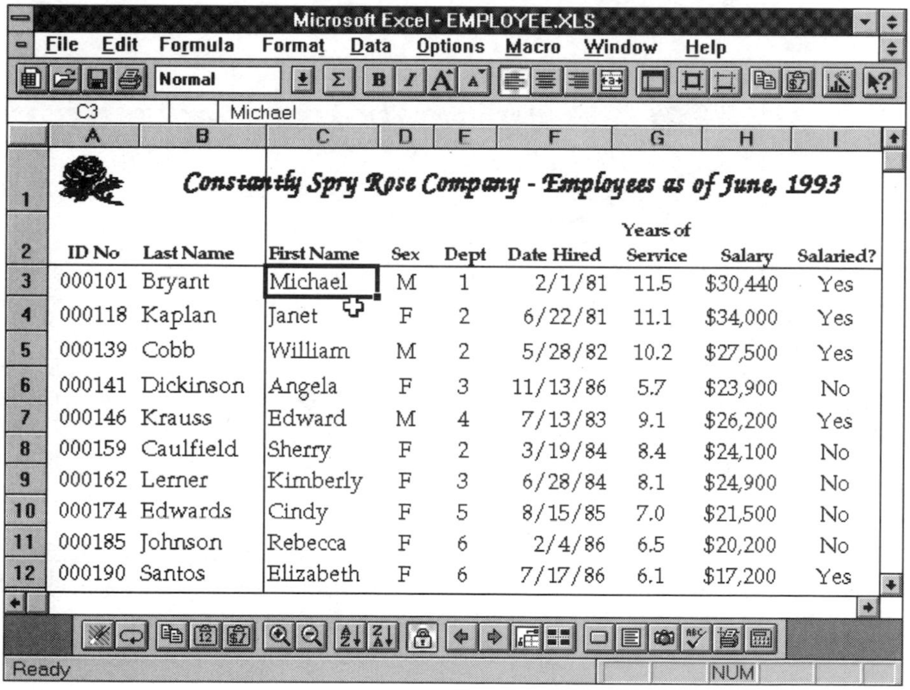

Figure 5-4:
Frozen panes to keep the column headings and last names on the screen at all times.

Figure 5-5 shows what happens when you scroll the worksheet up after freezing the window panes. In this figure, I scrolled the worksheet up so that rows 25 through 33 appear under rows 1 and 2. Because the vertical pane with the worksheet title and column headings is frozen, it remains on-screen (normally, rows 1 and 2 would have been the first to disappear as you scrolled the worksheet up).

Figure 5-6 shows what happens if you scroll the worksheet to the left. In this figure, I scrolled the worksheet so that columns F through L appear after columns A and B. Because the first two columns are frozen, they remain on-screen, helping you identify who belongs to what information.

To unfreeze the windows panes in a worksheet, choose Unfreeze Panes from the Window menu. If you want to remove the panes from the document window at the same time, choose Remove Split from the Window menu instead.

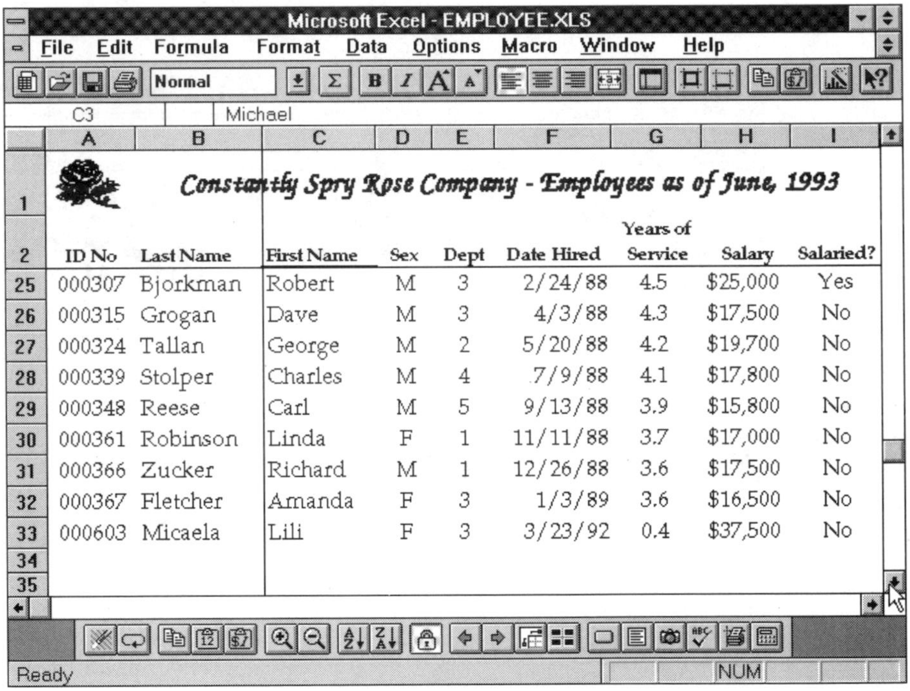

Figure 5-5:
The
employee
roster
scrolled up
to display
the last
rows of the
worksheet.

	A	B	C	D	E	F	G	H	I
1			Constantly Spry Rose Company - Employees as of June, 1993						
2	ID No	Last Name	First Name	Sex	Dept	Date Hired	Years of Service	Salary	Salaried?
25	000307	Bjorkman	Robert	M	3	2/24/88	4.5	$25,000	Yes
26	000315	Grogan	Dave	M	3	4/3/88	4.3	$17,500	No
27	000324	Tallan	George	M	2	5/20/88	4.2	$19,700	No
28	000339	Stolper	Charles	M	4	7/9/88	4.1	$17,800	No
29	000348	Reese	Carl	M	5	9/13/88	3.9	$15,800	No
30	000361	Robinson	Linda	F	1	11/11/88	3.7	$17,000	No
31	000366	Zucker	Richard	M	1	12/26/88	3.6	$17,500	No
32	000367	Fletcher	Amanda	F	3	1/3/89	3.6	$16,500	No
33	000603	Micaela	Lili	F	3	3/23/92	0.4	$37,500	No
34									
35									

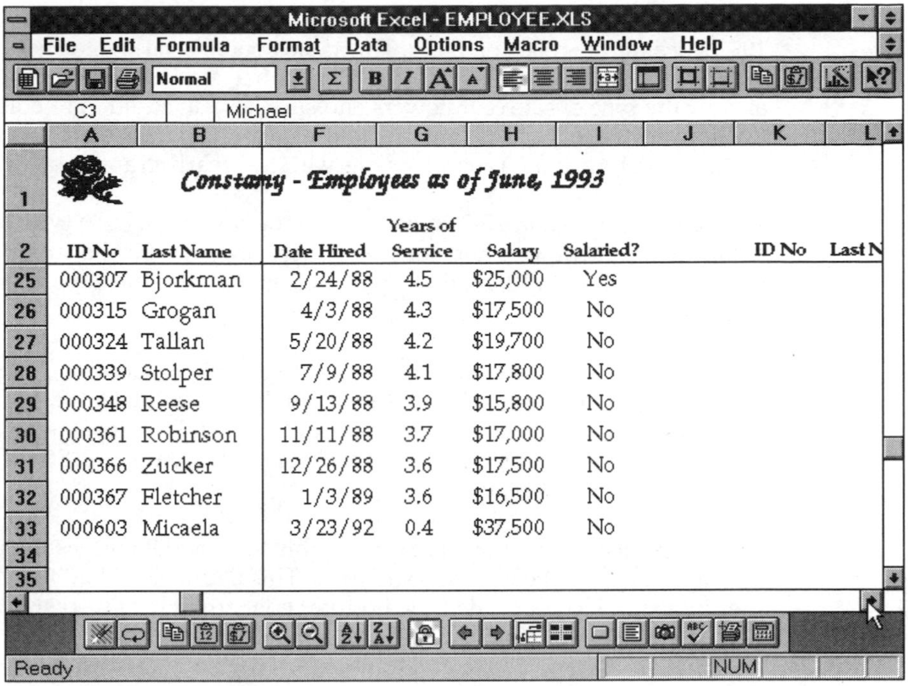

Figure 5-6: The employee roster scrolled left to display the worksheet columns F through L.

We'll Have an Outline in the Old Town Tonight

Remember when you had to outline your papers in school? Didn't it always seem like it would have been easier to work backwards and create the outline *after* you finished writing the paper instead of trying to create it before you knew what you were going to say?

Well, this is exactly the approach Excel takes when it outlines information in a worksheet table. After you enter all the information and formulas to calculate subtotals and grand totals for a table, the program then analyzes which columns and rows contain summary information (such as quarterly subtotals or department subtotals) and which columns and rows contain the supporting values. Excel then assigns outline levels to its columns and rows accordingly.

The purpose of outlining a worksheet table is so that you can display as much or as little supporting information as you want. To facilitate outlining, Excel adds a series of buttons to the table that you use to expand or collapse the outline. As you collapse the outline, Excel hides all the columns or rows with the supporting values for the level you are viewing. You can then view the summary information for that level all together — without the details.

Figure 5-7 shows a sample worksheet outline created for a sales table showing 1992 sales for the rose company. This table contains sales information broken out for each month (January through December) not only by department but also by the type of sale (cut flowers and supplies). In addition to columns with the monthly sales for all 12 months, there are columns for quarterly subtotals (columns E, I, M, and Q) as well as one with the yearly grand total (column R).

As you can see in Figure 5-7, in addition to the rows with each type of sale by department (cut flowers and supplies), there are rows for the subtotal of each department (rows 6, 10, 14, and 18) as well as one with the departmental grand total (row 19).

To outline this table, select its cells (the range A2:R19), choose Outline from the Formula menu, and then click on the Create button in the Outline dialog box. If you want, you can direct Excel to apply different styles to each level of the outline (while it creates the outline) by clicking on the Automatic Styles check box before you click on Create.

Figure 5-7 shows the outline created for this table and identifies the outline symbols added to the columns and rows. This figure also identifies the tools on the Utility toolbar (docked at the bottom) concerned with worksheet outlines. Click on the Show Outline Symbols tool to hide and redisplay the outline symbols that are located above and to the left of the document window. Click on the Promote and Demote tools to manually change the level of a particular column or row.

When creating the outline, sometimes Excel messes up and doesn't assign a particular column or row of subtotals to the correct outline level. To reassign an outline level to a row or column, choose from the following options:

✔ To assign one outline level up, click on the column letter or row number on the frame and then click on the Promote tool on the Utility toolbar. Excel moves the dot in front of that column or row to the next level up.

✔ To assign the next lower outline level, click on the column letter or row number on the frame and then click on the Demote tool.

✔ To remove an outline from a table, select all the rows by dragging through the row numbers on the frame and then click on the Promote tool repeatedly until all the row outline symbols disappear. Then select all of the columns and click on the Promote tool to remove the column outline symbols.

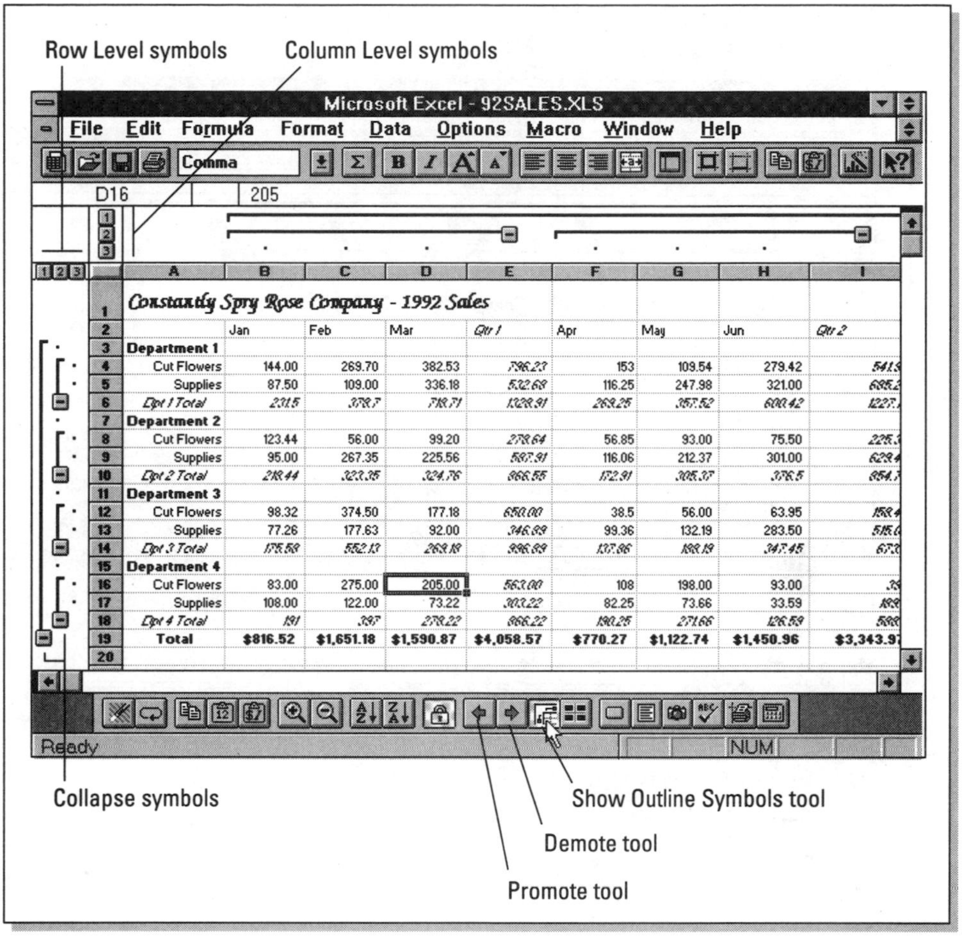

Figure 5-7: The sample 1992 sales table with outline symbols.

You can use the row level and column level symbols to display more or fewer
levels of detail in the table. Figure 5-8 shows the 1992 sales table after clicking
on the level 2 symbols for both the rows and columns. In this figure, only the
department subtotals by quarter are shown (instead of quarterly subtotals for
each type of sale — cut flowers and supplies).

Notice that at this level of detail, Excel places an Expand symbol above each
summary row and column in the table. To view the supporting figures in the
rows above or columns in front of a particular summary level, click on its Expand symbol (the Expand symbol then changes to a Collapse symbol attached
to a bar, showing which columns or rows are summarized).

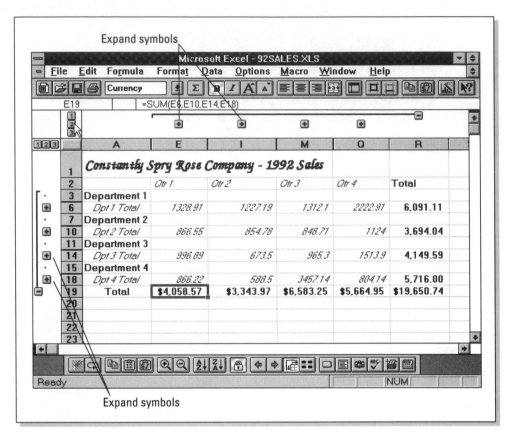

Figure 5-8: The sample 1992 sales table with quarterly totals by department.

Figure 5-9 shows the 1992 sales table after you click on the level 1 column symbol (leaving the level 2 row symbol selected). In this figure you see only the departmental totals for the entire year.

To print or chart just the outline levels displayed in the worksheet, click on the Select Visible Cells tool on the Utility bar (the one immediately to the right of the Show Outline Symbols tool) before you create the chart (see Chapter 7) or select the print area (see Chapter 6).

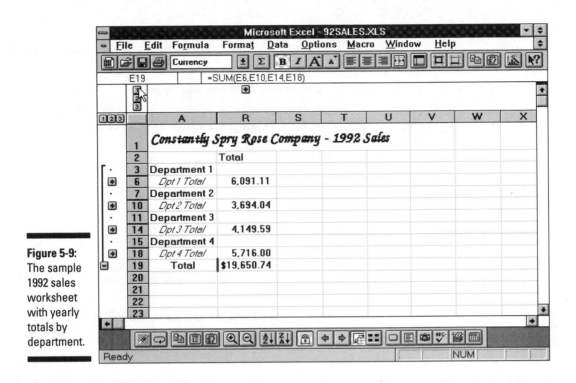

Figure 5-9:
The sample
1992 sales
worksheet
with yearly
totals by
department.

Electronic Post-it Notes

Excel lets you add notes to particular cells in a worksheet that work kind of like
electronic Post-it notes. For example, you can add a note to yourself to verify a
particular figure before printing the worksheet or to remind yourself that a particular value is only an estimate. In addition to using notes to remind yourself of
something you've done or that still remains to do, you can also use a note to
mark your current place in a large worksheet. You can then use the note's location to quickly find your starting place the next time you work with that
worksheet.

To add a note to a cell, follow these steps:

1. **Select the cell to which you want to add the note.**

2. **Choose Note from the Formula menu.**

   The Cell Note dialog box appears.

3. **Type the text of your note in the Text Note list box.**

   If you want to add notes to more than one cell, click on the Add button, select the cell to which you want to add the next note, and type its text.

4. **Choose OK or press Enter when you finish adding notes.**

   Excel marks the location of notes in a cell by adding a tiny square in the upper-right corner of the cell (this square appears in red on a color monitor).

5. **To display the note in a cell, double-click on the cell.**

   Alternatively, select the cell.

6. **Choose Note from the Formula menu.**

   Excel opens a Cell Note dialog box, similar to the one in Figure 5-10, where you can read the text of your note. This dialog box also shows the location of all other notes in the worksheet.

7. **To read other notes, select the note location from the Notes in Sheet list box.**

8. **After you finish looking over your notes, click on the Close button.**

   The Cell Note dialog box closes.

Adding notes that sound off

If you have one of the new Macs with built-in sound capabilities, you can use the microphone that came with your Mac (if you can find it) to record sound notes in cells. Just follow these steps:

1. Open the Cell Note dialog box.

2. Click on the Record button to open up a dialog box where you record the note.

3. Click on the Record button (the large dot) in this dialog box.

4. Speak the text of your note into the microphone.

5. Click on the Stop button (the square) when you've finished recording.

6. Click on the Save button to close the dialog box.

7. Click on the Add button in the Cell Note dialog box.

In the Notes in Sheet list box of the Cell Note dialog box, Excel indicates that you have a sound note by placing an asterisk after the cell reference. To play a sound note, double-click on the cell in the worksheet, or select the sound note from the Notes in Sheet list box, and then click on the Play button.

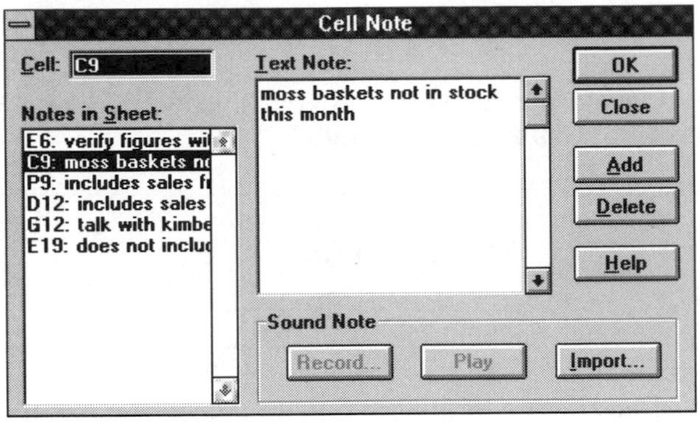

Figure 5-10:
The Cell
Note dialog
box.

Excel 4.0 for Windows is capable of recording and playing sound notes as described for Macintosh computers. However, to use this capability, you must be running Windows 3.1 and your IBM-compatible must be equipped with hundreds of dollars worth of separate equipment (in the form of at least a sound board and a microphone) — a typical IBM kluge!

If you used a note as a placeholder and want to go to that cell, first select all the cells in the worksheet that contain notes by choosing Select Special from the Formula menu and pressing Enter (the Notes radio button is automatically selected when you open the Select Special dialog box). After only the cells with notes are selected, move the cell pointer from one selected cell to the next by pressing Tab (press Shift+Tab to back up and revisit a previous cell).

To remove all notes from the worksheet, first select all the cells with notes by choosing Select Special. Press Del, click on the Notes radio button in the Clear dialog box, and then choose OK. To remove the notes in a particular cell range, select the range as you would any other range and click on the Notes radio button in the Clear dialog box.

When printing a worksheet, you can print the notes alone or the notes plus selected worksheet data. See Chapter 6 for details on choosing what information to print.

Name That Cell

By assigning descriptive names to cells and cell ranges, you can go a long way towards keeping on top of the location of important information in a worksheet. Rather than trying to associate random cell coordinates with specific information, you just have to remember its name. And best of all, after you name a cell or cell range, you can use this name with the Goto feature.

When assigning range names to a cell or cell range, you need to follow a few guidelines:

✔ Range names must begin with a letter of the alphabet, not a number. For example, instead of **93Profit**, use **Profit93**.

✔ Range names cannot contain spaces. Instead of a space, use the under-score (the Shifted hyphen) to tie the parts of the name together. For example, instead of **Profit 93**, use **Profit_93**.

✔ Range names cannot correspond to cell coordinates in the worksheet. For example, you can't name a cell **Q1** because this is a valid cell coordinate. Instead, use something like **Q1_sales**.

To name a cell or cell range in a worksheet:

1. **Select the cell or cell range.**

2. **Choose Define Name from the Formula menu.**

   Excel opens the Define Name dialog box (see Figure 5-11). The references for the selected cell or cell range appear in the Refers to text box (using absolute cell references).

3. **Type the name for the selected cell or cell range in the Name text box.**

4. **Choose OK or press Enter.**

If you want to define more than one range name at a time:

1. **Typing the name of the first range.**

2. **Click on the Add button.**

   Excel adds that name to the Names in Sheet list box.

3. **Replace the current range name in the Name text box with the name of the next range.**

4. **Press Tab to select the Refers to text box.**

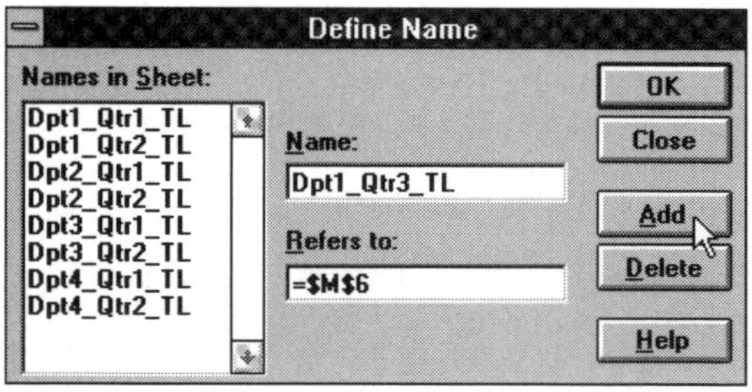

Figure 5-11:
The Define
Name dialog
box.

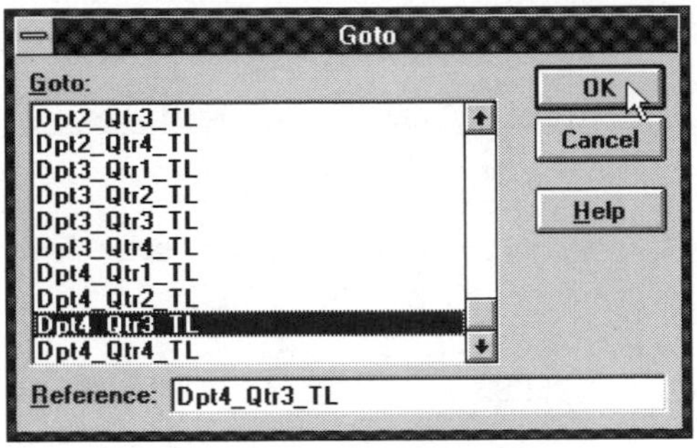

Figure 5-12:
The Goto
dialog box.

5. **Select the cell or cell range in the worksheet to which you want to apply this new range name.**

6. **Click on the Add button.**

7. **After you finish naming cells, click on the Close button.**

To select a named cell or range in a worksheet, press F5 or choose Goto from the Formula menu. The Goto dialog box appears (see Figure 5-12). Double-click on the desired range name in the Goto list box (alternatively, select the name and choose OK or press Enter). Excel moves the cell pointer directly to the named cell. If you selected a cell range, all the cells in that range are selected.

Finders Keepers

When all else fails, you can use Excel's Find command to locate specific information in the worksheet. When you choose Find from the Formula menu or press Shift+F5, Excel opens the Find dialog box (see Figure 5-13). In the Find What text box, enter the text or values you want to locate and then choose OK or press Enter to start the search.

When you search for a text entry with the Find command, be mindful of whether the text or number you enter in the Find What text box is separate in its cell or occurs as part of another word or value. For example, Figure 5-13 shows the characters mic in the Find What text box. Because the Part radio button is activated, Excel will find the first name Michael as well as the last name Micaela because they both contain mic as part of the cell entry. If you checked the Match Case check box in the Find dialog box before starting the search, Excel would not consider Michael or Micaela to be a match because of their capitalization.

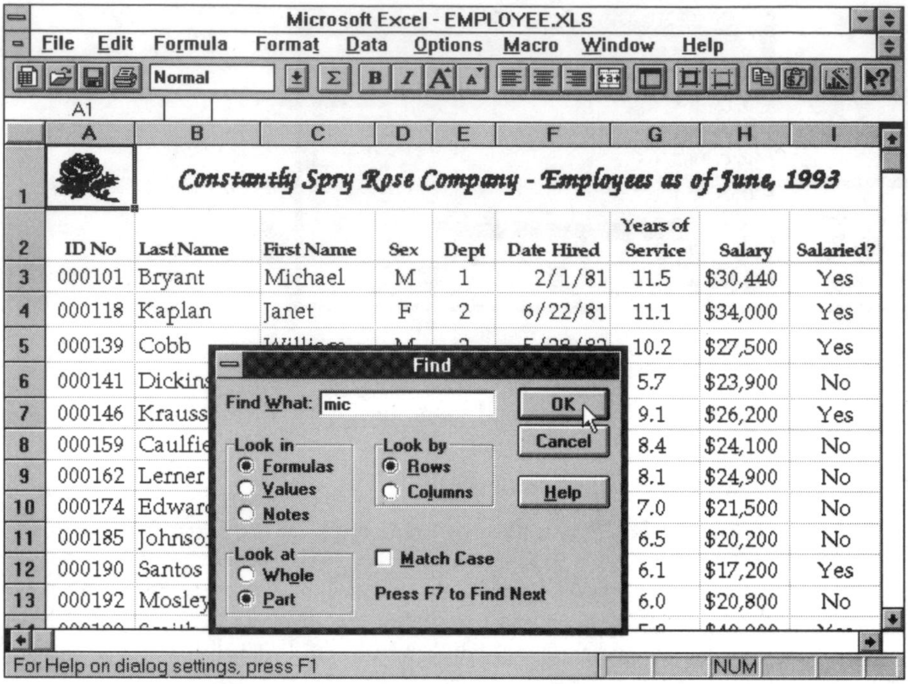

Figure 5-13:
The Find
dialog box.

When you search for values in the worksheet, be mindful of the difference between formulas and values. For example, Figure 5-13 shows the value 11.5 in cell G3 of the employee roster. However, if you enter **11.5** in the Find What dialog box and press Enter to start the search, Excel displays an alert box with the following message:

```
Could not find matching data
```

Excel does not find the value 11.5 in cell G3 because this value is calculated by the following formula, and Excel normally searches the formulas (not the values returned by the formulas):

```
=NOW()-F3/365
```

To search for the 11.5 calculated by the formula in G3, click on the Values radio button in the Find dialog box instead of the normally activated Formulas button. If you are looking for text or values entered in notes added to the worksheet cells, click on the Notes radio button to have Excel search them.

If you don't know the exact spelling of the word or name, or the precise value or formula you're searching for, you can use wildcards. Use the question mark (?)

to stand for a single unknown character; use the asterisk (*) to stand for any number of missing characters. Suppose that you enter the following in the Find What text box and choose the Values option:

```
7*4
```

Excel stops at cells that contain the values 74, 704, and 7,5234, and even finds the text entry 782 4th Street.

If you actually want to search for an asterisk in the worksheet, precede it with a tilde (~), as follows:

```
~*4
```

This arrangement enables you to search the formulas in the worksheet for one that multiplies by the number 4 (remember that Excel uses the asterisk as the times sign).

```
J?n*
```

This entry in the Find What text box finds cells that contain Jan, January, June, Janet, and so on.

When Excel locates a cell in the worksheet that contains the text or values you're searching for, it selects that cell. To search for the next occurrence of the text or value, press F7. Excel normally searches down the rows. To search across the columns, click on the Columns radio button (instead of Rows) in the Find dialog box. To revisit a previous occurrence of a found entry, press Shift+F7.

The shortcut keystroke you use on the Mac to open the Find dialog box is ⌘+J (for *Jump to?*). If you have the extended keyboard, Shift+F5 also works. To find the next occurrence of the text or value you're looking for, press ⌘+H (for *next Hit?*). To revisit a previous occurrence of a found entry, press ⌘-Shift+H — on the extended keyboard, Shift+F7 also works.

Replacement Costs

If your purpose for finding a cell with a particular entry is so that you can change it, you can automate this process by choosing Replace instead of Find from the Formula menu. After entering the text or value you want to replace in the Find What text box, enter the text or value you want as the replacement in the Replace With text box.

When you enter replacement text, enter it exactly as you want it to appear in the cell. In other words, if you replace all occurrences of Jan in the worksheet with **January,** enter the following in the Replace With text box:

```
January
```

Make sure that you use the capital *J* in the Replace With text box, even though you can enter the following in the Find What text box (providing you don't check the Match Case check box):

```
jan
```

After specifying what to replace and what to replace it with, you can have Excel replace occurrences in the worksheet on a case-by-case basis or globally. To replace all occurrences in a single operation, click on the Replace All button.

Be careful with global search-and-replace operations; they can really mess up a worksheet in a hurry if you inadvertently replace values, parts of formulas, or characters in titles and headings that you hadn't intended to change. As a precaution, ***never undertake a global search-and-replace operation on an unsaved worksheet.*** Also, verify which radio button in the Look at setting of the Replace dialog box is checked before you begin. You can end up with a lot of unwanted replacements if you leave the Part radio button activated when you should have chosen the Whole button. If you do make a mess, choose the Undo command to restore the worksheet. If you don't discover the problem in time to use Undo, close the messed-up worksheet without saving the changes and open the unreplaced version you saved — thanks to reading this warning!

To see each occurrence before you replace it, choose the Find Next button. Excel selects the next cell with the text or value you entered in the Find What text box. To have the program replace it, click on the Replace button. To skip this occurrence, click on the Find Next button to continue the search. When you finish replacing occurrences, click on the Close button to close the Replace dialog box.

To Calc or Not To Calc

Locating information in a worksheet — although admittedly extremely important — is only a part of the story of keeping on top of the information in a worksheet. In really large worksheets, you may want to switch to manual recalculation so that you can control when the formulas in the worksheet are calculated. You need this kind of control when you find that Excel's recalculation of formulas each time you enter or change information in cells has slowed the program's response to a crawl. By holding off recalculations until you are ready to save or print the worksheet, you find that you can work with the worksheet without interminable delays.

To put the worksheet on manual, choose Calculation from the Options menu, click on the Manual radio button in the Calculations Options dialog box, and choose OK or press Enter. Provided that you don't remove the *X* from the Recalculate Before Save check box when changing the calculation options (not generally a very smart idea), Excel still automatically recalculates formulas before saving the worksheet so that you are assured of saving only the most up-to-date values.

After switching to manual recalculation, Excel displays the message `Calculate` on the status bar. This is your signal that not all calculated values in the worksheet are correct. To bring formulas up to date before saving the worksheet (as you would before printing it), press F9 or Ctrl+= (the equal sign) or click on the Calculate Now tool on the Utility toolbar (the last one on the right with the picture of a calculator).

Excel then recalculates the formulas in all open documents. If you are working with more than one worksheet document and you don't want to wait around for Excel to recalculate every single document, you can restrict the recalculation to the current document by clicking on the Calc Document button in the Calculation Options dialog box or pressing Shift+F9.

If you've changed calculation from automatic to manual on the Mac, you recalculate open worksheets by pressing ⌘+= (the equal sign) to choose the Calc Now command. If you have an extended keyboard, you can also press F9.

Protect Yourself!

Once you've more or less finalized a worksheet by checking out its formulas and proofing its text, you often want to guard against any unplanned changes by protecting the document.

Each cell in the worksheet can be locked or unlocked. By default, Excel locks all the cells in a worksheet when you choose Protect Document from the Options menu and then choose OK or press Enter. Locking all the cells makes it impossible to make further changes anywhere in the entire worksheet.

Usually, your intention in protecting a document is not to prevent *all* changes but to prevent changes in certain areas of the worksheet. For example, in a budget worksheet, you may want to protect all the cells that contain headings and formulas but allow changes in all the cells where you enter the budgeted amounts. That way, you can't inadvertently wipe out a title or formula in the worksheet simply by entering a value in the wrong column or row (not an uncommon occurrence).

To leave certain cells unlocked so that you can still change them after protecting the document, follows these steps:

1. **Select the cells you want to be able to change.**

2. **Choose Cell Protection from the Format menu.**

3. **Remove the *X* from the Locked check box in the Cell Protection dialog box.**

   Alternatively, select the cells and click on the Lock Cell tool (the one with the picture of the lock, naturally) on the Utility toolbar.

4. **After unlocking the cells you want to be able to change, protect the document by choosing the Protect Document command on the Options menu.**

Excel displays an alert dialog box with the following message when you try to edit or replace an entry in a locked cell:

```
Locked cells cannot be changed
```

To remove protection from a document so that you can make changes to any of its cells (locked or unlocked), choose Unprotect Document from the Options menu.

To make it impossible to remove protection from a document unless you know the password, enter a password in the Password text box of the Protect Document dialog box. Excel masks each character you enter with a dot. After you choose OK, Excel makes you reenter the password before protecting the document. From then on, you can remove protection from a worksheet only if you can reproduce the password exactly as you assigned it (including any case differences). Be very careful with passwords. If you forget the password, you cannot change any locked cells and you cannot unlock any more cells in the worksheet.

Chapter 6
Getting the Information Down on Paper (or Spreadsheet Printing 101)

• •

In This Chapter

▶ How to use the Print Preview feature to see how a report will appear when printed

▶ How to use the Print tool to print a worksheet

▶ How to use the Set Print Area command to print only a particular section of the worksheet

▶ How to fit an entire report on a single page

▶ How to change the orientation of the printing of a report

▶ How to change the margins for a report

▶ How to add a header and footer to a report

▶ How to print column and row headings on every page of a report

▶ How to insert page breaks in a report

▶ How to print the formulas in a worksheet

• •

*G*etting it all down on paper — when all is said and done, this is really what it's all about. All the data entry, all the formatting, all the formula checking, all the things you do to get a worksheet ready, you do in preparation for printing its information. In this chapter, you learn how easy it is to print reports with Excel. And you find that by just following a few simple guidelines, you can produce top-notch reports the first time you send the document to the printer (instead of the second, or even the third, time around).

The only trick to printing a worksheet is getting used to the paging scheme and learning how to control it. Many of the worksheets you create with Excel are not only longer than one printed page but also wider. Unlike a word processor, which only pages the document vertically (because it won't let you create a document wider than the page size you're using), spreadsheet programs like Excel often have to break up pages both vertically and horizontally to print a worksheet document.

When paging a worksheet, Excel first pages the document vertically down the rows in the first columns of the print area (just like a word processor). After paging the first columns, the program pages down the rows of the second set of columns in the print area. Excel pages down and then over until all of the document included in the print area (which can include the entire worksheet or just sections) is paged.

When paging the document, keep in mind that Excel does not break up the information within a row or column. If all the information in a row won't fit at the bottom of the page, the program moves the entire row to the following page. So, too, if all the information in a column won't fit at the right edge of the page, the program moves the entire column to a new page. (Because Excel pages down and then over, chances are that the column will not appear on the next page of the report.)

There are several ways to deal with such paging problems — and you're going to learn them all! Once you have these page problems under control, printing, as you shortly see, is a proverbial piece of cake.

Look Before You Print!

Do the world a favor and save a forest or two by using the Print Preview feature before you print any worksheet. Because of the peculiarities in paging a worksheet, you should check the page breaks for any report that requires more than one page. Print Preview mode not only shows you exactly how the worksheet document will be paged when printed but also enables you to modify the margins, change the page settings, and even go ahead and print the document when everything looks okay.

To switch to Print Preview mode, choose the Print Preview command from the File menu. Excel displays all the information on the first page of the report in a separate window. Figure 6-1 shows the Print Preview window with the first page of a three-page sample report.

Excel has a Print Preview tool you can use to switch to Print Preview mode instead of choosing Print Preview from the File menu all the time. Unfortunately, the programmers forgot to put this tool on any of the built-in toolbars. If you jump to Chapter 11, however, you learn how to remedy this oversight in short order.

When Excel displays a full page in the Print Preview window, you can barely read its contents; increase the view to actual size if you need to verify some of the information. You can zoom up to 100 percent by clicking on the Zoom but-

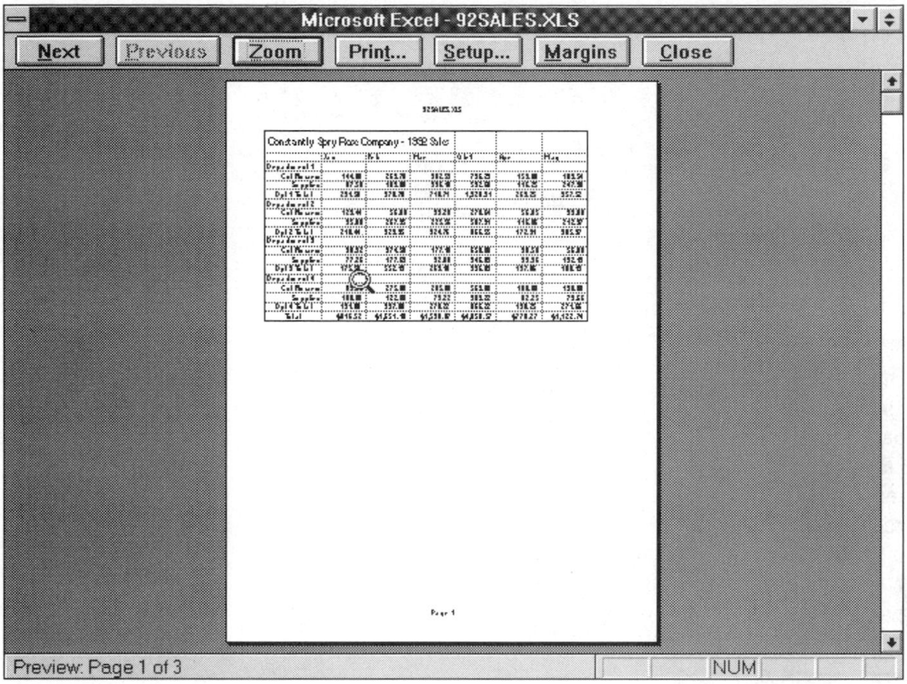

Figure 6-1:
The first
page of a
three-page
report in
Print
Preview
mode.

ton at the top of the window. Alternatively, click the mouse pointer (which assumes the shape of a magnifying glass) on the part of the page you want to see in full size. Figure 6-2 shows the first page of the three-page report after you click the magnifying-glass pointer in the lower-left portion of the page.

After a page is enlarged to actual size, use the scroll bars to bring new parts of the page into view in the Print Preview window. If you prefer to use the keyboard, press the ↑ and ↓ keys or PgUp and PgDn to scroll up or down the page; press ← and → or Ctrl+PgUp and Ctrl+PgDn to scroll left and right.

To return to the full-page view, click the mouse pointer (in its arrowhead form) anywhere on the page or click on the Zoom button at the top of the window. Excel indicates the number of pages in a report on the status bar of the Print Preview window. If your report has more than one page, you can view pages that follow the one you are previewing by clicking on the Next command button at the top of the window. To review a page you've already seen, back up a page by clicking on the Previous button. You can also advance to the next page by pressing the PgDn or ↓ key or move back to the previous page by pressing the PgUp or ↑ key when the page view is full-page rather than actual size.

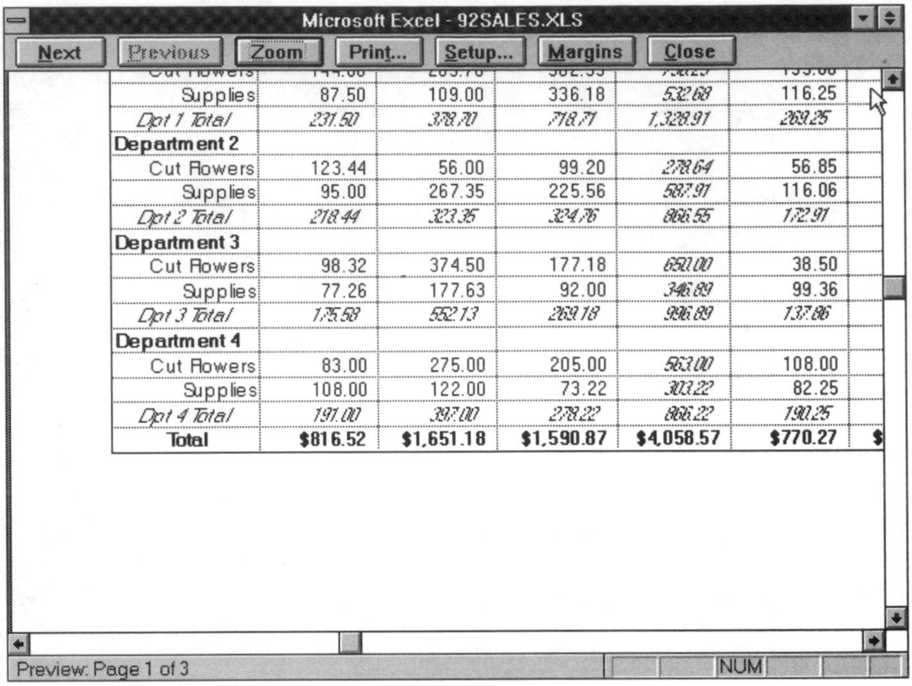

Figure 6-2:
The first page of a previewed report after zooming in on the bottom left part of the page.

When you finish previewing the report, you have the following options:

- ✔ If the pages look okay, you can click on the Print button to display the Print dialog box and start printing the report from there.

- ✔ If you notice some paging problems you can solve by choosing a new paper size, page order, orientation, or margins, or you notice a problem with the header or footer in the top or bottom margin of the pages, you can click on the Setup button and take care of these problems in the Page Setup dialog box.

- ✔ If you notice some problems with the margins or with the column widths and you want to adjust them in Print Preview mode, you can click on the Margins button and drag the margin markers into place (see "Marginal thinking" later in this chapter for details).

- ✔ If you notice any other kind of problem, such as a typo in a heading or a wrong value in a cell, click on the Close button and return to the normal worksheet document window; you cannot make any kind of editing changes in the Print Preview window.

- ✔ After you make corrections to the worksheet, you can print the report from the normal document window by choosing Print from the File menu. Alternatively, you can switch back to Print Preview mode to make a last-minute check and click on the Print button, or use the Print button (fourth from left) on the Standard toolbar.

The page breaks automatically

Excel automatically displays the page breaks in the normal document window after you preview the document. Page breaks appear on-screen as dotted lines between columns and rows that will appear on different pages.

To get rid of page breaks in the document window, choose Display from the Options menu, clear the X from the Automatic Page Breaks check box, and choose OK or press Enter.

Printing in a nutshell

As long as you want to use Excel's default print settings, printing a worksheet is uncomplicated: click on the Print tool on the Standard toolbar (the fourth tool on the left, with the picture of the printer) and the program prints one copy of all the information in the worksheet, including any charts and graphics — but not including notes you added to cells. (See Chapter 7 for details about charts and graphics.)

After you click on the Print tool, Excel routes the print job to the Windows Print Manager, which acts like a middleman to send the job to the printer. While Excel is sending the print job to the Print Manager, Windows displays a Printing dialog box to keep you informed of its progress (such as `Printing Page 2 of 3`). Once this dialog box disappears, you are free to go back to work in Excel (be aware, however, that Excel will probably move like a slug until the job is actually printed). To abort the print job while it's being sent to the Print Manager, click on the Cancel button in the Printing dialog box.

If you want to cancel the print job but you don't get it done before Excel finishes shipping it to the Print Manager (that is, while the Printing dialog box appears on-screen), you must leave Excel, activate the Print Manager window, and cancel printing from there. To cancel a print job from the Print Manager, follow these steps:

1. **Press Alt+Tab until Windows displays the Print Manager icon.**

   Release the Alt and Tab keys to open the Print Manager window.

2. **In the Print Manager window, select the print job you want to delete.**

3. **Click on the Delete button.**

   After you confirm that you want to delete the job, you can return to Excel by clicking somewhere on the Excel window (it should still be visible in the background) or by pressing Alt+Tab until you see the Microsoft Excel icon.

You can also print by clicking on the Print tool on the Standard toolbar; this approach is fine provided that you want to print all the pages in the report, don't want to print the cell notes, and only need one copy of the report. If any of

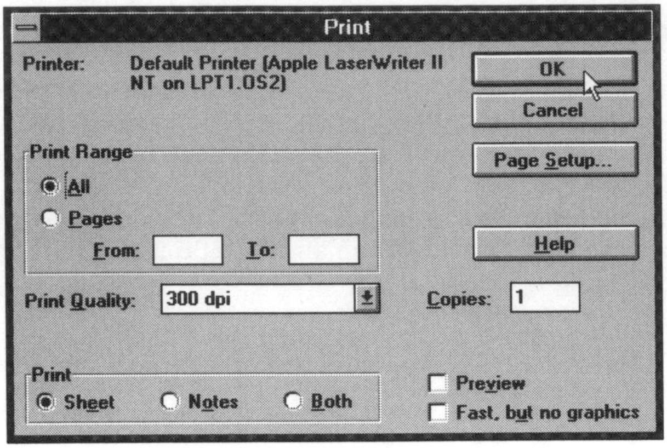

Figure 6-3:
The Print
dialog box.

these requirements changes, open the Print dialog box (shown in Figure 6-3) by choosing the Print command from the File menu or by pressing Ctrl+Shift+F12. Make your changes in the Print dialog box before you send the job to the printer.

On the Mac, the keystrokes you use to cancel a print job being sent to the Print Monitor are ⌘+. (period). To open the Print dialog box, press ⌘+P (for *Print*).

After you open the Print dialog box, you can make changes to any or all of the print settings before sending the job to the printer.

✔ To print a specific range of pages, click on the Pages radio button and enter the starting page number in the From text box and the ending page number in the To text box.

✔ To print the notes attached to cells rather than the cell entries, click on the Notes radio button.

✔ To print both the entries and the notes in the worksheet, click on the Both radio button.

✔ To print more than one copy of the report, enter the number of copies you want to print in the Copies text box (Excel collates each copy of the report for you).

After you finish choosing new print options, send the job to the printer by choosing OK or pressing Enter. To preview the document with your setting changes before you print, click on the Preview check box before you choose OK or press Enter. Excel then opens the document in the Print Preview window. If everything looks okay there, send the print job to the Print Manager by clicking on the Print button in the Print Preview window (Excel does not open the Print dialog box again).

If you keep the Preview check box activated in the Print dialog box, Excel automatically goes into Print Preview mode every time you print a worksheet (even when you click on the Print tool). That way, you get a chance to preview every printout without having to remember to choose Print Preview from the File menu.

Printing just the good parts

You don't always have to print everything in a worksheet. When you need to print only particular tables of information, you can select their cell ranges and choose Set Print Area from the Options menu. Alternatively, click on the Set Print Area tool on the Utility toolbar (the tool second from the right with a picture of a printer and two perpendicular lines along the left and top edges).

If you want to print another cell selection from the same worksheet, select that cell range and choose the Set Print Area command or tool before you print the new selection with the Print tool or Print command. When you choose the Set Print Area command again, Excel immediately redraws the page breaks (with dotted lines) in the worksheet document window to suit the new print selection.

If you later want to print the entire worksheet, select all the cells by clicking on the button in the upper-left corner of the document window (the thing at the intersection of the column letters and row numbers on the frame). Then choose the Remove Print Area command from the Options menu so that Excel prints all the information in the entire worksheet the next time you choose the Print tool or the Print command.

In Pursuit of the Perfect Page

As I said at the beginning of this chapter, about the only thing the slightest bit complex in printing a worksheet is figuring out how to get the pages right. Fortunately, the options in the Page Setup dialog box give you a great deal of control over what goes on which page. The particular options offered in the Page Setup dialog box may vary slightly with the type of printer you use. Figure 6-4 shows the Page Setup dialog box when the Apple LaserWriter is the current printer (all the options you see here are also present when using other laser printers such as the HP LaserJet printer).

To open the Page Setup dialog box for your printer, choose Page Setup from the File menu, click on the Page Setup button if the Print dialog box is open, or click on the Setup button if the Print Preview window is open.

The Print dialog box in Excel for the Macintosh doesn't contain a Page Setup button. To open the Page Setup dialog box, either choose Page Setup from the File pull-down menu or click on the Setup button in the Print Preview window.

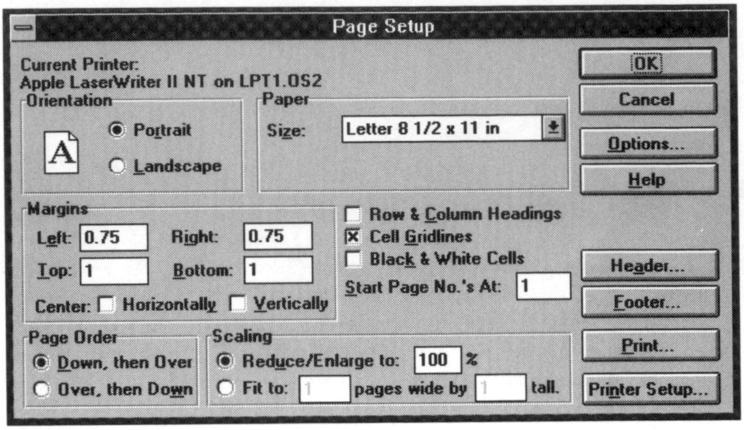

Figure 6-4:
The Page
Setup dialog
box.

With almost all printers, the Page Setup dialog box includes options for choosing a new paper size, changing the margins, centering the printing horizontally or vertically on the page (these options are great when you're printing a small table or form and you want it printed in the dead center of the page), and modifying the page order from down and over, to over and down.

The Page Setup dialog box normally includes a series of check boxes that let you choose the effects used in printing. Among these check boxes, you find the Row & Column Headings, Cell Gridlines, and Black & White Cells.

✔ Click on the Row & Column Headings check box when you want to print the worksheet frame with the column letters and row numbers to identify the location of the printed information (see "Printing by Formula," later in this chapter for an example).

✔ Click on the Cell Gridlines check box when you want the column and row gridlines displayed on-screen to print on the report (note that any borders you assigned to the cell ranges print regardless of whether this check box is activated).

✔ Click on the Black & White Cells check box when you have assigned different colors to cell ranges for a color monitor but want to print in monochrome on a black-and-white printer.

You also find a text box in the Page Setup dialog box for changing the starting page number when you want the first number to be higher than 1. You use this numbering option only when you're printing page numbers in the header or footer (see "My header don't know what my footer's doing," later in this chapter).

For many printers (including most of the dot-matrix, laser, or ink-jet persuasion), the Page Setup dialog box includes an option for changing the orientation of the printing from the more normal *portrait* (where the printing runs parallel to the short edge of the paper) to *landscape* (where the printing runs parallel to the long edge of the paper). With these types of printers, you can usually use the Page Setup dialog box to scale the size of the printing, making it possible to enlarge or reduce the printing by a particular percentage or to force all the information on a single page or a set number of pages.

Squeezing it all on one page

If your printer supports the scaling options, you're in luck. You can always get a worksheet to fit on a single page simply by clicking on the Fit to radio button. When you click on this radio button, Excel figures out how much to reduce the size of the information you're printing to get it all on one page.

If you preview this one page and find that the printing is just too small to read comfortably, reopen the Page Setup dialog box and try changing the number of pages in the pages wide by tall text boxes (to the immediate right of the Fit to radio button). For example, instead of trying to stuff everything on one page, check out how it looks to fit the worksheet on two pages across: enter **2** in the pages wide text box and leave 1 the in the pages tall text box. Alternatively, see how the worksheet looks on two pages down: leave the 1 in the page wide text box and enter **2** in the pages tall text box.

After using the Fit to option, you may find that you don't want to scale the printing. Cancel scaling by clicking on the Reduce/Enlarge radio button right above the Fit to button and enter **100** in the text box.

Orienting yourself to the landscape

Many worksheets are far wider than they are tall (consider budgets or sales tables that track expenditures over all 12 months). If your printer supports changing the orientation of the page, you may find that such worksheets page better if you switch the orientation from the normal portrait mode (which accommodates fewer columns on a page because the printing runs parallel to the short edge of the page) to landscape mode.

Figure 6-5 shows the Print Preview window with the first page of a report in landscape mode. For this report, Excel can get two more columns of information on this page in landscape mode than it can in portrait mode. Not only that, but the total page count for this report is reduced to two pages in landscape mode from the three pages it would take to print it in portrait mode.

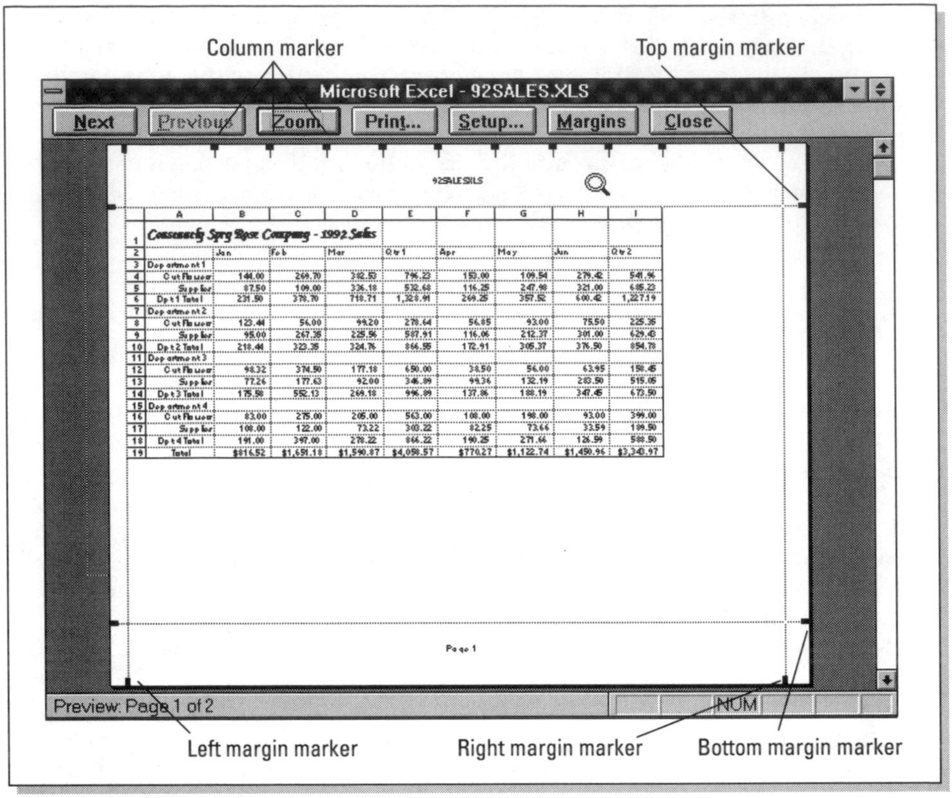

Figure 6-5: The Print Preview window with a page in landscape mode.

Marginal thinking

Frequently, you can squeeze the last column or the last few rows on a page just by adjusting the margins for the report. By default, Excel sets top and bottom margins of 1 inch and left and right margins of ¾ inch. To get more columns on a page, try reducing the left and right margins. To get more rows on a page, try reducing the top and bottom margins.

You can change the margins in two ways:

  ✔ Open the Page Setup dialog box and enter the new settings in the L̲eft, R̲ight, T̲op, and B̲ottom text boxes.

  ✔ Open the Print Preview window, click on the M̲argins button, and drag the margin markers to their new positions.

If you use the Margins button in the Print Preview window to change the margin settings, you can modify the column widths as well as the margins. (Figure 6-5 shows the margin and column markers that appear when you click on the Margins button in the Print Preview window). To change one of the margins, position the mouse pointer on the desired margin marker (the pointer shape changes to a double-headed arrow) and drag the marker in the appropriate direction. When you release the mouse button, Excel redraws the page using the new margin setting. You may gain or lose columns or rows, depending on what kind of adjustment you make. Changing the column widths is the same story: drag the column marker to the left or right to decrease or increase the width of a particular column.

My header don't know what my footer's doing

Headers and footers are simply standard text that appears on every page of the report. The header is printed in the top margin of the page, and the footer is printed in the bottom margin (both are centered vertically in the margins). You can use a header and footer in a report to identify the document used to produce the report and display the page numbers and the date and time of printing. Unless you specify otherwise, Excel automatically adds a header that shows the name of the document being printed and a footer that shows the current page number.

To remove the stock header or footer from the report or modify them in some way, open the Header and Footer dialog boxes and make your changes there. From the Page Setup dialog box, click on the Header or Footer button, depending on which one you want to change.

Figure 6-6 shows the standard Header dialog box (the Footer dialog box is set up just like this one). Notice that a header is divided into three sections: left, center, and right. All header text entered in the Left Section of this dialog box is justified with the left margin of the report. All header text entered in the Center Section box is centered between the left and right margins, and (you guessed it) all text entered in the Right Section box is justified with the right margin of the report.

Use the Tab key to advance from section to section in the header and to select the contents of that section. If you want to break the header text in one of the sections, press Alt+Enter to start a new line. Be careful: pressing Enter alone closes the Header dialog box.

Notice the appearance of the &F code (for *Filename*) in the center section of the standard header. This code is replaced with the filename of the document you are printing. You insert this code by clicking on the Filename tool in the Header dialog box. To delete the &F code from the header, select it in the Center Section and press Del.

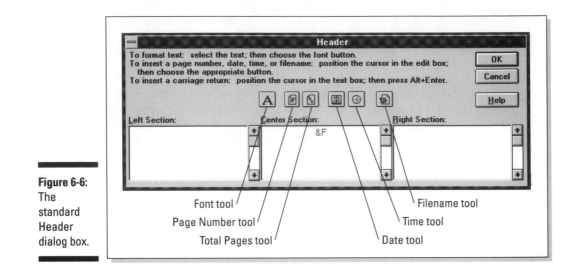

Figure 6-6:
The standard Header dialog box.

Figure 6-7 shows a header that uses all three sections and mixes standard text with all of the special codes as follows:

✔ Enter the &D code in the Left Section by using the Date tool; the code will be replaced by the date of the printout.

✔ Enter the &T code by using the Time tool; the code will be replaced by the time of the printout.

✔ Enter the &P code in the Right Section by using the Page Number tool; the current page number replaces the code. (The standard footer has Page &P in the Center Section.)

✔ Enter the &N code by using the Total Pages tool; the total number of pages in the report replaces the code.

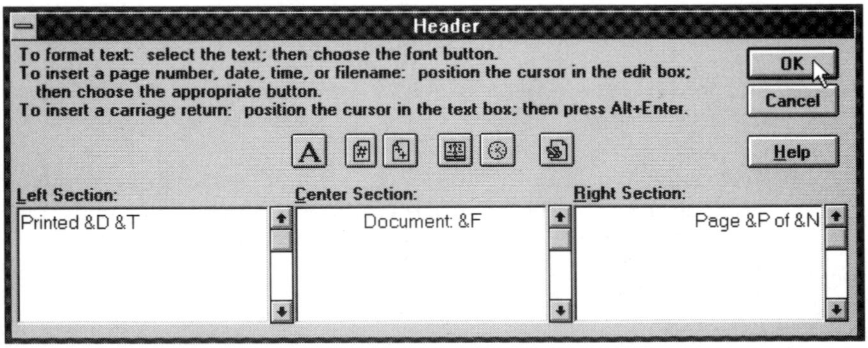

Figure 6-7:
The Header dialog box with a three-part header.

You can format any section of the header (or footer) with a new font, font size, or text style by selecting the text in that section and then clicking on the Font tool. Excel displays the standard Font dialog box, from which you can choose a new font, size, or style (see Chapter 3 for details).

Figure 6-8 shows how the header set up in Figure 6-7 appears on the printout of the first page of the report. For this report, because the individual page number and total page number appear in the right section of the header, I deleted the footer that normally displays the current page number. To delete a footer for a document, open the Footer dialog box, select the Center Section (the section with the text Page &P), and press Del.

Figure 6-8:
The first page of a printed report showing the three-part header.

Printed 8/10/93 3:56 PM   Document: EMPLOYEE.XLS   Page 1 of 6

Constantly Spry Rose Company - Employees as of June, 1993

ID No	Last Name	First Name	Sex	Dept	Date Hired	Years of Service	Salary	Salaried?
000101	Bryant	Michael	M	1	2/1/81	11.5	$30,440	Yes
000118	Kaplan	Janet	F	2	6/22/81	11.1	$34,000	Yes
000139	Cobb	William	M	2	5/28/82	10.2	$27,500	Yes
000141	Dickinson	Angela	F	3	11/13/86	5.7	$23,900	No
000146	Krauss	Edward	M	4	7/13/83	9.1	$26,200	Yes
000159	Caulfield	Sherry	F	2	3/19/84	8.4	$24,100	No
000162	Lerner	Kimberly	F	3	6/28/84	8.1	$24,900	No
000174	Edwards	Cindy	F	5	8/15/85	7.0	$21,500	No
000185	Johnson	Rebecca	F	6	2/4/86	6.5	$20,200	No
000190	Santos	Elizabeth	F	6	7/17/86	6.1	$17,200	Yes
000192	Mosley	Deborah	F	4	8/23/86	6.0	$20,800	No
000199	Smith	Steven	M	2	10/11/86	5.8	$40,900	Yes
000210	Morin	Victoria	F	2	12/20/86	5.6	$20,700	No
000211	Johnson	Stuart	M	1	12/29/86	5.6	$21,000	No
000220	Edwards	Jack	M	1	2/14/87	5.5	$32,200	Yes
000222	King	Mary	F	3	3/10/87	5.4	$18,100	No
000226	Rosenzweig	Adam	M	3	3/1/87	5.5	$19,000	No
000247	Savage	Elaine	F	4	5/27/87	5.2	$18,900	No
000262	Bird	Lance	M	4	8/13/87	5.0	$21,100	Yes
000281	Adamson	Joy	F	2	10/21/87	4.8	$34,400	Yes
000284	Morse	Miriam	F	6	11/2/87	4.8	$19,600	No
000297	Percival	James	M	6	12/18/87	4.7	$19,200	Yes
000307	Bjorkman	Robert	M	3	2/24/88	4.5	$25,000	Yes
000315	Grogan	Dave	M	3	4/3/88	4.4	$17,500	No
000324	Tallan	George	M	2	5/20/88	4.2	$19,700	No
000339	Stolper	Charles	M	4	7/9/88	4.1	$17,800	No
000348	Reese	Carl	M	5	9/13/88	3.9	$15,800	No
000361	Robinson	Linda	F	1	11/11/88	3.7	$17,000	No
000366	Zucker	Richard	M	1	12/26/88	3.6	$17,500	No
000367	Fletcher	Amanda	F	3	1/3/89	3.6	$16,500	No
000603	Micaela	Lili	F	3	3/23/92	0.4	$37,500	No
000262	Bird	Lance	M	4	8/13/87	5.0	$21,100	Yes
000281	Adamson	Joy	F	2	10/21/87	4.8	$34,400	Yes
000284	Morse	Miriam	F	6	11/2/87	4.8	$19,600	No

Entitlements

Just as you can freeze rows and columns of information on the screen so that you can always identify the data you're looking at, you can print particular rows and columns on each page of the report. Excel refers to such rows and columns in a printed report as *print titles.* Don't confuse print titles with the header of a report. Even though both are printed on each page, header information is printed in the top margin of the report; print titles always appear in the body of the report — at the top in the case of rows used as print titles and on the left in the case of columns.

To designate print titles for a report, follow these steps:

1. **Choose Set Print Titles from the Options menu.**

   The Set Print Titles dialog box appears (see Figure 6-9).

2. **Click on the row you want to use to enter its row number (with an absolute reference) in the Titles for Columns text box.**

   To designate multiple neighboring rows, drag through the rows in the worksheet.

   Excel enters the row range in the Titles for Columns text box in the form `$1:$2`.

   Excel indicates the print-title rows in the worksheet by placing a dotted line (that moves like a marquee) on the border between the titles and the information in the body of the report.

3. **Click on the Titles for Rows text box and then select the column or columns as you did in step 2 for rows.**

4. **Choose OK or press Enter.**

   After you close the Set Print Titles dialog box, the dotted line showing the border of the titles disappears from the worksheet.

In Figure 6-9, rows 1 and 2 containing the worksheet title and column headings for the employee roster are designated as the print titles for the report. Figure 6-10 shows the Print Preview window with the second page of the report. In this figure, you can see how these print titles appear in the report. (The Cell Gridlines check box in the Page Setup dialog box was deselected so that the worksheet gridlines are missing from this figure.)

To clear print titles from a report if you no longer need them, open the Set Print Titles dialog box and clear the row and column ranges from the Titles for Columns and Titles for Rows text boxes before you choose OK or press Enter.

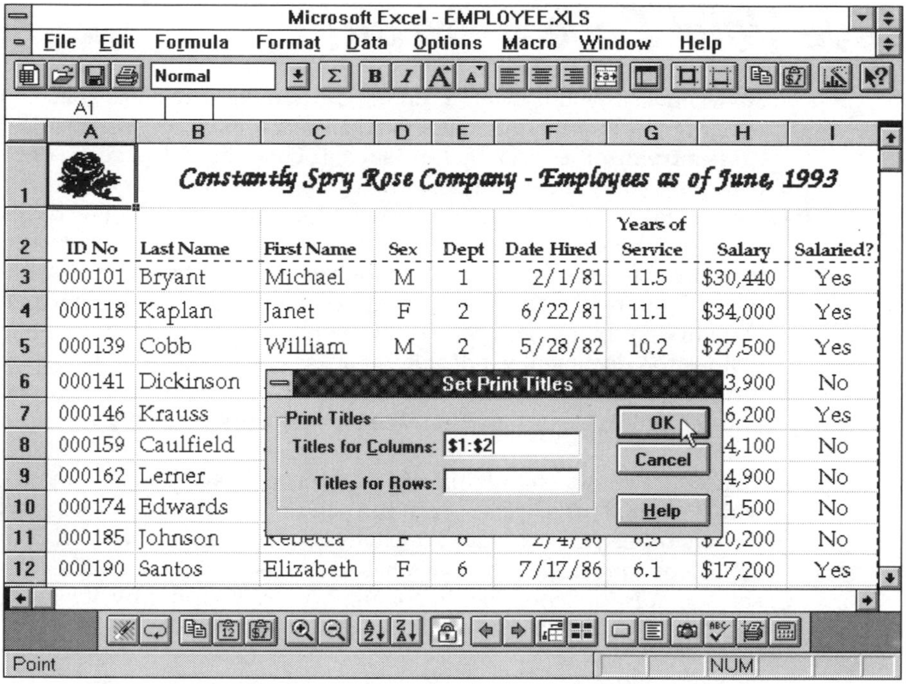

Figure 6-9:
Setting the print titles for the sample report.

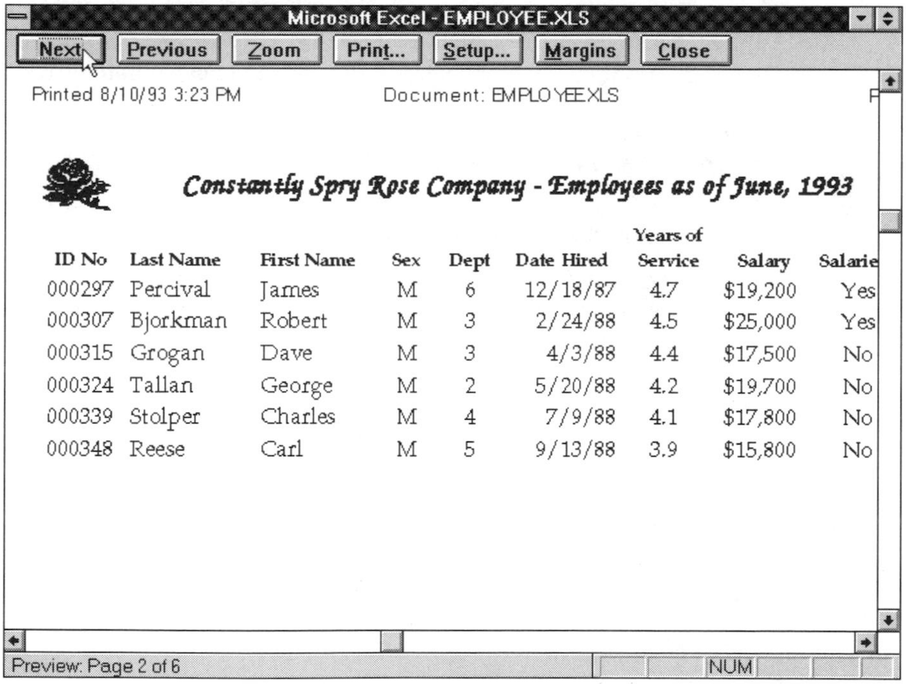

Figure 6-10:
The second page of the sample report showing the print titles set in Figure 6-9.

Give Your Page a Break!

Sometimes, as you preview a report, you see that Excel has split — onto different pages — information that should always appear together on the same page. If, after trying other approaches (such as changing the page size, orientation, or margins), you still can't remedy the bad page break, you can insert a manual page break to force Excel to print the information on the same page.

Inserting a manual page break is a lot like dividing the document window into panes. You use the top and left edges of the cell pointer to determine where the manual page break is placed just like you use them to determine how Excel divides the document window into panes. The top edge of the cell pointer determines where the page break occurs horizontally; the left edge of the cell pointer determines where the page break occurs vertically.

Figure 6-11 shows an example of a bad vertical page break that you can remedy with a manual page break. Given the page size, orientation, and margin settings for this report, Excel breaks the page between columns K and L. This break separates the sales figures for July and August in columns J and K from the sales figures for September in column L; more importantly, it separates the July and August figures from the third-quarter totals in column M.

To keep all the third-quarter figures on the same page, insert a manual page break so that the sales information in columns J and K is forced onto the page containing the figures in columns L and M. (This exercise assumes that none of the other treatments — short of using the Fit to setting — works to squeeze the sales information in columns L and M onto the page containing the information in columns for J and K.)

Figure 6-11 shows how you can create the vertical page break by following these steps:

1. **Position the cell pointer in cell J1.**

   Make sure that the pointer is in row 1 of column J; otherwise, Excel inserts a horizontal page break at the row as well as the vertical page break at column J.

2. **Choose Set Page Break from the Options menu.**

   Excel inserts a manual vertical page break between columns I and J (see Figure 6-12). The manual page break removes the automatic page break that appeared between columns and K and L, and forces all the third-quarter sales figures together on one page.

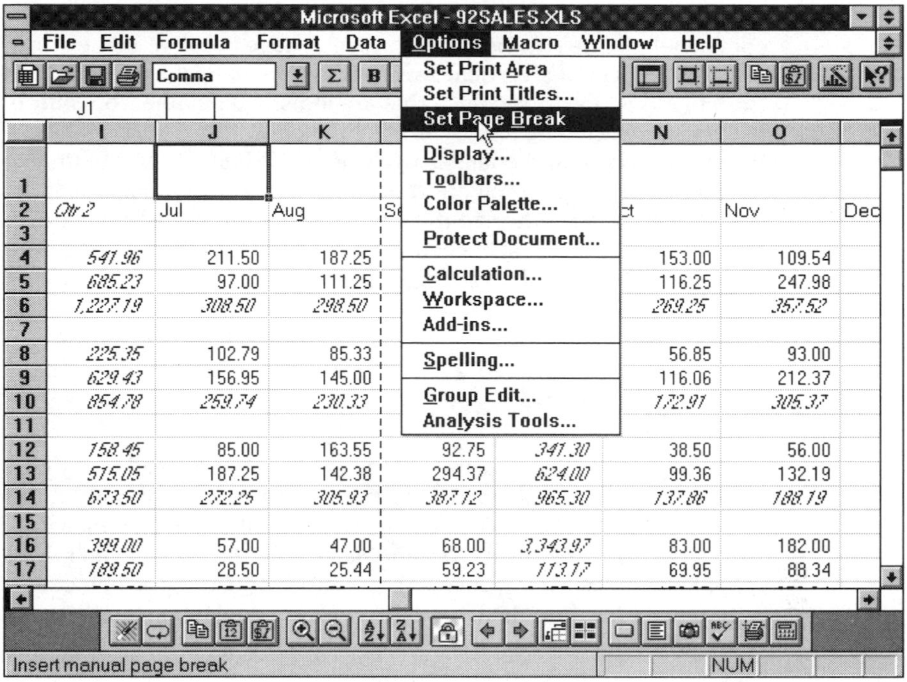

Figure 6-11: The Options menu used to insert a manual page break between columns I and J.

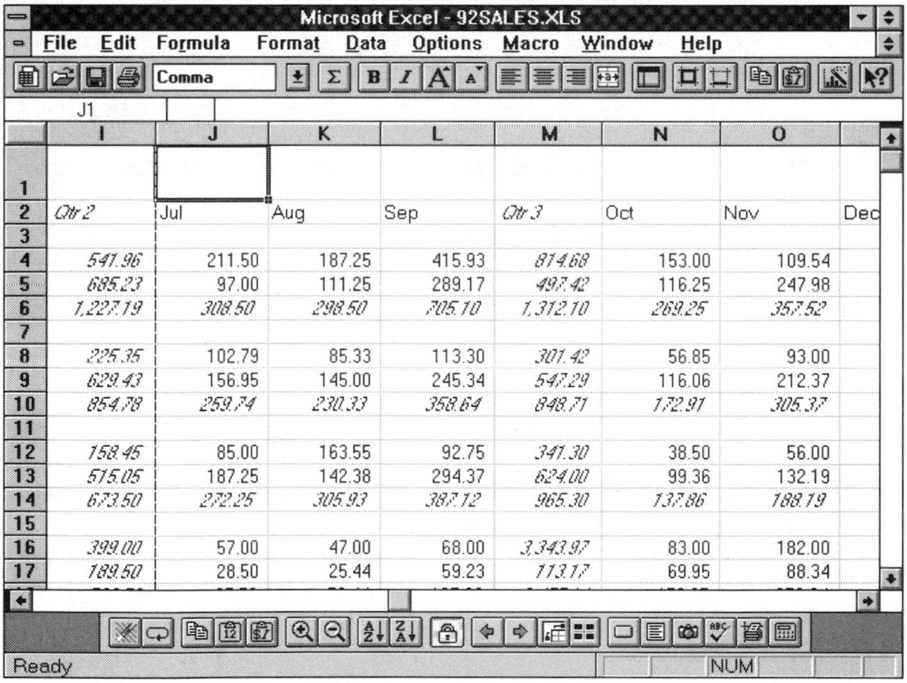

Figure 6-12: The worksheet after you insert the manual page break between columns I and J.

To remove a manual page break from a worksheet, position the cell pointer somewhere in the row below a horizontal page break or somewhere in the column to the right of a vertical page break. (Manual page breaks are indicated in the worksheet by dotted lines that are indistinguishable from automatic page breaks.) Then choose Remove Page Break from the Options menu. (The Set Page Break command changes to the Remove Page Break command on the Options menu, depending on where you place the cell pointer.) If you inserted both a vertical and a horizontal page break at the same time, you must position the cell pointer in the same cell you used to create the two page breaks in order to get rid of them both in a single operation.

Printing by Formula

There's one more basic printing technique you may need every once in a while: how to print the formulas in a worksheet (instead of printing the calculated results of the formulas). You can use a printout of the formulas in the worksheet to check them over and make sure that you haven't done anything stupid like replace a formula with a number or use the wrong cell references in a formula before you distribute the worksheet company wide (which can be really embarrassing).

Before you can print a worksheet with its formulas, you have to display the formulas, instead of their results, in the cells. To display the formulas, choose Display from the Options menu, click on the Formulas check box under Cells, and choose OK or press Enter. Excel displays the contents of each cell in the worksheet as they normally appear only in the formula bar. Notice that value entries lose their number formatting, formulas appear in their cells (Excel widens the columns with best-fit so that the formulas appear in their entirety), and long text entries no longer spill over into neighboring blank cells.

After Excel displays the formulas in the worksheet, you are ready to print it as you would any other report. You can include the worksheet frame in the printout so that if you *do* spot an error, you can pinpoint the cell reference right away. To include the frame in the printout, click on the Row & Column Headings check box in the Page Setup dialog box before you send the report to the printer. Figure 6-13 shows in the Print Preview window containing part of a report that prints the formulas and includes the worksheet frame.

When you display formulas in the cells, all entries — text, values, and formulas — are left-aligned in their cells, and all formatting for the values is missing.

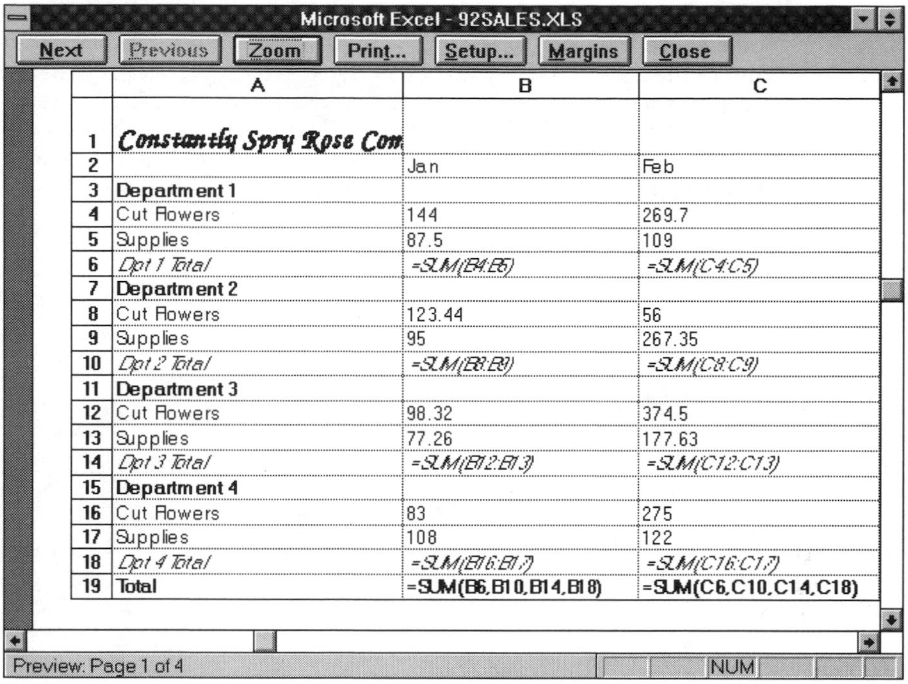

Microsoft Excel - 92SALES.XLS

| Next | Previous | Zoom | Print... | Setup... | Margins | Close |

	A	B	C
1	*Constantly Spry Rose Com*		
2		Jan	Feb
3	Department 1		
4	Cut Flowers	144	269.7
5	Supplies	87.5	109
6	*Dpt 1 Total*	*=SUM(B4:B5)*	*=SUM(C4:C5)*
7	Department 2		
8	Cut Flowers	123.44	56
9	Supplies	95	267.35
10	*Dpt 2 Total*	*=SUM(B8:B9)*	*=SUM(C8:C9)*
11	Department 3		
12	Cut Flowers	98.32	374.5
13	Supplies	77.26	177.63
14	*Dpt 3 Total*	*=SUM(B12:B13)*	*=SUM(C12:C13)*
15	Department 4		
16	Cut Flowers	83	275
17	Supplies	108	122
18	*Dpt 4 Total*	*=SUM(B16:B17)*	*=SUM(C16:C17)*
19	Total	=SUM(B6,B10,B14,B18)	=SUM(C6,C10,C14,C18)

Preview: Page 1 of 4 | NUM

Figure 6-13:
The first
page of a
four-page
report that
prints the
worksheet
formulas
(viewed in
the Print
Preview
window).

After you print the worksheet with the formulas, to return the worksheet to normal, choose Display from the Options menu, deselect the Formulas check box, and choose OK or press Enter.

You can toggle between displaying formulas and the normal display by pressing Ctrl + ' (the accent with the ~ key) — ⌘ + ' on the Mac.

Part IV
Amazing Things You Can Do with Excel (for Fun and Profit)

The 5th Wave

By Rich Tennant

"THE IMAGE IS GETTING CLEARER NOW... I CAN ALMOST SEE IT...YES! THERE IT IS—THE GLITCH IS IN A FAULTY CELL REFERENCE IN THE FOOTBALL POOL SPREADSHEET."

The part in which...

You get exposed to something more exciting than the standard anybody-can-do-it worksheet. First, you learn how easy it is to win friends and influence people by creating super-looking charts that make the folks who read them sit up and take notice of your otherwise mundane numbers. Next, you learn how to use Excel to maintain and organize the huge quantities of facts and figures that you need to track. You learn how to sort the data in any order you can dream up, as well as search for and retrieve only the information that you *really* want.

Finally, you learn how to work with more than one Excel document at a time: how to arrange your documents so that you can easily compare or transfer their information or how to organize them into a "book" form so that you can browse through them at the same time — anytime!

Chapter 7
A Picture Worth a Thousand Numbers

• •

In This Chapter

▶ How to create a chart in a worksheet with the ChartWizard

▶ How to change the chart type with the Chart toolbar

▶ How to edit a chart in its own chart window

▶ How to select a new chart type

▶ How to add a text box and arrow to a chart

▶ How to reposition the chart legend

▶ How to modify the chart's axes

▶ How to change the orientation of a 3D chart

▶ How to use the drawing tools to add graphics to charts and worksheets

▶ How to print charts

• •

*A*s Rod Stewart once observed, "Every picture tell a story, don't it." By adding charts to worksheets, you not only heighten interest in the worksheet but can also illustrate trends and anomalies that might not otherwise be apparent from just looking at the numbers. Because Excel makes it so easy to chart the information in a worksheet, you can experiment with different types of charts until you find the one that best represents the data — in other words, the picture that best tells the particular story.

Just a word about charts before you start learning how to make them in Excel. Remember your high school algebra teacher valiantly trying to teach you how to graph equations by plotting different values on an x-axis and a y-axis on graph paper? Of course, you were probably too busy with more important things like sex and rock 'n roll to pay too much attention to an old algebra teacher. Besides, you probably told yourself, "I'll never need this junk when I'm out on my own and get a job!"

Well, see, you just never know. It turns out that even though Excel automates almost the entire process of charting worksheet data, you may need to be able to tell the x-axis from the y-axis, just in case Excel doesn't draw the chart the way you had mind. To refresh your memory, the x-axis is the horizontal axis; the y-axis is the vertical one.

In most charts that use these two axes, Excel plots the categories along the x-axis and their relative values along the y-axis. The x-axis is sometimes referred to as the *time axis* because the chart often depicts values along this axis at different time periods such as months, quarters, years, and so on.

Charts as if by Magic

Well, that's enough background on charts. Now let's get on with the charting itself. Excel makes the process of creating a new chart in a worksheet as painless as possible with the ChartWizard. The ChartWizard walks you through a five-step procedure, at the end of which you have a complete and beautiful new chart.

Before you start the ChartWizard, first select the cell range that contains the information you want charted. Keep in mind that to end up with the chart you want, the information should be entered in standard table format. With the information in this format, you can select it all as a single range (see Figure 7-1).

If you create a chart that uses an x-axis and y-axis (as most do), the ChartWizard naturally uses the row of column headings in the selected table for the category labels along the x-axis. If the table has row headings, the ChartWizard uses these as the headings in the legend of the chart (if you choose to include one). The *legend* identifies each point, column, or bar in the chart that represents the values in the table.

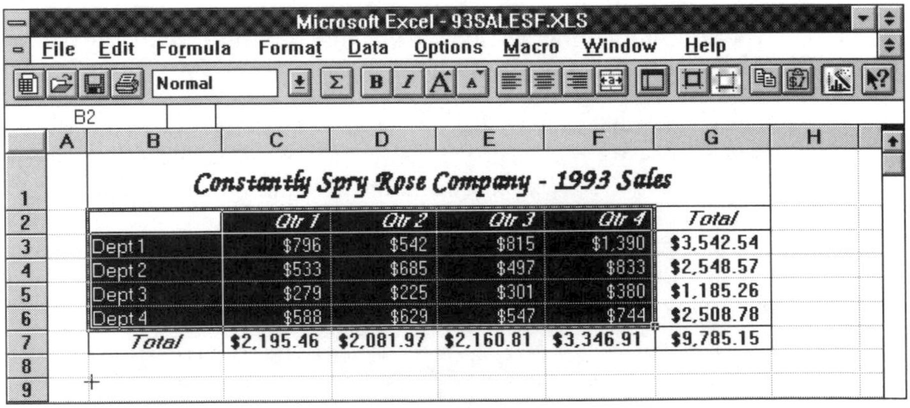

Figure 7-1:
Selecting
the
information
to be
charted.

	Microsoft Excel - 93SALESF.XLS

File Edit Formula Format Data Options Macro Window Help

Normal

B2

	A	B	C	D	E	F	G	H
1		*Constantly Spry Rose Company - 1993 Sales*						
2			*Qtr 1*	*Qtr 2*	*Qtr 3*	*Qtr 4*	*Total*	
3		Dept 1	$796	$542	$815	$1,390	**$3,542.54**	
4		Dept 2	$533	$685	$497	$833	**$2,548.57**	
5		Dept 3	$279	$225	$301	$380	**$1,185.26**	
6		Dept 4	$588	$629	$547	$744	**$2,508.78**	
7		*Total*	$2,195.46	$2,081.97	$2,160.81	$3,346.91	$9,785.15	
8								
9		+						

To chart an outlined table, collapse the outline to the level of row and column detail you want charted (see Chapter 5 for specific information on how to this). Select the collapsed range of cells before clicking on the Select Visible Cells tool on the Utility toolbar (the one to the immediate right of the Show Outline Symbols tool; it has what appears to be four selected cells slightly separated from one another). Then click on the ChartWizard tool on the Standard toolbar to create the chart as described in this section.

Once you select the information to chart, follow these steps to create the chart:

1. Click on the ChartWizard tool on the Standard toolbar.

The ChartWizard tool is the one second from the right with the picture of a magic wand over a column chart.

2. Indicate the size and shape of the finished chart in the worksheet.

To facilitate this, the mouse pointer changes shape to a crosshair that you drag in the document. To remind you that you're creating a chart, Excel displays the following message in the status bar:

```
Drag in document to create a chart
```

Position the crosshair at the upper-left corner of the place in the worksheet where you want the chart; drag diagonally down until you've drawn the outline of the chart. Don't worry if you don't get it exactly the right size or in the just right place — you can easily move or resize the chart after it's created.

3. Release the mouse button.

Excel displays the ChartWizard - Step 1 of 5 dialog box (see Figure 7-2). Notice that the outline of the shape of the finished chart no longer appears in the worksheet.

Notice, too, that the step numbers in this book don't correspond with the step numbers in the dialog boxes on-screen. Oh well.

4. Verify the cell range.

While the first ChartWizard dialog box is displayed, verify that the cell range surrounded by a marquee and specified in formula form (with absolute cell references) in the Range text box is correct. To modify this range (perhaps to include the row of column headings or the column of row headings), either reselect the range with the mouse or edit the cell references in the Range text box.

5. Click on the Next> button in the dialog box or press Enter when the selected range is correct.

Excel displays the ChartWizard - Step 2 of 5 dialog box (see Figure 7-3). Left to itself, the ChartWizard represents your data in a column chart. The Step 2 of 5 dialog box offers a wide range of chart types.

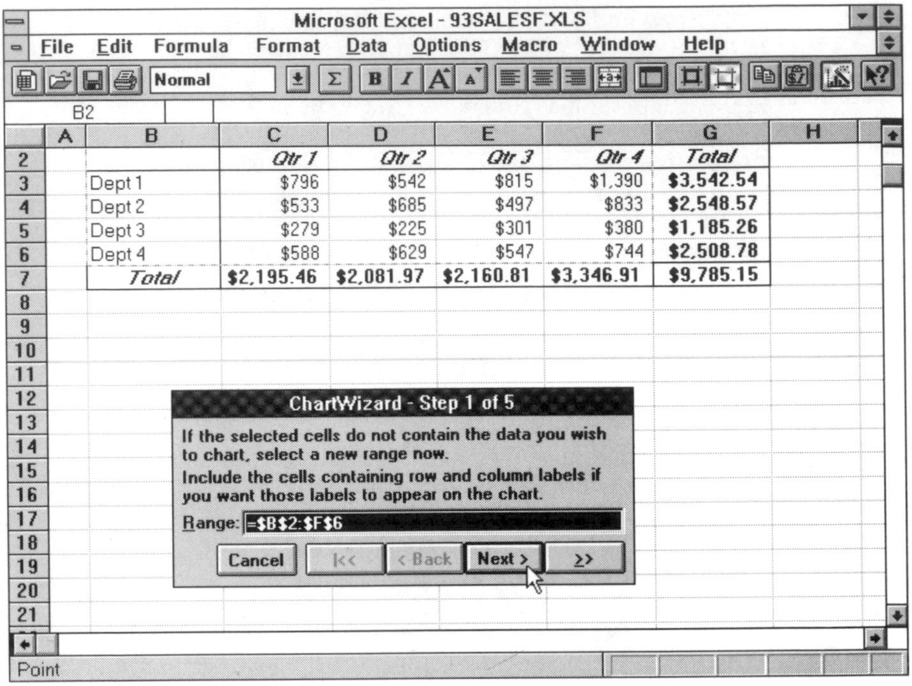

Figure 7-2:
Step 1:
Verify the
range to be
charted.

Microsoft Excel - 93SALESF.XLS

File   Edit   Formula   Format   Data   Options   Macro   Window   Help

Normal

B2

	A	B	C	D	E	F	G	H
2			*Qtr 1*	*Qtr 2*	*Qtr 3*	*Qtr 4*	*Total*	
3		Dept 1	$796	$542	$815	$1,390	**$3,542.54**	
4		Dept 2	$533	$685	$497	$833	**$2,548.57**	
5		Dept 3	$279	$225	$301	$380	**$1,185.26**	
6		Dept 4	$588	$629	$547	$744	**$2,508.78**	
7		*Total*	**$2,195.46**	**$2,081.97**	**$2,160.81**	**$3,346.91**	**$9,785.15**	

ChartWizard - Step 1 of 5

If the selected cells do not contain the data you wish
to chart, select a new range now.
Include the cells containing row and column labels if
you want those labels to appear on the chart.

Range: =$B$2:$F$6

Cancel |<<   < Back   Next >   >>

Point

6. **Select a chart type other than the default Column type if you want.**

To select another chart type, click on its sample chart or press the command letter associated with that chart-type name (for example, press E for a 3D Area chart).

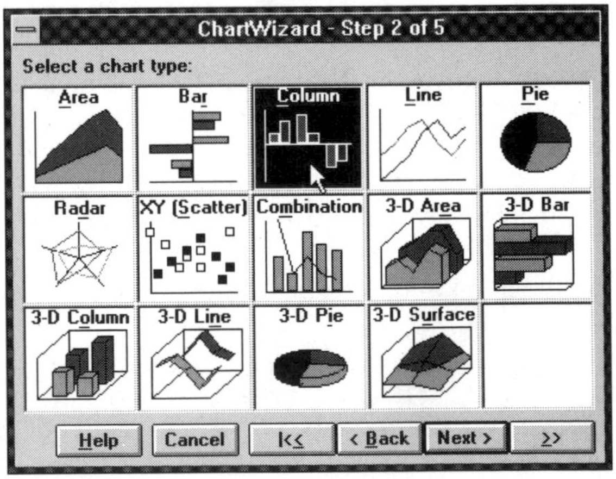

Figure 7-3:
Step 2:
Select the
type of chart
you want.

ChartWizard - Step 2 of 5

Select a chart type:

Area   Bar   Column   Line   Pie

Radar   XY (Scatter)   Combination   3-D Area   3-D Bar

3-D Column   3-D Line   3-D Pie   3-D Surface

Help   Cancel |<<   < Back   Next >   >>

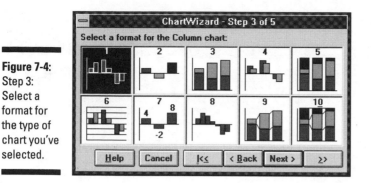

Figure 7-4:
Step 3:
Select a
format for
the type of
chart you've
selected.

7. **Click on the Next> button or press Enter.**

The ChartWizard - Step 3 of 5 dialog box appears (see Figure 7-4). Each chart type is available in one of many different formats. Each chart type has a default format (referred to as the *preferred format*).

8. **Choose a preferred format for your chart.**

To choose a new format, click on its sample in the dialog box or type its number (type **0** if you want to choose format 1<u>0</u>). Figure 7-4 shows the dialog box with format 1 selected as the preferred format for the column chart.

9. **Click on the Next> button or press Enter.**

The ChartWizard shows you a preview of the chart in the ChartWizard - Step 4 of 5 dialog box (see Figure 7-5).

10. **Verify that Excel has charted the data correctly.**

Normally, the ChartWizard makes each row of values in the selected table into a separate *data series* on the chart. The *legend* (the boxed area with samples of the colors or patterns used in the chart) identifies each data series in the chart. In Figure 7-5, the Dept 1 sales figures in row 3 (cell range C3:F3) form the first data series. This data series is represented in the chart by columns with diagonal crosshatching (the first column in every group).

Because the chart forms the data series by rows, the ChartWizard uses the entries in the first row (the column headings in cell range C2:F2) to label the x-axis (the so-called *category labels*). The ChartWizard uses the entries in the first column (the row labels in cell range B3:B6) as the headings in the legend.

If you want, switch the data series from rows to columns by clicking on the <u>C</u>olumns radio button. Doing this causes the ChartWizard to use the sales figures for each quarter (rather than each department) as the data series.

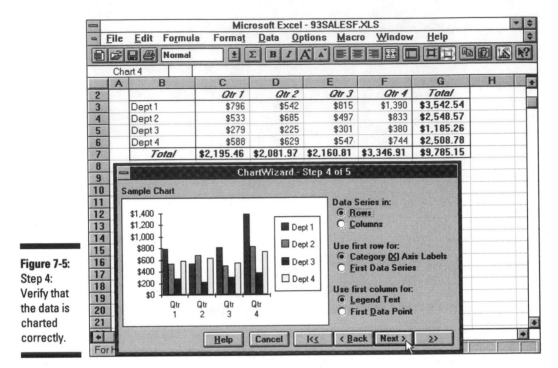

Figure 7-5:
Step 4:
Verify that
the data is
charted
correctly.

This means that the department numbers in the first column of the table are used as the x-axis labels and the quarter numbers in the first row are used as the headings in the legend.

11. **Click on the Next> button or press Enter.**

The ChartWizard - Step 5 of 5 dialog box appears (see Figure 7.6).

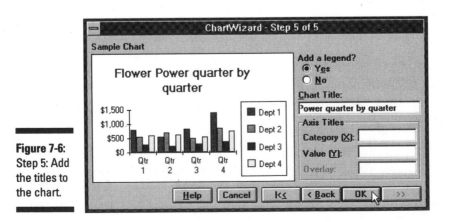

Figure 7-6:
Step 5: Add
the titles to
the chart.

12. Enter the titles for the chart.

You can enter a title for the entire chart as well as individual titles for the category axis (the x-axis) and the value axis (the y-axis). You can also remove the legend from the chart (not recommended for any chart that contains more than one data series) by clicking on the No radio button.

Figure 7-6 shows the dialog box after a title for the chart was entered in the Chart Title text box. The Sample Chart area shows the title as you enter it (because of space limitations in the dialog box, the text may not wrap in the worksheet the same way it does in the Sample Chart area). If you add a title for the x-axis in the Category (X) text box, it appears right under the category labels in the chart. If you add a title for the y-axis in the Value (Y) text box, it appears to the left of the values, running up the side of the chart.

13. Click on the OK button or press Enter to close the last ChartWizard dialog box.

The chart you have created appears in the worksheet in the area you selected earlier. Figure 7-7 shows the column chart created for the 93 sales worksheet.

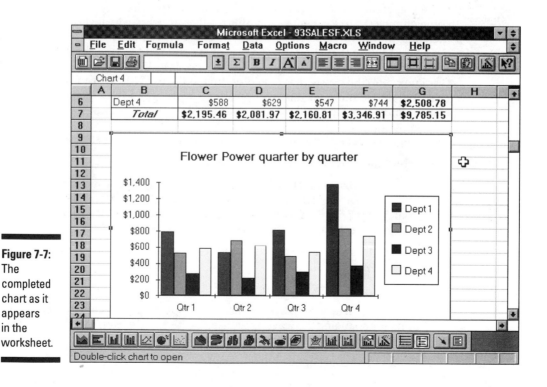

Figure 7-7:
The completed chart as it appears in the worksheet.

You can easily move or resize the chart right after creating it because the chart is still selected. (You can always tell when a graphic object like a chart is selected: you see *selection handles* — the tiny squares — around the edges of the object.) Immediately after creating the chart, the Chart toolbar is docked at the bottom of the document window. To move the chart, position the mouse pointer somewhere inside the chart and drag it to a new location. To resize the chart (you may want to make it bigger if it seems distorted in any way), position the mouse pointer on one of the selection handles. When the pointer changes from the arrowhead to a double-headed arrow, drag the side or corner (depending on which handle you select) to enlarge or reduce the chart.

When the chart is properly sized and positioned in the worksheet, set the chart in place by deselecting it (simply click the mouse pointer in any cell outside of the chart). As soon as you deselect the chart, the selection handles disappear as does the Chart toolbar from the bottom of the window. To reselect the chart (to edit, size, or move it), click anywhere on the chart with the mouse pointer.

A Little Change of Chart

Once you create a chart, you can use the tools on the Chart toolbar to make some changes to it. Remember that this toolbar appears whenever you select the chart in the worksheet. To change the chart type, simply click on the tool on the Chart toolbar that shows the type of chart you want to see. To add (or get rid of) gridlines for the major values (on the y-axis), click on the Horizontal Gridlines tool (the one with the pointer on it in Figure 7-8). Figure 7-8 shows the chart created in the preceding section after the chart type was changed from a simple-column to a stacked-column chart and horizontal gridlines were added.

To change the data represented in the chart, follow these steps:

1. **Select the chart and click on the ChartWizard tool.**

   The ChartWizard tool is located either on the Standard toolbar or on the Chart toolbar that appears as soon as you select the chart. The ChartWizard displays a ChartWizard - Step 1 of 2 dialog box that contains the Range text box with the current cell range being charted.

2. **Change this cell range to include more or less data or labels in the worksheet.**

3. **Click on the Next> button or press Enter.**

   The ChartWizard - Step 2 of 2 dialog box appears; it contains the same options for changing the way the data is charted as the Step 4 of 5 dialog box did when you created the chart.

4. **Change the chart options if you want.**

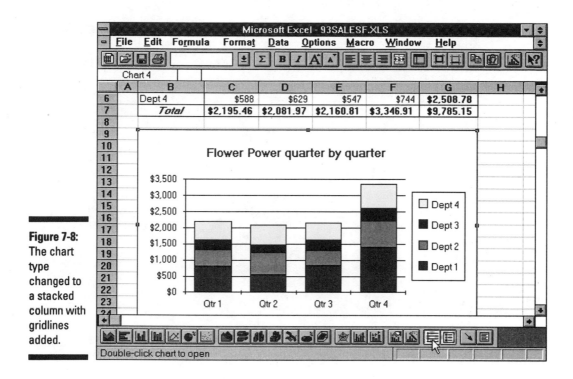

Figure 7-8:
The chart
type
changed to
a stacked
column with
gridlines
added.

5. Click on the OK button or press Enter.

Your changes show up immediately in the selected chart.

Figure 7-9 shows what happens if you convert the chart in the 93 sales worksheet from a stacked column to a 3D pie by clicking on the 3D-Pie tool (shown with the mouse pointer in this figure). Notice that Excel uses the totals for each quarter and converts them into percentages (a pie chart doesn't use x and y axes; instead it compares each part to the whole).

Accentuate the positive

Besides changing the type of chart or adding or removing gridlines with the tools on the Chart toolbar, you may want to make changes to specific parts of the chart (for example, selecting a new font for titles or repositioning the legend). To make these kinds of changes, you must work on the chart in a separate chart document window. To open a chart created in the worksheet in its own chart window, double-click on the chart.

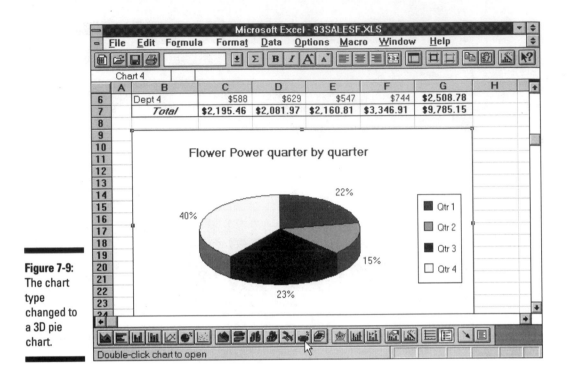

Figure 7-9:
The chart
type
changed to
a 3D pie
chart.

Once you open the chart in a chart document window, you can select the individual parts of the chart whose formatting need changing.

- ✔ To select one of these chart objects, click on it.

- ✔ You can tell when an object is selected because selection handles appear around it. Selection handles for most chart objects appear as white squares, indicating that you can neither move nor resize the object.

- ✔ Only those objects with black squares as selection handles can be moved or resized.

Once you select one object in the chart by clicking on it, you can cycle through and select the other objects in the chart by pressing the ↓ and ↑ keys. Pressing ↓ selects the next object; pressing ↑ selects the previous object.

All the parts of the chart you can select in a chart window have shortcut menus attached to them. Remember that to open a shortcut menu, you click on the object with the *right* mouse button. If you know that you want to select a command from the shortcut menu as soon as you select a part of the chart, you can both select the object and open the shortcut menu by clicking the chart object with the *right* mouse button. (You don't have to click on the object with the left button to select it and then click again with the right to open the menu.)

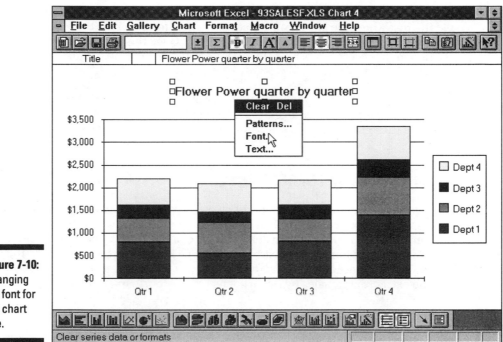

Figure 7-10:
Changing the font for the chart title.

In Excel 4.0 for the Macintosh, you press ⌘+Option as you click on an object to open its shortcut menu.

Figure 7-10 shows the stacked-column version of the chart for the 93 sales after I double-clicked on it to open it in its own chart document window. Here you also see the shortcut menu attached to the chart title, opened when I clicked on the title with the right mouse button.

- ✔ Use the Patterns command to place a border or change the pattern or color within the title area.

- ✔ Use the Font command to select a new font, size, or style for the title.

- ✔ Use the Text command to change the alignment or orientation of the title.

Notice the white selection handles around the chart title. They indicate that you can neither move nor resize the chart title (for this reason, title text is referred to as *attached text*).

Although you can't move the chart title (it is always centered over the *plot area* of the chart — the area that actually contains the graphed data), you can break the title up on several different lines. Then if you want, you can use the Text command on the title shortcut menu to change the alignment of the broken-up text.

To force part of the title on a new line, click the insertion point at the place in the text where the line break is to occur on the formula bar (the text of the title appears there whenever you select the title). Once the insertion point is positioned in the formula bar, press Alt+Enter (just like you do to start a new line in a worksheet entry).

In addition to changing the way the titles appear in the chart, you can modify the way the data series, legend, and x and y axes appear in the chart by opening their shortcut menus and selecting the appropriate commands from them.

Singularly unattached

Figure 7-11 shows a couple of other changes you can easily make to a chart. In this figure, you see the chart for the 93 sales worksheet (converted from a two-dimensional stacked-column chart to a 3D-column chart by clicking on the 3D Column Chart tool on the Chart toolbar). The legend has been moved to the lower-left corner and a *callout* (a text box with an arrow that calls attention to the extraordinary sales by Department 1 in the fourth quarter) has been added.

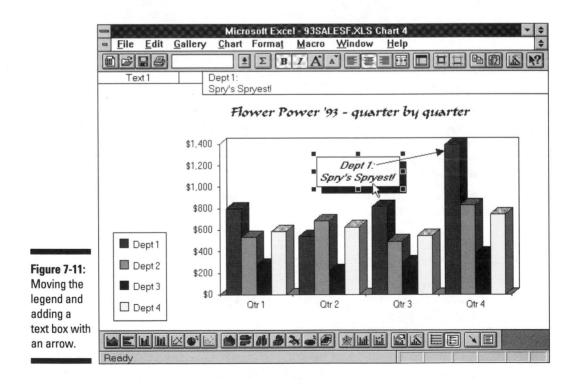

Figure 7-11: Moving the legend and adding a text box with an arrow.

The legend and the text box are among the few unattached objects in a chart (indicated by black instead of white selection handles when you select them). Although you can't resize a legend box, you can move it around by dragging it. In fact, you can dock the legend in a chart much like you dock a toolbar around the edges of a worksheet document window (see Chapter 3 for more on this nifty feature).

Simply drag the box to one of the sides of the chart (left, right, top, or bottom). When a long straight line appears, this is your signal that Excel will dock the legend (and shift the rest of the chart out of the way) when you release the mouse button.

To add a text box to the chart, click on the Text Box tool on the Chart toolbar (the very last one on the right with the picture of a box containing lines of text). Excel places a new text box containing the word TEXT in the exact middle of the plot area of the chart (the text box is already selected as indicated by the black selection handles that appear around it). Start typing the message you want to appear in the box (remember to press Alt+Enter to force text onto a new line). The text you type appears only on the formula bar until you click on the enter box or press the Enter key. Then the text you typed replaces the word TEXT in the text box in the middle of the chart.

- ✔ You can move the text box to a new location in the chart by dragging it.
- ✔ You can resize the text box by dragging the appropriate selection handle.
- ✔ To put a border around the text box or add a pattern to its area, choose the Patterns command from its shortcut menu.
- ✔ To add the drop-shadow effect shown in Figure 7-11, click on the Shadow check box in the Patterns dialog box.

When annotating a particular part of the chart with a text box, you may want to add an arrow to point directly to the object or part of the chart you are describing. To add an arrow, click on the Arrow tool (immediately to the left of the Text Box tool) on the Chart toolbar or choose the Add Arrow command from the Chart pull-down menu.

Excel then draws a new arrow in the upper-left part of the plot area with its arrowhead pointing down. The arrow is already selected and contains two black selection handles, one in front of the tip of the arrowhead and the other on the end of the shaft.

- ✔ To move the arrow, drag it into position.
- ✔ To change the length of the arrow, drag one of the selection handles.
- ✔ As you change the length, you can also change the direction of the arrow by pivoting the mouse pointer around the stationary selection handle.
- ✔ If you want to change the shape of the arrowhead or the thickness of the arrow's shaft, choose the Patterns command from the arrow's shortcut menu and make changes to the Patterns dialog box.

As soon as you finish modifying the chart in the chart window, you can return to the worksheet document window, where the changes are immediately reflected. Close the chart document window either by double-clicking on its Control-menu box (the one immediately to the left of the File pull-down menu, not the one on the left of the title bar for the Excel window) or by choosing the Close command from the File pull-down menu.

You can also switch to the worksheet document window that contains the chart without actually closing the chart window. To do this, choose the name of the worksheet from the Window pull-down menu (either by typing its number or clicking on its name). Notice that the name of the worksheet document always immediately precedes that of its chart document in the Window pull-down menu because Excel simply appends a chart number to the worksheet filename when naming the chart window.

Figure 7-12 shows the 93 sales worksheet with its updated chart. To save the changes to the chart, save the worksheet with the Save command on the File pull-down menu or with the Save File tool on the Standard toolbar. If you see something that isn't quite right in the updated chart, open it in a separate chart window by once again double-clicking somewhere in the chart in the worksheet.

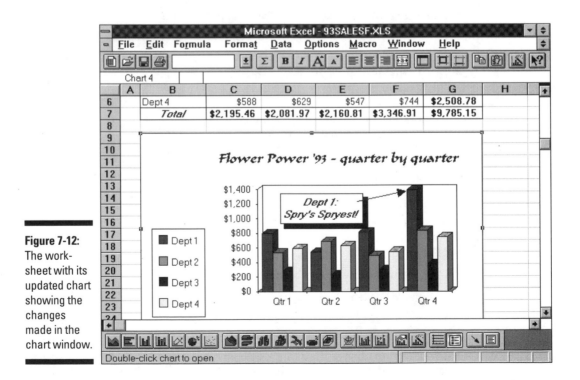

Figure 7-12:
The worksheet with its updated chart showing the changes made in the chart window.

Getting a new perspective on things

Figure 7-13 shows the chart in a chart window in yet another guise: this time as a 3D-area chart. When you select this kind of chart (as well as the 3D-column, 3D-line, and 3D-surface charts), Excel draws the chart in perspective view by adding a third axis to the chart. Now you have the category (x) axis with the quarters running along the bottom of the closest side, the data series (y) axis with the departments running along the bottom of the other side, and the values (z) axis with the dollar amounts running up the left wall.

These three axes form a kind of open box with the category and series axes on the two sides of the floor and the values axis on the left side of the wall of the box. You can modify the view of this type of 3D-perspective chart by rotating the box, thereby changing the viewing angles of its walls and floor.

To do this, open the 3D chart in a chart window and select the chart by clicking on one its corners. When the black selection handles appear (if you get white selection handles, try clicking on the corner again), drag one of the handles (the lower one at the front corner is a good one to use). As you drag and rotate the mouse pointer, Excel shows you the effect on the viewing angles by rotating and repositioning an outline of the box that contains the chart (see Figure 7-14).

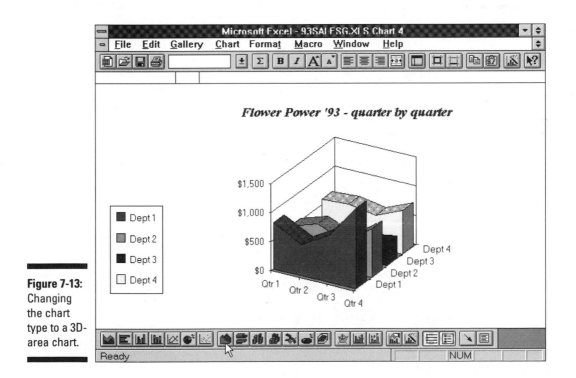

Figure 7-13:
Changing the chart type to a 3D-area chart.

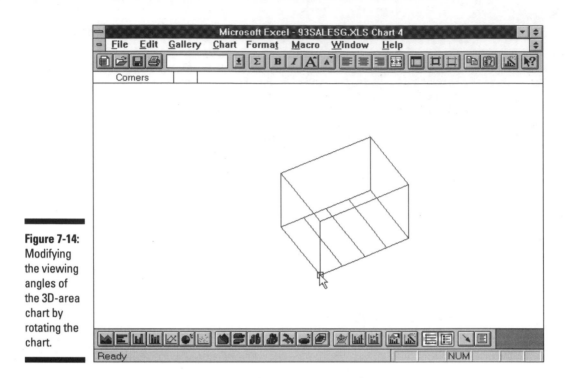

Figure 7-14:
Modifying the viewing angles of the 3D-area chart by rotating the chart.

When the outline of the frame of the 3D chart is the way you want it, release the mouse button. Excel draws the 3D chart using the new viewing angles. Figure 7-15 shows the 3D-area chart after the chart's frame was rotated down just a little and slightly to the left.

Notice how this change in perspective gives you a better view of the Department 3 data series (which was almost totally obscured in the original 3D chart). Also notice how Excel has shifted the orientation of the category and series headings and repositioned the values (z) axis on the right side of the chart.

A Worksheet without Graphics Is Like . . .

Charts are not the only kind of graphics you can add to a worksheet. Indeed, Excel lets you spruce up a worksheet with drawings, text boxes, and even graphic images imported from other sources, like scanned images or drawings created in other graphics programs.

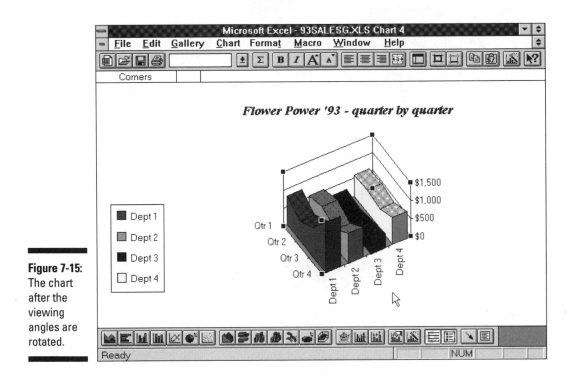

Figure 7-15:
The chart after the viewing angles are rotated.

Figure 7-16 shows some of the other types of graphics you can include in the worksheet. In the upper-left corner of the table is a drawing of a rose. This graphic was scanned and then brought into the worksheet after being copied to the Clipboard with the Paste command on the Edit pull-down menu. When you paste a graphic image in the worksheet from the Clipboard, the image appears in Excel as a selected graphic that you can both resize and move.

In addition to the imported rose graphic, the worksheet shown in Figure 7-16 also contains other graphics: a text box with a drop shadow, an arrow, and an oval drawn around the yearly total sales figure in cell G7. These three graphics were added with the tools on the Drawing toolbar (shown as a floating toolbar in the lower-right corner of the worksheet document window).

The Drawing toolbar contains all sorts of drawing tools you can use to draw outlined or filled shapes. Here are some examples:

✔ To draw the oval around the yearly total in cell G7, click on the Oval tool on the Drawing toolbar and drag the crosshair pointer until the oval is the size and shape you want (to draw a circle rather than an oval with this tool, hold the Shift key as you drag the pointer). If you shift as you select, Excel creates a filled circle or oval.

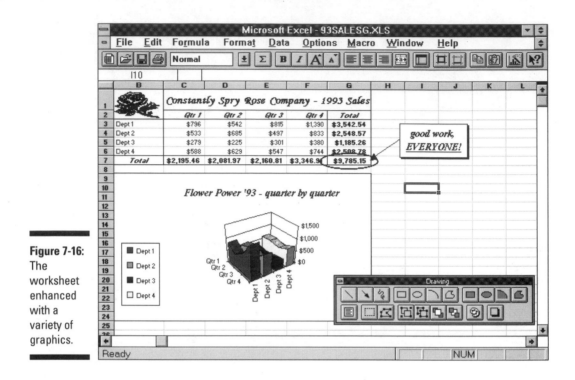

Figure 7-16:
The
worksheet
enhanced
with a
variety of
graphics.

✔ To create the text box with the drop shadow, click on the Text Box tool on the Drawing toolbar (this tool uses the same picture as its counterpart on the Chart toolbar) and drag the crosshair pointer to create the size and shape of the box. When you release the mouse button, Excel draws the text box in the worksheet and positions the insertion point inside it where you can enter text. When you're done entering text, click the mouse pointer somewhere outside of the new text box to deselect the box. If you want, you can change the font and alignment of the text in the box by using the Font and Text commands from the box's shortcut menu.

✔ To draw the arrow from the text box to the yearly total, click on the Arrow tool on the Drawing toolbar, drag the crosshair from the box to the oval, and then release the mouse button. When drawing an arrow in the worksheet with the Arrow pointer, the direction you drag the pointer determines which end of the shaft gets the arrowhead. If you drag the crosshair pointer from the oval to the text box, the arrowhead points up to the box instead of down to the cell with the yearly total.

Putting one in front of the other

In case you haven't noticed, graphic objects float on top of the cells of the work-sheet. Most of the objects (including charts) are opaque, meaning that they hide (*without* replacing) information in the cells beneath. If you move one opaque graphic on top of another, the one on top hides the one below, just as putting one sheet of paper over another hides the information on the one below. This means that most of the time, you should make sure that graphic objects don't overlap one another or overlap cells with worksheet information you want to display.

Sometimes, however, you can create some interesting special effects by placing a transparent graphic object (such as a circle) in front of an opaque one. The only problem you might encounter is if the opaque object gets on top of the transparent one. If this happens, switch their positions by selecting the opaque object and then choosing the Send to Back command from the Format pull-down menu.

Now you see them, now you don't

There's just one more thing you'll want to know about the graphics you add to a worksheet: how to hide them. You see, adding graphics to a worksheet can appreciably slow down the screen response because Excel has to take time to redraw each and every little picture in the document window whenever you scroll the view even slightly. To keep this sluggishness from driving you crazy, either hide the display of all the graphics (including charts) while you edit other things in the worksheet, or replace them with gray rectangles that continue to mark their places in the worksheet but don't take nearly as long to redraw.

To hide all the graphics or replace them with gray placeholders, choose the Display command from the Options pull-down menu to open the Display Options dialog box. Click on the Hide All radio button to get rid of the display of all graphics entirely. Click on the Show Placeholders radio button to replace the graphics with shaded rectangles (this is the safest bet because the placeholders give you a general idea of how changes to the cells of the worksheet impact the graphics).

Before you print the worksheet, be sure that you redisplay the graphic objects: open the Display Options dialog box again and click on the Show All radio button.

Putting Out the Chart

To print the charts in a worksheet, first make sure that the graphic objects are displayed. Then choose the Print command from the File pull-down menu or click on the Print tool on the Standard toolbar. If you've used the Set Print Area command on the Options menu to print a particular cell range in the worksheet, use the Print Preview feature to make sure that the print range includes all of the chart. If the whole chart is not included in the print range, expand the print range to include the entire range of cells under the chart (as well as the ranges of data you want printed) and choose the Set Print Area command again. Then print the worksheet with the Print command on the File menu or the Print tool.

If you want, you can print the chart alone on its own page without any attendant worksheet information. To do this, double-click on the chart to open it in its own chart document window. Then choose the Print command from the File pull-down menu on the chart window menu bar.

The page setup options for printing a chart vary slightly from the standard options you use to print a worksheet. In the Page Setup dialog box, you can choose one of three chart-size option buttons: Size On Screen (to print the chart in the size it assumes on the screen), Scale to Fit Page (the default, which scales the chart so that it prints on whatever page size selected), or Use Full Page (to have Excel expand the chart, if necessary, to fill the page size selected). Other than these chart-size options, all the other page-setup and printing options are the same as those you use when printing worksheets (see Chapter 6 for details on using them).

If you decide to print information in a worksheet without attendant graphics, select the object you don't want to print and then choose the Object Properties command from the graphics shortcut menu. In the Object Properties dialog box, remove the *X* from the Print Object check box and close the dialog box. Remember, however, to reselect the Print Object check box when you decide to include the graphic in the printed report.

Chapter 8
Facts and Figures at Your Fingertips

● ●

In This Chapter
▶ How to set up a database in Excel
▶ How to create a data form for a database
▶ How to add records with the data form
▶ How to find, edit, and delete records with the data form
▶ How to sort records in the database
▶ How to set up selection criteria
▶ How to locate records with Data Find
▶ How to extract records with Data Extract

● ●

*T*he purpose of all the worksheet tables you've been exposed to up till now has been to perform essential calculations (such as to sum monthly or quarterly sales figures) and then present the information in an understandable form. But there's another kind of worksheet table you can create in Excel: a *database*. The purpose of a database is not so much to calculate new values but to store lots of information in a consistent manner. For example, you can create a database that contains the names and addresses of all your clients, or you can create a database that contains all the essential facts about your employees.

Believe it or not, you already know everything you need to know about setting up and creating a database from your experience with creating other types of worksheet tables. When setting up a database, you start by entering a row of column headings (technically known as *field names* in database parlance) to identify the different kinds of items you need to keep track of (such as First Name, Last Name, Street, City, State, and so on). After you enter the row of field names, you start entering the information for the database in the appropriate columns of the rows immediately below the field names.

As you proceed, notice that each column of the database contains information for a particular item you want to track in the database, such as the client's company name or an employee's telephone extension. Each column is also known as a *field* in the database. In looking back over your work, you see that each row of the database contains complete information about a particular person or thing you're keeping track of in the database, whether it's a corporation such as PBC Broadcasting, Inc., or a particular employee such as Michael Bryant. The individuals or entities described in the rows of the database are also known as the *records* of the database. Each record (row) contains many fields (columns).

Maintaining vast quantities of data in a tabular format is but one small part of the database story in Excel. You will find that Excel provides you with very powerful features for organizing the data as well as for locating just the information you need.

For example, suppose that you entered the clients in a database alphabetically by company name but now want to see them listed alphabetically by company name *and* grouped by states and cities. No problem: sort the records of the database by their State, City, and then Company fields.

Suppose that you want a list of only the clients in Boston and New York who purchased at least $10,000 worth of merchandise from you. It's simple: enter the city names **Boston** and **New York** under the City field name and >=**10000** under the Total Sales field name in a special region of the worksheet known as a *criteria range*. Then perform an operation called a *data extract*. Presto! Excel searches the fields in the database and extracts only those records that meet your criteria (in this case, where the city is Boston or New York and the total sales is $10,000 or more); Excel copies these records to a special place in the worksheet called the *extract range*.

Data in What Form?

Setting up and maintaining a database is easy with Excel's handy, built-in *data form*. You use the data form to add, delete, or edit records in the database. To create a data form for a new database, you first enter the row of column headings used as field names and one sample record in the following row (check out the personnel database in Figure 8-1).

Format each field entry just like you want those that follow in that same column to appear throughout the database. Then select the two rows of cells, choose the Set Database command from the Data pull-down menu, and then choose the Form command from the Data menu.

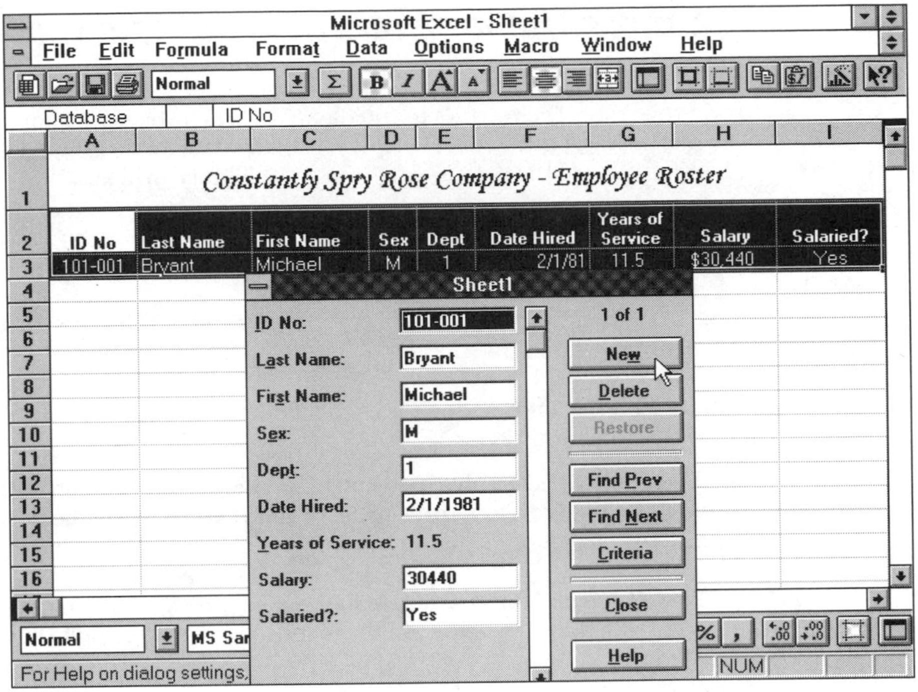

Figure 8-1:
Creating the
data form
for a new
database.

As soon as you choose the Form command, Excel analyzes the row of field names and lists them down the left side of the data form it creates. Figure 8-1 shows the data form for this new database; it looks kind of like a customized dialog box. The data form Excel creates includes the entries you made in the first record. The data form also contains a series of buttons on the right side that you use to add, delete, or find specific records in the database. Right above the first button (New), the data form lists the number of the record you're looking at followed by the total number of records (1 of 1 when you first create the data form).

Calling a Database a Database

When you choose the Set Database command from the Data menu, Excel assigns the name Database to the selected cell range. Each time you add a record to the database using the data form, Excel automatically redefines the Database range to include the new record. To quickly select the entire database (for example, if you want to print it), use the Goto feature (F5) and select Database from the Goto list box.

The more the merrier: adding new records

After you create the data form with the first record, you can then use the form to add the rest of the records to the database. The process is simple. When you click on the New button, Excel displays a blank data form (marked New Record at the right side of data form). You get to fill this form in.

After you enter the information for the first field, you press the Tab key to advance to the next field in the record.

Whoa! Don't press the Enter key. If you do, you'll insert the new, incomplete, record into the database.

Continue entering information for each field and pressing Tab to go to the next field in the database.

- ✔ If you notice that you've made an error and want to edit an entry in a field you've already passed, press Shift+Tab to return to that field.

- ✔ To replace the entry, just start typing.

- ✔ To edit some of the characters in the field, press ← or click the I-beam pointer in the entry to locate the insertion point; then edit the entry from there.

When entering information in a particular field, you can copy the entry made in that field for the previous record by pressing Ctrl+" (quotation mark). Press Ctrl+", for example, to carry forward the same entry in the State field of each new record when entering a series of records for people who all live in the same state.

When entering dates in a date field, use a consistent date format that Excel knows (for example, enter something like **2/19/93**). When entering numbers that use leading zeros that you don't want to disappear from the entry (such as ZIP codes like **00102**), put an ' (apostrophe) before the first **0**. The apostrophe tells Excel to treat the number like a text label.

Press the ↓ key when you've entered all the information for the new record. Instead of the ↓ key, you can press Enter or click on the New button (see Figure 8-2). Excel inserts the new record as the last record in the database and displays a new blank data form where you can enter the next record (see Figure 8-3).

When you finish adding records to the database, press the Esc key or click on the Close button to close the data form. Then save the worksheet with the Save command on the File pull-down menu or click on the File Save tool on the Standard toolbar.

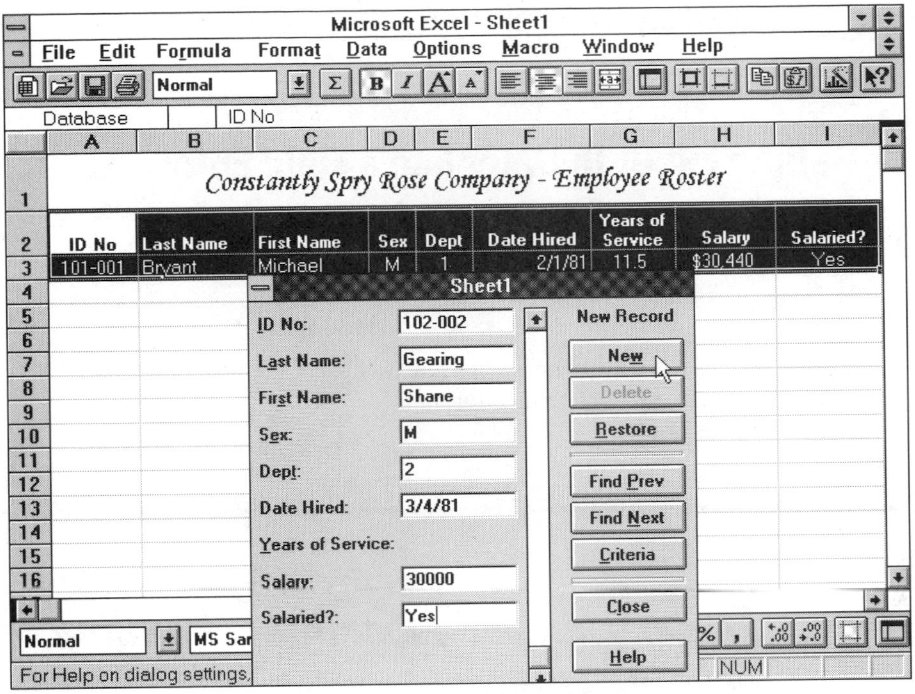

Figure 8-2:
Entering
information
in the data
form for the
second
record.

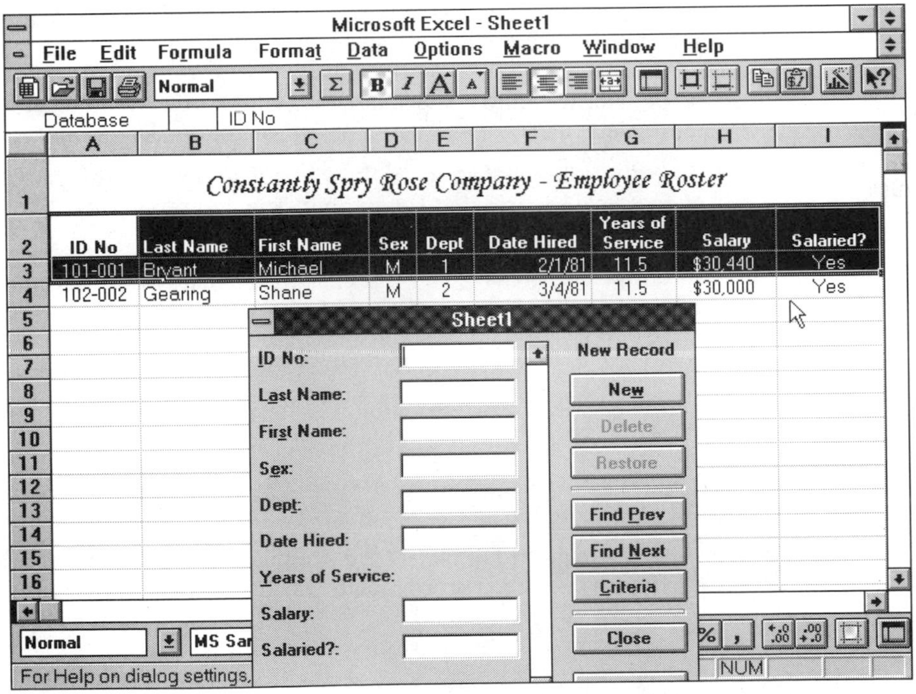

Figure 8-3:
The
worksheet
after the
second
record was
entered
in the
database.

TECHNICAL STUFF

Getting Excel To Calculate a Field Entry

If the entry in a particular field can be calculated, enter the formula for that field in the first record of the database. Excel copies the formula for this field to each new record you add with the data form.

In the personnel database, for example, the Years of Service field in cell G3 of the first record is calculated by the formula =(NOW()-F3)/365.

As you can see, Excel adds the calculated field, Years of Service, to the data form but doesn't provide a text box for this field (calculated fields can't be edited). When you enter additional records to the database, Excel calculates the formula for the Years of Service field. If you then redisplay the data for these records, you see the calculated value following Years of Service (although you won't be able to change it).

Finder's keepers: locating, changing, and deleting records

Once the database is underway and you're caught up with entering new records, you can start using the data form to perform routine maintenance on the database. For example, you can use the data form to locate a record you want to change and then make the edits to the particular fields. You can also use the data form to find a specific record you want to remove and then delete it from the database.

- ✔ To edit the fields of a record that already appears in the data form, move to that field by pressing Tab or Shift+Tab and replace the entry by typing a new one.

- ✔ Alternatively, press ← or → or click the I-beam cursor to reposition the insertion point and then make your edits.

- ✔ To clear a field entirely, select it and then press the Del key.

To delete the entire record from the database, click on the Delete button. Excel displays an alert box with the following dire warning:

```
Displayed record will be deleted permanently
```

To go ahead and get rid of the record displayed in the data form, choose OK. To play it safe and keep the record intact, choose Cancel.

Please keep in mind that you *cannot* use the Undo feature to bring back a record you removed with the <u>D</u>elete button! Excel is definitely *not* kidding when it uses words like `deleted permanently`. As a precaution, always save a backup version of the worksheet with the database before you start removing old records.

"Scroll me up, Scotty"

Once you display the data form in the worksheet by choosing the F<u>o</u>rm command from the <u>D</u>ata pull-down menu, you can use the scroll bar to the right of the list of field names or various keystrokes (both summarized in Table 8-1) to move through the records in the database until you find the one you want to edit or delete.

- To move to the data form for the next record in the database, press ↓, press Enter, or click on the ↓ scroll arrow at the bottom of the scroll bar.

- To move to the data form for the previous record in the database, press ↑, press Shift+Enter, or click on the ↑ scroll arrow at the top of the scroll bar.

- To move to the data form for the first record in the database, press Ctrl+↑, press Ctrl+PgUp, or drag the scroll box to the very top of the scroll bar.

- To move to a blank data form beyond the last record, press Ctrl+↓, press Ctrl+PgDn, or drag the scroll box to the very bottom of the scroll bar.

Table 8-1:	Ways To Get to a Particular Record
Keystrokes or Scroll Bar Technique	**Result**
Press ↓ or Enter, or click on the ↓ scroll arrow or the Find <u>N</u>ext button.	Moves to the next record in the database and leaves the same field selected
Press ↑ or Shift+Enter, or click on the ↑ scroll arrow or the Find <u>P</u>rev button.	Moves to the previous record in the database and the same field selected
Press PgDn.	Moves 10 records forward in the database
Press PgUp.	Moves 10 records backward in the database
Press Ctrl+ ↑ or Ctrl+PgUp, or drag the scroll box to the top of the scroll bar.	Moves to the first record in the database
Press Ctrl+↓ or Ctrl+PgDn, or drag the scroll box to the bottom of the scroll bar.	Moves to a blank record beyond, or after the last record in the database

Eureka! (or Look me up when you're in town)

In a really large database, trying to find a particular record by moving from record to record — or even moving ten records at a time with the scroll bar — can take all day. Rather than waste time trying to manually search for a record, you can use the Criteria button in the data form to look it up.

When you click on the Criteria button, Excel clears all the field entries in the data form (and replaces the record number with the word *Criteria*) so that you can enter the criteria to search for in the blank text boxes. For example, suppose that you need to edit Martha Carr's salary (she got a raise!). Unfortunately, her paperwork doesn't include her employee number so you can't use that to find her record. You do know that she works in Department 2, and although you don't remember exactly how she spells her last name, you're pretty sure that it begins with a *C* instead of a *K*.

To find her record, you can at least use this information to narrow the search down to all the records where the department is 2 and the last name begins with the letter *C*. To do this, open the data form for the personnel database, click on the Criteria button, and then enter the following in the text box for the Last Name field:

```
C*
```

Also enter the following in the text box for the Dept field (see Figure 8-4):

```
2
```

When you enter search criteria for records in the blank text boxes of the data form, you can use the ? (question mark) and * (asterisk) wildcard characters. Remember that you used these wildcard characters with the Find command on the Formula menu to locate cells with particular entries (see Chapter 5 for more on using these wildcard characters with the Find feature).

Now click on the Find Next command button or press Enter. Excel displays in the data form the first record in the database where the last name begins with the letter *C* and the department is 2. As shown in Figure 8-5, the first record in this database that meets these criteria is for Thomas Campbell. To press on and find Martha's record, click on the Find Next button or press Enter. Figure 8-6 shows Martha Carr's record. Having located Martha's record, edit her salary in the text box for the Salary field. When you click on the Close button, Excel records her well-deserved raise in the database itself.

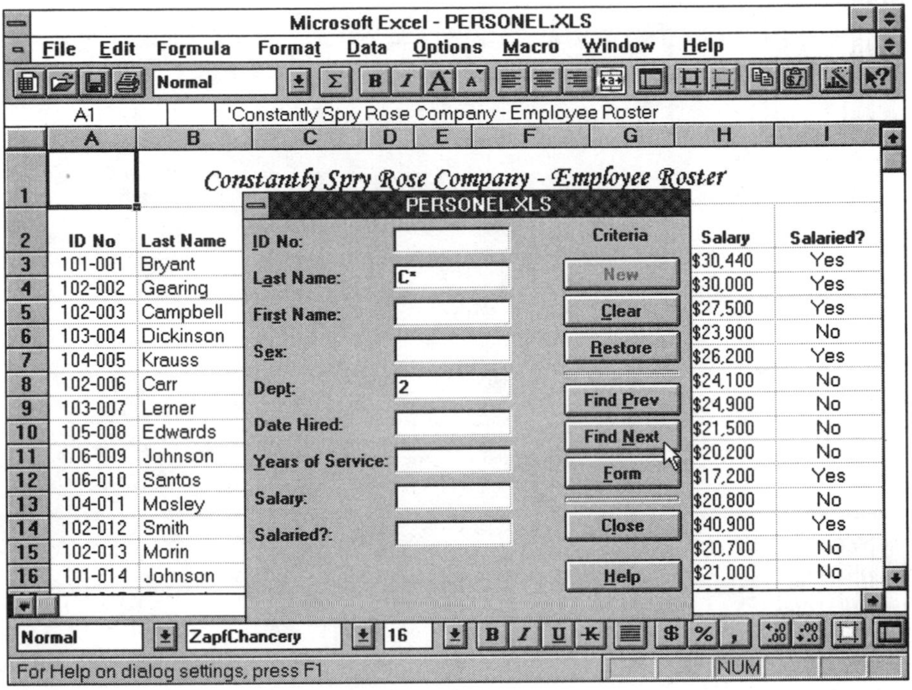

Figure 8-4:
The data form after Criteria was selected. The search criteria was entered in the blank field boxes.

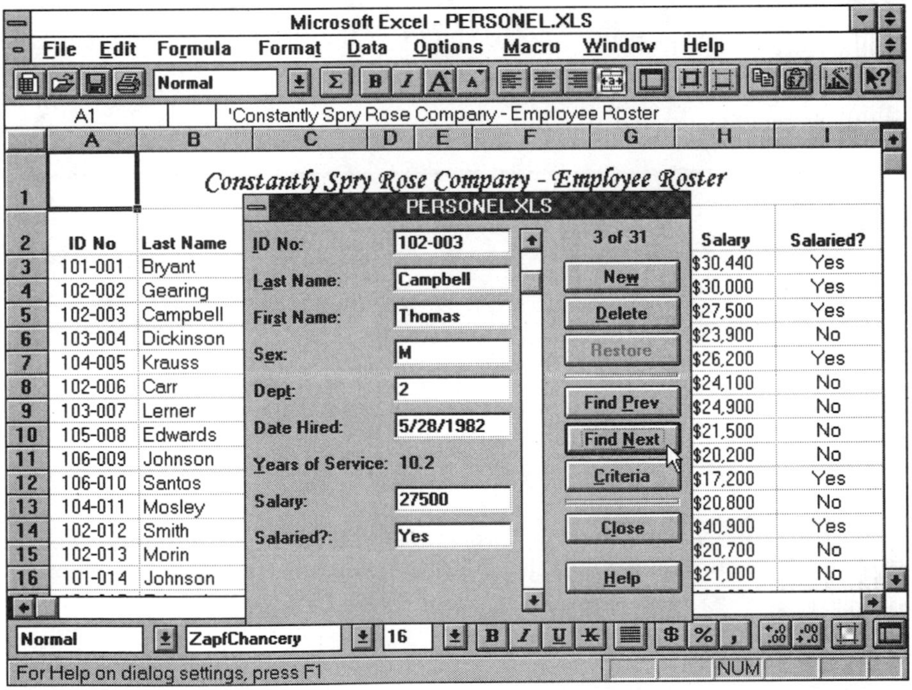

Figure 8-5:
The first record in the database that meets the search criteria.

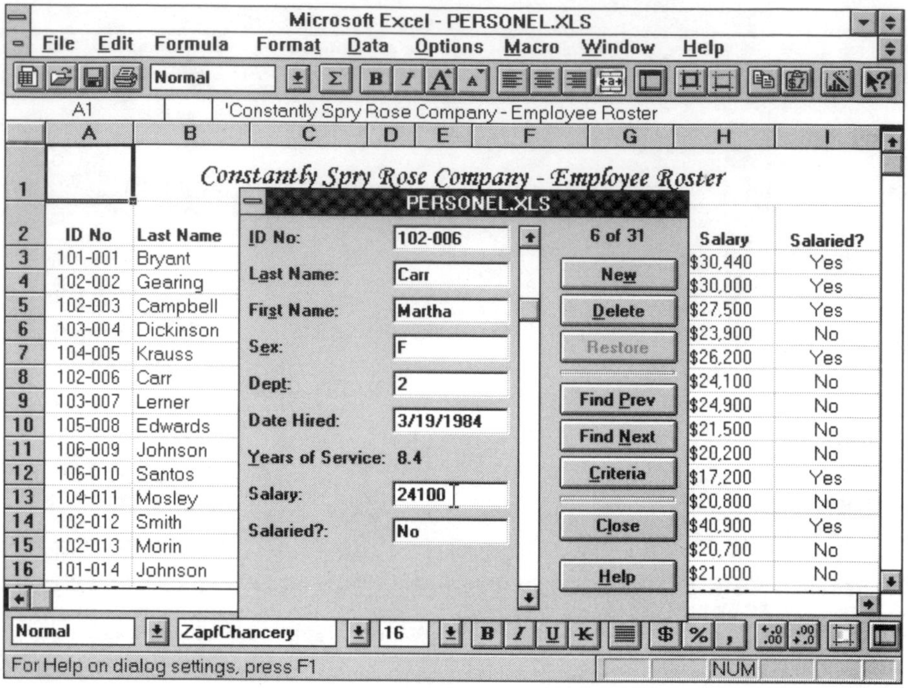

Figure 8-6:
Eureka! The
long-lost
record
appears.

When you use the Criteria button in the data form to find records, you can in-clude the following operators in the search criteria you enter to locate a spe-cific record in the database:

Operator	Meaning
=	Equal to
>	Greater than
>=	Greater than or equal to
<	Less than
<=	Less than or equal to
<>	Not equal to

For example, to display only those records where the employee's salary is greater than or equal to $30,000 a year, enter **>=30000** in the text box for the Salary field before clicking on the Find Next button.

When specifying search criteria that fit a number of records, you may have to click on the Find Next or Find Prev button several times to locate the record you want. If no record fits the search criteria you enter, the computer beeps at you when you click on one of these buttons.

To change the search criteria, if necessary, first clear the data form by clicking on the Criteria button again. Then select the appropriate text boxes and clear out the old criteria before you enter the new. (You can just replace the criteria if you're using the same fields.)

To switch back to the current record without using the search criteria you enter, click on the Form button (this button replaces the Criteria button as soon as you click on the Criteria button).

Data from A to Z (or "So, Sort Me!")

Every database you put together in Excel will have some kind of preferred order for maintaining and viewing the records. Depending on the database, you may want to see the records in alphabetical order by last name. In the case of a database of clients, you may want to see the records arranged alphabetically by company name. In the sample personnel database used in this chapter, the preferred order is numerical order by the employee number assigned to each employee when he or she is first hired.

When you initially enter records for a new database, you no doubt enter them in whatever order is the preferred one. However, as you will soon discover, you don't have the option of adding subsequent records in that preferred order. Whenever you add a new record with the New button in the data form, Excel tacks that record onto the bottom of the database by adding a new row.

This means that if you originally enter all the records in alphabetical order by company (from *ABC Supplies* to *Zastrow and Sons*) and then you add the record for a new client named *Digital Products of America,* Excel puts the new record at the bottom of the barrel, in the last row right after *Zastrow and Sons* instead of inserting it in its proper position somewhere after *ABC Supplies* but definitely before Zastrow and his wonderful boys!

And this is not the only problem you can have with the order used in originally entering records. Even if the records in the database remain fairly stable, the preferred order merely represents the order you use *most* of the time. But what about those times when you need to see the records in another, special order?

For example, although you usually like to work with the database in alphabetical order by company name, when you use the records to generate mailing labels for a mass-mailing, you want the records in ZIP-code order. When you want to generate for your account representatives a list that shows which clients are in whose territory, you need the records in alphabetical order by state and maybe even city.

It seems like flexibility in the record order is exactly what's required to keep up with the different needs you have for the data. This is precisely what the Sort command offers you, once you understand how to use it.

To have Excel correctly sort the records in a database, you must specify which fields are the key to the new order (therefore, these fields are rightfully known as the *sorting keys*). Further, you must specify what type of order should be created using the information in these fields. There are two possible orders: *ascending order,* in which text entries are placed in alphabetical order (A to Z) and values are placed in numerical order (from smallest to largest), and *descending order,* which is the exact reverse of alphabetical order (Z to A) and numerical order (largest to smallest).

When you sort records in a database, you can specify up to three fields (keys) on which to sort (you can also choose between ascending and descending order for each key you use). You only need more than one key when the field you really want to sort (technically known as the *primary key*) contains duplicates and you want a say in how the records with duplicate entries are arranged. (If you don't specify another key, Excel just puts the records in the order in which you entered them.)

Ascending and Descending

When you use the ascending sort order with a key field that contains many different kinds of entries, Excel places numbers (from smallest to largest) before text entries (in alphabetical order), followed by any logical values (TRUE and FALSE), error values, and finally, blank cells. When you use the descending sort order, Excel arranges the different entries in reverse: numbers are still first, arranged from largest to smallest, text entries go from Z to A, and the FALSE logical value precedes the TRUE logical value.

The best and most common example of when you need more than one key is when sorting a large database alphabetically in last-name order. Consider a database that contains several people with the last name Smith, Jones, or Zastrow (as is the case when you work at Zastrow and Sons). If you specify the Last Name field as the only sorting key (using the default ascending order), all the duplicate Smiths, Joneses, and Zastrows are placed in the order in which their records were originally entered. To better sort these duplicates, you can specify a second key. For example, you can specify the First Name field (again using the default ascending order) as the *secondary* or *tie-breaker* key, so that Ian Smith's record precedes that of Sandra Smith, and Vladimir Zastrow's record comes after that of Mikhail Zastrow.

To sort records in an Excel database, follow these steps:

1. **Select all the records in the database to be sorted.**

   Make sure that you include *all* the fields (columns) in each record (row), not just the field you want to sort on. At the same time, make sure *not* to include the row of field names at the top of the database in the cell selection. If you do, Excel sorts the field names in with the other database records — not good!

2. **Choose the Sort command from the Data menu.**

   Excel opens the Sort dialog box (see Figure 8-7). By default, the Rows radio button is selected as the method of sorting, and the address of the active cell is listed in the 1st Key text box.

3. **Select a cell in the field (column) you want to use as the primary key.**

   Remember that you can drag the Sort dialog box out of the way of the cell you want to click on. For example, to specify the Last Name field as the primary key, select any cell in column B.

4. **Click on the radio button that specifies the sort order you want for this key.**

   To sort the records in descending order by last name, for example, click on the Descending radio button in the 1st Key box.

5. **Specify a secondary key if necessary.**

   If the primary key field contains duplicates, and you want to specify how the duplicate records are sorted, click in the 2nd Key box and select a cell in the field to be used as the secondary key. For example, to specify a secondary key of the First Name field, select any cell in column C.

   To sort records in descending order using the secondary key, click on the Descending radio button in the 2nd Key box.

6. Specify a third key if necessary.

If the secondary key field contains duplicates, and you want to specify how the duplicate records are sorted, click in the 3rd Key box and select a cell in the field to be used as the third key. For example, to specify a third key of the ID No field, click on any cell in column A.

To sort records in descending order using the third key, click on the Descending radio button in the 3rd Key box.

7. Choose OK or press Enter.

Excel sorts the selected records. If you see that you sorted the database on the wrong fields or in the wrong order, choose the Undo Sort command from the Edit menu or press Crl+Z to immediately restore the database records to their previous order.

Figure 8-7 shows the Sort dialog box after a primary and secondary key were specified for sorting the records in the personnel database. The dialog box specifies that records are sorted in alphabetical (ascending) order by last name and then first name. Figure 8-8 shows the database right after sorting.

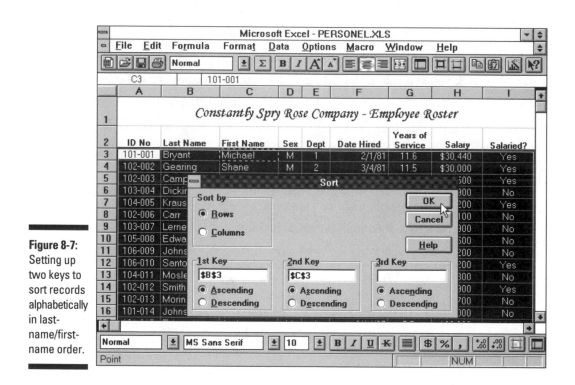

Figure 8-7:
Setting up two keys to sort records alphabetically in last-name/first-name order.

		Microsoft Excel - PERSONEL.XLS						

File Edit Formula Format Data Options Macro Window Help

A3   102-020

	A	B	C	D	E	F	G	H	I
1			*Constantly Spry Rose Company - Employee Roster*						
2	ID No	Last Name	First Name	Sex	Dept	Date Hired	Years of Service	Salary	Salaried?
3	102-020	Adamson	Joy	F	2	10/21/87	4.8	$34,400	Yes
4	104-019	Bird	Lance	M	4	8/13/87	5.0	$21,100	Yes
5	103-023	Bjorkman	Robert	M	3	2/24/88	4.5	$25,000	Yes
6	101-001	Bryant	Michael	M	1	2/1/81	11.6	$30,440	Yes
7	102-003	Campbell	Thomas	M	2	5/28/82	10.2	$27,500	Yes
8	102-006	Carr	Martha	F	2	3/19/84	8.4	$24,100	No
9	103-004	Dickinson	Angela	F	3	11/13/86	5.8	$23,900	No
10	105-008	Edwards	Cindy	F	5	8/15/85	7.0	$21,500	No
11	101-015	Edwards	Jack	M	1	2/14/87	5.5	$32,200	Yes
12	101-030	Fletcher	Amanda	F	3	1/3/89	3.6	$16,500	No
13	102-002	Gearing	Shane	M	2	3/4/81	11.5	$30,000	Yes
14	103-024	Grogan	Dave	M	3	4/3/88	4.4	$17,500	No
15	106-009	Johnson	Rebecca	F	6	2/4/86	6.5	$20,200	No
16	101-014	Johnson	Stuart	M	1	12/29/86	5.6	$21,000	No

Normal   MS Sans Serif   10   B I U

Ready   NUM

Figure 8-8: The database sorted in alphabetical order by last name and first name.

You can use the Sort Ascending tool (the one with the *A* above the *Z*) or the Sort Descending tool (the one with the *Z* above the *A*) on the Utility toolbar to sort records in the database. These tools use either the very first field or the very last field in the database as the sorting key.

- ✔ To sort the database using the *first* field as the primary key, make the first entry in the first field active, select all the records in the database, and then click on the Sort Ascending tool or Sort Descending tool.

- ✔ To sort the database using the *last* field as the primary key, make the first cell in the last field active, select the database, and click on the Sort Ascending tool or Sort Descending tool.

Going for the Record

As mentioned previously, Excel provides you with several tools for finding and retrieving just the information you need from the database. Before you can use these tools to locate information in a database, you must set up a special cell range in the worksheet called the *criteria range*. You use this range to specify search criteria.

The criteria range consists of cells containing selection criteria entered beneath appropriate field names. To facilitate multiple searches with different selection criteria, copy all the field names to a new section of the worksheet and then place the criteria you want to use under the appropriate field names.

For example, to find all the employees in Department 3 in the personnel database, enter **3** in the cell below the field name Dept. Then you define as the criteria range the cells with the field names along with those in the row below by choosing the Set Criteria command from the Data pull-down menu. When you choose the Find, Extract, or Delete command from the Data menu, Excel uses Department equals 3 as the criteria for locating, retrieving, or removing records from the database.

When locating the criteria range in the same worksheet as the database, position it in columns *to the right* of those containing the database instead of in the rows *below* the database. That way, you can add new records to the database without continually relocating the criteria range, and you can modify the size and shape of the criteria range without affecting any of the records in the database. Just remember to select the cells in the criteria range and choose the Set Criteria command from the Data menu any time that changes to the selection criteria appreciably alter the size and shape of the original criteria range.

Not just any criteria

Entering selection criteria in a criteria range is much like entering search criteria in a data form after clicking on the Criteria button. When you want to locate records that contain a particular text entry or value, type this entry under the appropriate field name in the criteria range.

In addition to looking for records that contain a particular phrase or that are equal to a particular number, you can also use the other operators (>, >=, <, <=, and <>) in the selection criteria to find records less than, greater than, or not equal to a particular value. Table 8-2 provides examples of some of the ways you can use these operators in selection criteria.

When you enter two or more criteria in the same row beneath their field names in the criteria range, Excel selects only those records that meet *both* these selection criteria. Figure 8-9 shows an example of a criteria range with just such a condition (ignore the information in rows 6 through 9 for now). Row 3 of this figure tells Excel to select only those records where the department is 3 *and* the date hired is sometime after January 1, 1988. Both criteria are used in the search because both selection criteria **3** and **>1/1/88** are placed in the same row of the criteria range.

Table 8-2:	How To Use Operators in Selection Criteria		
Operator	*Meaning*	*Example*	*What It Locates in the Database*
>	Greater than	ZIP Code>42500	Records where the number in the ZIP Code field comes after 42500
>=	Greater than or equal to	Hired>=1/11/92	Records where the date in the Hired field is on or after January 11, 1992
<	Less than	Last Name<d	Records where the name in the Last Name field begins with a letter before *D* (that is, begins with *A, B,* or *C*)
<=	Less than or equal to	Joined<=2/15/91	Records where the date in the Joined field is on or before February 15, 1991
<>	Not equal to	State<>"NY"	Records where the entry in the State field is not *NY* (New York)

When you enter two or more criteria in different rows of the criteria range, Excel selects records that meet *any one of* the criteria. Figure 8-10 shows an example of this type of selection criteria (ignore the information in rows 6 through 16 for now).

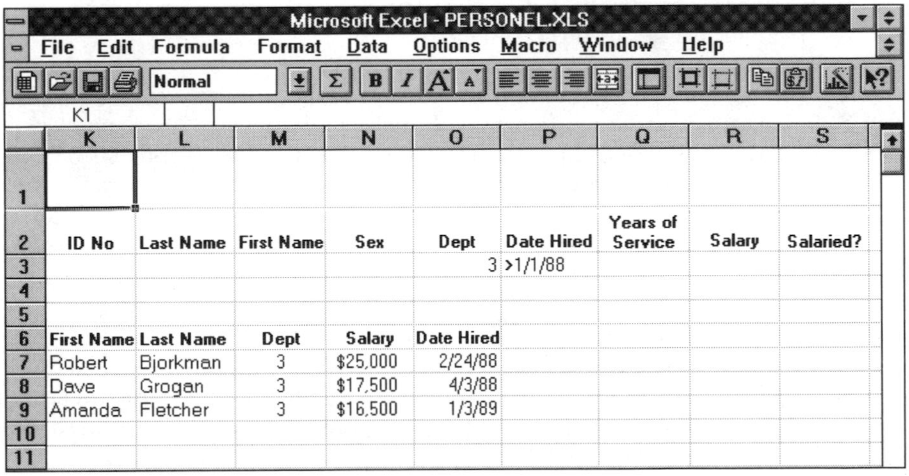

Figure 8-9: Using two selection criteria, *both* of which must be met, to select a record.

	K	L	M	N	O	P	Q	R	S
1									
2	ID No	Last Name	First Name	Sex	Dept	Date Hired	Years of Service	Salary	Salaried?
3					3	>1/1/88			
4									
5									
6	First Name	Last Name	Dept	Salary	Date Hired				
7	Robert	Bjorkman	3	$25,000	2/24/88				
8	Dave	Grogan	3	$17,500	4/3/88				
9	Amanda	Fletcher	3	$16,500	1/3/89				
10									
11									

	Microsoft Excel - PERSONEL.XLS							

File Edit Formula Format Data Options Macro Window Help

Normal Σ B I A A

K1

	K	L	M	N	O	P	Q	R	S
1									
2	ID No	Last Name	First Name	Sex	Dept	Date Hired	Years of Service	Salary	Salaried?
3					4				
4					6				
5									
6	First Name	Last Name	Dept	Salary	Date Hired				
7	Edward	Krauss	4	$26,200	7/13/83				
8	Rebecca	Johnson	6	$20,200	2/4/86				
9	Elizabeth	Santos	6	$17,200	7/17/86				
10	Deborah	Mosley	4	$20,800	8/23/86				
11	Elaine	Savage	4	$18,900	5/27/87				
12	Lance	Bird	4	$21,100	8/13/87				
13	Miriam	Morse	6	$19,600	11/2/87				
14	James	Percival	6	$19,200	12/18/87				
15	Charles	Stolper	4	$17,800	7/9/88				
16	Lili	Micaela	4	$24,500	9/2/92				
17									
18									

Ready   NUM

Figure 8-10: Using two selection criteria, *either* of which may be met, to select a record.

Column O of this figure tells Excel to select records where the Department is either 4 or 6. Either criteria is used because they are entered in separate rows in the criteria range. When you create these kinds of conditions, remember to redefine the criteria range with the Set Criteria command to include all the rows that contain criteria. If you forget to do this before you perform a Find, Extract, or Delete operation, Excel uses only the criteria in the rows previously selected with the Set Criteria command.

What if you want to find all the records in a database that fall within a range, say all those records where the salary is between $20,000 and $35,000 or all those records where the ZIP code is between 56000 and 66000? To enter these types of selection criteria, create a formula in the criteria range that uses the built-in AND function (a so-called *logical function*). For information on how to use a logical function to do this, see Chapter 13.

Using Data Find

Select the Find command from the Data menu when you want to review, one at a time, the records that match the selection criteria in the criteria range. After you set up the criteria range, place the selection criteria there, and choose the Find command, Excel highlights matching records in the database.

✔ To see whether any more records match and to move to the next one in the database, press ↓ or click on the ↓ scroll arrow in the vertical scroll bar. (When you choose the Find command, the scroll bars become striped, indicating that their function is modified.)

✔ To move to the previous matching record, press ↑ or click on the ↑ scroll arrow in the vertical scroll bar.

In a really large database, you can drag the scroll box in the vertical scroll bar to skip to the next matching record in a completely different part of the database. You can also use the horizontal scroll bar to scroll left and right to view different fields. Excel does not allow you, however, to scroll the entire database out of sight; at least the first or last field must remain on the screen when you scroll from side to side.

After you finish viewing any matching records, choose the Exit Find command from the Data menu, press Esc, or just click on a cell outside the database to return the functioning of the scroll bars to normal and once again be able to move the cell pointer out of the database. If, after you choose the Find command from the Data menu, none of the records in the database match the selection criteria entered in the criteria range, Excel displays an alert box indicating that there are no matching records.

To edit a field in a record highlighted during a Find operation, click on the cell that contains the entry to select it and edit its contents as you would any other entry. If you want to search the database for other records matching the search criteria after you edit a record, select the Find command from the Data menu again and then press ↓ or ↑ until Excel highlights the record.

Excerpts from the database

The Find command is good when you need to locate only a record or two for editing. For the times when you want to see just the records that meet the selection criteria, use the Extract command on the Data menu instead. Before you can extract records from a database, you must set up and define an *extract range* that indicates where the records that match the selection criteria are to be copied.

When setting up an extract range, copy the field names for all the fields you want to copy from the database. The field names in the extract range do not have to follow the order used in the database itself. For example, if the Last Name field precedes the First Name field in the database, you can reverse this order in the extract range and have the First Name field precede the Last Name field (refer back to row 6 of Figures 8-9 and 8-10).

You also do not have to include all of the field's names in the extract range. For example, to create mailing labels for a client database, include in the extract range just the First Name, Last Name, Street Address, City, State, and ZIP Code fields so that Excel copies only this information from the database.

After you enter the field names you want to include in the extract range, you then let Excel know the whereabouts of the extract range with the Set Extract command on the Data menu. Before you perform an Extract operation using the selection criteria, you usually don't have any idea how many records will match and be copied to the extract range. To leave unspecified the number of rows in the extract range below the field-name row, select only the cells in the field-name row before you choose the Set Extract command. When the extract range consists of only field names, Excel uses as many rows beneath the names as required to copy all the matching records from the database.

Be careful, however, that you don't have existing entries in the rows below the extract-range field names — Excel replaces any existing entries with information extracted from the database. So to avoid losing data during an Extract operation, locate the extract range in an area of the worksheet where there is no possibility of overwriting existing cell entries.

If you include blank rows in the extract range you specify with the Set Extract command, you restrict the extract range to just those blank rows. Although this prevents Excel from overwriting existing entries, you may find that you didn't select sufficient blank rows to hold all matching records. If Excel fills the extract range before it finishes copying all matching records, the program indicates this condition by displaying an alert message box stating that the Extract range is full.

After you set up and define both the extract and the criteria ranges, select the Extract command from the Data menu. Excel displays the Extract dialog box. To have Excel extract only unique records into the extract range, click on the Unique Records Only check box. (Normally, you want *all* the matching records rather than just the first one that matches the criteria. In this case, leave the check box unselected.) When you choose OK or press Enter, Excel locates information in the database that matches the criteria in the criteria range and copies it to the extract range. (Refer back to Figures 8-9 and 8-10, which show typical Extract operations.)

If you change the selection criteria and perform another Extract operation without changing the extract range, Excel clears the existing contents of the extract range before copying new information there. Therefore, if you want to save the results of one Extract operation before performing another one, you must either copy the contents of the extract range to a new part of the worksheet (or an entirely new worksheet) or set up and define another extract range in a different part of the worksheet.

You can save the results of an Extract operation to a new worksheet quite easily by following these steps:

1. **Select the contents of the extract range (including the field names if you want them in the new worksheet).**

2. **Click on the Copy tool in the Standard toolbar to copy the range to the Clipboard.**

3. **Click on the New Worksheet tool in the Standard toolbar to open a new worksheet.**

4. **Select the first cell of the range to contain the extracted database information.**

5. **Press Enter.**

After copying extracted records to a new worksheet, you can use the Sort command on the Data menu to sort the records or fields into the desired order.

Chapter 9
Coping with More Than One Document at a Time

In This Chapter

▶ How to open more than one worksheet at a time

▶ How to arrange the document windows you have open

▶ How to create a new worksheet from a template

▶ How to edit a group of worksheets at the same time

▶ How to consolidate the values in a group of worksheets

▶ How to create a workbook containing all the documents you want to use at the same time

*W*hen you are brand new to spreadsheets, you have enough trouble keeping track of a single worksheet; the very thought of working with more than one document is more than you can deal with. As soon as you get a little experience under your belt, though, you will find that keeping track of two or more Excel documents isn't any more taxing than working with one.

Assuming that you are doing reasonably well with a single worksheet, you should have no trepidation about moving on and opening two, three, or even four worksheets. It does, however, get pretty confusing when you try to keep track of more than four worksheets at once because there's no way to display them all on the screen at one time. Luckily, you seldom need more than two, let alone four.

Before you see *how* to work with more than one Excel document, I'll talk about *why* you'd want to do such a thing in the first place. There are a couple of situations where you want more than one worksheet document open: when you need to copy information from one worksheet to another and when you need to compare the information in the two documents side by side. (It's pretty hard to know what's inside a worksheet when it's still closed on the disk!) To copy information from one worksheet to another open one, you use the Windows Clipboard. To compare information, you arrange the windows containing the documents side by side on the screen.

Arranging Documents for Fun and Profit

To open more than one document, click on the File Open tool on the Standard toolbar or choose the Open command from the File menu; then specify the name of the document to open. Excel enables you to continue opening as many documents as you want, provided that the computer has sufficient memory to hold it all.

Each time you open a new Excel document, the program opens it in its own window that either partially or completely (depending on whether or not the first window's been maximized) obscures the display of the document opened before it. The layered effect of the windows is much like placing one piece of paper on another to block out the display of the information on the paper beneath. To bring a buried Excel document to the top of the stack, open the Window menu and choose the document you want to see. (You can choose the document either by clicking on its name in the menu or by typing its number.)

If you ever get wild enough to open more than nine documents at a time, Excel adds a More option to the bottom of the Window menu which you can choose to get to documents 10 and up). You can also cycle through the open documents, displaying each one on top in the order in which you opened them. To display the next document in the stack, press Ctrl+F6.

Unfortunately, the standard arrangement of document windows — one on top of the other — makes it virtually impossible to compare information in two open documents. To successfully compare information, you must resize and arrange the document windows side by side on the screen. You do this with the Arrange command on the Window pull-down menu. When you choose this command, Excel displays the Arrange Windows dialog box (see Figure 9-1).

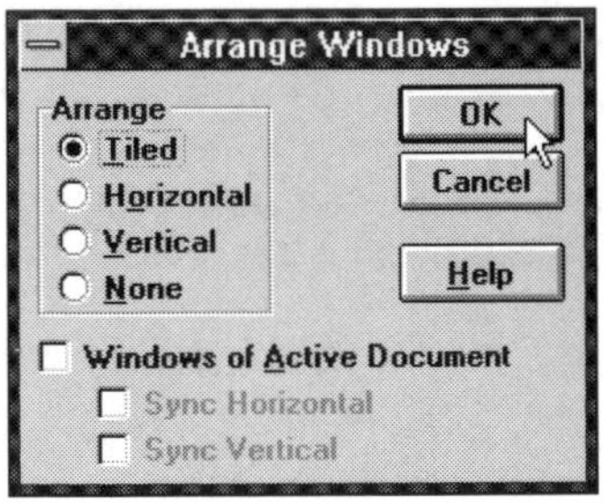

Figure 9-1:
The Arrange
Windows dialog
box lets you
display a little
part of all the
open documents.

To have Excel arrange and size the open document windows so that they all fit side by side on the screen (in the order in which they appear on the <u>W</u>indow pull-down menu), click on the <u>T</u>iled radio button (Figure 9-2 shows the screen after clicking on this button when three document windows are open).

✔ Click on the H<u>o</u>rizontal radio button when you want Excel to size the document windows equally and then tile them one above the other.

✔ Click on the <u>V</u>ertical radio button when you want Excel to size the document windows equally and then tile them one next to the other (Figure 9-3 shows the screen after the <u>V</u>ertical radio button was clicked when three document windows were open.)

Once the windows are tiled in one arrangement or another, you can activate the one you want to use (if it's not already selected) by clicking on it or by pressing the Ctrl+F6 keystrokes you use to display full-size open windows. When you select a window in this manner, Excel indicates that it's been selected by highlighting its title bar and adding scroll bars to the window. You can temporarily zoom the window up to full size by clicking on the Maximize button in the window's upper-right corner. When you finish the work you need to do in the full-size window, return it to the tiled view by clicking on the Restore button.

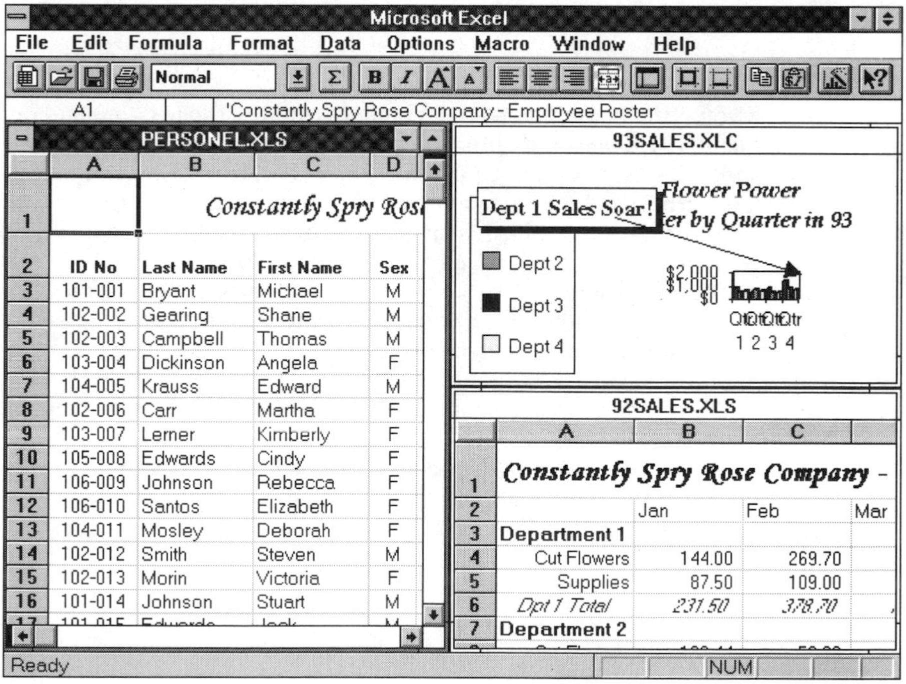

Figure 9-2: The screen after the open document windows were tiled.

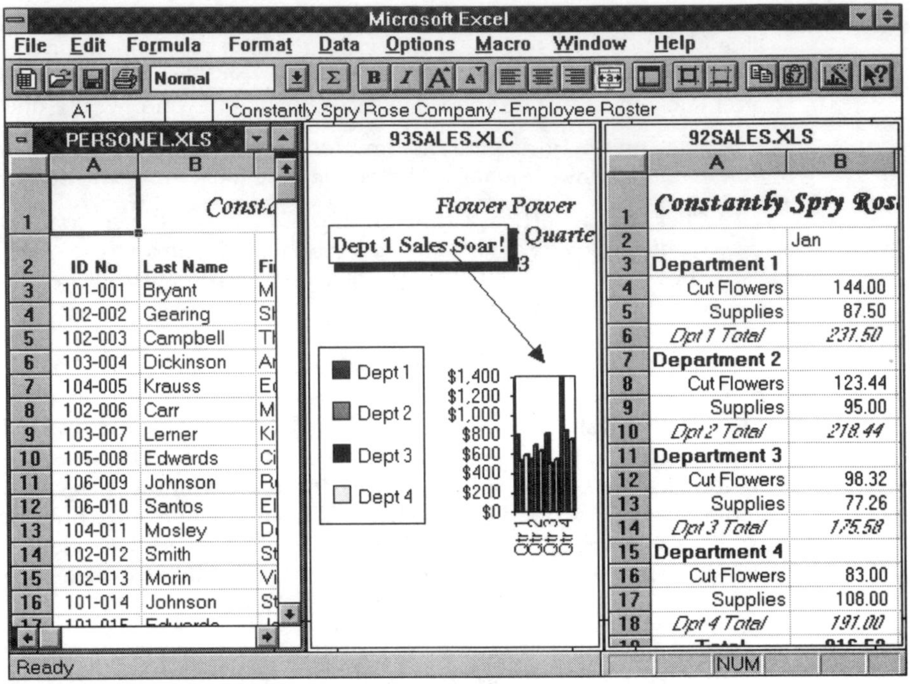

Figure 9-3: The screen after the open document windows were vertically tiled.

If you close one of the tiled documents with the Close command on the File menu, Excel does not automatically resize the other open windows to fill in the gap. Likewise, if you open another document, Excel does not automatically tile it in with the others (in fact, it just sits on top of the other open windows). To fill in the gap created by closing a window or to integrate a newly open window into the current tiled arrangement, open the Arrange Windows dialog box and click on the OK button or press Enter. (The same radio button you clicked on last time is still selected; if you want to choose a new arrangement, click on the new radio button before you click on OK.)

When you save your documents, Excel saves the window-arrangement setting along with the data. If you don't want the current tiled setting (Tiled, Horizontal, or Vertical) saved with the document, open the Arrange Windows dialog box, click on the None radio button, close the dialog box, and then close and save the changes to the document.

Something borrowed

Sometimes you want to borrow headings or formulas or a range of values already entered in one worksheet and reuse them in another. Copying data between worksheets is much like copying data within a worksheet using the Copy and Paste commands. You must use the Clipboard to take data across worksheets; the drag-and-drop copy variation does not work.

To copy information from one worksheet to another, follow these steps:

1. **Open both worksheets.**

   Use the Open File tool on the Standard toolbar or select the Open command from the File menu.

2. **Tile the document windows.**

   So that you can see what you're doing, tile the windows using one of the options in the Arrange Windows dialog box (see the preceding section in this chapter for details).

3. **Activate the worksheet window containing the information you want to copy.**

   Select the window either by clicking on it or by choosing its name from the Window pull-down menu.

4. **Select the cells containing the information you want to copy to the other document.**

5. **Copy the selected cells to the Clipboard.**

   Copy information to the Clipboard with one of these methods: click on the Copy tool on the Standard toolbar, select the Copy command from the Edit menu, or press Ctrl+C.

6. **Switch to the document window where you want to copy the information.**

   Switch to the other window by clicking on it or by choosing its name from the Window pull-down menu.

7. **Select the cell in the upper-left corner of the range where you want the copied information to appear.**

8. **Paste the contents of the Clipboard into the new worksheet.**

   Paste starting with the current cell by pressing the Enter key, choosing the Paste command from the Edit menu, or pressing Ctrl+V.

When copying information between two existing worksheet documents, you have to open both documents. If you want to copy part of an existing worksheet to a brand-new worksheet, open the worksheet with the data to be copied, click on the New Worksheet tool on the Standard toolbar (or choose the New command from the File menu), and then select Worksheet from the New dialog box. Then switch back to the worksheet with the goodies and begin the copy procedure just outlined.

Copy a chart

You can copy a chart from one worksheet to another or from a chart window to another worksheet. If the chart is placed somewhere in the worksheet, click on the chart somewhere to select it and then choose the Copy command to copy it to the Clipboard. After switching to the worksheet where you want the copy of the chart to appear, position the cell pointer in the cell in the upper-left corner of the range where the chart should appear and then choose the Paste command. When Excel pastes the chart into the worksheet, it is selected; you can move or resize it if you need to.

To copy a chart from its chart window, choose the Select Chart command from the Chart pull-down menu and then choose the Copy command. Excel places selection handles around the chart when you choose the Select Chart command and a marquee around it when you choose the Copy command. After copying the chart to the Clipboard, switch to the window containing the worksheet where it is to be copied and paste it into place.

Here Come the Worksheet Clones!

Sometimes you may need to create a worksheet so similar in layout and content to another you've already finished that you might be tempted to copy the entire thing to a new worksheet and just make appropriate editing changes to the headings and values in the new worksheet. For example, you may develop an invoice form for a particular sale and then want to copy the original and adapt it for the next sale. Or you may create a budget or sales-tracking worksheet for a particular year and then want to use the original to create the budget or track sales for the next year.

Instead of copying an entire worksheet (or opening the original, modifying it, and saving it under a new name), you can use the original document to create a worksheet template. A *template* is a special Excel document that generates a copy of itself each time you open it with the Open File tool or the Open command on the File menu. These copies (or clones) are given numbered temporary document names, reflecting the name you gave to the template file. If you open a template saved with the file name BUDGET.XLT (the extension stands for *Excel Template*), the first copy of the template is called *Budget1,* the second copy *Budget2,* and so on.

To create a template from an original file, simply replace with zeros any of the numbers you know will change in each new worksheet you generate, while leaving the formulas intact. If the worksheet contains any titles to be updated in each new worksheet, such as the year of the budget or the number of the invoice, delete the characters in them that you know will change (I usually replace them with *X*s).

To replace all the numbers in a large worksheet with zeros, select all the ranges that have values (be careful not to include cells with formulas, however) and enter 0 in all the selected cells by typing **0** and pressing Ctrl+Enter (Control+Enter on the Mac).

After replacing all the numbers with zeros and editing the titles that need changing, you can, if you want, protect the cells that contain formulas and labels that never change. To do this, follow these steps:

1. **Select all the ranges with the zeros and headings that *do* need modifying.**

2. **Choose the Cell Protection command from the Format menu or click on the Lock Cell tool on the Utility toolbar to unlock them.**

3. **Choose the Protect Document command from the Options menu.**

   If you want the user to have to know a password to unprotect the document (letting him or her at the formulas and other goodies in the still-locked cells), enter a password in the Password text box before choosing OK or pressing Enter.

After unlocking the sections that require data entry and protecting the document (if you want to add this level of security), you are ready to create the template file. To do this, choose the Save As command from the File menu, enter the main filename for the template in the Save File Name text box (for example, *budget, sales, invoice*, and the like), select Template from the File as Type pop-up list box (Excel automatically changes the file extension from XLS to XLT in the File Name list box), and then choose OK or press Enter.

On the Macintosh, of course, Excel doesn't add the file extension XLT to the document name when you select Template as the file format. As you may know, the clever Macintosh has no need for filename extensions. But to make it easier to identify a document as a template rather than a regular worksheet, however, it's a good idea to give the document a name like *Budget Template* or *Invoice Template* when creating it in the Save As dialog box.

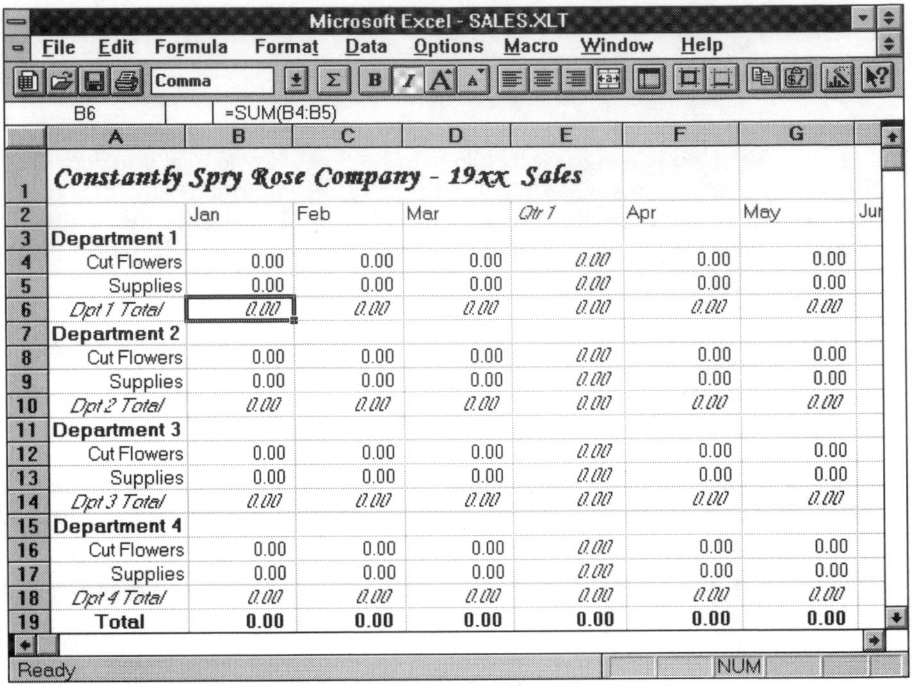

Figure 9-4: A template for generating worksheets that track yearly sales.

Figure 9-4 shows a template for generating new sales worksheets. It was created from the 92 sales sample worksheet you've seen elsewhere in this book. I created this template from the 92SALES.XLS worksheet by zeroing out the cells that contained the sales figures. In this template, protection is turned on and all the cells that contain formulas or labels that don't change from worksheet to worksheet remain locked.

Figure 9-5 shows a new 1993 sales worksheet being created from the sales template. To create this new worksheet, you would simply unprotect the document and edit the title in cell A1 to show the current year and then fill in the sales figures for the different departments in the appropriate columns. Because the worksheet generated from the template already contains all the formulas, that's all there is to it! When you finish entering sales figures, save the worksheet. When you do, you can then assign a permanent filename (replacing the temporary document name Sales1).

If, after creating a template file, you find that you need to make some changes to it (that is, you want to make modifications that should appear in all the worksheets you create from the template, rather than in just one particular worksheet), open the original template file by holding down the Shift key as you select the template document name from the Open dialog box that opens when you select Open from the File pull-down menu.

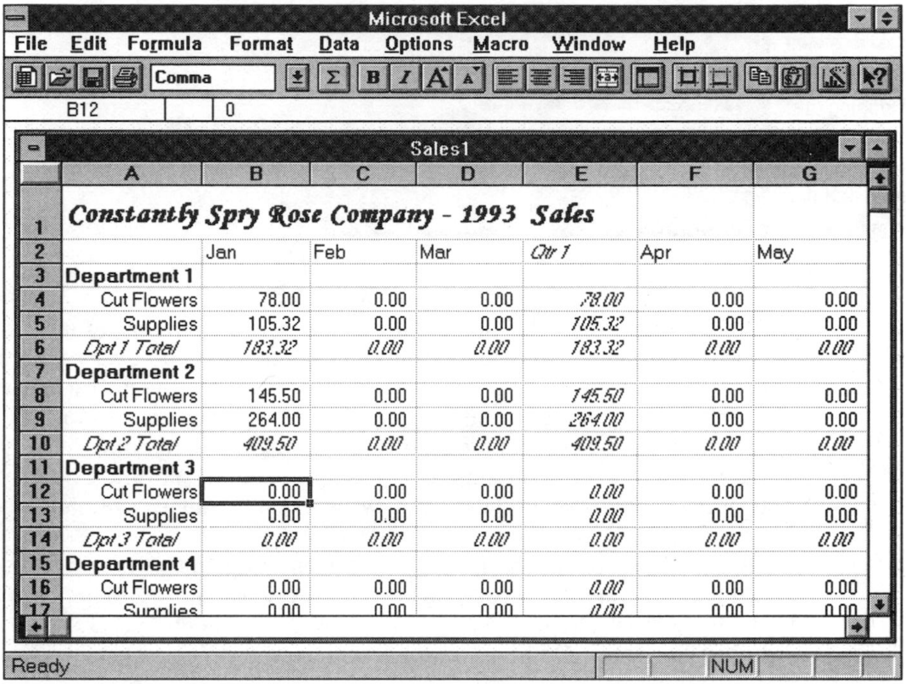

Figure 9-5: Creating a new sales worksheet for recording 1993 sales from the SALES template.

Modifications en masse

Because worksheets created from templates share the same layout, you can edit them at the same time. To edit more than one worksheet at a time, you open all the worksheets you want to make the same changes to (such as adding italics and bold to the same column headings) and select the worksheet you actually want to work on. Then choose the Group Edit command from the Options menu.

Excel displays the Group Edit dialog box (see Figure 9-6). Notice that the program has automatically selected in the Select Group list box all the documents you have open.

✔ To designate all the open documents as a single group that will get the same edits, choose OK or press Enter.

✔ To deselect any of the documents in the Select Group list box, click on the document in the list box to remove the highlighting from it.

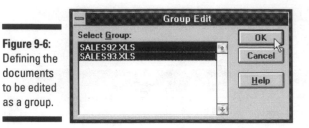

Figure 9-6:
Defining the
documents
to be edited
as a group.

After specifying several documents as a group, any changes that you make to the active worksheet, Excel will promptly make to each and every other document in the group (make sure that none of the documents in the group are protected). Excel makes group edits such as entries and deletions as well as any formatting. Excel indicates that you are editing in group mode by adding [Group] to the title bars of the open documents (of course, you see this addition only in the active window unless you tiled the windows with the Arrange command).

Figure 9-7 shows an example of group formatting. In this example, both SALES92.XLS and SALES93.XLS are included in the group. When you make bold the worksheet title in cell A1 of the SALES92.XLS document, Excel bolds the title in cell A1 of the SALES93.XLS document as well.

Figure 9-7:
Bolding the
titles in both
worksheets
in the group.

	Microsoft Excel							
File	Edit	Formula	Format	Data	Options	Macro	Window	Help

A1   'Constantly Spry Rose Company - 1992 Sales

SALES92.XLS [Group]

	A	B	C	D	E	F	G	H
1	*Constantly Spry Rose Company - 1992 Sales*							
2		Jan	Feb	Mar	Qtr 1	Apr	May	Jun
3	**Department 1**							
4	Cut Flowers	144.00	269.70	382.53	796.23	153.00	109.54	279.42
5	Supplies	87.50	109.00	336.18	532.68	116.25	247.98	321.00
6	*Dpt 1 Total*	231.50	378.70	718.71	1,308.91	269.25	357.52	600.42
7	**Department 2**							

SALES93.XLS [Group]

	A	B	C	D	E	F	G	H
1	*Constantly Spry Rose Company - 1993 Sales*							
2		Jan	Feb	Mar	Qtr 1	Apr	May	Jun	Q
3	**Department 1**							
4	Cut Flowers	78.00	146.00	45.56	269.56	67.45	84.65	72.45
5	Supplies	105.32	68.70	154.00	328.02	134.00	145.25	205.67
6	*Dpt 1 Total*	183.32	214.70	199.56	597.58	201.45	229.90	278.12
7	**Department 2**							
8	Cut Flowers	145.50	86.50	89.00	321.00	114.00	90.45	92.50
9	Supplies	264.00	133.25	200.15	597.40	175.54	200.00	276.00

Ready   NUM

When you finish doing the editing that needs to take place in all documents in the group, disband the group by selecting one of the other documents you have open (it doesn't matter which one). Remember that you can do this by selecting the document from the Window pull-down menu or by pressing Ctrl+F6. If you have tiled the windows with one of the options in the Arrange Windows dialog box, you can select another window simply by clicking on it. Excel removes [Group] from the title bars of the open documents and you once again can edit each worksheet independently of the others.

Don't select another open document window until you are ready to disband the group. If you select one just to check something, you have to define which documents are to be group-edited all over again. Try to think ahead when you arrange the windows and select the one you really want to work with before you go to the trouble of defining the group.

Consolidate your holdings

Not only can you edit as a unit the worksheets generated from a template, you can also consolidate their values. For example, you can use the Consolidation feature with a group of budget worksheets, each of which contains the planned expenses for a particular department, to produce a summary worksheet that contains a company-wide budget. Or you can use the Consolidation feature to produce a summary worksheet that totals the sales made in the last few years.

Figure 9-8 shows how easy it is to consolidate values from worksheets generated from a common template. To re-create this example, you would open the SALES92.XLS and SALES93.XLS worksheets and then open a brand new sales worksheet with the SALES.XLT worksheet template. After positioning the cell pointer in the first cell where you want consolidated values to appear (cell B4 with the cut flowers sales for the month of January), you would choose the Consolidate command from the Data menu.

The Consolidate dialog box appears (see Figure 9-8). Use this dialog box to indicate which cell ranges in the various worksheet documents are to be totaled. You can tell that Excel will total the values because SUM is listed in the Function drop-down list box.

To indicate the first cell range to be added (cell range B4:R19 from the SALES92.XLS worksheet), make sure that the insertion point is in the Reference text box of the Consolidate dialog box, switch to the SALES92.XLS document window (either by choosing it from the Window menu or by pressing Ctrl+F6), and select the cell range B4:R19. Once the cell range is selected (it appears in a marquee rather than highlighted in the worksheet), click on the Add button in the Consolidate dialog box.

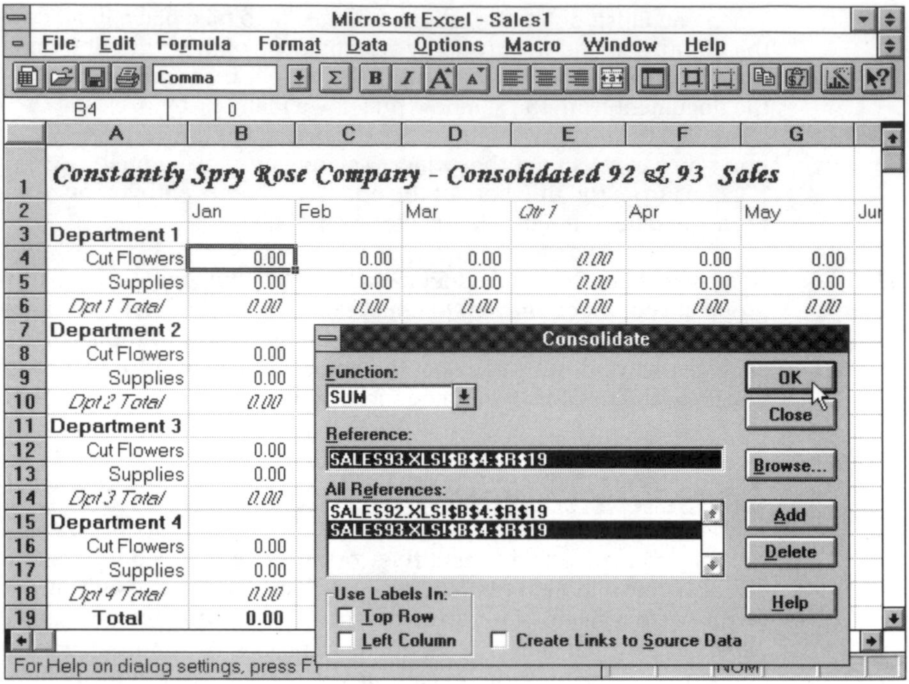

Figure 9-8:
Indicating
the cell
ranges to
consolidate.

As soon as you click on the Add button, Excel switches back to the new worksheet (the one with all zeros) and adds the following cell reference, listed in the Reference text box, to the All References list box:

```
SALES92.XLS!$B$4:$R$19
```

This cell reference looks awfully ugly and complicated, but it's really not. All it says is that you want to use the cell range B4:R19 (in absolute terms) from the document SALES92.XLS.

All you have to do next is repeat this procedure, this time switching to the SALES93.XLS document window where you select the same cell range B4:R19 (you always want to consolidate the same ranges of data). When you click on the Add button and Excel switches back to the new worksheet, the program adds this cell reference to the All References list box:

```
SALES93.XLS!$B$4:$R$19
```

Now that you've told Excel which ranges to sum together, all you have to do is choose OK or press Enter to have the program perform the consolidation. The program adds all the values in corresponding cells and places their totals in the

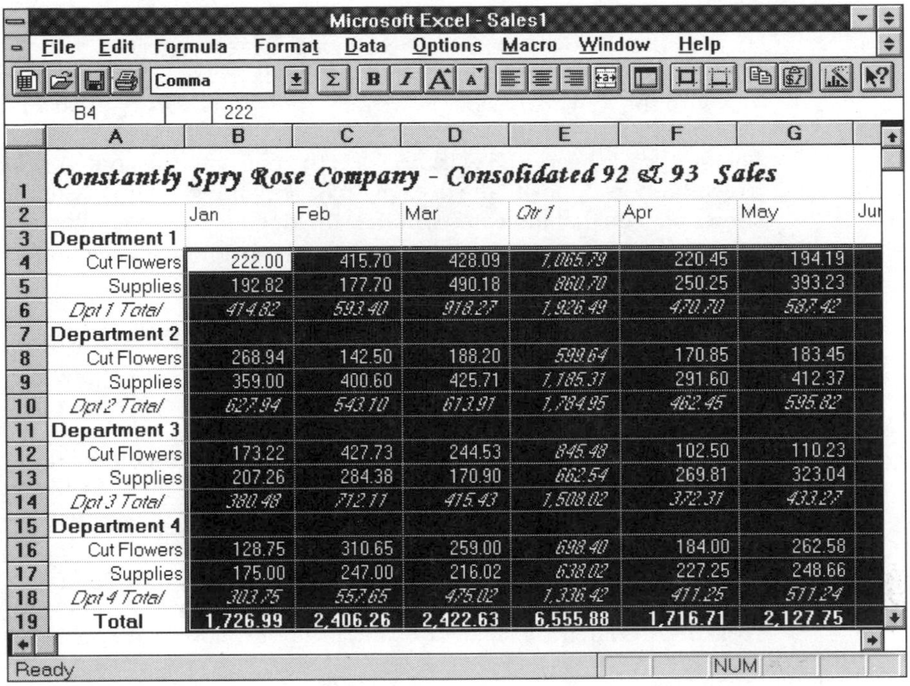

Figure 9-9: A worksheet that consolidates the 1992 and 1993 sales.

	Microsoft Excel - Sales1						
File	**Edit**	**Formula**	**Format**	**Data**	**Options**	**Macro**	**Window**	**Help**

B4 — 222

	A	B	C	D	E	F	G
1	*Constantly Spry Rose Company - Consolidated 92 & 93 Sales*						
2		Jan	Feb	Mar	Qtr 1	Apr	May	Jun
3	Department 1						
4	Cut Flowers	222.00	415.70	428.09	1,065.79	220.45	194.19
5	Supplies	192.82	177.70	490.18	860.70	250.25	393.23
6	Dpt 1 Total	414.82	593.40	918.27	1,926.49	470.70	587.42
7	Department 2						
8	Cut Flowers	268.94	142.50	188.20	599.64	170.85	183.45
9	Supplies	359.00	400.60	425.71	1,185.31	291.60	412.37
10	Dpt 2 Total	627.94	543.10	613.91	1,784.95	462.45	595.82
11	Department 3						
12	Cut Flowers	173.22	427.73	244.53	845.48	102.50	110.23
13	Supplies	207.26	284.38	170.90	662.54	269.81	323.04
14	Dpt 3 Total	380.48	712.11	415.43	1,508.02	372.31	433.27
15	Department 4						
16	Cut Flowers	128.75	310.65	259.00	698.40	184.00	262.58
17	Supplies	175.00	247.00	216.02	638.02	227.25	248.66
18	Dpt 4 Total	303.75	557.65	475.02	1,336.42	411.25	511.24
19	Total	1,726.99	2,406.26	2,422.63	6,555.88	1,716.71	2,127.75

Ready — NUM

new worksheet, starting at the cell with the cell pointer. Figure 9-9 shows the results of the consolidation of the 1992 and 1993 sales figures. Note how these consolidated values have overwritten the zeros that were put in the new worksheet when the new worksheet was generated from the Sales template.

After consolidating your documents, save the results in the new worksheet with the File Save tool on the Standard toolbar or the Save command on the File menu. Then close up the other open documents.

Jot This Down in Your Workbook

Excel's workbook feature offers a super way to store different documents that you always use together so that they are always open and available to you. By saving Excel documents in a workbook, you ensure that they are kept together and that they all open up whenever you open the workbook file.

To create a workbook, open all the documents you want in the workbook and choose the Save Workbook command from the File menu. Excel creates a Work-book Contents sheet that lists the documents you have open (in the order they appear on the <u>W</u>indow menu) and then displays a dialog box (see Figure 9-10). Use this dialog box to name the workbook (Excel suggests a name like *BOOK1.XLW* — where *XLW* stands for *Excel Workbook*). Edit this name (don't fool with the XLW extension, however), and choose OK or press Enter.

The first worksheet in all workbooks is the one with the contents. Instead of page numbers opposite the document names, the Workbook Contents sheet shows an icon that indicates whether the document is bound or unbound. When you create a new workbook, all documents are automatically bound in their workbook (more about this binding stuff shortly).

Not only does the Workbook Contents sheet list the Excel documents the workbook contains, it also enables you to add new documents to the workbook, remove them, or rename them.

Yes! Here's where you dump DOS's cryptic eight-character names and all their weird extensions and assign nice, long, descriptive names up 32 characters long including spaces, just like you can on the Macintosh!

Besides doing all these great things, you can also change the order of the documents in the workbook just by changing the order in which they appear in the Workbook Contents sheet. For example, in the Sales workbook, the worksheet

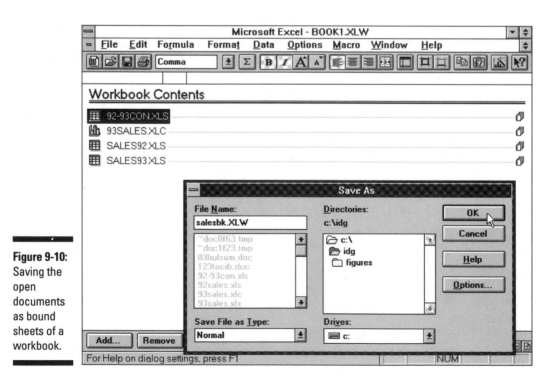

Figure 9-10:
Saving the open documents as bound sheets of a workbook.

document that consolidates the 1992 and 1993 sales is ahead of the individual worksheets with the 1992 and 1993 sales; the chart document with the 3D-column chart illustrating the 1993 sales comes before the worksheet with the 1993 sales. Remember that the order of documents in the Workbook Contents sheet is based purely on the order in which these documents were opened.

Suppose, however, that you want to change the order of the sheets in the workbook to make the consolidation worksheet the last sheet in the worksheet and to place the chart document after its supporting worksheet.

No problem! The key is dragging the icons on the Workbook Contents sheet. Each document in a workbook is preceded by a different icon that denotes its type: worksheet, chart, macro, or slides. To move the 92-93CON.XLS document to the last page of the workbook, drag its icon below the last sheet listed in the Workbook Contents sheet and release the mouse button.

As you drag the document's icon, you see a bar (just like the one that appears when you insert data you are copying or moving with drag-and-drop). The bar shows where Excel will insert the document when you release the mouse button (see Figure 9-11). In this figure, the Workbook Contents sheet for the Sales workbook is shown as the chart document is moved down to follow the 1993 sales worksheet (the consolidation worksheet was already moved to the bottom).

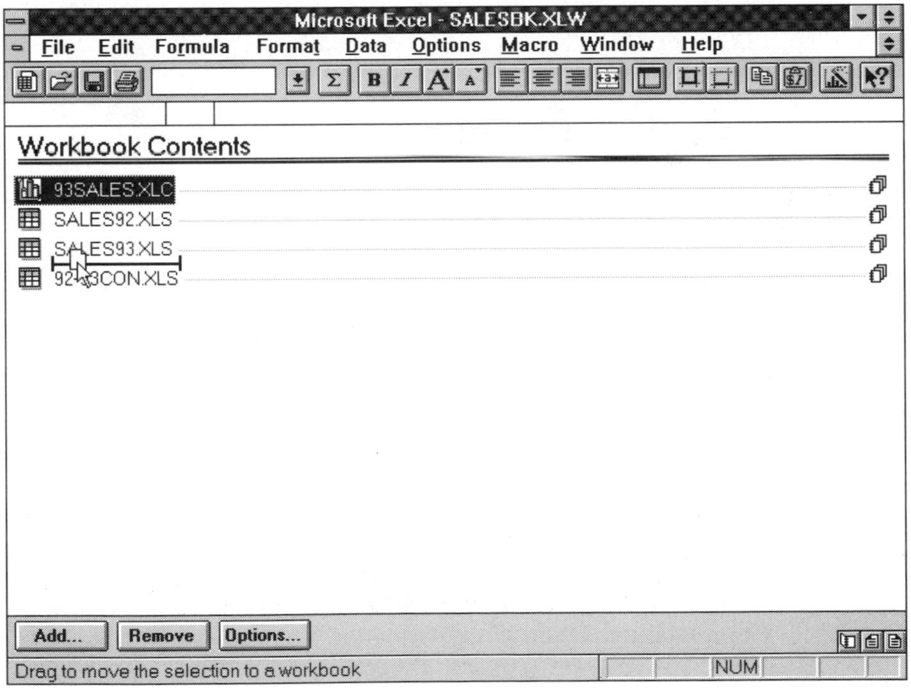

Figure 9-11:
Moving a
sheet in the
workbook's
table of
contents.

After you add documents to a workbook, Excel opens them (in the order they appear in the Workbook Contents sheet) whenever you open the workbook. You may wonder whether documents you add to one workbook can still be used on their own or be added to other workbooks that you create. Normally, the answer is *no*. In the parlance of Excel, the documents are said to be "bound" to their workbook and are, therefore, not available outside the workbook or for inclusion in other workbooks.

Documents unbound!

If you want to retain the ability to use a document in a workbook independently or to use it in another workbook (as you might if you wanted to include a work-sheet template in a couple different workbooks), you can unbind a document.

To unbind a document, either click on its bound icon (the one opposite the document name on the right side of the Workbook Contents sheet with the picture of the spiral-bound sheets of paper) or select the document (by clicking on its name in the Workbook Contents sheet), click on the Options button at the bottom of the window, and click on the Separate file (Unbound) radio button in the Document Options dialog box, or use the right mouse button and the option.

Excel shows that a document is unbound by changing the icon opposite its name. The icon picture changes from one that shows all the sheets nicely bound to one with a couple of fly-away sheets, representing, of course, your "document unbound."

By any other name

I have great news for those of you who can't stand the filename limitations (eight characters, no spaces, and so on) imposed by DOS onto Windows. When naming your documents, these limitations force you to come up with abbreviations so cryptic that even the Secret Service couldn't decode them afterward. The news is that you can assign descriptive file names up to 32 characters long (yes, Virginia, including spaces!) to any bound document in a workbook.

Of course, on the Macintosh you can always give documents the long, newsy names described in this section, so for you Mac users, this feature is no big deal. You guys can just chortle (to yourself please) at us Windows/DOS users and then pass on to the next section, which *is* relevant to your situation.

To rename a bound document, simply select it by clicking on its name in the Workbook Contents sheet, click on the Options button at the bottom of the sheet, enter your descriptive filename in the Document text box, and select OK or press Enter. That's all there is to that!

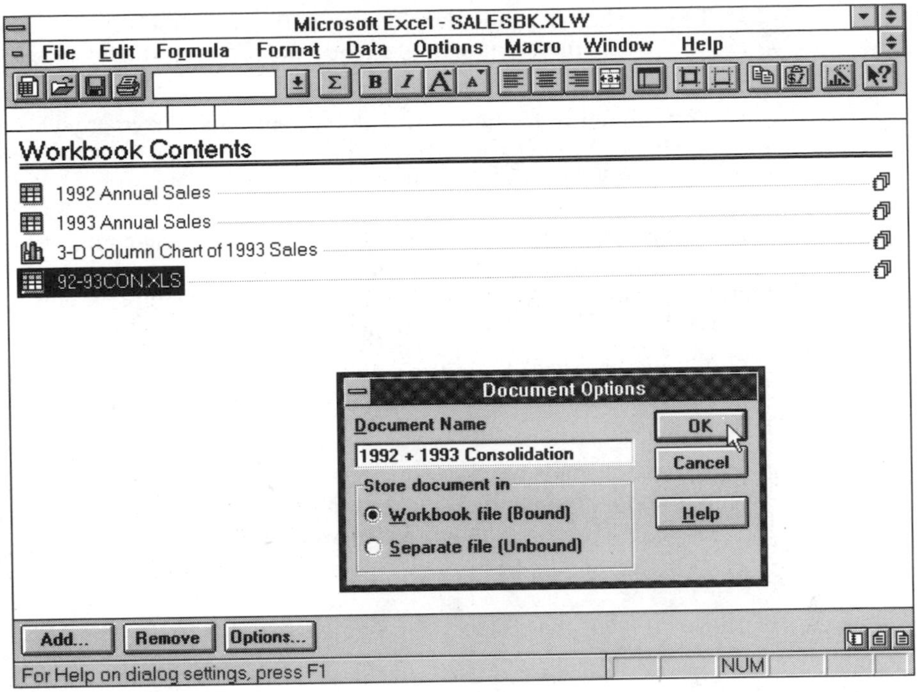

Figure 9-12: Giving sensible names to the documents in the workbook's table of contents.

Figure 9-12 shows how downright civilized the Workbook Contents sheet can appear with the help of some long filenames. In this figure, the last document, 92-93CON.XLS, is just about to be converted to 1992 + 1993 Consolidation. As you can see, the other (bound) documents have already been given names that the average person can make sense of.

Going to and fro

The real beauty of a workbook is that you can open all its files simply by opening the single workbook document. Once the workbook is open, you can use a number of methods to move from document to document or to a specific document in the workbook.

✔ To move to the next document in the workbook, click on the next-document icon (the one in the lower-right corner of the Workbook Contents sheet; it's the page with a dog-eared upper-right corner).

✔ To move to the previous document in the workbook, click on the previous-document icon (it's the icon that looks like a page with a dog-eared upper-left corner).

- ✔ To go right to a particular document in the workbook, either double-click on the document name in the Workbook Contents sheet or select it and press Enter.

- ✔ You can return to the Workbook Contents sheet from anywhere in the workbook by clicking on the first icon in the lower-right corner of the window (the icon with the picture of open pages).

You can also display a particular document by choosing its name from the Window pull-down menu (the document name — long or short — follows the workbook name in this menu). Once you display a document, you make changes to it as you do to any independent Excel document.

- ✔ To save changes to just the active document in the workbook, click on the Save tool in the Standard toolbar or select the Save command from the File menu.

- ✔ To save changes to all the documents in the workbook, choose the Save Workbook command (Excel dutifully asks whether you want to save changes to each document in the workbook).

Part V
Excel — Have It Your Way

The 5th Wave   By Rich Tennant

"IT WAS CLASHING WITH THE SOUTHWESTERN MOTIF."

The part in which...

You learn how to put your own personality into the way Excel works for you and how it looks on the screen. You start by learning how to streamline the do-it-time-after-time tasks, composing and recording macros that you can play back any time you need them — at the touch of a couple of keys.

You learn how to customize the toolbars both by modifying Excel's own and by creating toolbars of your own design. And you learn how to jazz up the look of the Excel window and the look of your documents!

Chapter 10
Excel Made to Order

• •

In This Chapter

▶ How to record and play back simple macros that perform common tasks

▶ How to change the display options in Excel

▶ How to change the workspace options in Excel

▶ How to customize the colors available in Excel

• •

*N*ow that you're familiar with the basics of Excel and how it normally appears and operates, it's high time you learned how to add your own touches to the program. First, you learn how to automate some of those everyday tasks that take up so much of your valuable time. Then you take a look at how to control what's displayed on the screen in each individual document window as well as in the Excel window itself.

As you will soon see, "doing your own thing" with Excel is quite easy. Not only can it help you be more productive with the program but it also makes you feel more like you're the one in control of Excel and not vice versa!

Holy Macros!

Macros! Just hearing the word can be enough to make you want to head for the hills. Rather than think of this term as so much technobabble, keep in mind that *macro* is short for *macro instruction* and that the word *macro* refers to the **big** picture. A macro (at least, at the level of this book) is nothing more than a way to record the actions you take to get a particular task done (such as to enter a company name in a worksheet, save and print a worksheet, or format row headings) and have Excel play them back for you.

Using a macro to perform a routine task rather than doing it by hand has some definite advantages. First, Excel can execute the commands involved much faster than you can (no matter how good you are at the keyboard or how familiar you are with Excel). Also, Excel performs the task flawlessly each and every time (because the macro plays back your actions exactly as recorded, you only have to worry that you record them correctly). Besides, you can even streamline the playback process by assigning keystroke shortcuts to your favorite macros, essentially reducing common tasks that otherwise require quite a few steps to just two keystrokes.

The process of creating a macro is surprisingly straightforward:

✔ Name the macro and assign shortcut keystrokes to it in the Record Macro dialog box to turn on the macro recorder.

✔ Perform the sequence of actions you want recorded in the macro just as you normally do in Excel (you can choose commands from the pull-down or shortcut menus, click on tools in the toolbars, or use shortcut keystrokes).

✔ Select a command to turn off the macro recorder.

✔ Perform the task simply by pressing the keystroke shortcut assigned to the macro.

You'll be happy to know that when recording your actions, Excel doesn't record mistakes (don't you wish everyone else was so forgiving?). In other words, if you're entering the heading **January** in the macro and you type **Janaury** by mistake and then correct your error, Excel does not record your pressing of the Backspace key to delete the characters **aury** and then typing **uary.** The only thing the macro records is the final, corrected result of January!

To record your actions, Excel uses its own macro language (a language, by the way, that you don't have to know in order to create and use *simple* macros — the only kind you're going to get involved with in this book). The commands in this language are recorded in a separate macro sheet. A *macro sheet* is just a special kind of worksheet document that uses wider columns than the normal worksheet and has turned on the display of formulas (so that you can see the macro commands in their cells instead of their results). Excel saves macro sheets with the filename extension XLM (for *Excel Macro*).

Before you start recording a macro, along with naming the macro and assigning shortcut keystrokes, you have to decide whether or not to record it in a regular macro sheet or in a special global macro sheet. Macros you save in the global macro sheet are available for use as soon as you start Excel, but macros you record in a regular macro sheet (that you name like any other Excel document and to which the program appends the extension XLM) are not available until you open that macro sheet.

For this reason, record all the macros you ordinarily use in your work with Excel in the global macro sheet. Record the macros you need to use only in special situations in a particular macro sheet you open just before performing the specific tasks.

A macro a day

The best way to get a feel for how easy it is to record and play back a simple macro is to follow along with the steps for creating a couple of them. The first sample macro enters and formats a company name in a cell. In these steps you turn on the macro to record as you enter the company name, **Constantly Spry Rose Company**, change the font to 16-point Zapf Chancery, and finally increase the row height and center the name vertically in the cell. You can easily adapt this basic macro to enter the name of your company and use the font and type size you want to use.

The very first thing you need is a place in which to perform the steps you want to record in the macro. For this example, open a new worksheet (although you can also use a blank cell in an existing worksheet). Then follow these steps:

1. **Position the pointer in the cell where you want to enter the company name.**

   For this example, position the pointer in cell A1 in the new worksheet.

2. **Choose the Record command from the Macro pull-down menu.**

   The Record Macro dialog box appears (see Figure 10-1).

   If you display the Macro toolbar (shown spanning columns F through H in Figure 10-1), you can also open this dialog box by clicking on the Record Macro tool (the one second from the right; it's the one with the dot).

3. **Assign a name to the macro in the Name text box.**

   The name you type replaces the temporary name Record1 in this example. When naming a macro, follow the same guidelines as when naming ranges (for a refresher on these guidelines, see Chapter 5).

   For this example, enter **Company_Name.**

4. **Click on the Key text box and enter a single letter (between A and Z) or a single number (between 0 and 9).**

   This number or letter is the key you use (in combination with the Ctrl key) when playing back the macro. Try to avoid using letters already assigned to shortcuts (such as Ctrl+P for displaying the Font dialog box or Ctrl+S to select the Style box on the Standard toolbar).

   For this example, enter **N.**

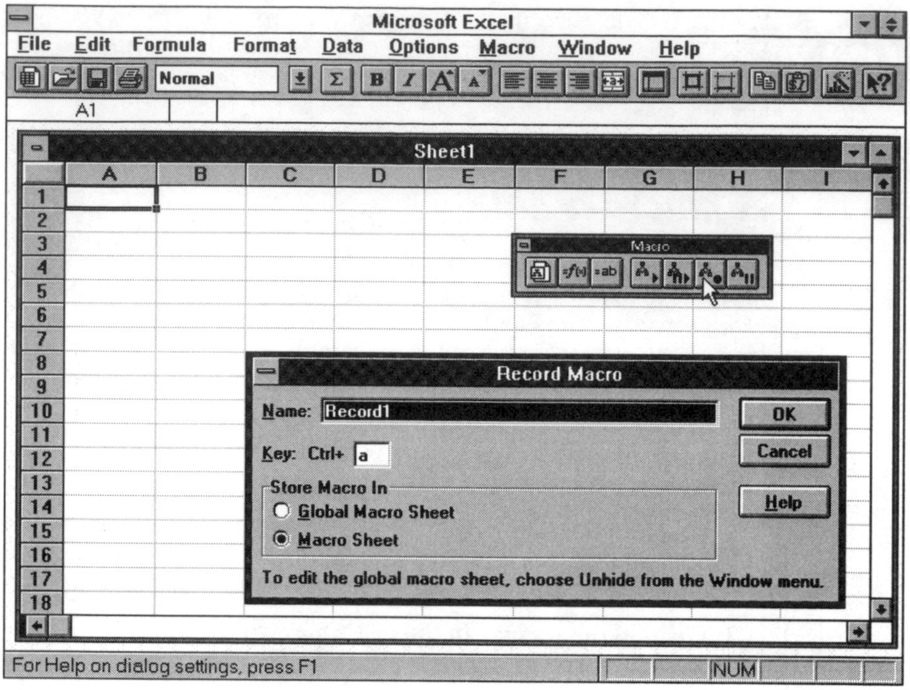

Microsoft Excel

File   Edit   Formula   Format   Data   Options   Macro   Window   Help

Normal

A1

Sheet1

	A	B	C	D	E	F	G	H	I
1									
2									
3						Macro			
4									
5									
6									
7									
8					Record Macro				
9									
10				Name: Record1			OK		
11									
12				Key: Ctrl+ a			Cancel		
13				Store Macro In					
14				○ Global Macro Sheet			Help		
15				● Macro Sheet					
16									
17				To edit the global macro sheet, choose Unhide from the Window menu.					
18									

Figure 10-1:
The Record
Macro
dialog box
and the
Macro
toolbar.

For Help on dialog settings, press F1   NUM

Shortcut keystrokes for Excel macros on the Macintosh consist of a
combination of the Option or ⌘ key and a single letter of the alphabet;
sorry, Excel for the Mac can't use the numbers 0 to 9!

5. Click on the Global Macro Sheet radio button if you want the macro to be available to you any time you use Excel.

If you want to save the macro in another macro sheet (which you have to
open before you can use the macro), skip this step.

Figure 10-2 shows the Record Macro dialog box just before the dialog box
was closed to record the macro. As you can see, the macro is named
Company_Name and the shortcut keystroke is Ctrl+N (for *Name*). Also, because the company name is so often added to new worksheets, the Global
Macro Sheet radio button is selected so that this macro is saved as a global
macro.

6. Choose OK or press Enter.

The Record Macro dialog box closes, and Excel shows you that the macro
recorder is turned on by displaying the message Recording on the status
line.

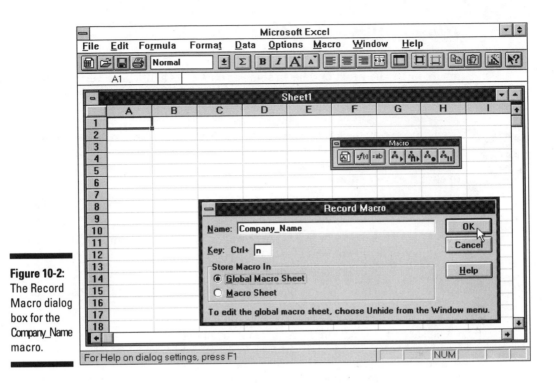

Figure 10-2:
The Record
Macro dialog
box for the
Company_Name
macro.

7. Perform the task you want to record.

For the Company_Name sample macro, you enter the company name in cell
A1. Next, select a new font and font size for it, increase the height of its row
(row 1), and then change the alignment to center it vertically.

As you record a macro, you can temporarily stop the recording if you need
to do some things you don't want included in the macro (like checking
some facts and figures in another part of the worksheet or a different document before you take any further steps in the macro). To temporarily inter-
rupt the recording of the macro, select the Stop Recorder command from
the Macro menu. When you're ready to once again resume the recording,
choose the Start Recorder command from the Macro menu.

8. Turn off the macro recorder when you finish the task the macro is sup-
posed to record.

Choose the Stop Recorder command from the Macro pull-down menu. The
Recording message disappears from the status bar.

Play you back with interest

After you turn off the macro recorder, you are ready to test the macro. If your macro enters new text or deletes some as part of its actions, be very careful where you test it out: be sure that the pointer's in a part of the worksheet where existing cell entries can't be trashed when you play back the macro.

If, when you play back the macro, you find it running amok, press Esc to stop the macro prematurely. Excel displays a macro error dialog box indicating the point at which the macro was interrupted. Click on the Halt button in this dialog box to shut the macro down.

✔ The easiest way to play back a macro is to press the shortcut keystrokes (Ctrl+N for the sample Company_Name macro).

✔ You can also play back a macro by choosing the Run command from the Macro pull-down menu; when the Run Macro dialog box appears, double-click on the name of the macro in the Run list box.

✔ Alternatively, select the macro name from the list box and choose OK or press Enter.

If you saved the macro in the global macro sheet (named GLOBAL.XLM — a document that's not created until the first time you save a macro as a global macro), you can run it any time after you start Excel. (Excel automatically opens the global macro sheet and hides it as soon as it starts up.) To see the contents of the global macro sheet, choose the Unhide command from the Window pull-down menu and then choose GLOBAL.XLM from the Unhide dialog box.

If you saved the macro in a new macro sheet, Excel gives the sheet a temporary document name like Macro1, Macro2, and the like. To save the macro sheet with a more descriptive document name, switch to the macro sheet by selecting it from the Window pull-down menu and then choose the Save As command from the File menu.

When you exit Excel, the program asks whether you want to save changes to any open macro sheets that contain unsaved changes. Be sure to click on the Yes button so that you can use the macros the next time you work in Excel.

January, February, June, and July

The second sample macro enters the 12 months of the year (from January to December) across a single row of the worksheet. After entering the names, the macro makes the names bold and italic before it widens their columns with the best-fit feature. Because this macro is used a lot less frequently than the one that enters and formats the company name, this macro is not saved in the global macro sheet.

As with the first macro, first find a place in a worksheet where you can enter and format the names. For this macro, use a new worksheet. You might also use a region of an existing worksheet that has 12 unused columns so that existing cell entries don't skew how wide the best-fit feature makes the columns. (You want the length of the name of the month to determine how wide to make each column.)

Figure 10-3 shows the Record Macro dialog box for this macro. Its name, appropriately enough, is Months_of_the_Year, and its shortcut keystroke is Ctrl+M. Notice that this time, the <u>M</u>acro Sheet radio button is selected.

Once the macro recorder is turned on, follow these steps:

1. **Enter the 12 months.**

   Type **January** in the first blank cell (cell A1), and then use the AutoFill feature to extend the names out to December (by dragging the fill handle across to cell L1).

2. **Then click on the Bold and Italic tools on the Standard toolbar.**

   This step adds these enhancements to the entries (the cell range A1:L1 with the month names is still selected).

3. **Select the range of columns containing the months (columns A through L) and double-click on the right border of one of them to widen the columns with best-fit.**

   Click in the first cell of the range to deselect the range of columns.

Now turn off the macro recorder and test the macro. To adequately test the macro, use some new columns to the right. For example, I tested this macro on the virgin columns N through Y in Sheet1 by placing the cell pointer in cell N1 and then pressing Ctrl+M. As expected, the macro entered in cell range N1:Y1 the names of the 12 months, January through December, and then dutifully made them bold and italic. Unfortunately, however, the macro did not select columns N through Y and use best-fit to match the column widths to their entries as I had intended. Instead, the macro selected and applied best-fit to columns A through L a second time, before selecting cell A1.

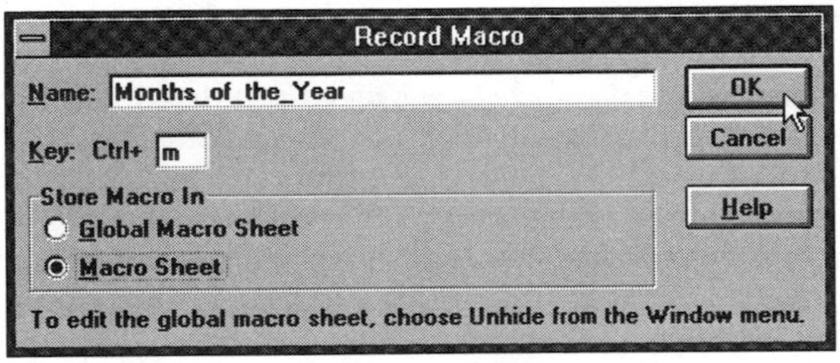

Figure 10-3:
The Record
Macro dialog
box for the
Months_of_
the_Year
macro.

The relative record

What, you may ask, causes the Months_of_the_Year macro to screw up so that it always applies best-fit to the columns A through L instead of applying best-fit to the columns where the 12 months were actually entered? Remember back in Chapter 4 where you learned about the differences between copying a formula with relative cell references and one with absolute cell references? There you learned that Excel adjusts cell references in copies of a formula unless you take steps to convert them to *absolute* (or unchanging) references.

When recording macros, just the opposite is true: when you select a cell range (or a range of columns in this case), Excel records the cell references as absolute references rather than relative ones. This is the reason that the Months_of_the_Year macro keeps selecting columns A through L instead of the columns where the months are entered.

To change this macro so that it works correctly, you have to rerecord the macro, this time using relative cell references. Open up a new worksheet where you can perform the actions to be recorded, choose the Record command from the Macro menu, and set up the Macro Record dialog box the same way you did when you first created the macro. Excel prompts whether you want to overwrite the existing macro; click on the Yes button.

Before you start recording the macro steps, choose the Relative Record command from the Macro pull-down menu. Then perform all actions (typing **January,** using AutoFill to generate the rest of the months, applying bold and italics to the cell range, and then selecting their columns and adjusting their widths with best-fit). This time, Excel records the command for selecting the columns with relative column references so that the selection of the columns in the macro is always relative to the cell range containing the names of the months.

After stopping the macro, test it in columns in the worksheet. Now, no matter where you enter the names of the months, the Months_of_the_Year macro always adjusts the widths of the columns that contain them.

The Vision Thing

You use macros to customize how Excel *works*. In addition, you can use macros to customize the way Excel *looks*. The options for controlling the appearance of Excel are split between the Display Options and the Workspace Options dialog boxes. Changes you make in either of these dialog boxes are saved as part of the program and become a standard part of the Excel environment.

Putting on a good display

Figure 10-4 shows the Display Options dialog box. To open this dialog box, choose the Display command from the Options menu. With display options, you can control how various elements appear in a *particular document window*.

You are already familiar with many of the check-box options in the Cells portion of the dialog box: Formulas displays formulas in the cells instead of the results (Chapter 6); Gridlines displays the column and row gridlines (Chapter 3); Outline Symbols displays the various row/column level, collapse, and expand symbols for a worksheet outline (Chapter 5); and Automatic Page Breaks displays page breaks after you preview or print a report on the screen (Chapter 6).

This leaves only two new cell-display options in the Display Options dialog box you might want to become familiar with:

✔ The Row & Column Headings check box controls whether or not the worksheet frame with the column letters and row numbers is displayed. Deselect this check box if you want to remove the display of the frame (seldom done).

✔ The Zero Values check box controls whether or not zero entries are displayed in the worksheet. Deselect this check box if you want to suppress the display of all zeros in a worksheet (as you might in a worksheet template if you don't want to see all those zeros in a new worksheet generated from the template).

Chapter 7 introduced you to the Objects radio buttons in the Display Options dialog box. Remember that these settings determine how graphic objects (including charts and other types of graphics) are displayed in the worksheet. To speed up the screen-response time when making editing changes, you can replace the detailed display of graphic objects with placeholders (shaded

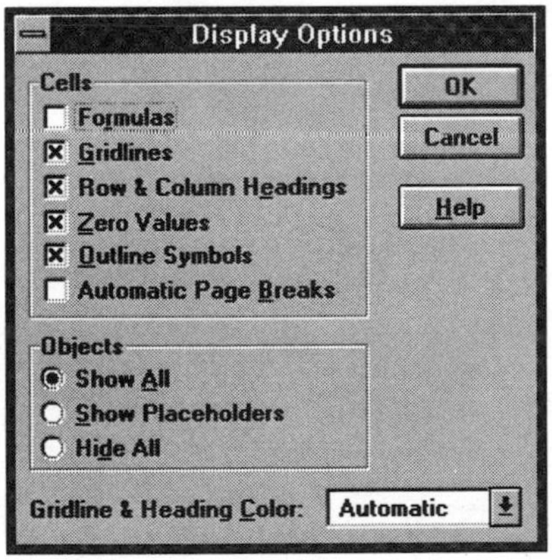

Figure 10-4:
The Display
Options
dialog box.

rectangles) by clicking on the Show Placeholders radio button. To hide the graphic objects altogether, click on the Hide All radio button instead. When you finish editing and are again ready to display the charts and graphics in a worksheet, click on the Show All radio button.

The last option in the Display Options dialog box is the Gridline & Heading Color option. This setting controls the color used to display the worksheet frame (column letters and row numbers) and the gridlines — provided that the Gridlines and Row & Column Headings check boxes are selected so that these two items are displayed.

The color setting is normally Automatic, meaning that Excel uses whatever color (black in most color schemes) is assigned to Window Text in the Windows Colors dialog box (accessed from the Control Panel). To change this setting in Excel, select the Gridlines & Heading Color option in the Display Options dialog box and then choose the appropriate color bar from the pop-up menu (for information on how to customize these color selections, see "Colors for every palette," later in this chapter).

Maintaining your own (Work)space

Figure 10-5 shows the options you control from the Workspace Options dialog box. To display this dialog box, choose the Workspace command from the Options pull-down menu. Below the Fixed Decimal option (which automatically fixes the decimal point at so many places — see Chapter 2 for details), you find a number of Display check-box options. These options control what elements are shown in the *entire Excel window* (as opposed to any one particular document window).

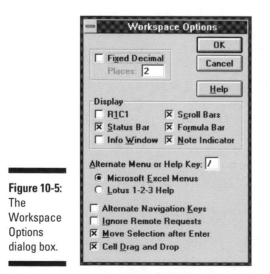

Figure 10-5:
The
Workspace
Options
dialog box.

The R1C1 check box controls whether the normal cell-reference system of column letter/row number is used (for example, B2) or the R1C1 system is used (for example, R2C2 instead of B2). Don't select the R1C1 check box unless you are used to a spreadsheet program that gives cell coordinates by row and cell number.

If you were reading the Technical Stuff sidebars in Chapter 1, you may recall some talk about Excel's support for an alternate system of cell references called the *R1C1 cell-reference system*. In this system, both the columns and rows in the worksheet are numbered, and the row number precedes the column number. For example, in this system, cell A1 is called R1C1 (row 1, column 1), cell A2 is R2C1 (row 2, column 1), and B1 is R1C2 (row 1, column 2).

The Status Bar, Scroll Bars, and Formula Bar check boxes control whether or not these different elements are displayed in the Excel window. If you ever start Excel and one of these elements is missing (you sure can't do too much to a worksheet when the formula bar's gone!), you'll know the reason. Just open the Workspace Options dialog box and select the appropriate check box to restore the missing part of the screen.

The Note Indicator check box determines whether or not Excel displays a dot when you add a note to a particular cell (see Chapter 5 for information on how to add notes). If you ever add a note to a cell and it's missing a little dot in its upper-right corner, you know right away that some wisenheimer has deselected the Note Indicator check box. All you have to do is reselect the box to restore the display (the only problem may be remembering that the Note Indicator check box is located in the Workspace Options dialog box).

The Info Window check box controls whether or not Excel displays information about the current cell on the screen in a separate window. The Info window lists the address of the current cell, its contents, and the text of any note added to the cell. You can use this option to review the contents of particular cells in a worksheet. Simply select the cell whose contents and note you want to review, open the Workspace Options dialog box, and click on the Info Window check box. To review the contents of another cell, select the cell (this causes the Info window to temporarily disappear from the screen), and then choose the Info window (or type its number) from the Window pull-down menu.

When you are finished doing your review with the Info window, close it by choosing the Close command from the File pull-down menu or by double-clicking on the Control-menu box on the Info window itself.

Colors for every palette

If you're fortunate enough to have a color monitor on your computer, you can spruce up the on-screen appearance of a document by applying various colors to different parts of worksheets or charts. Excel lets you choose from a palette of 16 predefined colors; you can apply these colors to specific cells, cell borders, fonts, or graphic objects (such as a particular data series in a chart or a text box or an arrow).

To apply a new color to a cell selection or a selected graphic object, choose the Patterns command from the object's shortcut menu or the Patterns command from the Format pull-down menu and then select the desired foreground and background colors. To change the color of the borders of a cell or cell selection, select the Border command from the shortcut menu or choose Border from the Format pull-down menu and then select the new color from the Color drop-down list box. To change the color of the font used in a cell selection or for a selected graphic object (such as a chart title or text box), choose the Font command from the object's shortcut menu or the Font command from the Format pull-down menu.

If the 16 predefined colors don't exactly suit your artistic tastes, you can customize colors on the palette. Although you can't place additional colors on the palette, you can change any or all of the predefined colors, depending on how ambitious you want to get.

To customize a color on the palette, choose the Color Palette command from the Options menu. The Color Palette dialog box appears. This box shows you the 16 existing colors (shown at the left of Figure 10-6). To modify any of the colors displayed in this dialog box, simply select one of the 16 color bars and then click on the Edit button.

Excel opens the Color Picker dialog box (shown to the right of the Color Palette dialog box in Figure 10-6) where you can modify the selected color. If you know something about color theory, you can modify the color by adjusting its hue (Hue), saturation (Sat), and luminosity (Lum) or its red (Red), green (Green), and blue (Blue) content.

If you don't have the foggiest idea what to do with these individual settings, you can still customize the color by dragging the crosshair around the color square or the triangle up and down the color bar on the right.

- ✔ When you drag the crosshair, you change the color's hue and saturation.
- ✔ When you drag the triangle up and down the color bar, you change the color's luminosity as well as its mixture of red, green, and blue.

As you change the color settings, check how the color will appear by looking at the Color/Solid rectangle in the Color Picker dialog box. When you've got the color just the way you want it, choose OK or press Enter to close the Color

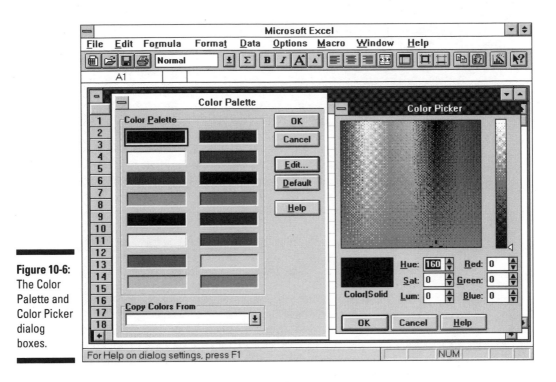

Figure 10-6:
The Color
Palette and
Color Picker
dialog
boxes.

Picker dialog box and return to the Color Palette dialog box. The custom color
now appears in this dialog box.

The Macintosh version of Excel has a color wheel that works almost identi-
cally to the Color Picker in the Windows version. To change the hue and
saturation, drag the black dot (with a hole in its center) to a new position
within the wheel. To modify the green, red, and blue content, drag the scroll
box or click on the scroll arrows in the accompanying scroll bar.

To customize other colors in the palette, select them and repeat the editing process. To restore the predefined colors to Excel, click on the Default button.

Once you customize the colors for a particular document, you can then copy
them to another document (saving you all the time and effort of modifying each
color individually again). To do this, open the document with the customized
palette, switch to the document to which you want to copy the palette, open
the Color Palette dialog box in the second document, and then select the first
document from the Copy Colors From drop-down list box.

Excel modifies the colors in the Color Palette dialog box to match the ones in
the document you selected. You can use them in the new document as soon as
you close the Color Palette dialog box by choosing OK or pressing Enter.

Chapter 11
Tooling Around

. . . .

In This Chapter

▶ How to customize the built-in toolbars in Excel

▶ How to create new toolbars

▶ How to assign macros to blank tools

▶ How to assign your own pictures to tools

. . . .

*U*p to now, you've used the tools on the various built-in toolbars that come with Excel 4.0 exactly as they were configured. Now it's time to learn how to customize the toolbars so that they contain only the tools you need and how to create toolbars of your own.

As you discover, the tools found on the built-in toolbars represent just a small part of the total number of tools supplied with Excel. You can add unused tools to any of the existing toolbars or use them to create new toolbars of your own design.

Not only can you customize Excel toolbars by creating new combinations using various built-in tools, you can also customize toolbars by assigning macros (see Chapter 10 for details) to any of the unassigned tools that come with Excel. Further, if none of the pictures used on the unassigned tools suit the function of the macro you're adding to a toolbar, you can use a graphic created in another program (such as a clip-art image or one that you created yourself with another graphics program).

The Right Tool for the Job

As you learned in previous chapters, Excel comes with a set of several built-in toolbars. Each toolbar consists of a group of tools that the program designers thought would be most helpful in getting particular tasks done. As you know, the Standard toolbar, the all-purpose toolbar, contains a wide variety of general tools for creating, formatting, and printing documents. It is automatically displayed at the top of the Excel window when you start the program.

Excel offers additional specialized toolbars: the Formatting, Utility, Chart, Drawing, and Macro toolbars.

- ✔ The Formatting toolbar brings together more formatting features than are available on the Standard toolbar (although it does contain some duplicate tools).

- ✔ The Utility toolbar has a potpourri of tools such as those for outlining, spell checking, and calculating the worksheet.

- ✔ The tools on the Chart, Drawing, and Macro toolbars are specialized for performing their particular mission, be it charting, adding graphics, or creating macros for a worksheet.

The Microsoft Excel 3.0 toolbar is included in version 4.0 as a courtesy to people who learned Excel 3.0 and got used to that arrangement of tools. (There was only one toolbar available in Excel 3.0!) If Excel 4.0 is the first version of Excel you've been exposed to, there's no need to use the 3.0 toolbar at all; its hodgepodge of tools are spread among the Standard, Drawing, and Utility toolbars (where they're more logically arranged by function).

Although the arrangements on most of the built-in toolbars may satisfy your needs, it's easy to modify the arrangement of any of them. For example, if there are tools you seldom or never use, replace them with ones more useful for the type of work you do. If you use a tool quite often but are not happy with its position in the toolbar — or even the toolbar it's on — move it to a more convenient position.

Before you can modify any toolbar, you must display it somewhere in the Excel window. You can display any toolbar by opening the toolbar shortcut menu and selecting the name of the desired toolbar. To hide a displayed toolbar, open the toolbar shortcut menu and select its name from the list again. Of all the toolbars, only the Chart toolbar appears and disappears automatically (it appears whenever you select a chart in the worksheet or open a chart window and disappears when you deselect the chart or switch back to a worksheet window).

After displaying the toolbar you want to modify, choose the Toolbars command from the toolbar shortcut menu or the Toolbars command from the Options pull-down menu. Excel displays the Toolbars dialog box (see Figure 11-1). Click on the Customize button in this dialog box. The Customize dialog box appears (see Figure 11-2).

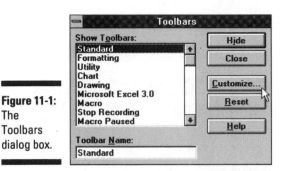

Figure 11-1:
The
Toolbars
dialog box.

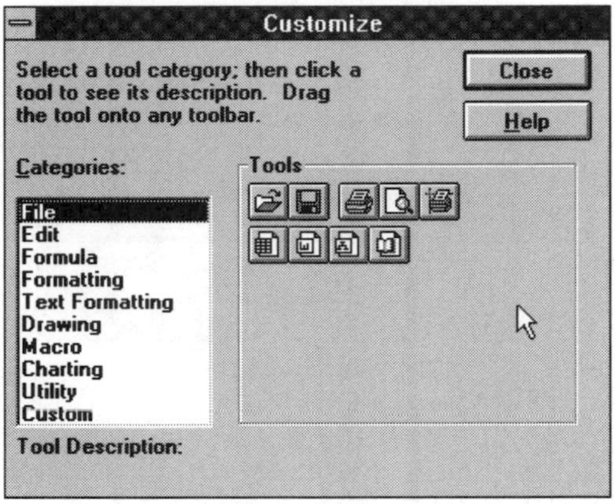

Figure 11-2:
The
Customize
dialog box.

Musical toolbars

Once the Customize dialog box is displayed, you can select individual tools on any of the displayed toolbars just as you would any graphic object in a worksheet window.

- ✔ To remove a tool after selecting it, simply drag the tool off the toolbar and release the mouse button.

- ✔ To reposition a tool on the same toolbar, drag it until it is positioned slightly in front of the tool it is to precede and release the mouse button.

- ✔ To move a tool to a different toolbar, drag it to the desired position on the new toolbar.

- ✔ To copy a tool to a different toolbar, hold down the Ctrl key as you drag the tool (you see a small plus sign next to the arrowhead pointer, just as you do when copying a cell selection with the drag-and-drop feature).

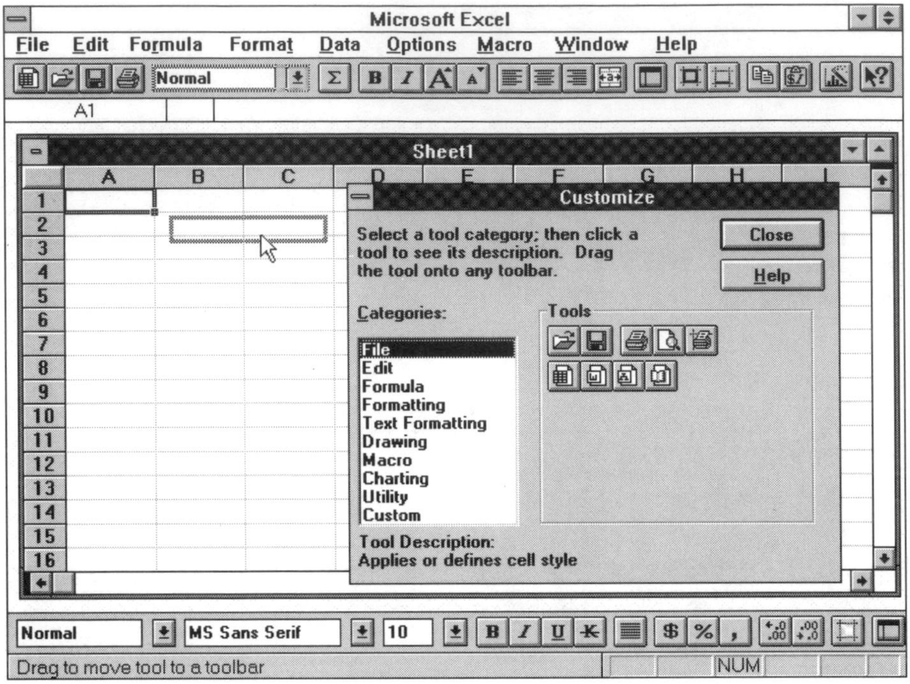

Figure 11-3:
Removing
the Style
box from the
Standard
toolbar.

Figure 11-3 shows the Standard toolbar with its Style box being removed (remember that the Style box tool is duplicated on the Formatting toolbar). After you drag this tool off the toolbar, Excel removes it when you release the mouse button. Figure 11-4 shows the Standard toolbar right after the mouse button was released.

Where's That Toolbar?

Whenever you exit Excel, the program saves the current toolbar layout and display shown in the Excel window in a special file named EXCEL.XLB. This file is located in the Windows directory (C:\WINDOWS on most computers).

To preserve the toolbar arrangement and display you had before you started making changes, use the Windows File Manager to locate and rename the old EXCEL.XLB file with a new filename (such as CUST.XLB). When you exit Excel, the program saves the current toolbar arrangement in the EXCEL.XLB file. If you renamed the original toolbar arrangement, you can switch between the original (CUST.XLB) and the customized (EXCEL.XLB) toolbars by selecting the desired XLB file in the Windows File Manager window and choosing the Open command from the File Manager's File pull-down menu.

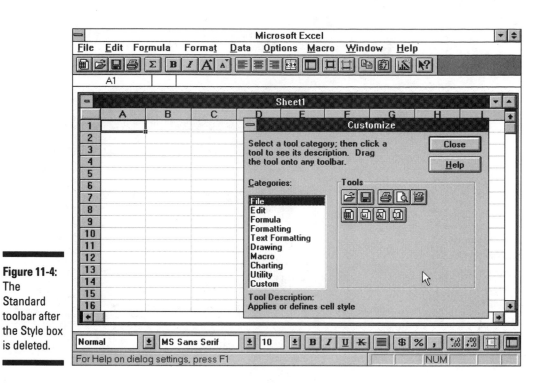

Figure 11-4:
The
Standard
toolbar after
the Style box
is deleted.

New tools for old jobs

Removing and moving tools are just a small part of the story of customizing the built-in toolbars. You'll find the capability to add new tools to the toolbars even more important. The new tools I'm talking about are tools that come with Excel but for some reason or other didn't make it to the built-in toolbars.

All the Excel tools are grouped into the following categories: File, Edit, Formula, Formatting, Text Formatting, Drawing, Macro, Charting, Utility, and Custom. All tools — with the exception of those in the Custom category — perform specific tasks. Custom tools are blank so that you can assign macros to them; see "A Blank Tool Is a Terrible Thing To Waste," later in this chapter.

   ✔ To display the tools for a particular category in the Tools area of the Customize dialog box, select the name of the category in the Categories list box.

   ✔ To find out what a particular tool does, click on the tool in the Tools area; Excel displays a short description of its function in the Tool Description area at the bottom of the dialog box.

   ✔ To add a tool to a toolbar, drag the tool from the Tools area to the desired position on the toolbar and release the mouse button.

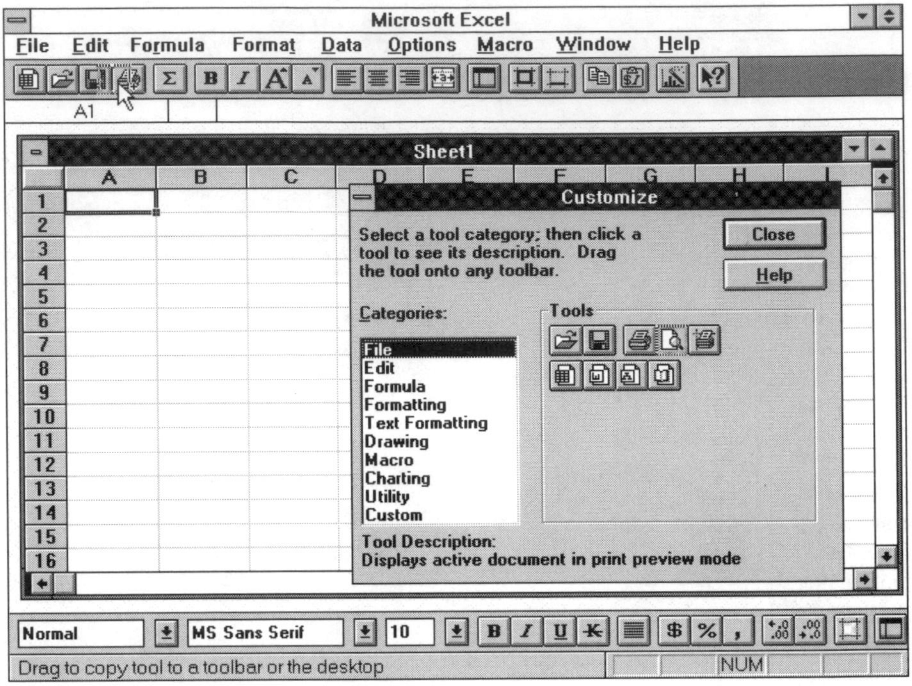

Figure 11-5: Adding the Print Preview tool to the Standard toolbar.

Figure 11-5 shows the process of adding a new tool to the Standard toolbar. In this figure, the Print Preview tool, from the File category, is being added to the Standard toolbar (right in front of the Print tool). Figure 11-5 shows the tool being dragged into position. Figure 11-6 shows the Standard toolbar after the Print Preview tool was added.

Spaced-out tools

You may have noticed how tools on various built-in toolbars are grouped together with little spaces before and after the group of tools. You too can group various tools when customizing a toolbar.

You can insert a space on the left or right side of a tool to separate it from other tools. To do this, drag the tool slightly in the opposite direction of where you want the space to appear (to the right to insert a space on its left side, and to the left to insert a space on its right side) and release the mouse button. Excel inserts a space before or after the tool you just dragged.

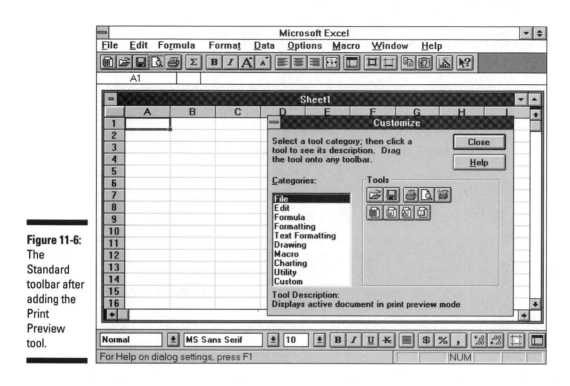

Figure 11-6:
The Standard toolbar after adding the Print Preview tool.

To delete a space in front of or after a tool so that the tool abuts the tool next to it, drag the tool in the appropriate direction until it touches or slightly overlaps the neighboring tool and then release the mouse button. Excel redraws the toolbar to remove the space from the tool you just dragged.

Toolbar restoration

Sometimes, you may make changes to a built-in toolbar that you don't want to keep. No matter what wild changes you make to a built-in toolbar, you can always restore the toolbar to its original form by choosing the Toolbars command from the Options menu, selecting the toolbar you want to restore from the Show Toolbars list box, and clicking on the Reset button.

If the toolbar you restored to its original form is not currently displayed, you can display it in the Toolbars dialog box by clicking on the Show button (the Show button appears if you click on a toolbar that is not displayed). If the toolbar is displayed, Excel redraws the toolbar with its initial layout. If you then want to hide the toolbar, click on the Hide button. Otherwise, just go ahead and close the Toolbars dialog box by clicking on the Close button.

A Toolbar for Every Occasion

You are by no means limited to the built-in toolbars that come with Excel. You can create your own toolbars to combine any of the available tools — those used in the built-in toolbars as well as those that are not.

To create a toolbar of your very own, follow these steps:

1. **Choose the Toolbars command from the Options pull-down menu.**

   The Toolbars dialog box appears.

2. **Enter a name for the new toolbar in the Toolbar Name text box.**

3. **Click on the Add command button or press the Enter key.**

   The Customize dialog box opens, and a small toolbar dialog box appears in the upper-left corner of the document window. Use the toolbar dialog box to add the tools to the new toolbar.

4. **Choose the category containing the first tool you want to add to the new toolbar from the Categories list box.**

5. **Drag the tool from the Tools area in the Customize dialog box to the tiny toolbar dialog box in the upper-left corner of the document window. Release the mouse button.**

6. **Repeat steps 4 and 5 until you have added all the tools you want to the new toolbar.**

   Once the tools are in the toolbar, you can rearrange and space them as you want.

7. **Press the Esc key or click on the Close command button to close the Customize dialog box.**

As you add tools to the new toolbar, Excel automatically widens the toolbar dialog box. When the dialog box is wide enough, the name you assigned to the toolbar appears in the title bar. If the toolbar dialog box starts running into the Customize dialog box, just drag the new toolbar down by its title until it's entirely clear of the Customize dialog box.

You can also create a new toolbar simply by dragging a tool from the Customize dialog box to somewhere in the document window and releasing the mouse button. Excel creates a new toolbar dialog box for the tool and assigns a name (like `Toolbar1`) to the toolbar. You can then add more tools to the new toolbar. Unfortunately, when you create a toolbar in this manner, you can't rename the toolbar later to give it a more descriptive title.

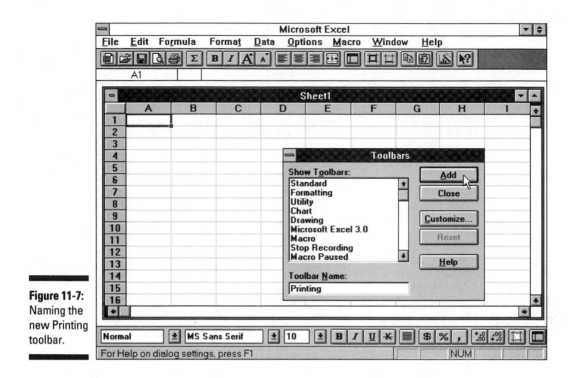

Figures 11-7 through 11-9 show the process of creating a new toolbar. Figure 11-7 shows the Toolbars dialog box after the name for the new toolbar was entered. Figure 11-8 shows the new toolbar after clicking on the Add button on the Toolbars dialog box. This action adds a blank toolbar dialog box and activates the Customize dialog box. Figure 11-9 shows the Printing toolbar after tools for spell checking, calculating, and printing a worksheet were added.

After creating a toolbar, you can display, hide, move, resize, and dock it just like you do any of the built-in toolbars. If you don't want to keep a toolbar you've created, delete it by opening the Toolbars dialog box and selecting the toolbar from the Show Toolbars list box. As soon as you select the name of a toolbar you created, Excel replaces the Reset button with a Delete button (the program won't let you delete any built-in toolbar). When you click on Delete, Excel displays an alert dialog box, in which you confirm the deletion by choosing OK or pressing Enter.

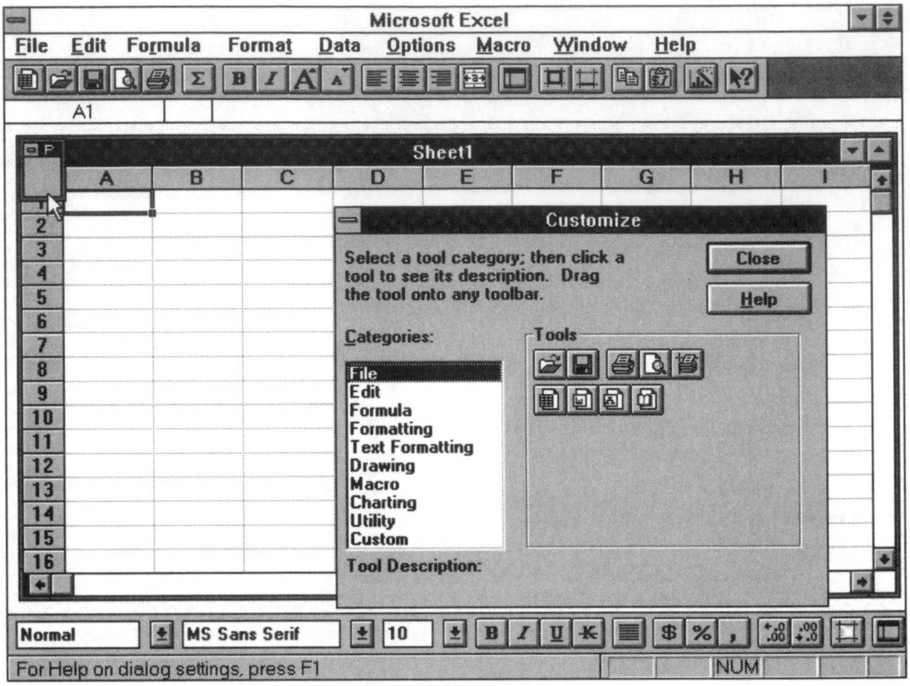

Figure 11-8:
The new Printing toolbar before tools were added.

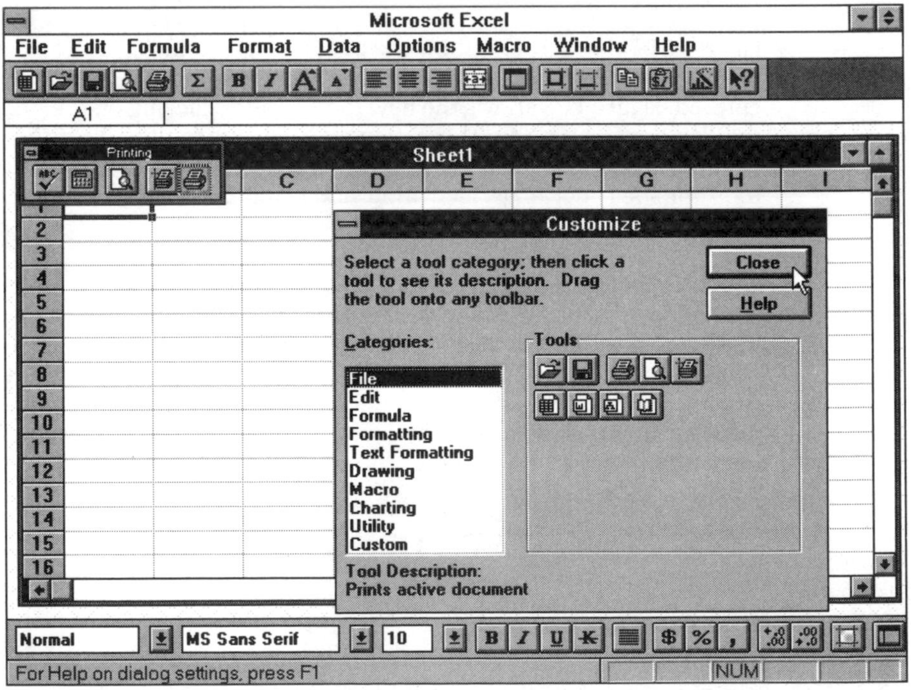

Figure 11-9:
The completed Printing toolbar.

A Blank Tool Is a Terrible Thing To Waste

As hinted at earlier, you can assign macros (covered back in Chapter 10) to tools and then place these tools on toolbars (either on one of the built-ins or on one of your own creation). That way, you can play back a macro by clicking on its tool. This is particularly helpful when you've assigned all 26 letters (A through Z) and 10 numbers (0 through 9) as shortcut keystrokes in a particular macro sheet.

Excel has a variety of blank tools in the Custom category (shown in Figure 11-10) to which you can assign macros. Unfortunately, these tools use a mixed bag of pictures, many of which you will be hard put to associate with the function of a macro. Come on, what's a happy-face macro supposed to do?!

To assign a macro to a tool, follow these steps:

1. **Display the toolbar where you intend to put the macro tool.**

   If the macro is not a global macro, open the macro sheet containing the macro you want to assign to a tool.

2. **Open the Customize dialog box.**

   Choose the Customize option from the toolbar shortcut menu or choose the Toolbars command from the Options pull-down menu and click on the Customize command button to open the dialog box.

3. **Select the Custom category from the Categories list box.**

   Excel displays the Custom tools shown in Figure 11-10.

4. **Drag one of the Custom tools in the Tools area to the desired position on your toolbar. Release the mouse button.**

   Excel opens the Assign To Tool dialog box (see Figure 11-11). From this dialog box, select or record the macro you want to assign to the tool.

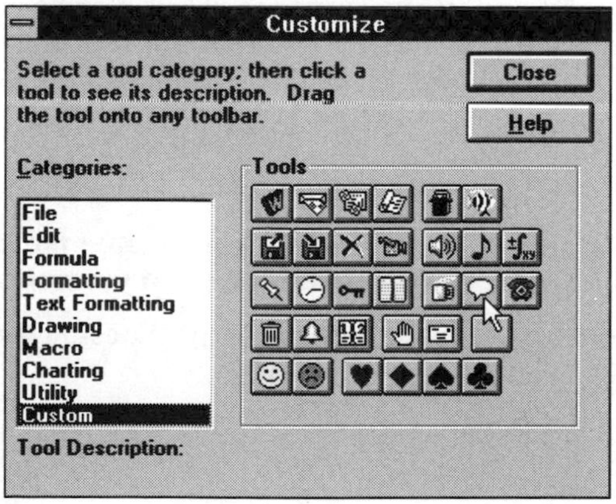

Figure 11-10:
The
Customize
dialog box
with the
Custom tools.

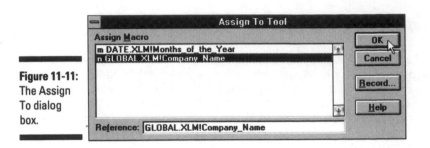

Figure 11-11:
The Assign
To dialog
box.

5. **Select or record the macro to be assigned to the tool.**

To assign an existing macro to the selected tool, double-click on the macro name in the Assign Macro list box or select the macro and choose OK or press Enter.

To record a new macro for the tool, click on the Record command button and record a macro just like you would record any other (see Chapter 10).

6. **Repeat steps 4 and 5 for every macro you want to assign to a tool.**

7. **Click on the Close button or press Enter to close the Customize dialog box.**

Just Put on a Happy Toolface

Fortunately, you aren't stuck with customized tools that have pictures of smiley faces, hearts, and coffee mugs. You can paste onto the face of a blank tool a picture from another source, like clip art or images you create with a graphics program like the Paintbrush application that comes with Windows.

When choosing pictures, keep in mind how small the face of the tool is. A graphic that looks fine in the graphics program at full size may be completely unintelligible when reduced to fit on the face of a tool. For that reason, make sure that whatever picture you choose is sufficiently simple to remain visible when made tiny.

To paste a picture onto a tool, follow these steps:

1. **First switch to the graphics program where you created the image or where you can view the image if you didn't draw it yourself.**

2. **Select the image and copy it to the Clipboard by choosing the Copy command from the File menu.**

3. **Switch back to Excel and display the toolbar with the custom tool whose face you want to change (this assumes you've already assigned the macro to one of the tools, as described in the previous section).**

4. **Open the Customize dialog box, click with the right mouse button on the tool whose face you want to replace to open the tool shortcut menu, and then choose the Paste Tool Face command.**

That's all there is to it. Excel replaces the face of the selected tool with the picture stored in the Clipboard, automatically resizing the image, if necessary, to fit the toolface.

Part VI
Excel Function Reference (for Real People)

The 5th Wave
By Rich Tennant

THUMP
THUMP
THUMP

RICHTENNANT

"I TELL YA I'M STILL GETTING INTERFERENCE—
— COOKIE, RAGS? RAGS WANNA COOKIE? —
THERE IT GOES AGAIN."

The part in which...

You learn how to use an array of Excel worksheet functions. You start with the most common functions such as SUM, AVERAGE, MAX, and MIN and you progress easily to the more specialized functions, such as the financial functions PV and PMT. This part takes you all the way to the logical functions of IF, AND, and OR!

Chapter 12
I Love Everyday Functions

In This Chapter

▶ How to use the SUM, PRODUCT, and SUMPRODUCT functions to total figures

▶ How to use the AVERAGE function to find the average of the values in a list

▶ How to use the COUNT function to find the number of items in a list

▶ How to use the MAX and MIN functions to find the highest and lowest values in a list

▶ How to use the ROUND function to round values up or down

▶ How to use the NOW function to stamp a worksheet with the date and time

*L*et's face it, if you do a lot of work with formulas, you need to become as familiar as possible with the built-in worksheet functions. As you undoubtedly recall, functions perform specific predefined calculations based on the type of information (called, for the sake of argument, *arguments*) you supply. To use an Excel function, all you have to know are the arguments the function takes.

This chapter looks at the more common, everyday functions that you use most often. It should come as no surprise that the bulk of these functions are statistical in nature. After all, bean-counting is what most worksheets are all about.

To SUM Up

You are already familiar with the SUM function, at least as it's applied with the AutoSum tool on the Standard toolbar. Being the most commonly used function in the world of spreadsheets, it's only fitting that this chapter start with a brief discussion of the way it can be used (besides with AutoSum).

Take a look at your *Excel Function Reference* (part of the documentation provided with your program). You will see the following form (which they insist on calling *syntax*) of the SUM function:

SUM(***number1***,*number2,...*)

As is standard practice, the arguments of the function (remember that the arguments are the text between the parentheses) are shown in italics, signifying that they are *variables*. This means that in place of the *number1* argument, you can substitute such things as the cell reference **B5**, the value **100**, or even a simple calculation like **100*B5**.

In the *Excel Function Reference,* any argument shown in ***bold italics*** is required to get the function to work at all. All the arguments in regular *italics* are optional ones you can use when you need them but are not required to get the blasted thing to work.

In terms of the SUM function, all this bold/italic/variable lingo simply means that you must substitute something for the ***number1*** argument but that the *number2* argument is purely optional. The three periods (a.k.a. ellipsis) after the *number2* argument just mean that you can add more number-type arguments to the SUM function (up to 30 total).

The thing that's the most confusing about the way the *Excel Function Reference* presents the arguments of the SUM function is that it's easy to misinterpret ***number1,*** *number2,* and so on as representing only individual values (whether they are in the cells referenced, numbers you enter, or numbers calculated by formulas). If you remember how you total up a row or column of numbers with the AutoSum tool, you will realize that this is clearly not the case. The ***number1*** and *number2* arguments can just as well refer to ranges of cells that contain numbers or formulas.

Suppose that you need to figure the grand total of the values in three different columns of a worksheet, say in the ranges C3:C15, G3:G19, and H2:H25. To do this with the SUM function, replace the ***number1*** argument with the first cell range C3:C15; the *number2* argument with the second cell range G3:G19; and the *number3* argument with the third range H2:H25. Do this by entering the following formula in the cell where you want the total of all the numbers in these cells to appear:

```
=SUM(C3:C15,G3:G19,H2:H25)
```

When creating formulas like this, keep in mind that you must separate each argument with a comma and no space. After you type the comma, remember that Excel allows you to select the individual cell ranges with the mouse or keyboard so that you don't have to type cell references unless you want to.

I'm Just a *PRODUCT* of My Times

You use the SUM function when you want to add values together. When you want to multiply them together, you use the PRODUCT function. This function works just like the SUM function; it follows the same form with the same kind of arguments:

```
PRODUCT(number1,number2,...)
```

Again, the *number* arguments can be cell ranges, individual cell references, or numbers that you enter or Excel calculates. You can include up to 30 such arguments in the function.

For example, if you want to know the product of a value in cell D4 and the value in cell E4, you can use the following PRODUCT function:

```
=PRODUCT(D4,E4)
```

Alternatively, you can create the following formula, which returns the very same result:

```
=D4*E4
```

You can use the PRODUCT function to multiply all the values in a range by each other. For example, if you want to find the product of all the values in the cell range B23:F23, enter the following function in the cell where you want the product:

```
=PRODUCT(B23:F23)
```

The *SUMPRODUCT*

The SUMPRODUCT function combines multiplication and addition. Figure 12-1 shows how you can use this function to add two columns of figures that are first multiplied together. This sample invoice for training and consulting services takes the numbers of hours in column B, multiplies them by the hourly rates in column C, and then places the results (the products) in column E.

The total due for this invoice is the sum of the products in column E. Cell E5 contains the formula with the SUMPRODUCT function. It calculates the amount due by multiplying the cells in column B with their counterparts in column C and then summing these products. The actual formula reads as follows:

```
=SUMPRODUCT(B7:B14,C7:C14)
```

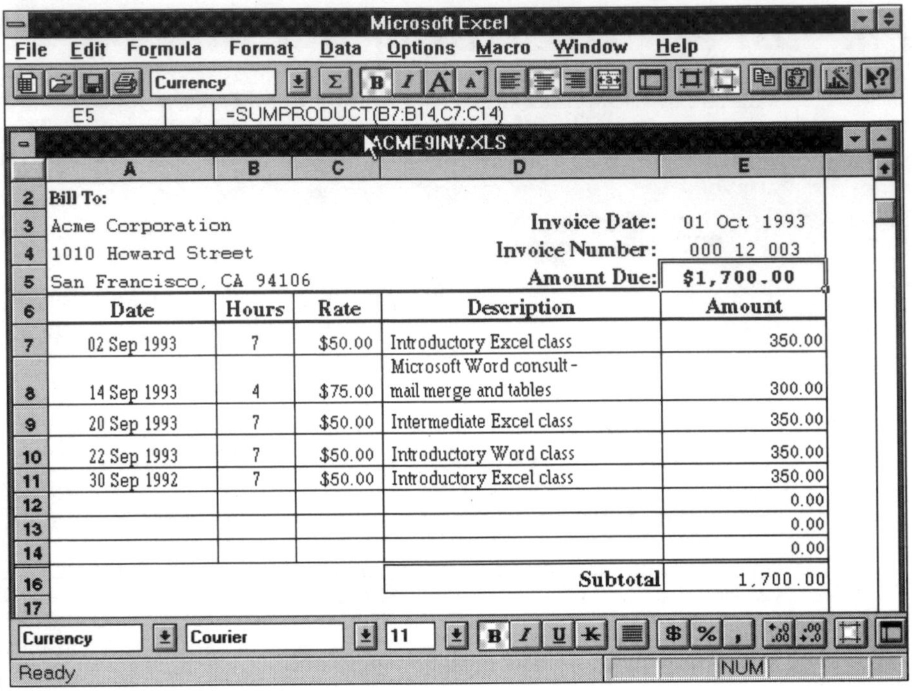

Figure 12-1:
Using
SUMPRODUCT
to multiply
across
columns and
then add
down rows.

In essence, this single formula does the same thing as the several formulas in column E that calculate the amount for each training or consulting session across each row and the standard SUM formula in E16 that totals the amounts in column E.

I'm Just Your AVERAGE Joe

The AVERAGE function calculates what's technically known as the *arithmetic mean*. The AVERAGE function follows the same form as the SUM function:

> AVERAGE(**number1,**number2,...)

Excel calculates the average by adding up all the values specified by the number arguments, counting how many values there are, and dividing the total by the result of this tally (just like you were taught in grade-school math class).

The only catch with using the AVERAGE function is how Excel counts (or miscounts, depending on how you look at it) the number of entries. The easiest way to explain this little quirk is by way of an illustration.

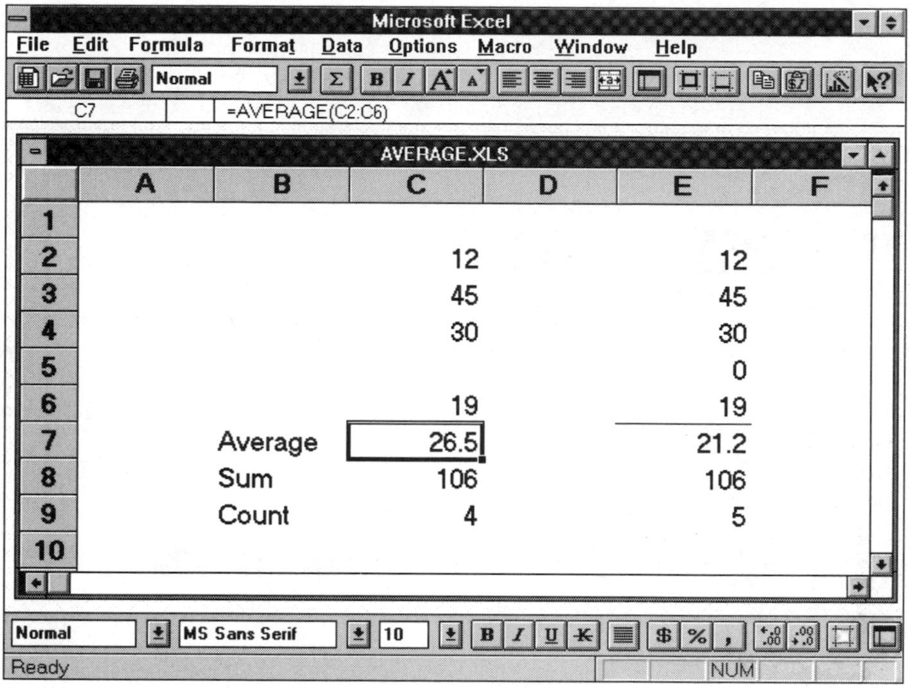

Figure 12-2:
Averaging, summing, and counting two ranges identical except for a zero.

	A	B	C	D	E	F
1						
2			12		12	
3			45		45	
4			30		30	
5					0	
6			19		19	
7		Average	26.5		21.2	
8		Sum	106		106	
9		Count	4		5	
10						

Microsoft Excel — C7 = AVERAGE(C2:C6) — AVERAGE.XLS

Figure 12-2 shows two ranges of figures in separate columns. The numbers are identical except that the fourth cell of the first range (C6) is empty and the fourth cell in the second range (E6) has a 0 in it.

Although the addition of 0 to the second range makes no difference in the sum of these two ranges, it does change the count (zeros in cells are counted but blank cells are not). The different count is the reason Excel calculates a different average for the second range. What a difference a zero makes!

COUNT Me In!

The COUNT function is useful when you are dealing with a really large cell range and need to know how many items it contains. For example, you can use it to get an accurate count of the number of records in a database.

The COUNT function, like the AVERAGE function, counts cells that contain a zero; it does not count blank cells. If you designate a range that has blank cells, the COUNT function doesn't include them in the tally. This means that when counting records in a database, make sure that you don't select a field (or column) that is missing a lot of entries; this skews the result. Excel would tell you that you have fewer records than you actually do because it would fail to count the records that are missing entries in that particular field. For this reason, always choose a field that has an entry in each and every record; select its cell range as the argument for COUNT.

The MEDIAN Strip

Sometimes, instead of knowing the average value in a series of numbers, you want to know the *median value,* that is, the value truly smack dab in the middle of the series. There are just as many values higher than the median as there are values lower. The MEDIAN function is set up just like the AVERAGE function (which in turn is set up just like the SUM function).

How To Get the MAXimum in the MINimum Time

Although the MEDIAN function gives you the value in the middle of those in a list of arguments, the MAX function returns the highest value and the MIN function returns the lowest one. Like COUNT, these two functions are most useful when dealing with a large range of values (especially when they haven't been sorted) and you need to quickly find out which one is highest or lowest. The MAX and MIN functions take the same argument series as the SUM or AVERAGE functions.

Going ROUND About

In Chapter 3, I made a great big deal about how formatting values in a worksheet affects only their display on the screen and not how they are stored in the cell. Back then, I recommended clicking on the Precision as Displayed check box in the Calculations Options dialog box to have Excel round off all the values to the number of decimal places allowed by their number formats. The only trouble with this solution is that it is universal (it applies to all values in the entire worksheet).

For those situations where you only want to round off *some* of the values in a worksheet, use the ROUND function instead. The ROUND function has two required (see, they're shown here in ***bold italic*** type) arguments that are entered according to the following pattern:

ROUND(***number,num_digits***)

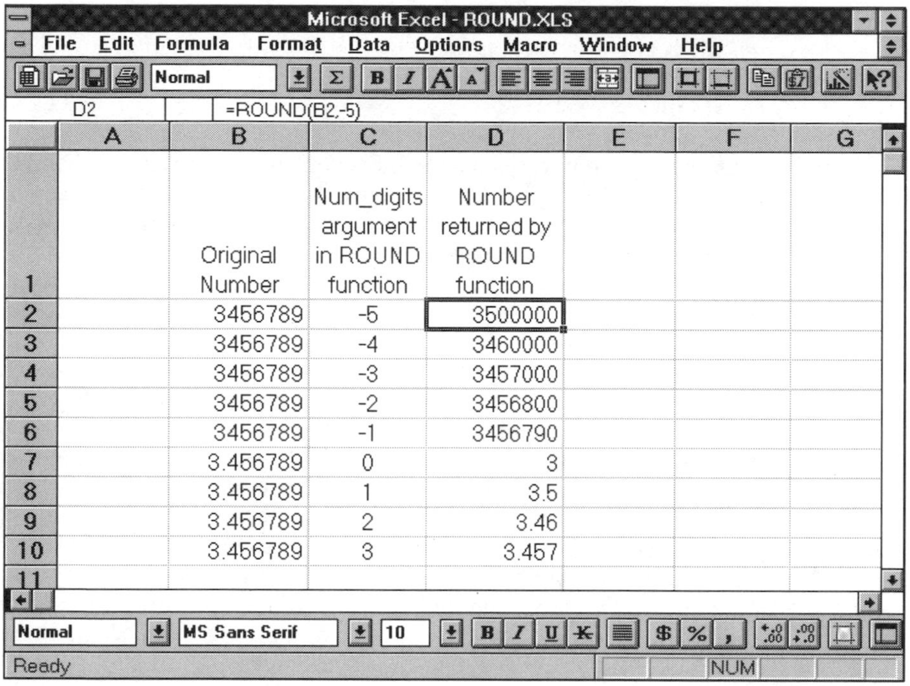

Figure 12-3:
Using the ROUND function with positive and negative values.

The first argument, *number,* indicates the value you want rounded (or its cell reference). The second argument, *num_digits,* indicates the number of decimal places you want in the rounded number.

To round a value to a specific number of decimal places, enter a positive value for the *num_digits* argument that represents the number of decimal places to round to the right of the decimal point. To round a decimal value to the nearest whole number (integer), enter **0** as the *num_digits* argument. To round off a whole number, enter a negative value for the *num_digits* argument that represents the number of places to round to the left of the decimal point.

Figure 12-3 shows the effect of changing the *num_digits* argument when rounding two values: one a large whole number with seven digits and the other a small decimal value with six decimal places.

I Want It NOW!

The last function you learn in this chapter is the date function NOW that returns the current date and time to the worksheet. Because this function gets its date and time information directly from your computer's clock/calendar, it doesn't require any arguments; you simply enter (or paste) the following in a cell when you want to stamp the worksheet with the current date and time:

```
=NOW( )
```

When you first enter this function, Excel returns both the date and time and selects a date/time format that displays them both. If today were September 3, 1993, and you entered the NOW function in a cell exactly at 3:45 PM, the following entry would appear in the worksheet:

```
9/3/93 15:45
```

You can modify what the NOW function displays in the cell by selecting a new date or time format. If you aren't concerned with the time and only want to see the date, open the Number Format dialog box and choose a format code in the Date format category. On the other hand, if you don't care about the date and only want to see the time, choose one of the format codes available for the Time format category.

When using the NOW function, keep in mind that Excel enters the date and time in a dynamic fashion. Each time the program recalculates the worksheet, it updates the date and time. To test this out, enter the NOW function in a blank cell of a worksheet, wait a minute, and then press F9 (the Calculate Now key) or click on the Calculate tool on the Utility toolbar. When Excel recalculates the worksheet, the program updates the time in the cell with the NOW function, adding a minute to it.

This automatic updating is useful when you have formulas you need to keep up to date (or up to the minute, as the case may be). For example, you can use the NOW function to calculate the age of various equipment purchases by subtracting the date of purchase from the current date supplied by the NOW function. This gives you the number of days; divide by 365.25 to convert this figure into years. Every time you open the worksheet with these formulas, Excel updates them, advancing the ages by the number of days that elapsed between now and the last time you worked with the document.

But what if you don't want the date or time to change? What if your purpose is to record a sale or a purchase in a worksheet that you made today? In such a case, you freeze the date/time entry made with the NOW function so that it is never again subject to being updated. To do this, position the cell pointer in the cell with the NOW function, press F2 to activate the formula bar, press F9 to calculate the formula, and then press the Enter key.

To freeze a formula on the Mac, press ⌘+U to activate the formula bar and then press ⌘+= (or F9 if you have the extended keyboard) to calculate the formula.

Chapter 13
Functions for the More Adventurous

* *

In This Chapter

▶ How to use financial functions like PV and PMT

▶ How to use text functions like PROPER

▶ How to use lookup and reference functions like VLOOKUP

▶ How to use logical functions like IF

* *

*B*eyond the pale of run-of-the-mill functions like SUM, AVERAGE, and NOW lies a whole world of specialized worksheet functions. This chapter exposes you to a few of these functions in the financial, text, lookup and reference, and logical categories. Although some of these worksheet functions are full of arguments that at first glance may look like so much gobbledygook, you don't have to be a spreadsheet guru to comprehend and use them. Believe me, you are ready for them, even if you have limited experience with formulas and functions.

When learning a more complex function, concentrate mostly on what arguments it uses and their order of appearance in the function. Then look at which arguments are required and which are optional. By mastering the few functions covered in this chapter and learning how their calculations can help you create more effective worksheets, you will be in great shape for proceeding on your own to learn any other functions you need later on.

High Finance (or I Want My PMT)

As you'd expect from any good spreadsheet program, Excel offers many sophisticated financial functions. This section takes a look at just two of the most common financial functions: PV (Present Value) and PMT (Payment).

You use the PV function to calculate the current worth of a series of future payments (the very definition of the term *present value*). You can use this function to determine whether the return on a particular investment is a sound one considering the initial cost to you. The PV function follows this pattern:

PV(***rate,nper,pmt,****fv,type*)

Note that the arguments ***rate*** (the interest rate per period), ***nper*** (the total number of payment periods), and ***pmt*** (the payment made each period) are all required. (Any required argument to a command is formatted in ***bold italic type.***)

The arguments *fv* (future value or cash balance you want to realize after the last payment) and *type* (0 if the payment is made at the end of the period, 1 if made at the beginning) are optional. (These optional arguments are formatted in plain *italic* type.) If you omit the *fv* argument, Excel assumes that the future value is 0 (as would be the case when paying off a loan). If you omit the *type* argument, Excel assumes that you make the payment at the end of each period.

When using other financial functions like PV (such as PMT, FV, and the like), first make sure that you're dealing with a true *annuity*, which in English just means an investment where all the payments are the same and are made at regular intervals (such as monthly, quarterly, or yearly). The best example of an annuity is a fixed-rate mortgage where you pay a set amount each month for a continuous fixed period. An adjustable-rate mortgage, however, where the interest rate is adjusted annually or semi-annually, is not a true annuity.

REMEMBER

For the Sake of Argument

If you were paying attention in Chapter 12, you know this already. If not, here's a refresher on functions and arguments.

Functions perform specific predefined calculations based on the type of information (called *arguments*) you supply. To use an Excel function, all you have to know are the arguments the function takes. When you put together the function itself and the arguments it takes, you have what is called the *syntax* of the function.

Remember the SUM function? Here's the syntax:

SUM(***number1****,number2,...*)

The arguments (the text between the parentheses) of the function are considered *variables*, and they are shown in italic type. In computer lingo, a *variable* is something you replace with your own thing. So in place of the ***number1*** argument, you can put in cell references like **B5**, values like 100, or even a calculation like **100*B5.**

When an argument is shown in *bold italics*, this means that you *must* use something for that argument or the function won't work at all. All the arguments in regular *italics* are optional ones you can use when you need them but are not required to get the function to work.

The three periods (a.k.a. ellipsis) after the *number2* argument just mean that you can add more number-type arguments to the SUM function (up to 30 total).

The most common mistake when working with annuity functions is not expressing the *rate* argument in the same time units as the *nper* argument. Most interest rates are quoted as annual rates, but payment periods are monthly. When this is the case, divide the annual interest rate by 12 to get a monthly interest rate to go with the monthly payments. Likewise, if you make payments on a monthly basis but the payment period is in years (as in 30 for a standard 30-year mortgage), convert this payment-period value into equivalent monthly periods by multiplying the value by 12.

With annuities, keep in mind that the money you pay out is always expressed as a negative number (hey, it comes out of your account); money you earn (for example, a dividend you put in your account) is expressed as a positive number. For example, if you make an initial investment of $5000 for a term-life insurance policy, it shows up as –5000 on your worksheet but as 5000 on the insurance company's worksheet.

Figure 13-1 shows an example of the PV function used to determine the advisability of an annuity by comparing its present value against the initial cash outlay. Here you evaluate the present value of an annuity that pays $150.00 at the end of each month for the next 10 years at an annual interest rate of 7 percent. Assume an initial investment of $10,000. The PV function calculates the present value for this annuity at $12,918.95. Because you're only required to invest $10,000, it's not such a bad deal at all.

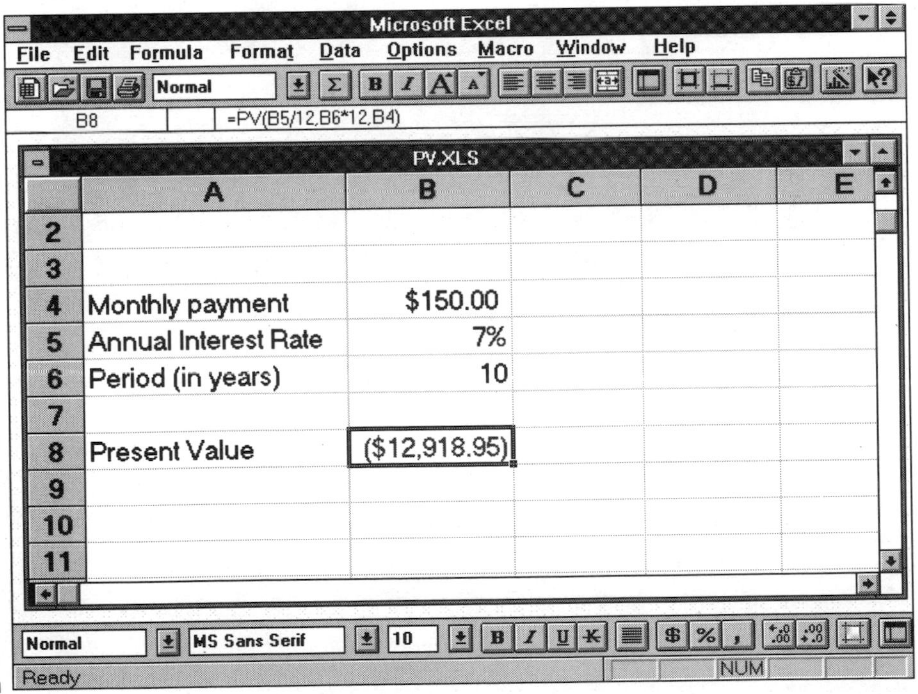

Figure 13-1:
Using the PV function to determine the present value of an annuity.

The PMT function is another commonly used annuity function. It uses almost the same arguments as the PV function except that instead of a *pmt* argument (which is what the function finds), it requires a *pv* (present value) argument as follows:

PMT(***rate,nper,pv,****fv,type*)

The PMT function is most often used to calculate loan payments. To do this, you enter the interest rate as the ***rate*** argument, the period as the ***nper,*** and the amount of the loan as the ***pv*** argument. Again make sure that the ***rate*** and ***nper*** arguments are expressed in the same time units (monthly interest rate and a number of monthly payments if you want to calculate the amount of a monthly payment).

Figure 13-2 shows an example of the PMT function used to calculate a monthly mortgage payment. Here the amount of the loan is $150,000, the annual interest is 8.75%, and the period is a standard 30 years. To calculate a monthly mortgage payment, you must divide the annual interest in cell B5 by 12 and multiply the period in years in cell B6 by 12.

You can also use the PMT function to determine how much you need to save to realize a certain return. For example, suppose that you just had a new baby and you want to start a college savings account for her. To find out how much to

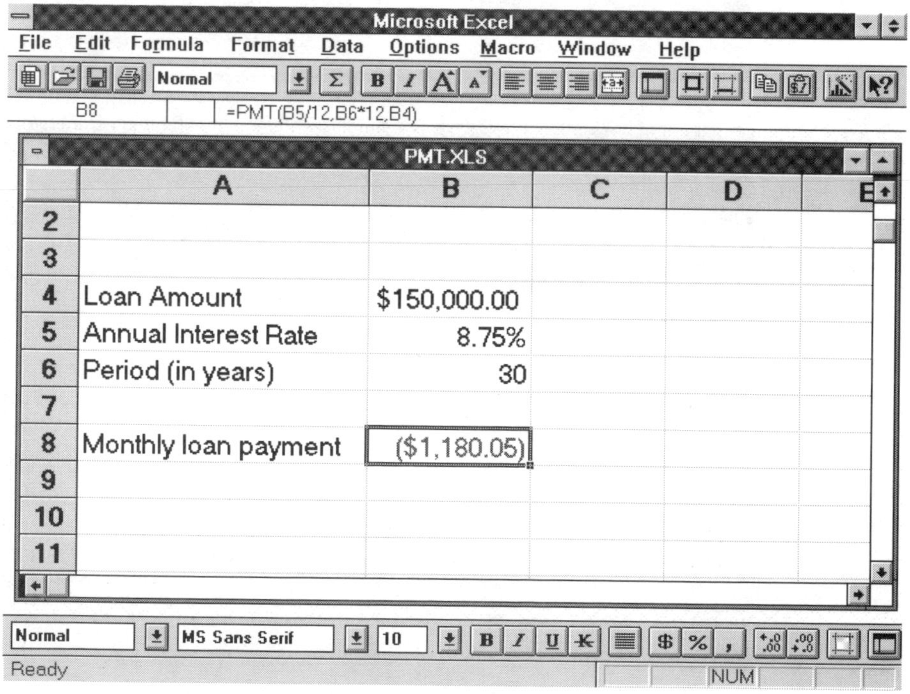

Figure 13-2:
Using the
PMT
function to
calculate a
monthly loan
payment.

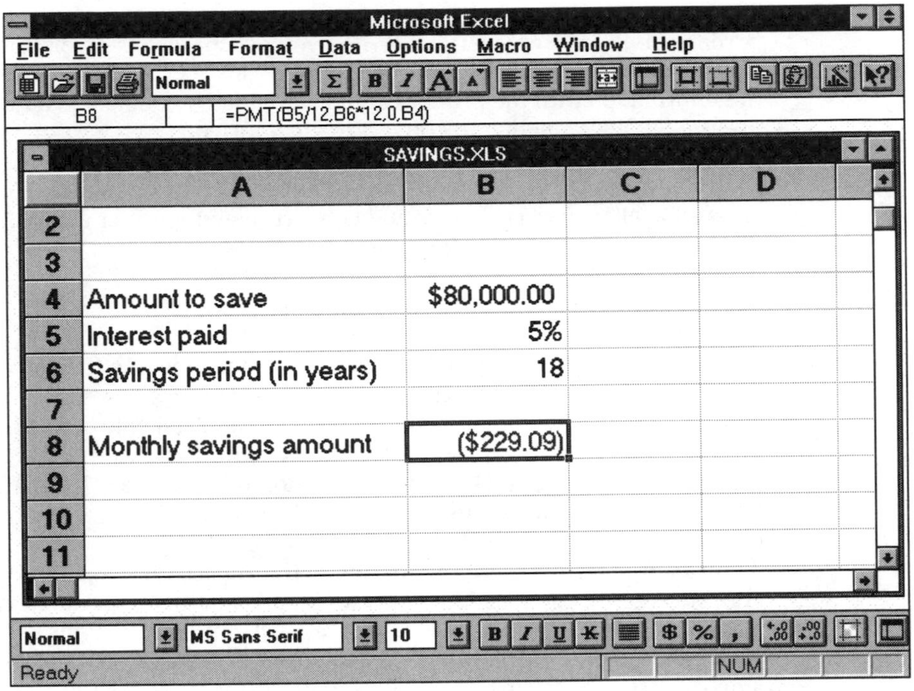

Figure 13-3:
Using the PMT function to calculate the amount you must save each month to reach a target.

put away each month, assuming a tuition for a four-year state school of $80,000 (this may not be enough in 2010 dollars!) and assuming that you have 18 years to save, you can use the PMT function as shown in Figure 13-3. If the bank pays you 5 percent interest on your savings account (as of this writing, this may be a bit optimistic), you have to cough up a mere $229.09 a month. (Does she really have to go to a four-year school?)

In the example that uses the PMT function to determine how much to save to reach a target amount, you enter 0 as the required *pv* (present value) argument; the target amount ($80,000) is entered as the optional *fv* (future value) argument.

Just for the Text of It

It may come as a bit of a surprise to learn that you can construct formulas to perform various operations on text because you associate calculations quite naturally enough with numbers. Well, believe it or not, Excel includes a wide variety of text functions that work exclusively with text arguments. Admittedly, you may not find too many uses for the text functions unless you routinely import information into worksheets from other sources like on-line services (Dow Jones, for example) where you don't have any control over how the information is formatted.

For example, you may find that the text you take into the worksheet is in all uppercase or all lowercase letters. (When you purchase lists on disk, it's not unusual to find the text in all uppercase letters.) Instead of wasting time retyping the information with the proper capitalization (say, for mailing labels), you can use the PROPER function to convert the text for you.

Figure 13-4 shows how you can use the PROPER function to take a list of names entered in all uppercase letters and convert them to proper capitalization. To do this, enter the following formula in cell B2:

```
=PROPER(A2)
```

Then use the AutoFill feature to copy this formula down to the cell range B3:B12. The PROPER function capitalizes all the entries correctly — with the exception of Diane's Place, where the function mistakenly capitalizes the S following the apostrophe. (The PROPER function uppercases the first letter of each word as well as any letter that does not follow another letter.) You must fix this by editing this particular entry on the formula bar.

If you want to do any more processing to the entries (like sorting or spell-checking them), you must convert the formulas to their calculated values (that means converting them to text in this case). If you don't convert the formulas to their text values, Excel sorts or spell-checks the formulas in the cells (for example, =PROPER(A2) in cell B2) instead of the text (J.D. Powers).

Figure 13-4: Using the PROPER function to change to proper capitalization.

To convert the formulas to their text values, first select the cell range containing the PROPER functions: B2:B12. Then choose the Copy command from the Edit menu. In this example, you can replace the original all-capitals range with the properly capitalized text by pasting the values in range B2:B12 over the original entries in range A2:A12. (Remember that Excel always replaces existing entries with new ones.)

To replace the uppercase range with the properly capitalized range, select the first cell, A2, in response to the prompt to select the destination. Then press Enter or choose Paste. To convert the PROPER formulas to their text values, choose the Paste Special command from the Edit menu and click on the Values radio button before you choose OK or press Enter (see Figure 13-5).

Figure 13-6 shows the results of pasting the values in the cell range A2:A12. Notice the contents of cell A2 on the formula bar: it reads *J.D. Powers* just as though you typed it rather than calculated it with an Excel function! After you copy the values to the range A2:A12, delete the formulas in B2:B12, edit the entry in cell A10, and save the worksheet.

In addition to the PROPER function, Excel includes an UPPER and LOWER function.

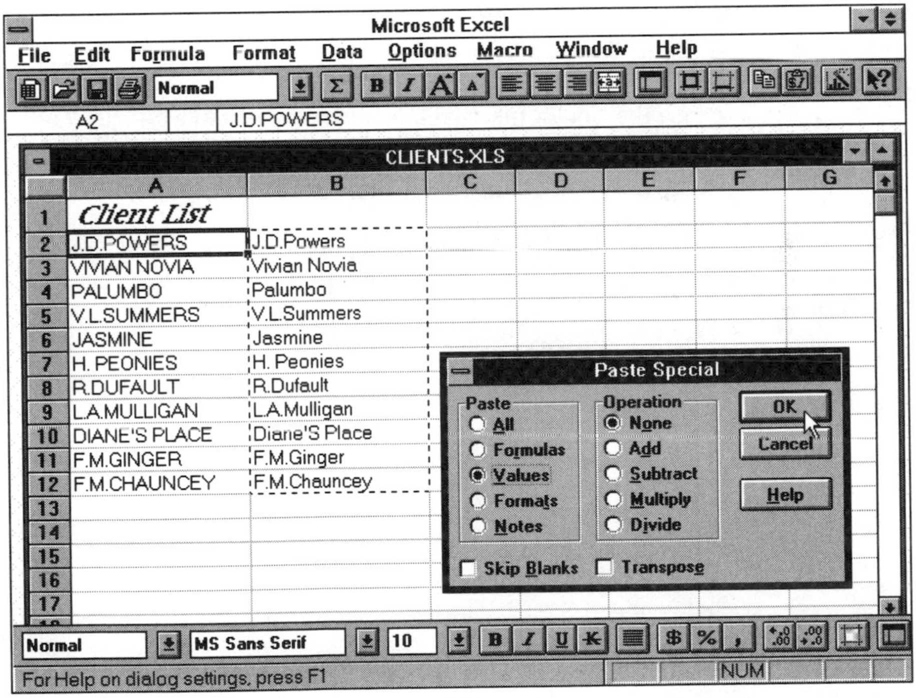

Figure 13-5: Using the Paste Special dialog to convert to text the formulas with the PROPER function.

```
                        Microsoft Excel
 File   Edit  Formula  Format  Data  Options  Macro  Window  Help
 [toolbar]  Normal  [Σ] B I A A  [alignment buttons]

        A2              J.D.Powers

                           CLIENTS.XLS
          A                B           C      D      E      F      G
 1   Client List
 2   J.D.Powers       J.D.Powers
 3   Vivian Novia     Vivian Novia
 4   Palumbo          Palumbo
 5   V.L.Summers      V.L.Summers
 6   Jasmine          Jasmine
 7   H. Peonies       H. Peonies
 8   R.Dufault        R.Dufault
 9   L.A.Mulligan     L.A.Mulligan
10   Diane'S Place    Diane'S Place
11   F.M.Ginger       F.M.Ginger
12   F.M.Chauncey     F.M.Chauncey
13
14
15
16
17

 Normal    MS Sans Serif    10    B I U K    $ % ,
 Select destination and press ENTER or choose Paste          NUM
```

Figure 13-6: The worksheet after the formulas are converted with the PROPER functions.

⊭ Use the UPPER function to convert the text in a cell to all uppercase letters.

⊭ Use the LOWER function to convert the text to all lowercase letters.

Just as with the PROPER function, remember to convert UPPER or LOWER formulas to their resulting text if you want to perform further text-based operations like sorting on these cells.

Hey, Look Me Over!

The functions in the lookup and reference category offer a rather mixed bag of tricks. The reference-type functions return various kinds of information about your current whereabouts in a worksheet. (These functions are primarily used in complex macros that process worksheet data. The functions keep track of the current cell position during the processing.) The lookup-type functions can return particular information from a series or a table of data and, therefore, have more practical uses for the average spreadsheet user.

The most common lookup functions are VLOOKUP (for vertical lookup) and HLOOKUP (for horizontal lookup). Both these functions look up a particular value or text entry in a table and return related information from the table. They differ simply in the way they do their work:

- The VLOOKUP function moves vertically down the rows of the lookup table looking for matching information in the first column of the table.

- The HLOOKUP function moves horizontally across the columns of the lookup table looking for matching information in the top row of the table.

To get an idea of how handy these lookup functions can be, I'll tell you how I would go about using the VLOOKUP function to return specific information to a worksheet. Figure 13-7 shows a simple vertical lookup table that relates the description and cost of various items sold to an item number. When setting up a vertical lookup table like the one shown in this figure, always place the information you will use to look up other information in the first (leftmost) column. In this case, because you want to look up the description and cost of an item by its item code, make the column with the item codes the first column.

Further, after entering all the information in a lookup table, you must sort its data in ascending order using the first column of the table as the sorting key (see Chapter 8 for a complete rundown on sorting with keys).

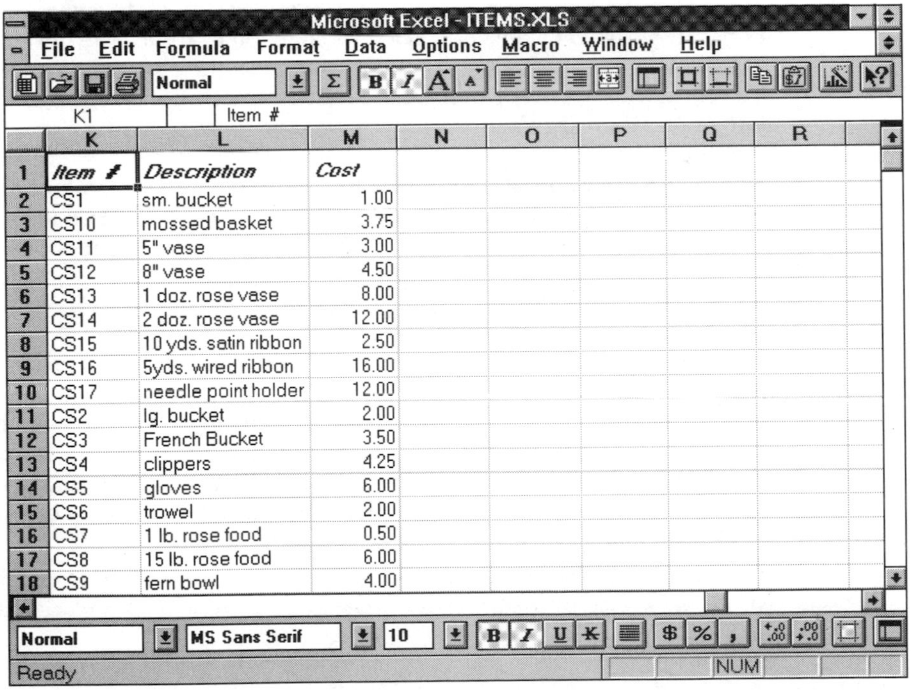

Figure 13-7:
The lookup table with descriptions and costs of items arranged by item number.

Item #	Description	Cost
CS1	sm. bucket	1.00
CS10	mossed basket	3.75
CS11	5" vase	3.00
CS12	8" vase	4.50
CS13	1 doz. rose vase	8.00
CS14	2 doz. rose vase	12.00
CS15	10 yds. satin ribbon	2.50
CS16	5yds. wired ribbon	16.00
CS17	needle point holder	12.00
CS2	lg. bucket	2.00
CS3	French Bucket	3.50
CS4	clippers	4.25
CS5	gloves	6.00
CS6	trowel	2.00
CS7	1 lb. rose food	0.50
CS8	15 lb. rose food	6.00
CS9	fern bowl	4.00

Notice how the lookup table in Figure 13-7 is sorted in ascending order by item number. At first glance, this table looks out of order because the information on item CS10 immediately follows that for item CS1 instead of that for item CS2 as you might expect. This sort order occurs because the item numbers mix text and numbers and are therefore entered as labels rather than as numbers. Excel does not sort them according to the values they contain but rather in alphabetical order.

After you create and sort the information in a vertical lookup table, use the VLOOKUP function to return any of its information. The arguments for this function are as follows:

VLOOKUP(***lookup_value,table_array,col_index_num***)

The ***lookup_value*** argument in this example is the cell that contains the item number you want to look at in the sample table in Figure 13-7.

The ***table_array*** argument is the cell range that contains the lookup table itself (excluding column headings). In this example, the lookup table occupies the cell range K2:M18. To make things simpler, give the range the name ***cost_table;*** you can use this range name in place of the ***table_array*** argument rather than using actual cell references.

The ***col_index_num*** argument is the number of the column in the lookup table whose information you want returned by the VLOOKUP function. To derive this number, count the columns in the lookup table from left to right, starting with 1. For example, if you want the VLOOKUP function to return the description of an item when you enter its item number, enter **2** as the ***col_index_num*** argument. To return the cost of the item instead of the description, enter **3** as the ***col_index_num*** argument.

Figure 13-8 shows the use of the VLOOKUP function to return both the description and the cost of an item by entering just the item-number code. Cell B3 contains the following formula:

```
=VLOOKUP(A3,cost_table,2)
```

This formula takes the item-number code you enter in cell A3 (item number CS8 in Figure 13-8) looks it up in the first column of the lookup table named ***cost_table*** (cell range K2:M18) by moving vertically down the rows in the first column of the table. When Excel locates the item number in the lookup table, the VLOOKUP function returns the description entered in column 2 of this table (15 lb. rose food for item number CS8) to cell B3, the one containing the VLOOKUP function.

Figure 13-8:
Using the
VLOOKUP
function to
return the
description
and cost of
an item from
the lookup
table.

The cost of the item is returned to cell C3 from the lookup table with a similar formula that uses the following VLOOKUP function:

```
=VLOOKUP(A3,cost_table,3)
```

The only difference between the formula in cell C3 and the one in cell B3 is that the second formula uses **3** as the *col_index_num* argument; therefore, this formula returns the cost (6.00 for item number CS8) instead of the description.

By copying the formulas entered in cells B3 and C3 down their columns, you can continue to use the lookup table to find the description and cost for whatever item-number code you enter in column A.

Is That Logical? (or IF I Were a Rich Man)

The logical-functions category is a small group, consisting of just six functions in all. These function are noted for their black-or-white result. A logical function can return only one of two possible results: TRUE or FALSE.

The most common and powerful of the logical functions is the IF function. This function is particularly powerful because it can test for a particular condition in the worksheet and use one value if the condition is true and another value if the condition is false.

To use the IF function, you use the following arguments:

IF(*logical_test*,*value_if_true*,*value_if_false*)

The *logical_test* argument can be any expression that, when evaluated, returns either a TRUE or FALSE response. For example, you can test whether a value in one cell is greater than or equal to a particular value by entering this formula:

```
=IF(B2>=1000)
```

In this example, the IF condition is TRUE when B2 contains a value of 1000 or larger; the condition is FALSE when the value in cell B2 is anything less than 1000.

To indicate what value should be used when the *logical_test* argument is TRUE, enter the *value_if_true* argument right after the *logical_test* argument. To indicate what value should be used when the *logical_test* argument is FALSE, enter the *value_if_false* argument right after the *value_if_true* argument.

For example, if you want Excel to put the value 100 in the cell when B2 contains a value greater than or equal to 1000, but you want 50 in the cell when B2 is less than 1000, enter the following formula:

```
=IF(B2>=1000,100,50)
```

If you want Excel to put 10% of the value in B2 in the cell when B2 contains a value greater than or equal to 1000 but only 5% of the value when B2 is less than 1000, enter the following formula:

```
=IF(B2>=1000,B2*10%,B2*5%)
```

Although you usually want an IF function to enter or calculate a particular value when the *logical_test* argument returns TRUE or FALSE, you can also have the IF function enter text. Do this by entering the different text alternatives as the *value_if_true* and *value_if_false* arguments of the IF function. For example, suppose that you want Excel to enter the text A grand or better when B2 contains a value greater than or equal to 1000 but the text Less than a grand when B2 contains any lesser value. To do this, enter the following formula:

```
=IF(B2>=1000,"A grand or better","Less than a grand")
```

When you use text as the *value_if_true* or *value_if_false* argument, you must enclose the text in a pair of double quotation marks (" ").

Figure 13-9 shows a typical use for the IF function. Here the IF function calculates the price of a particular item based on what it costs. If the item costs $5.00 or more, the markup is 75%. If the item costs less than $5.00, the markup is only 50%.

You enter the IF function that determines which markup percentage to use in calculating the price in cell D3 as follows:

```
=IF(C3>5,C3*1.75,C3*1.5)
```

In this formula, the *logical_test* argument, C3>5, tests whether or not the price entered in cell C3 is greater than $5.00.

✔ If the value is greater than $5.00, Excel uses the *value_if_true* argument, C3*1.75 (it's 1.75 because the resulting price is the total cost plus a markup of 75% of that cost), and returns the calculated value to cell D3.

✔ If the value is less than $5.00, Excel uses the *value_if_false* argument, C3*1.50 (total cost plus a markup of 50% of that cost), and returns the calculated value to cell D3 instead.

In this particular example, the IF function calculates the price in cell D3 according to the *value_if_true* argument because the cost in cell C3 is $6.00.

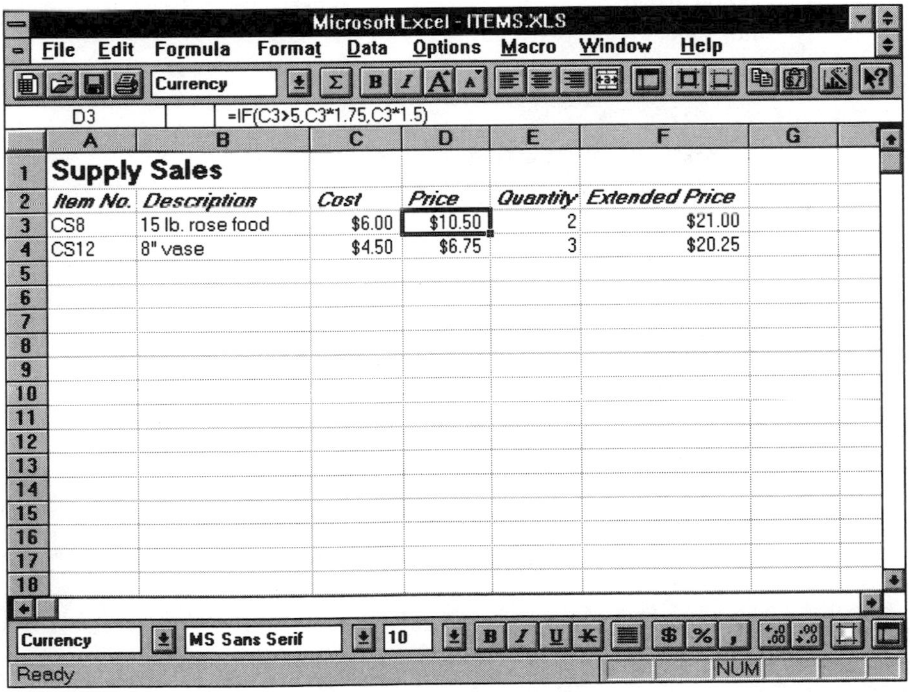

Figure 13-9: Using the IF function to determine the price of an item.

After creating the IF formula in cell D3, you can copy it down column D to calculate the prices for the other items in the worksheet based solely on the cost. Figure 13-9 shows the formula copied to cell D4. There, the IF function returns the price according to the *value_if_false* argument because the cost in cell C4 is only $4.50.

Part VII
The Part of Tens

The 5th Wave — By Rich Tennant

"COMPATABILITY? NO PROBLEM. THIS BABY COMES IN OVER A DOZEN DESIGNER COLORS."

The part in which...

You learn that like a baker's dozen, in which 12 equals 13, 10 doesn't always equal 10! Each chapter in this part is a list of 10, or 7, or 13 neat things to know. And as a special bonus, the final chapter includes 10,000 (well, more or less) keystroke shortcuts guaranteed either to save you time or drive you crazy, or both!

Chapter 14
Ten Beginner Basics

- ✔ To start Excel from the Windows Program Manager, double-click on the Microsoft Excel program icon in the Microsoft Excel 4.0 window.

- ✔ To start Excel from DOS when Windows isn't running, type **win**, press the spacebar, then type **excel**, and press Enter.

- ✔ To open a document at the same time you start Excel, locate the document in the Windows File Manager and double-click on it.

- ✔ To locate a part of the worksheet that you cannot see on-screen, use the frame that labels the columns and rows. Columns are assigned letters of the alphabet from A through IV; rows are assigned numbers from 1 through 16384.

- ✔ To find out exactly where you are working in the Excel worksheet, check the current cell reference in the formula bar. The cell reference lists the column letter followed by the row number, such as A100.

- ✔ One of the fastest ways to move the cell pointer to a particular cell is to use the Goto feature: press F5, type the cell reference, and press Enter.

- ✔ To choose one of the many commands on the pull-down menus, click on the menu name (on the menu bar) to open the menu, and then click on the command name on the pull-down menu.

- ✔ If the command name on a pull-down menu is followed by three periods (an ellipsis), you know that a dialog box will appear when you select the command. If the command name is dimmed, you know that the command is temporarily out of commission.

- ✔ To choose a command from a shortcut menu, click on the object (cell, toolbar, chart, and so on) with the right mouse button to open the menu, and then click on the command with the left mouse button.

- ✔ To get help on the use of a command or a tool, click on the Help tool on the Standard toolbar; then use its question mark pointer to click on the command or tool for which you want help.

- ✔ To exit Excel when you're done working with the program, choose the Exit command from the File menu or press Alt+F4. If you have documents open that contain unsaved changes, Excel will ask if you want to save the changes in each document before closing and returning to Windows.

Chapter 15
Ten Excel Commandments

- ✔ Work small. To conserve computer memory, construct tables close to each other, rather than separating them with more than a single blank column or row.

- ✔ Formulas always, always, always, always, every time, and without exception begin with = (the equal sign).

- ✔ You enter dates and times as values by using date or time formats that Excel knows. Entering dates and times as values instead of as text enables you to use dates and times in calculations performed by formulas.

- ✔ Use AutoFill to extend a series either sequentially or by a specific value. Select the cells with the initial entries and then drag the fill handle in one direction (right, down, left, or up).

- ✔ Repeat after me: select, then apply; select, then apply; select, then apply; select, then apply. This is the key to successful formatting. *Select* the cell(s) and then click on the formatting tool or choose the appropriate menu command to *apply* the desired formatting to the selection.

- ✔ Whenever you goof up and things don't go as planned, use the Undo feature *right away*. Excel offers many ways to get to this command: you can choose the Undo command from the Edit menu, press Ctrl+Z, or click on the Undo tool on the Utility toolbar (if it's displayed).

- ✔ Leave yourself little to-do lists and markers by adding notes to cells. To zip around among all the notes, use the Select Special command on the Formula menu and then tab from note to note.

- ✔ Here's a way to use your right brain a little now and then: assign names to cells and cell ranges. Descriptive names can help you recognize the information in your worksheet; to get to it quickly, use the Goto command with the range names.

- ✔ If you're working a large worksheet with a lot of formulas and Excel gets really sluggish on you, switch to manual recalculation. Then when you're ready to recalculate a worksheet (like right before you print it), press F9 or click on the Calculate Now tool on the Utility toolbar.

- ✔ Click on the Criteria button in a data form to search for records that meet particular search criteria (such as all the records where the City is Chicago or the ZIP Code is 94500).

- To keep several Excel documents together at all times, bind them in a workbook document. When you open a workbook file, Excel automatically opens all the documents listed on its Workbook Contents sheet.

- Record a macro to automate any task you commonly perform in Excel.

Chapter 16
Ten Printing Pointers

. . . .

✔ Preview the Coming Attractions at a theater near you: You can take a good look at what you've created with the Zoom feature, check the header and footer, change margins and column widths, take care of certain setup items, and print the thing from the Print Preview window. (Any editing goes on back in the document window.)

✔ When the big moment finally arrives, click on the Print tool on the Standard toolbar to print the whole shebang. To print more than one copy, to print just selected pages, to print without cell notes, or to print just cell notes, use the Print dialog box.

✔ To print only particular areas of a worksheet, select the cell range or ranges, choose the Set Print Area command from the Options menu, and then click on the Print tool.

✔ The Page Setup dialog box is indispensable: this is where you dictate what goes on which page and how. Depending on your printer, this dialog box is where you handle the dyslexic wonders of page ordering on a spreadsheet, set orientation, paper size, margins, scaling, visibility of gridlines, column and row headings, black-and-white cells, not to mention headers and footers.

✔ Use headers and footers in multipage reports to print running heads (in the top or bottom margin of each page) that contain such information as the page number, date and time of printing, and document name.

✔ Designate headings in rows and columns of the worksheet as print titles to appear at the top or left edge of each page in multipage reports by using the Set Print Titles command on the Options menu.

✔ To keep Excel from splitting up information that should always appear together on the same page, insert a manual page break by selecting the Set Page Break command from the Options menu.

Chapter 17
Ten Clever Customizers

- ✔ To chart a cell range of data, select the range, wave your ChartWizard wand, and follow the yellow-brick road through its five steps. You will soon have the chart of your choosing.

- ✔ Whenever you select a chart in a worksheet, you have instant access to tools on the Chart toolbar. You can use the tools in the Chart toolbar to change the chart type at any point, and add gridlines, text, arrows, and a legend.

- ✔ Double-click on a chart, and its very own Chart window opens. While in the Chart window, you can edit to your heart's content, changing the chart type (go ahead — try 3D just this once!), rearranging axes, adding text boxes and arrows, and formatting the various objects in the chart.

- ✔ Call up the Drawing toolbar and use its tools to add more graphics to your charts and worksheets.

- ✔ To customize the elements displayed in a particular document window, use the options in the Display Options dialog box (you open it by selecting the Display command from the Options pull-down menu).

- ✔ To customize the elements displayed in the Excel window, use the display options in the Workspace Options dialog box (you open it by selecting the Workspace command from the Options pull-down menu).

- ✔ To customize the colors in a document's color palette, click on the Edit button in the Color Palette Options dialog box (you open it by selecting the Color Palette command from the Options pull-down menu).

- ✔ You can customize any of Excel's built-in toolbars by removing tools, adding new tools, or rearranging the tools.

- ✔ To create a new toolbar, open the Toolbars dialog box, enter the name for the new toolbar in the Toolbar Name text box, and click on the Add button. Drag the tools you want on your new toolbar from the Customize dialog box to the appropriate position on the new toolbar, and then close the Customize dialog box.

- ✔ To assign a macro to a tool, open the Customize dialog box, and then choose Custom from the Categories list box. Next drag the tool you want to hitch the macro to all the way to the desired toolbar. Finally, double-click on the name of the macro in the Assign To Tool dialog box.

Chapter 18
Ten Welcome Warnings

✔ Remember that you can have NO SPACES in filenames and that filenames can have no more than eight characters. Excel automatically adds the file extension XLS to the main filename you assign to your document, indicating that the file contains an Excel worksheet. When you edit a filename (as opposed to replacing it), be careful that you leave the XLS extension intact.

✔ If you introduce a space into an otherwise completely numeric entry, Excel categorizes the entry as text (indicated by its alignment at the left edge of the cell). If you feed that entry into a formula, the text classification completely throws off the answer because text entries are treated like zeros (0) in a formula.

✔ When nesting parentheses in a formula, pair them properly so that you have a right parenthesis for every left parenthesis in the formula. If you do not include a right parenthesis for every left one, Excel displays an alert dialog box with the message `Parentheses do not match` when you try to enter the formula. After you close this dialog box, Excel goes right back to the formula bar, where you can insert the missing parenthesis and press Enter to correct the unbalanced condition. By the way, Excel always highlights matched parentheses.

✔ You can reenter edited cell contents by clicking on the enter box or pressing Enter, but you can't use the arrow keys. When you are editing a cell entry, the arrow keys only move the insertion point through the entry.

✔ Be sure that you don't press one of the arrow keys to complete a cell entry within a preselected cell range instead of clicking on the enter box or pressing Enter. Pressing an arrow key deselects the range of cells when Excel moves the cell pointer.

✔ The Undo command on the Edit menu changes in response to whatever action you just took. Because it keeps changing after each action, you've got to remember to strike when the iron is hot, so to speak, by using the Undo feature to restore the worksheet to its previous state *before* you choose another command.

✔ Deleting entire columns and rows from a worksheet is risky business unless you are sure that the columns and rows in question contain nothing of value. Remember, when you delete an entire row from the worksheet, you delete ***all information from column A through IV*** in that row (and you can see only a very few columns in this row). Likewise, when you delete an entire column from the worksheet, you delete ***all information from row 1 through 16384*** in that column.

✔ Be careful with global search-and-replace operations; they can really mess up a worksheet in a hurry if you inadvertently replace values, parts of formulas, or characters in titles and headings that you hadn't intended to change. As a precaution, ***never undertake a global search-and-replace operation on an unsaved worksheet.*** Also, verify which radio button in the Look at setting of the Replace dialog box is checked before you begin. You can end up with a lot of unwanted replacements if you leave the Part radio button activated when you should have chosen the Whole button. If you do make a mess, choose the Undo command to restore the worksheet. If you don't discover the problem in time to use Undo, close the messed-up worksheet without saving the changes and open the unreplaced version you saved — thanks to reading this warning!

✔ To make it impossible to remove protection from a document unless you know the password, enter a password in the Password text box of the Protect Document dialog box. Excel masks each character you enter with a dot. After you choose OK, Excel makes you reenter the password before protecting the document. From then on, you can remove protection from a worksheet only if you can reproduce the password exactly as you assigned it (including any case differences). Be very careful with passwords. If you forget the password, you cannot change any locked cells and you cannot unlock any more cells in the worksheet.

✔ You *cannot* use the Undo feature to bring back a database record you removed with the Delete button! Excel is definitely *not* kidding when it uses words like `deleted permanently`. As a precaution, always save a backup version of the worksheet with the database before you start removing old records.

✔ When doing group editing, don't select another open document window until you're ready to disband the group. If you select one just to check something, you have to define which documents are to be group-edited all over again. Try to think ahead when you arrange the windows and select the one you really want to work with before you go to the trouble of defining the group.

Chapter 19
Ten Ways To Work Smarter, Faster, and Get That Promotion!

- ✔ Close that window and you won't catch cold! As soon as you've finished with a document window, put it away so that you have enough memory to keep working on the documents you do have to keep open.

- ✔ Name any often used cell range in the worksheet and then use its name to move to it, select its cells, or print it. Remember, you can press the Goto key (F5), and then select the range name in the Goto dialog box. When you choose OK, Excel will not only move you to the first cell in that range, but select all its cells as well.

- ✔ Don't waste all day scrolling through a seemingly endless table of data. Instead, use the Ctrl+arrow key (or End, then arrow key) to jump from one edge of the table to another or to jump from the edge of one table to the other.

- ✔ Switch to manual recalc when editing a really big worksheet so that Excel doesn't keep getting in your way by recalculating all those #*@%! formulas every time you make a simple editing change. Then, when you've made all your changes, don't forget to bring the worksheet up-to-date by pressing the Calc Now key (F9) — that's what the Calc thing on the status bar is trying to tell you!

- ✔ Lose the graphics in the worksheet by replacing their display with place-holders when you find that Excel just can't keep up with your movements in a worksheet. Screen response time is greatly improved by this trick — just don't forget to put the graphics back before you print the worksheet, or you'll end up with shaded rectangles where the pictures ought to be!

- ✔ When making editing and formatting changes in your Excel documents, don't overlook the shortcut menus attached to the things that need fixing. This can save a lot of time that you would otherwise waste searching the menus on the menu bar to find the editing or formatting command you need. Also, don't forget how much time you can save by displaying and using the tools on the various toolbars to get things done!

✔ Before making changes to an unfamiliar worksheet, use the <u>Z</u>oom command from the <u>W</u>indow menu to zoom out so that you can get a good idea of how the information is laid out. When inserting or deleting cells in an unfamiliar worksheet, resist the temptation to insert or remove entire columns and rows which can damage unseen tables of data. Instead, just insert or cut out the cell ranges in the region you're working in — you know, think globally, but act locally!

✔ After you've got a new worksheet just the way you want it, save yourself a lot of hassle and heartache by protecting the document. That way, neither you nor any other well-meaning coworker can wreak havoc on your masterpiece without at least taking the time to unprotect the document!

✔ Give yourself a break and record a macro for doing those little tasks that you end up doing over and over and over again. Using macros to get these kinds of things done will not only alleviate the boredom but also free you up to do truly important things (like playing another game of Solitaire).

✔ Put together in a workbook file all the Excel documents (like the chart and macro sheets) that you end up having to open up individually each time you work with a particular worksheet. That way, you can simply open the workbook, and Excel will open them all up for you, giving you instant access to all related information.

Chapter 20
Ten Thousand (More or Less) Useful Keystroke Shortcuts

• •

When You Need Help

On an IBM Press	On a Mac Press	To
F1	⌘ + /	Open the Excel Help window
Shift+F1	⌘ + Shift + ?	Get context-sensitive Excel Help

When You Want To Move Through the Worksheet

On an IBM Press	On a Mac Press	To
Arrow keys (←, →, ↑, ↓)	Arrow keys (←, →, ↑, ↓)	Move left, right, up, down one cell
Home	Home	Move to the beginning of the row
PgUp	PgUp	Move up one screenful
Ctrl + PgUp	⌘ + PgUp	Move left one screenful
PgDn	PgDn	Move down one screenful
Ctrl + PgDn	⌘ + PgDn	Move right one screenful
Ctrl + Home	⌘ + Home	Move to the first cell in the worksheet (A1)
Ctrl + End	⌘ + End	Move to the last active cell of the worksheet
Ctrl + Arrow key	⌘ + Arrow key	Move to the edge of a data block

When You Need To Select Cells in the Worksheet

On an IBM Press	On a Mac Press	To
Shift + Spacebar	Shift + Spacebar	Select the entire row
Ctrl + Spacebar	⌘ + Spacebar	Select the entire column
Ctrl + Shift+Spacebar	⌘ + Shift + Spacebar or ⌘ +A	Select the entire worksheet
Shift + Home	Shift + Home	Extend the selection to the beginning of the current row

When You Want To Move Around a Cell Selection

On an IBM Press	On a Mac Press	To
Enter	Return	Move the cell pointer down one cell in the selection when more there's than one row, or move one cell to the right when the selection has only one row
Shift + Enter	Shift + Return	Move the cell pointer up one cell in the selection when there's more than one row, or move one cell to the left when the selection has only one row
Tab	Tab	Move the cell pointer one cell to the right in the selection when there's more than one column, or move one cell down when the selection has only one column
Shift + Tab	Shift + Tab	Move the cell pointer one cell to the left in the selection when there's more than one column, or move one cell up when the selection has only one column
Ctrl + Period (.)	⌘ + Shift + A	Move to the next corner of the current cell range
Ctrl+Tab	⌘ + Tab	Move to the next cell range in a nonadjacent selection
Ctrl+Shift + Tab	⌘ + Shift + Tab	Move to the previous cell range in a nonadjacent selection
Shift + Backspace	Shift + Delete	Collapse the cell selection to just the active cell

When You Need To Scroll Through a Document

On an IBM Press	On a Mac Press	To
Arrow key	Arrow key	Scroll one row up or down or one column left or right
PgUp	PgUp	Scroll up one screenful
PgDn	PgDn	Scroll down one screenful
Ctrl+PgUp	⌘ + PgUp	Scroll left one screenful
Ctrl + PgDn	⌘ + PgDn	Scroll right one screenful

When You Need To Format a Cell Selection

On an IBM Press	On a Mac Press	To
Ctrl + S	⌘ + Shift + L	Select the style box in the Standard toolbar
Ctrl + Shift + ~	Control + Shift + ~	Apply the General number format to the cell selection
Ctrl + Shift + $	Control + Shift + $	Apply the currency format with two decimal places to the cell selection

(continued)

When You Need To Format a Cell Selection *(continued)*

On an IBM Press	On a Mac Press	To
Ctrl + Shift + %	Control + Shift + %	Apply the percentage format with no decimal places to the cell selection
Ctrl + Shift + ^	Control + Shift + ^	Apply the scientific (exponential) number format with two decimal places to the cell selection
Ctrl + Shift + #	Control + Shift + #	Apply the date format with the day, month, and year to the cell selection as in 27-Oct-93
Ctrl + Shift + @	Control + Shift + @	Apply the time format with the hour, minute, and indicating AM or PM to the cell selection as in 12:05 PM
Ctrl + Shift + &	⌘ + Option + 0 (zero)	Apply an outline border to the cell selection
Ctrl + Shift + _ (underscore)	⌘ + Option + - (hyphen)	Get rid of all borders in the cell selection
Ctrl + 1	⌘ + Shift + P	Apply the Normal font to the cell selection
Ctrl + B	⌘ + Shift + B	Apply or get rid of bold in the cell selection
Ctrl + I	⌘ + Shift + I	Apply or get rid of italics in the cell selection
Ctrl + U	⌘ + Shift + U	Apply or get rid of underlining in the cell selection
Ctrl + 5	⌘ + Shift + _ (underscore)	Apply or get rid of strikeout in the cell selection
Ctrl + 9	Control + 9	Hide selected rows
Ctrl + Shift + ((left parenthesis)	Control + Shift + ((left parenthesis)	Unhide all hidden rows
Ctrl + 0 (zero)	Control + 0 (zero)	Hide selected columns
Ctrl + Shift +) (right parenthesis)	Control + Shift +) (right parenthesis)	Unhide all hidden columns
Ctrl + F	N/A	Select the Font Name list in the Formatting toolbar if displayed; otherwise, open the Font dialog box
Ctrl + P	N/A	Select the Font Size list in the Formatting toolbar if displayed; otherwise, open the Font dialog box

When You're Editing the Worksheet

On an IBM Press	On a Mac Press	To
Enter	Enter	Carry out your action
Esc	⌘ + . (period)	Cancel a command or close the displayed dialog box
Alt + Enter	⌘ + Y	Repeat your last action

(continued)

When You're Editing the Worksheet *(continued)*

On an IBM Press	On a Mac Press	To
Ctrl + Z	⌘ + Z	Undo your last command or action
Ctrl+ Shift + Plus sign (+)	⌘ + I	Display the Insert dialog box to insert new cells, columns, or rows in the worksheet
Ctrl + Minus sign (−)	⌘ + K	Display the Delete dialog box to delete cells, columns, or rows from the worksheet
Delete	Delete	Display the Clear dialog box to clear the contents or formatting from your cell selection
Ctrl+Del	⌘ + B	Clear the entries in your cell selection
Ctrl + X	⌘ + X	Cut the selection to the Clipboard
Ctrl + C	⌘ + C	Copy the selection to the Clipboard
Ctrl + V	⌘ + V	Paste the contents of the Clipboard
Shift + F2	⌘ + Shift + N	Display the Cell Note dialog box
Ctrl + F2	⌘ + F2	Switch between the Info window with information about the active cell and the active document window
F3	N/A	Display the Paste Name dialog box so that you can paste a range name into a formula
Shift + F3	Shift + F3	Display the Paste Function dialog box so that you can paste a function and its arguments into a formula
Ctrl + F3	⌘ + L	Display the Define Name dialog box so that you can assign a range name to the cell selection
Ctrl + = (equal sign) or F9	⌘ + = (equal sign) or F9	Recalculate the formulas in all open worksheets
Shift + F9	⌘ + Shift + = (equal sign)	Recalculate the formulas in just the active worksheet document
Alt + = (equal sign)	⌘ + Shift + T	Create a sum formula (same as clicking the AutoSum tool on the Standard toolbar)
Ctrl + 8	⌘ + T	Toggle the outline symbols on and off or, if no outline exists, display an alert dialog box prompting you to create an outline
Alt+Shift + →	⌘ + Shift +K	Select the Demote tool in the Utility toolbar if displayed; otherwise, display the Demote dialog box

(continued)

When You're Editing the Worksheet *(continued)*

On an IBM Press	On a Mac Press	To
Alt + Shift + ←	⌘ + Shift + J	Select the Promote tool in the Utility toolbar if displayed; otherwise, display the Promote dialog box
Alt + ;	⌘ + Shift + Z	Select only the visible cells in the cell selection (same as clicking the Visible Cells Only tool in the Utility toolbar)

When You're Editing an Entry in the Formula Bar

On an IBM Press	On a Mac Press	To
F2	⌘ + U	Activate the formula bar and position the insertion point at the end of the current entry
Ctrl + ; (semicolon)	⌘ + - (hyphen)	Insert the current date in the formula bar
Ctrl + Shift + ; (semicolon — same as Ctrl + :)	⌘ + ; (semicolon)	Insert the current time in the formula bar
Ctrl + ' (single quote)	⌘ + ' (single quote)	Copy the formula from the cell above the active cell into the formula bar
Ctrl + Shift + ' (single quote — same as Ctrl + ")	⌘ + Shift + " (double quote)	Copy the value from the cell above the active cell into the formula bar
Ctrl + Enter	Option + Enter	Enter the contents of the formula bar in all cells in the current selection
Arrow key (↑, ↓, ←, →)	Arrow key (↑, ↓, ←, →)	Move the insertion point one character up, down, left, or right
Home	Home	Move the insertion point to the beginning of the formula bar
F4	⌘ + T	Convert the current cell reference from relative to absolute, from absolute to mixed, and from mixed back to relative
Alt + Enter	⌘ + Option + Return	Insert a new paragraph in the formula bar
Ctrl + Tab	⌘ + Option + Tab	Insert a tab in the formula bar
Backspace	Delete	Delete the preceding character in formula bar or activate and clear formula bar when a cell is selected
Ctrl + Shift + Delete	N/A	Delete the text to the end of the line in the formula bar

When You Need To Open or Save Excel Documents

On an IBM Press	On a Mac Press	To
Alt + Shift + F1 or Shift + F11	Shift + F1	Open a new worksheet document window
Alt + F1 or F11	F11	Open a chart document window
Alt + Ctrl + F1 or Ctrl + F11	⌘ + F11	Open a new macro sheet window
Alt + F2 or F12	⌘ + Shift + S	Save the active file with the Save As command on the File menu
Alt + Shift + F2 or Shift + F12	⌘ + S	Save the active file with the Save command on the File menu
Ctrl + F12	⌘ + O	Display the Open dialog box so that you can open an existing Excel document

When You Need To Size or Switch to a New Document Window

On an IBM Press	On a Mac Press	To
Alt or F10	/ (forward slash)	Activate the Menu bar
Alt + - (hyphen)	N/A	Select the Control menu for the active document window
Ctrl + F7, arrow keys	N/A	Move the active document window
Ctrl + F8, arrow keys	N/A	Size the active document window
Ctrl + F10	⌘ + F10	Maximize the active document window
Ctrl + F9	N/A	Minimize the active document window
Ctrl + F5	⌘ + F5	Restore the active document window
Ctrl + F4	⌘ + W	Close the active document window
Ctrl + F6	⌘ + M	Switch to the next open document window
Ctrl + Shift + F6	⌘ + Shift + M	Switch to the previous open document window
Alt + PgDn	Option+PgDn	Switch to the next document window in a workbook
Alt + PgUp	Option + PgUp	Switch to the previous document window in a workbook
F6	F6	Move to next pane in a split document window
Shift + F6	Shift + F6	Move to previous pane in a split document window
Alt + F4	⌘ + Q	Exit Excel

Glossary

• •

absolute cell reference

A cell reference that Excel cannot automatically adjust. If you're about to copy a formula and you want to prevent Excel from adjusting one or more of the cell references (the program has a tendency to change the column and row reference in copies), make the cell references absolute. Absolute cell references are indicated by a dollar sign (yes, a $) in front of the column letter and the row number — $K$11, for example. You can convert a relative reference to an absolute reference with the F4 key. See also *relative cell reference*.

active

The program window, document window, or dialog box currently in use. The color of the title bar of an active window or dialog box is different from the color of nonactive windows' title bars. When several document windows are displayed, you can activate an inactive window by clicking on it.

arguments

Not what you have with your spouse but rather the values you give to a worksheet function to compute. Arguments are enclosed in parentheses and separated from one another by commas. See also *function*.

attached text vs. unattached text

Two types of text you can add to a chart. *Attached text* is attached to a part of the chart and is automatically resized and moved with the chart. *Unattached text* can be placed anywhere in the chart; unattached text is not automatically resized and does not move when you make changes to the position or size of the chart.

borders

The different types of lines Excel can draw around the edges of each cell or the outside edge of a bunch of cells. Excel offers a wide variety of different line styles and colors for this purpose.

bound/unbound documents

Excel documents in a workbook file, which brings together documents you always use together. *Bound documents* are stored in the workbook document and can't be used outside of the workbook. *Unbound documents* remain separate so that, although they open automatically with the workbook, they can still be used independently. See also *workbook*.

cell

The basic building block of plant and animal life and also of the Excel worksheet. The *worksheet cell* is a block formed by the intersections of column and row gridlines displayed in the sheet. Cells are where all worksheet data is stored. Each cell is identified by the letter of its column and the number of its row, the so-called *cell reference*.

cell pointer

A heavy outline that indicates which cell in the worksheet is selected. You must move the cell pointer to a particular cell before you can enter or edit information in that cell.

cell range

A bunch of cells that are all right next to each other. To select a range of cells with the mouse, you simply point at the beginning of the range, click the mouse button, and drag through the cells.

cell reference

Identifies the location of a cell in the worksheet. Normally, the cell reference consists of the column letter followed by the row number. (For example, *B3* indicates the cell in the second column and third row of the worksheet.) When you place the cell pointer in a cell, Excel displays its cell reference at the beginning of the formula bar. See also **relative cell reference** and **absolute cell reference.**

chart

Also known as a *graph*. This is a graphic representation of a set of values stored in a worksheet. You can create a chart right on a worksheet, where it is saved and printed along with the worksheet data. You can also display a chart in its own document window, where you can edit its contents or print it independently of the worksheet data. (Such a chart is called, appropriately enough, a *chart document.*)

check box

Turns an option on or off in a dialog box. If the check box contains an X (sorry, not a check mark), the option is turned on. If the check box is blank, the option is turned off. The nice thing about check boxes is that you can select more than one of the multiple options presented as a group. See also **radio button.**

click

The simplest mouse technique. You press and immediately release the mouse button. See also **double-click.**

Clipboard

The Windows equivalent of a hand-held clipboard to which you attach papers and information you need to work with. The Windows Clipboard is a special area of memory, a holding place, where text and graphics can be stored to await further action. You can paste the contents of the Clipboard into any open Excel document (or any document in other Windows programs). The contents of the Clipboard are automatically replaced as soon as you place new information there (whether in Excel or some other program).

command button

A dialog-box button that initiates an action. The default command button is indicated by a dotted rectangle and a darker border. A button with an ellipsis (. . .) opens another dialog box or window. Frequently, after you choose options in the dialog box, you click on the OK or Cancel command button.

Control menu

A standard pull-down menu attached to all Windows program and document windows. It contains commands that open, close, maximize, minimize, or restore a window or dialog box. You can display a Control menu by clicking on the Control-menu box — the one with a minus sign in the upper-left corner of the program or document window.

criteria range

A special area you create for a database worksheet that indicates what information Excel is to locate for you in the database.

database

A tool for organizing, managing, and retrieving large amounts of information. A database is created right on a worksheet. The first row of the database contains column headings called *field names,* which identify each item of information you are tracking (like First Name, Last Name, City, and the like). Below the field names, you enter the information you want to store for each field (column) of each record. See also **field** and **record.**

default

Don't be alarmed; we're not talking blame here. A *default* is a setting, value, or response that Excel automatically provides unless you choose something else. Some defaults can be changed and rearranged. If you like controlling everything, see Chapter 10.

dialog box

A box containing various options that appears when you select Excel commands followed by an ellipsis (. . .). The options in a dialog box are presented in groups of buttons and boxes. (Oh, boy!) A dialog box can also display warnings and messages. Each dialog box contains a title bar and a Control menu but has no menu bar. You can move a dialog box around the active document window by dragging its title bar.

docking

Has nothing at all to do with the space shuttle. Docking in Excel refers to dragging one of the toolbars to a stationary position along the perimeter of the Excel window with the mouse. See also **toolbar.**

document

A file where you store the information you generate in Excel. The program currently supports five different types of documents (worksheet, chart, macro sheet, workbook, and slides), each of which opens in a separate document window. To save the information in a document, you must name the document in accordance with the horrid DOS naming conventions. To retrieve a document so that you can do more work on it or print it, you must remember the name you gave it. See also **window.**

double-click

To click the mouse button twice in rapid succession. Double-clicking opens things like a program or a document. You can double-click to close things, too.

drag and drop

A really direct way to move stuff around on a worksheet. Select the cell or range (bunch) of cells you want to move, position the pointer on one of its edges, and then press and hold the left mouse button. The pointer assumes the shape of an arrowhead pointing up toward the left. Hold the mouse button as you move the mouse and drag the outline of the selection to the new location. When you get where you're going, let it all go.

drop-down list box

A text box that displays the currently selected option, accompanied by an arrow button. When you click on the associated arrow button, a list box with other options that you can choose from drops down (or sometimes pops up) from the text box. To select a new option from this list and close the drop-down list box, click on the option.

error value

A value Excel displays in a cell when it cannot calculate the formula for that cell. Error values start with # and end with !, and they have various capitalized informative words in the middle. An example is #DIV/0!, which appears when you try to divide by zero. (So, should this be censored?)

field

A column in an Excel database that tracks just one type of item (like a city, state, ZIP code, and so on). See also *database* and *record.*

file

Any document saved to a computer disk. See also *document.*

font

Shapes for characters. A typeface. Fonts have a point size, weight, and style, such as Helvetica Modern 20-point bold italic. You can pick and choose fonts used to display information in an Excel worksheet and change their settings at any time.

footer

Information you specify to be printed in the bottom margin of each page of a printed report. See also *header.*

formula

Ready for some math anxiety? A sequence of values, cell references, names, functions, or operators that is contained in a cell and produces a new value from existing values. In other words, a mathematical expression. Formulas in Excel always begin with an equal sign (=).

formula bar

Sounds like a high-energy treat. Well, it is, sort of. Located at the top of the Excel window under the menu bar, the formula bar is used for entering or editing values and formulas in a cell or chart. When activated, the formula bar displays an enter box and a cancel box between the current cell reference on the left and the place where you enter information on the right. Click on the enter box or press the Enter key to complete an entry or edit. Click on the cancel box or press Esc to leave the contents of the formula bar unchanged.

function

(Let's see, I know what *dis*function is. . . .) A function simplifies and shortens lengthy calculations. Functions have built-in formulas that use a series of values called *arguments* to perform the specified operations and return the results. Functions can be entered or pasted into the formula bar.

graphics object

Any of the various shapes or graphics images you can bring into a worksheet document (including charts). All graphics objects remain in a separate layer on top of the cells in the worksheet so that they can be selected, moved, resized, and formatted independently of the information stored in the worksheet.

header

Information you specify to be printed in the top margin of each page of a printed report. See also *footer.*

I-beam cursor

The I-beam shape (looks just like the end of a girder or a capital *I*) that the mouse pointer assumes when you position it somewhere on the screen where you can enter or edit text. Click the I-beam cursor in the formula bar or a text box in a dialog box, for example, to insert the insertion point where you want to add or delete text.

insertion point

The blinking vertical bar that indicates your current location in the text. The insertion point shows where the next character you type will appear or the next one you delete will disappear.

list box

A boxed area in a dialog box that displays a list of choices you can choose from. When a list is too long for all the choices to be displayed, the list box has a scroll bar you can use to bring new options into view. Most list boxes are already open and have the list on display. Those that you must open by clicking on an arrow button are called *drop-down list boxes*.

macro

A sequence of frequently performed, repetitive tasks and calculations that you record. At the touch of a couple keystrokes, Excel can play back the steps in the macro much faster than is humanly possible.

marquee

That moving dotted line around the movie stars' names, right? Well, a marquee exists in Excel in a slightly toned-down version. It's the moving dotted line around a selection that shows what information is selected when you move or copy data with the Cut, Copy, and Paste commands on the Edit menu.

Maximize button

A little teeny box at the right of a window's title bar containing an upward-pointing triangle. When you click on the Maximize button, the document or program window that has been at a medium size expands to full size and fills the screen. See also **Minimize button** and **Restore button.**

menu

A vertical list of commands that can be applied to the active window or application. Also known as a *pull-down menu* because the menu opens down from the menu bar when you select the menu name. When an option is currently unavailable on a pull-down menu, the option is dimmed. See also **shortcut menus.**

menu bar

The row at the top of a program window that contains the names of the menu items available for the active document window.

message box

Also known as an *alert box.* This is a type of dialog box that appears when Excel gives you information, a warning, or an error message, or when it asks for confirmation before carrying out a command.

Minimize button

A minuscule box containing a downward-pointing triangle, located next to the Maximize button at the right end of a window's title bar. When you click on a Minimize button, the document window or application shrinks to an icon at the bottom of the screen. See also **Maximize button** and **Restore button.**

mode indicators

The information on the right side of the status bar (the row at the bottom of the screen) that tells you what keyboard modes are currently active. Some examples are ADD, NUM, and CAPS.

mouse pointer

Indicates your position on-screen as you move the mouse on the desk. It assumes various forms to indicate a change in the action when you use different features: the *arrowhead* when you point, select, or drag; the *I-beam* when you place the insertion point in text; the *double-headed arrow* when you drag to adjust row height or column width; and the *hourglass* when you need to wait. The most common shapes of the mouse pointer are revealed in Chapter 1.

nonadjacent selection

Also called a *discontinuous selection* (is that any better?). A nonadjacent selection is one composed of various cells and cell ranges that don't all touch each other. To accomplish this feat, click on the first cell or click and drag through the first range; then hold down Ctrl as you click on or drag through the remaining cells or ranges you want to select.

notes (text and sound)

Comments you attach to a particular worksheet cell to remind yourself of something important (or trivial) about the cell's contents. Text notes can be displayed in a separate dialog box or printed with the worksheet. If your computer is wired for sound, you can record sound notes to be played back directly through your computer's speaker for all the world to hear.

option button

See **radio button.**

pane

A part of a divided document window. You can display different parts of the same worksheet together on one window in different panes. Horizontal and vertical split bars are involved with creating and sizing.

paste

Yum, yum, remember kindergarten? Alas, in the computer age, paste means to transfer the cut or copied contents of the Clipboard into a document, either in the cell with the cell pointer or in a line of text at the location of the insertion point.

pointing

Babies do it, politicians do it, and so can you. Now that I've had my little digression, let me also say that *pointing* is selecting a cell or cell range as you enter a formula in the formula bar to automatically record cell references.

program icon

A graphical representation of an application, such as Excel, that appears in the Windows Program Manager. Not the idol for our new cult. To start a program from the Program Manager, you either double-click on the program icon or click on it and then press the Enter key.

radio button

Also known as an *option button.* A radio button looks like an old-fashioned radio push button in a dialog box when it's selected (because it has a dot in the middle). Radio buttons are used for dialog box items that contain mutually exclusive options. This means that you can select only one of the options at a time (only one can have the dot in the middle). See also **check box.**

range

Also called a *cell range.* A range is a bunch of neighboring cells that form some type of solid block when selected with the mouse or the keyboard.

record

A single row in a database that defines one entity (like an employee, a client, or a sales transaction). See also **database** and **field.**

relative cell reference

The normal cell reference (like A2) that is automatically adjusted when you copy formulas that refer to the cell. Row references are adjusted when you copy up or down; column references are adjusted when you copy to the left or right). See also **absolute cell reference** and **cell reference.**

Restore button

The double-triangle button at the right edge of the title bar. Mouse users can click on the Restore button to shrink a window or return a window to the size and location it had before being sized. See also **Maximize button** and **Minimize button.**

scroll bar

The vertical or horizontal bar in the active document window and in some list boxes. Use a scroll bar to move rapidly through a document or list by clicking on the scroll arrows or dragging the slider box.

selection

The chosen element, such as a cell, cell range, nonadjacent selection, file, directory, dialog box option, graphics object, or document text. To make a selection, highlight it by dragging the mouse or pressing keystroke shortcuts. You normally select an element before choosing the actions you want to apply to that element.

shortcut menus

Nutritious meals for the whole family in 30 minutes or less. Food fantasies aside, these menus are attached to certain things on the screen — namely, the toolbar, worksheet cell, or parts of a chart open in a chart window. They contain a quick list of command options related to the object they're attached to. You must use the mouse to open a shortcut menu and choose its commands. In Windows, you click on the object with the right mouse button; on the Mac, you hold the ⌘+Option keys as you click on the object.

size box

The little square box in the lower-right corner of the document window with the scrolling arrows pointing to it. Use the size box to manually size any open document window by dragging it until the window is the size and shape you want.

spreadsheet

A type of computer program that enables you to develop and perform all sorts of calculations between the text and values stored in a document. Most spreadsheet programs like Excel also include charting and database capabilities. *Spreadsheet* is also commonly used as alternate term for *worksheet* — so see also **worksheet.**

status bar

The line at the bottom of the Excel window. The status bar displays messages, such as Ready, or a short description of the menu option you have chosen, and it indicates any active modes, such as CAPS or NUM when you press the Caps Lock or Num Lock key.

style

If you've got it, flaunt it. Also known to some of us as a group of formatting instructions, all combined, that you can apply to the cells in a worksheet. Use styles to save time and keep things consistent. Styles can deal with the number format, font, alignment, border, patterns, and protection of the cells.

template

A special version of a worksheet document used to generate other, similar worksheets. When you open a template file, Excel opens a copy of the original document. Templates normally contain formulas and standard text and are filled out somewhat like a blank form.

text box

The area in a dialog box where you type a new selection or edit the current one.

title bar

The top bar of a program window, document window, or dialog box that contains its title. You can move an active window or dialog box around the screen by dragging its title bar.

toolbar

A series of related tools (buttons with icons) that you simply click on to perform common tasks like opening, saving, or printing a document. Excel 4.0 comes with several built-in toolbars you can use as-is or customize. You can create toolbars of your own design, using predefined tools or blank tools you assign macros to. Toolbars can be displayed in their own little dialog boxes that float around the active document window; they can also dock along the perimeter of the screen. See also *docking*.

window

A framed area on the screen that contains the program (called a *program window*) or the document (called a *document window*) you're working with. The Excel program window typically contains a title bar, Control menu, menu bar, Standard toolbar, open document windows (with the active one on top), and status bar. The program and document windows can be resized and moved around the screen as needed.

workbook

A type of Excel file in which you combine multiple documents such as worksheets, charts, and macro sheets that you regularly work with to keep related information together.

worksheet

Also called a *spreadsheet*. This is the primary document for recording, analyzing, and calculating data. The Excel worksheet is organized in a series of 256 columns and 16,384 rows, making for a heck of a lot of cells.

Index

&D code for Date, 166
&F code for Filename, 165
&N code for Total Pages, 166
&P code for Page Number, 166
&T code for Time, 166
* (asterisk) for multiplication, 54
* (asterisk) as wildcard with databases, 204
* (asterisk) as wildcard with Find command, 151
^ (caret) for raising a number to a power, 54
, (comma) with numeric values, 50
⌘+= (equal sign) for calculating formulas on Macintosh, 276
⌘+= (equal sign) for recalculating Macintosh worksheet, 153
⌘+F and missing files, 113
⌘+Option keys and shortcut menus, 37
⌘+Option for Macintosh toolbar shortcut menu, 81
⌘+Option for opening Macintosh shortcut menu, 187
⌘+P for printing with Macintosh, 160
⌘+. (period) for cancelling Macintosh print job, 160
⌘+T as shortcut for changing cell references, 122
⌘+U for activating Macintosh formula bar, 58
⌘+U for freezing formulas on Macintosh, 276
⌘ key on Macintosh equals Ctrl, 32
$ (dollar sign) as indicator for absolute cell reference, 122
$ (dollar sign) with numeric values, 50
= (equal sign) in formulas, 54
/ (forward slash) on Macintosh pull-down menus, 42

> (greater than sign) operator, 213
>= (greater than or equal to sign) operator, 213
< (less than sign) operator, 213
<= (less than or equal to sign) operator, 213
- (minus sign) for entering negative values, 50
- (minus sign or hyphen) for subtraction, 54
<> (not equal to sign) operator, 213
() (parentheses) for entering negative values, 50
+ (plus sign) for addition, 54
# (pound sign) as placeholder, 91
####### (pound signs) in Excel cells, 86
#DIV/0! error value message, 57
#NAME? error value message, 57
#NULL! error value message, 57
#NUM! error value message, 57
#REF! error value message, 57
#VALUE! error value message, 57
? (question mark) as wildcard with Find command, 150-151
? (question mark) as wildcard with data-bases, 204
;;; (semicolons) in Codes text box, 92
/ (slash) for division, 54
0 (zero) as placeholder, 91
3D charts, 191-192
32-character descriptive filenames, 232
1900 date system, 51
1904 date system for Macintosh, 51

—A—

About Microsoft Excel command, 46
absolute cell reference, $ (dollar sign) as indicator for, 122

active area of worksheet, 31
adding
    borders to cell selection, 105
    new records to database,
        200-201
    notes to cells, 145-147
    titles to charts, 182-183
addition, + (plus sign) for, 54
adjusting heights of rows, 95
alert boxes for messages and warnings, 42
aligning cell entries, 100-105
alignment
    data entry, 48
    options, Horizontal, 103
    tools, 100
Alignment dialog box, 101-103
alphabetical sort order, 208
Alternate Navigation Keys option, 37
Alt key for accessing menu bar, 35
Apple LaserWriter, 98, 161
applying new colors, 250
arguments for VLOOKUP function, 286
Arrange Windows dialog box, 220
arrowhead pointer, 27
ascending sort order, 208
Assign To dialog box, 264
AutoFill
    for copying adjacent cells, 119
    for copying formulas, 119-124
    feature, 60-62
AutoFormat, 77-79
    tool, 21
automatic page breaks, 159
AutoSelect
    feature, 74
    keyboard equivalent of, 75-76
AutoSum tool
    on Standard toolbar, 43, 65-67
    for summing lists of values, 20
AVERAGE function, 54, 272-273
avoiding loss of information, 133-154

— B —

background colors, 250
Backspace
    for correcting typos, 57
    for editing cell entries, 59

bar
    Control-menu on title, 19-20
    sizing buttons on title, 19-20
    status, 25
    title, 19-20
    vertical scroll, 30
    See also formula bar; menu bar(s)
beginner basics, 293
beginning new worksheets, 45-46
best-fit method for adjusting column widths,
        93-95
Best Fit button for sizing columns, 95
blank tools
    clip art for, 264
    in Custom category, 263
block to block, moving from, 33
Bold tool, 20, 99
book
    conventions used in, 5-6
    organization of, 3-5
    using this, 2
Border
    command for opening Help window, 43
    dialog box, 105-106
    style, 106
border colors, 250
borrowed headings, formulas, or range of
        values, 223
Bottom Border tool, 21
bottom margins, 164
built-in cell styles, 107-108
built-in toolbars, 253
button, Copy command, 44
bypassing Windows, 18

— C —

calculating field entries in databases, 202
cancel box for clearing wrong entry, 48
cell-reference system, R1C1, 15, 249
cell address, formula bar and, 21-22
cell entries
    accepted as text, 49
    aligning, 100-105
    keystrokes for editing, 59
Cell Gridlines check box, 105

cell pointer
    advancement, Workspace command for,
        48
    and current cell, 15
    as highlighter, 14
    keystrokes for moving, 31-32
    moving, 293
    versus mouse pointer, 28
cell ranges
    copying of, 117-118
    descriptive names for cells and, 147-149
    discontinuous selection of, 73
    as equivalent of cell selection, 72
    I-beam for inserting, 118
    moving of, 116
    nonadjacent selection of, 72
    printing selected, 161
    See also cell selections
cell reference, current, 293
cell references
    adjustments of, 121-124
    editing formula for, 124
    relative, 121
cells
    adding notes to, 145-147
    AutoFill for copying adjacent, 119
    and cell ranges, descriptive names for,
        147-149
    editing contents of, 110
    for emphasis, shading, 106
    for formatting, selecting, 71-78
    inserting new, 128
    removing shading from, 107
cell selections
    adding borders to, 105
    with Cut and Paste commands, moving,
        124-125
    with Cut and Paste commands, copying,
        125
    by keyboard, 75-76
    by mouse, 73-74
    pointing and, 54
    shortcuts for formatting,
        306-307
    See also cell ranges; selecting cells
cell styles, built-in, 107-108

Center Across Selected Columns tool, 21,
    100, 103
Center Align tool, 21, 100-101
changes
    to charts, 184-188
    to worksheets, 109-129
changing
    default margins, 164-165
    directories, 112
    font colors, 100
    orientation of text, 104-105
chart
    resizing, 184
    selecting format for, 181-182
    selecting type of, 180
    selection handles for, 184
charting outlined tables, 179
Charting tool, 257
charts, 177-196
    3D, 191-192
    adding titles to, 182-183
    changes to, 184-188
    legend in, 189
    page setup options for printing, 196
    in perspective view, 191-193
    printing, 195-196
    text box in, 189
chart title, immovable, 187
ChartWizard
    procedure, 178-180
    tool, 21
Check Box, 41
Classic table-format selection, 78-79
clearing cells in editing worksheets, 126, 127
clicking on objects, 26
clip art for blank tools, 264
Codes text box, ;;; (semicolons) in, 92
Colorful table-format selection,
        78-79
color monitor and on-screen appearance of
        documents, 250
Color Palette command, 250
Color Picker dialog box, 250
colors
    applying new, 250
    customizing, 250

hue and saturation of, 250
Patterns command and, 250
columns
 Best Fit button for sizing, 95
 as fields, 198
 labeling of, 15
 printing particular rows and, 168
 and rows, hiding and unhiding, 96-98
 and rows, selecting, 74
Column Width dialog box, 93-95
column widths, adjusting, 92-93
Column Width text box, 95
col_index_num argument, 286
Comma cell style, 107-108
Comma format, 87-88
command
 for editing, Redo, 114-115
 for editing, Undo, 114-115
 for opening Help window, Border, 43
 Workspace, 52-53
Command Button, 41
commandments, Excel, 295
command names
 dimmed, 36
 on pull-down menus, 293
commands
 on pull-down menus, 293
 on shortcut menus, 293
Comma Style tool, 84
comprehensive number format, 85
Consolidate dialog box and editing, 229-231
constants, text and values as, 48
Control-menu on title bar, 19-20
control of paging scheme, 155-156
Control Panel and Windows settings, 19-20
Copy command from Edit menu, 44
copying
 cell selections with Cut and Paste
  commands, 125
 charts between worksheets, 224
 with Cut and Paste commands, replicated, 125
 information across documents, 124
 information between worksheets, 223-224
Copy tool, 21
correcting typos, 57-59

COUNT function, 273-274
creating
 data form for new databases, 199
 directory for Excel documents, 112
 text box, 194
 toolbars, 260-262
Criteria button, finding records in database
  with, 204-207
criteria for locating records, selection,
  212-214
cross pointer, 27
Ctrl+down arrow for moving cell pointer, 32
Ctrl+End for moving cell pointer, 32
Ctrl+Home for moving cell pointer, 32
Ctrl+left arrow
 for editing cell entries, 59
 for moving cell pointer, 32
Ctrl+PgDn for moving cell pointer, 32
Ctrl+PgUp for moving cell pointer, 32
Ctrl+right arrow
 for editing cell entries, 59
 for moving cell pointer, 32
Ctrl+up arrow for moving cell pointer, 32
Currency cell style, 107-108
Currency Style tool, 83, 86, 90
current cell
 cell pointer and, 15
 reference, 293
current directory, 111
current disk drive, 111
Custom category, blank tools in, 263
custom dictionary in spelling checker, 129
custom format, 92
Customize dialog box with Custom tools,
  263
customizers, clever, 299
customizing
 appearance of Excel, 246-248
 colors, 250
 toolbars, 253
custom number formats, 91, 108
Custom tool, 257
Cut and Paste commands
 copying cell selections with, 125
 moving cell selections with, 124-125

— D —

databases
  adding new records to, 200-201
  calculating field entries in, 202
  creating data form for new, 199
  creating in Excel, 197-217
  data form for setting up and maintaining, 198-202
  date format in, 200
  sorting, 207-211
  sorting large, 209
  wildcard characters for searching in, 204
data classification, 48
data entry
  ABCs of, 47-48
  alignment, 48
  formula bar and, 47
  restrictions to, 59-60
data extract operation, 198
data form
  for new databases, creating, 199
  for setting up and maintaining databases, 198-202
date, dd for displaying, 91-92
date formats, 52, 200
dates, numbers representing, 50
date system
  1900, 51
  for Macintosh, 1904, 51
Date tool, 165, 166
date value format, 84
date values, 51
dd for displaying date, 91-92
decimal places
  fixing, 52-53
  increasing or decreasing, 88-89
decimal point with numeric values, 51
Decrease Decimal tool, 84, 88
Decrease Font Size tool, 20
default margins, changing, 164-165
default print settings, 159
deleting cells in editing worksheets, 126, 127-128
deletion options in editing worksheets, 126-128

Del for editing cell entries, 59
descending sort order, 208
descriptive names for cells and cell ranges, 147-149
designer series with AutoFill feature, 61
dialog box
  Alignment, 101-103
  Arrange Windows, 220
  Assign To, 264
  Border, 105-106
  Color Picker, 250
  Column Width, 93-95
  with Custom tools, Customize, 263
  Display Options, 40, 246-248
  and editing, Consolidate, 229-231
  Font, 99
  on Formula menu, Goto, 34
  Group Edit, 227
  Header, 165-166
  Number Format, 91-92
  OK button for closing, 42
  parts of, 40-41
  Paste Function, 64
  Patterns, 106-107
  and pull-down menus, 36
  Save As, 39
  Workspace Options, 53, 246-248
dimmed command names, 36
directories, changing, 112
directory
  current, 111
  for Excel documents, creating, 112
discontinuous keyboard selections, 76
discontinuous selection of cell ranges, 73
disk drive, current, 111
Display Options dialog box, 40, 246-248
division, / (slash) for, 54
docking toolbars, 81-83
document protection, 153-154
documents
  color monitor and on-screen appearance of, 250
  opening multiple, 220-224
  saving active, 36
  saving consolidated, 231

switching, 111
with Windows File Manager, opening, 18, 293
from workbook, unbinding, 234
workbook feature for saving Excel, 231-234
document window, 22-25
Control-menu in, 23
dragging objects with mouse, 24
losing title bar in, 24
maximizing, 24-25
mouse pointer and, 23
restoring original dimensions of, 24
sizing and moving, 22
sizing buttons in, 23-24
status bar in, 25
DOS
eight-character filenames, 232
Lotus 1-2-3 for, 36-37
starting Excel from, 18, 293
dot display and Note Indicator check box, 249
double-clicking
on objects, 26
speed for mouse, 28
Double-Click Speed, changing, 28
double words, flagging with spelling checker, 129
down arrow
for editing cell entries, 59
for moving cell pointer, 32
drag-and-drop
editing technique, 115-119
in insert mode, 118-119
dragging
icons on Workbook Contents sheet, 233
on objects, 26
Drawing tool, 257
Drawing toolbar, 193
Drives drop-down list box, 112
Drop-Down List Box, 40

— E —

editing
cell entries, keystrokes for, 59
entries in formula bar, shortcuts for, 309

locating records for, 215
multiple worksheets, 227-229
Redo command for, 114-115
and Replace command, 151-152
Undo command for, 114-115
editing techniques, drag-and-drop, 115-119
editing worksheets
clearing cells in, 126, 127
deleting cells in, 126, 127-128
deletion options in, 126-128
on different levels, 110
shortcuts for, 307-309
Edit menu
Copy command from, 44
Paste command on, 44
Edit tool, 257
End
down arrow for moving cell pointer, 32
for editing cell entries, 59
Home for moving cell pointer, 32
left arrow for moving cell pointer, 32
right arrow for moving cell pointer, 32
up arrow for moving cell pointer, 32
entering information into cell, 47
entries
interference with existing, 118-119
repeated, 62
entry, cancel box for clearing wrong, 48
error messages
"Can't Undo," 115
"Cut and paste areas are different shapes," 125
"Parentheses do not match," 56
See also messages
error value messages, 57
error values returned by formulas, 56-57
Excel 3.0 toolbar, 254
Excel 4.0, special icon for, 6
Excel Function Reference, 269
Excerpts from database, 215-217
exiting Excel, 293
Extract command, 215-217
extract operation, saving results of, 217
extract range in worksheet, 198

— F —

features, formatting, 71-76
field entries in databases, calculating, 202
field names, rows of column headings known as, 197-198
file-opening methods, 110-111
file extension, XLS, 18
File Manager icon (picture of file cabinet), 113
File menu, Print Topic command from, 44
filename limitations, 234-235
filenames
    32-character descriptive, 232
    DOS eight-character, 232
files
    searching for missing, 111-113
    Windows For Dummies and moving, 112
    in workbook, opening multiple, 235-236
File Save tool, 231
File tool, 257
fill handle, 27
Fill option, 103
financial value format, 84
Find command, 149-151, 214-215
finding
    missing files, 112-113
    records in database with Criteria button, 204-207
    and retrieving information, 211-212
Fixed Decimal setting, 52-53
floating toolbars, 81
font
    attributes, 99
    changes, making, 99-100
    colors, changing, 100
Font command on Format pull-down menu, 99-100
Font dialog box, 99
Font Name box, 83
Font Size box, 83
Font tool for headers and footers, 167
footers, 165, 165-167
foreground colors, 250
Format Codes list box, 91

formats
    custom number, 91, 108
    for every value, 84-90
formatting
    cell selections, shortcuts for, 306-307
    features, 71-76
Formatting tools, 79-80, 257
formula bar, 14
    data entry and, 47
    editing entries in, shortcuts for, 309
    and cell address, 21-22
    and data entry, 47
formula data, 48
Formula menu
    Goto dialog box on, 34
    opening, 35
    Show Active Cell command on, 34
formula problems, 56-57
formulas, 53-55
    AutoFill for copying, 119-124
    functions as predefined, 63
    printing, 172-173
    recalculation of, 152-153
    updating of, 48
    for use in another worksheet, borrowed, 223
Formula tool, 257
fractions as numeric values, 51
freezing headings, 138-140
Full Month style for making custom number format, 108
function(s), 269-276
    AVERAGE, 272-273
    COUNT, 273-274
    entering a specific, 5
    HLOOKUP, 285
    logical, 287-290
    MAX, 274
    MEDIAN, 274
    NOW, 275-276
    as predefined formulas, 63
    PRODUCT, 271
    ROUND, 64, 274-275
    SUM, 269-270
    SUMPRODUCT, 271-272

VLOOKUP, 285-287
See also specialized functions
function keys, F10 for accessing menu
bar, 35

— **G** —

getting around worksheet, 29
global macro sheet, 240, 244
global search-and-replace operations, 152
glossary term in Help system, 43
Goto
dialog box on Formula menu, 34
feature and descriptive names, 147, 149
feature, selecting cells with, 76
graphic images for sprucing up worksheets,
192-195
graphic objects
opaque, 195
transparent, 195
graphics
gray placeholders for, 195
hiding, 195
printing information without attendant,
196
replacing, 195
gray placeholders for graphics, 195
Gridline & Heading Color option, 248
Gridlines check box, 105
gridlines displayed in worksheets, 105
Group Edit dialog box, 227

— **H** —

hazards of using Undo command, 115
Header dialog box, 165-166
headers, 165-167
headings
freezing, 138-140
unfreezing, 140
for use in another worksheet, borrowed,
223
help
on-line, 43-44
pointer, 27
shortcuts, 305

Help tool on Standard Toolbar, 21, 43, 293
hidden format, 92
Hidden style as custom number format, 108
hiding
columns with mouse, 95-96
graphics, 195
and unhiding columns and rows, 96-98
HLOOKUP function, 285
Home
for editing cell entries, 59
for moving cell pointer, 32
Horizontal alignment options, 103
horizontal printing, 155-156
horizontal scroll bar, 30
HP LaserJet printer, 98, 161
hue and saturation of colors, 250

— **I** —

I-beam
for inserting cell range, 118
pointer, 27
icons, special, 6
immovable titles, 138-141
Increase Decimal tool, 84, 89
Increase Font Size tool, 20
information
across documents, copying, 124
across documents, moving, 124
avoiding loss of, 133-154
between worksheets, copying, 223-224
finding and retrieving, 211-212
locating specific, 149-151
in worksheet tables, outlining, 141-145
inserting new cells, 128
insert mode, drag-and-drop in,
118-119
Ins keystroke for editing cell entries, 59
Italic tool, 20, 99

— **J** —

jump term in Help system, 43
Justify Align tool, 103, 83

—K—

keyboard
    cell selections by, 75-76
    equivalent of AutoSelect, 75-76
    scrolling, 34
    selections, discontinuous, 76
    shortcut keys, 5
keys, sorting, 208
keystrokes
    for editing cell entries, 59
    for moving cell pointer, 31-32
    for moving to particular record, 203
keystroke shortcuts, 305-310

—L—

labeling of columns, 15
labels, text entries as, 48
landscape orientation of printing, 163-164
laser printer, 98
left-hand mouse users, 29
Left Align tool, 20, 100-101
left arrow
    for editing cell entries, 59
    for moving cell pointer, 32
left margins, 164
legend in charts, 189
Light Shading tool, 84
List Box, 40
list box option, selecting, 42
List table-format selection, 78-79
locating
    parts of worksheets, 293
    records for editing, 215
locking cells, 153
logical functions, IF among, 287-290
lookup_value argument, 286
Lotus 1-2-3 for DOS, 36-37
luminosity of colors, 250

—M—

Macintosh
    ⌘+= (equal sign) for recalculating
        worksheet, 153
    ⌘+= for calculating formulas, 276

    ⌘+Option for opening shortcut menu, 187
    ⌘+Option for toolbar shortcut menu, 81
    ⌘+. (period) for cancelling print job, 160
    ⌘+P for printing, 160
    ⌘+U for activating formula bar, 58
    ⌘+U for freezing formulas, 276
    ⌘ key equals Ctrl, 32
    / (forward slash) on pull-down menus, 42
    1904 date system for, 51
    repeated entries with Control key, 62
    starting documents from Finder, 18
    starting Excel for, 17
    toolbar shortcut menu, ⌘+Option for, 81
    See also MAC Tracks
macros, 239-246
    assigning, to tools, 263
    creating, 240
    display options, 246-248
    for entering months of the year, 244-246
    error dialog box, 244
    naming, 240
    playing back, 263
    pull-down menu, 246
    recording, in regular macro sheet, 240
    recording, in special global macro sheet, 240
    and Record Macro dialog box, 242-243
    for routine tasks, 240
    testing, 244
    and workspace options, 246-248
Macro tool, 257
MAC Tracks
    ⌘+Option for opening shortcut menu, 187
    ⌘+Option for toolbar shortcut menu, 81
    ⌘+U for activating formula bar, 58
    ⌘ key equals Ctrl, 32
    built-in sound capabilities, 146
    cancelling print jobs, 160
    copying with drag-and-drop, 117

data entry, 47
filenames, 68
Find command on System 7, 113
freezing formulas, 276
Help commands under System 7, 43
identifying templates, 225
keystroke shortcut for changing cell
        references, 122
long filenames, 234
menu bar, 42
microphone, 146
opening Print dialog box, 160
Page Setup dialog box, 161
recalculating open worksheet, 153
repeated entries with control keys, 62
shortcut keystroke for opening Find
        dialog box, 151
shortcut keystrokes for macros, 242
shortcut menus, 37
special icon for, 6
starting documents from Finder, 18
starting Excel, 17
zoom button, 25
See also Macintosh
magnification settings in Zoom command,
        134-136
magnifying-glass pointer, 157
margins, 164
math co-processor chip, presence of, 46
mathematical operations, order of, 55-56
mathematical operators, 54
MAX function, 274
MEDIAN function, 274
memory available to Excel, 46
menu
    Options, 52-53
    Paste Function command on Formula,
        63-64
    Save As command on File, 36
    Save option on File, 36
    Toolbar shortcut, 37-38
menu bar(s)
    Alt key for accessing, 35
    in Excel window, 20
    pull-down, 35
    See also bar

menus
    ⌘+Option keys and shortcut, 37
    dialog box and pull-down, 36
    mouse and shortcut, 38-39
    shortcut, 35, 37
messages
    "Calculate" on status bar, 153
    "Could not find matching data," 150
    "Displayed record will be deleted
        permanently," 202
    "Drag in document to create a chart," 179
    "Locked cells cannot be changed," 154
    "Overwrite non blank cells in destina-
        tion?," 117
    "Select destination and press Enter or
        choose Paste," 124
    See also error messages
messages and warnings, alert boxes for, 42
microphone for sound capabilities, 146
Microsoft Product Support Services, 44
missing files
    searching for, 111-113
    Windows File Manager and, 112
mmmm for spelling name of month, 91
mode, Print preview, 156-158
mode indicator, SCRL, 34
modifying
    stock headers or footers, 165
    tracking speed, 28
monitor and on-screen appearance of
        documents, color, 250
month, mmmm for spelling name of, 91
Months_of_the_Year macro, 246
mouse
    buttons, switching left and right, 29
    cell selections by, 73-74
    movement, 5
    pointer, cell pointer versus, 28
    pointer shapes, 27
    redisplaying columns with,
        95-96
    and shortcut menus, 38-39
    techniques, basic, 26
    techniques, learning, 27
    users, left-hand, 29
    users, south-paw, 29

Mouse Tracking Speed, changing, 28
moving
    from block to block, 33
    around cell selection, shortcuts for, 306
    cell selections with Cut and Paste
        commands,
        124-125
    information across documents, 124
    through worksheets, shortcuts for, 305
multiple worksheets, working with, 219-236
multiplication, * (asterisk) for, 54
musical toolbars, 255

— N —

negative values, entering, 50
new macro sheet, 244
New Worksheet tool, 20
nonadjacent selection of cell ranges, 72
Normal cell style, 107-108
Note Indicator check box, dot display
        and, 249
notes
    to cells, adding, 145-147
    electronic Post-it, 145-147
NOW function, 275-276
Number Format dialog box, 91-92
number formats, 90-92
number sign (#) as placeholder, 91
numbers with zeros, replacing all, 225
numerical sort order, 208
numeric entries, spaces in, 50
numeric values, entering, 50

— O —

Object properties command, 196
objects, clicking on, 26
OK button for closing dialog box, 42
on-line
    help, 43-44
    support telephone number, 44
opaque graphic objects, 195
Open File tool, 20, 224
opening
    documents, shortcuts for, 310
    documents with Windows File Manager,
        18, 293

multiple documents, 220-224
multiple files in workbook,
        235-236
operations, pasting particulars and related,
        126
operators in selection criteria, 213
Options menu, 52-53
order of mathematical operations, 55-56
orientation
    of printing, 163
    of text, changing, 104-105
Outline Border tool, 21
outline levels, printing, 144
outlining information in worksheet tables,
        141-145

— P —

page breaks
    bad, 170-172
    display of, 159
Page Number tool, 166
pages, printing perfect, 161-163
page setup options for printing charts, 196
paging scheme, control of, 155-156
palette, color, 250
parentheses, nesting, 56
Paste command on Edit menu, 44
Paste Formats tool, 21
Paste Function
    command on Formula menu,
        63-64
    dialog box, 64
pasting
    particulars and related operations, 126
    pictures on blank tools, 264
Patterns
    command and colors, 250
    dialog box, 106-107
pecking order of mathematical operations,
        55-56
percentages as numeric values, 51
percentage value format, 84
Percent cell style, 107-108
Percent number format, 88
Percent Style tool, 83
perspective view, charts in, 191-193

PgDn for moving cell pointer, 32
PgUp for moving cell pointer, 32
placeholder
    for graphics, gray, 195
    number sign (#) as, 91
    # (pound sign) as, 91
    zero (0) as, 91
pointer
    cell, 14
    help, 27
    magnifying-glass, 157
pointing and cell selection, 54
portrait orientation of printing, 163
pound signs (#######) in Excel cells, 86
predefined colors, 250
preferred sort order, 207
printer, laser, 98
printing
    charts, 195-196
    formulas, 172-173
    help topics, 44
    hints for, 297
    horizontal, 155-156
    information without attendant graphics,
        196
    orientation of, 163
    outline levels, 144
    particular rows and columns, 168
    perfect pages, 161-163
    spreadsheet, 155-173
    vertical, 155-156
    worksheets, 159-161
Print Preview
    mode, 156-158
    tool, 258, 259
    window, 163-164
print settings, default, 159
print titles, 168-169
Print tool, 20
Print Topic command from File menu, 44
problems, formula, 56-57
PRODUCT function, 271
Product Support command, 44
Program Manager window, 17
protection, document, 153-154
pull-down menu bars, 35
pull-down menus, commands on, 293

— Q —
quantities, numbers representing, 50

— R —
R1C1 cell-reference system, 15, 249
Radio (Option) button, 41
raising a number to a power,
    ^ (caret) for, 54
range
    selection criteria, 213-215
    of values for use in another worksheet,
        borrowed, 223
ranges, cell, 72
reader, assumptions about, 3
recalculation of formulas, 152-153
record, keystrokes for moving to particular,
    203
records
    to database, adding new,
        200-201
    in database, changing, locating and
        deleting, 202-207
    for editing, locating, 215
    scroll bar for moving through, 203
    selection criteria for locating, 212-214
    sorting, 209-211
Redo command for editing, 114-115
Reference text box, 34
regular macro sheet, 240
relative cell references, 121
Remember, special icon for, 6
removing
    manual page breaks, 172
    panes from window, 138
    shading from cells, 107
    stock header or footer, 165
repeated entries, 62
Replace command, editing and, 151-152
replacing
    all numbers with zeros, 225
    graphics, 195
replicated copying with Cut and Paste
        commands, 125
resizing chart, 184
restrictions to data entry, 59-60

retrieving information, finding and, 211-212
Right Align tool, 21, 100-101
right arrow
    for editing cell entries, 59
    for moving cell pointer, 32
right margins, 164
ROUND function, 64, 274-275
rows
    adjusting heights of, 95
    and columns, printing particular, 168
    selecting columns and, 74

— S —

Save As
    command on File menu, 36
    dialog box, 39
Save File tool, 20
Save option on File menu, 36
saving
    active documents, 36
    consolidated documents, 231
    Excel documents, shortcuts for, 310
    Excel documents, workbook feature for, 231-234
    results of extract operation, 217
    worksheets, 67-68
scaling options, printer support of, 163
scanned images for sprucing up worksheets, 192-195
scientific notation, 50
screens, scrolling, 31
SCRL mode indicator, 34
scroll bar
    horizontal, 30
    for moving through records, 203
    vertical, 30
scrolling
    through documents, shortcuts for, 306
    keyboard, 34
    screens, 31
    through worksheets, 30-32
Scroll Lock key, 34
searching for missing files, 111-113
selecting
    columns and rows, 74
    format for chart, 181-182

type of chart, 180
selecting cells
    for formatting, 71-78
    with GoTo feature, 76
    in worksheets, shortcuts for, 305
    See also cell selections
selection criteria
    for locating records, 212-214
    range, 213-215
selection handles for chart, 184
separating tools, 258
serial number of Excel, 46
serial numbers, dates stored as, 51
series created with AutoFill feature, designer, 61
Set Database command, 199
Set Extract command, 216
shading cells for emphasis, 106
shapes, mouse pointer, 27
Shift+F12 for saving active documents, 36
Shift+Tab for moving cell pointer, 32
shortcut menus
    commands on, 293
    for faster access to menu commands, 35
    using mouse, 37
shortcuts, keystroke, 305-310
Show Active Cell command on Formula menu, 34
sizing buttons on title bar, 19-20
sizing new document window, shortcuts for, 310
Solitaire card game in Windows, 27
Sort Ascending tool, 211
Sort Descending tool, 211
sorting
    databases, 207-211
    keys for, 208
    large databases, 209
    records, 209-211
sort order
    alphabetical, 208
    ascending, 208
    descending, 208
    numerical, 208
    preferred, 207
    specifying, 208

sound capabilities, microphone for, 146
south-paw mouse users, 29
spaces in numeric entries, 50
specialized functions
    HLOOKUP (horizontal lookup), 285
    LOWER, 283-284
    PMT (Payment), 277-281
    PROPER, 282-284
    PV (Present Value), 277-279
    UPPER, 283-284
    VLOOKUP (vertical lookup), 285-287
    See also function(s)
specialized toolbars, 254-255
specialized worksheet functions, 277-290
spelling checker, 129
spill-over text, 49
splitting worksheet window
    into four panes, 138
    horizontally, 136-137
    vertically, 137
spreadsheet, electronic
    description of, 13
    origin of, 12-13
spreadsheet printing, 155-173
sprucing up worksheets, 192-194
Standard toolbar
    AutoSum tool on, 43, 65-67
    formatting tools, 79-80
    Help tool on, 43
    tools on, 20-21
Standard Width text box, 93-95
starting Excel
    from DOS, 18, 293
    from Windows Program Manager, 16-17,
        293
starting Windows, 16-17
status bar, 25
stock header or footer, 165
Strikeout tool, 83, 99
structure of worksheets, editing, 110
Style Box
    removing, 256-257
    on Standard Toolbar, 20
subtraction, – (minus sign or hyphen) for, 54
SUM as built-in function, 54
SUM function, 65, 269-270

SUMPRODUCT function, 271-272
support, on-line telephone, 44
switching
    documents, 111
    left and right mouse buttons, 29
    to new document window, shortcuts
        for, 310

— T —

Tab for moving cell pointer, 32
table-format selection, Colorful,
        78-79
table of information, entering, 59-60
tables, charting outlined, 179
table_array argument, 286
tabular format, data in, 198
Technical Stuff, special icon for, 6
telephone number, on-line support, 44
template for cloning, worksheet, 224-227
testing macros, 244
text
    attached, 187
    box in charts, 189
    box, creating, 194
    box, Reference, 34
    boxes for sprucing up worksheets,
        192-195
    changing orientation of, 104-105
    data, 48-50
    entries, long, 49
    unattached, 188-190
    wrap, 103
Text Box, 40
Text Formatting tool, 257
time
    formats, 52
    values, 51
Time tool, 166
Tip, special icon for, 6
title bar, 19-20
titles, immovable, 138-141
tool
    AutoDum, 20
    Bold, 20, 99
    Bottom Border, 21

Center Across Selected columns, 21, 100, 103
Center Align, 21, 100-101
Custom, 257
Date, 165, 166
Decrease Decimal, 84, 88
Decrease Font Size, 20
File, 257
File Save, 231
Formatting, 257
for headers and footers, Font, 167
Help, 43
Increase Decimal, 84, 89
Increase Font Size, 20
Justify Align, 83
Light Shading, 84
Macro, 257
New Worksheet, 20
Open File, 20, 224
Outline Border, 21
Page Number, 166
Paste Formats, 21
Percent Style, 83
Print, 20
Print Preview, 258, 259
Right Align, 21, 100-101
Save File, 20
Sort Ascending, 211
Sort Descending, 211
Strikeout, 83, 99
Text Formatting, 257
Time, 166
Total Pages, 166
Underline, 83, 99
Utility, 257
toolbar
    Drawing, 193
    Excel 3.0, 254
    restoration, 259
    shortcut menu, 254
    Standard, 20-21
toolbars, 253-265
    adding new tools to, 257
    built-in, 253
    creating, 260-262
    Customize dialog box, 255
    customizing, 253
    docking, 81-83
    floating, 81
    Formatting, 83-84
    modifying, 254
    musical, 255
    restoring, 259
    specialized, 254-255
    undocking, 82
    versus menu commands, 35
Toolbars command, 259
Toolbar shortcut menu, 37-38
tools
    alignment, 100
    blank, in Custom category, 263
    categories of, 257
    Customize dialog box with Custom, 263
    Formatting, 79-80, 257
    on Formatting toolbar, 83-84
    pasting pictures on blank, 264-265
    separating, with spaces, 258
    on Standard Toolbar, 20-21
top margins, 164
Total Pages tool, 166
tracking speed, steps for modifying, 28
transparent graphic objects, 195
type size, uniform font and, 98
typos
    correcting, 57-59
    finding with spelling checker, 129

— U —

unbinding documents from workbook, 234
Underline tool, 83, 99
Undo
    command for editing, 114-115
    feature, 110, 114-115
undocking toolbars, 82
unfreezing headings, 140
unhiding and hiding columns and rows, 96-98
uniform font and type size, 98
Unique Records Only check box, 216
unlocking cells, 153, 154

unsaved worksheet and global
        search-and-replace operation, 152
up arrow
    for editing cell entries, 59
    for moving cell pointer, 32
Use Standard Width check box, 95
Utility tool, 257

— V —

value
    data, 48
    formats for every, 84-90
vertical printing, 155-156
vertical scroll bar, 30
viewing angles of 3D charts,
        192-193
visible number format, 92

— W —

Warning!
    completing cell entries, 60
    deletions in worksheets, 128
    disbanding group of documents, 229
    editing a cell entry, 58
    extract range, 216
    filenames, 68
    global search-and-replace operations, 152
    inserting incomplete record into data-
        base, 200
    nesting parentheses, 56
    password for protecting documents, 154
    restoring worksheet to previous state,
        114
    space in numeric entry, 50
    special icon for, 6
    table-format selections, 78
    Undo feature, 203
warnings, welcome, 301-302
ways for working smarter, 303-304
wildcard characters for searching in
        database, 204
wildcards with Find command,
        150-151

window
    Print Preview, 163-164
    Program Manager, 17
    removing panes from, 138
Windows
    bypassing, 18
    File Manager, opening documents with,
        18
    File Manager and missing files, 112
    starting, 16-17
Windows File Manager
    opening documents with, 293
    and renaming old EXCEL.XLB file, 256
Windows For Dummies and moving files, 112
Windows Print Manager, 159
Windows Program Manager, starting Excel
        from, 293
Windows settings, Control Panel and, 19-20
workbook
    feature for saving Excel documents,
        231-234
    opening multiple files in,
        235-236
    unbinding documents from, 234
Workbook Contents sheet, 232
working smarter, ways for, 303-304
worksheet
    active area of, 31
    extract range in, 198
    functions, specialized, 277-290
    getting around, 29
    outline, creating, 142
    scrolling through, 30-32
    tables, outlining information in, 141-145
    template for cloning, 224-227
worksheets
    beginning new, 45-46
    changes to, 109-129
    clearing cells in editing, 126, 127
    copying charts between, 224
    copying information between, 223-224
    deleting cells in editing, 126, 127-128
    deletion options in editing,
        126-128

drawings for sprucing up, 192-195
editing multiple, 227-229
editing structure of, 110
locating parts of, 293
printing, 159-161
saving, 67-68
sprucing up, 192-194
working with multiple, 219-236
worksheet window
splitting horizontally, 136-137
splitting into four panes, 138
splitting vertically, 137
Workspace command
for cell pointer advancement, 48
choosing, 52-53
Workspace Options dialog box, 53, 246-248
Wrap Text check box, 104

— X —

XLS file extension, 18

— Y —

year, yyyy for displaying, 92

— Z —

zero (0) as placeholder, 91
Zoom command, 134-136
zooming in print preview mode, 156-157

REMEMBER

Files I Should Never Delete

Filename	In English

TECHNICAL STUFF

Computer Guru	Phone #	Favorite Snack-Food Bribe

REMEMBER

Stupid Computer Mistakes I've Done (And Should Never Do Again!)

TECHNICAL STUFF

Computer Toys I'd Like to Own Someday

TIP

Important Stuff I Learned in This Book

Notes

Important Notes

Very Important Notes

Notes

Very, Very Important Notes

IDG Books Worldwide Registration Card
Excel For Dummies

Fill this out — and hear about updates to this book and other IDG Books Worldwide products!

Name _____

Company/Title _____

Address _____

City/State/Zip _____

What is the single most important reason you bought this book? _____

_____

Where did you buy this book?
- ❏ Bookstore (Name _____)
- ❏ Electronics/Software store (Name _____)
- ❏ Advertisement (If magazine, which? _____)
- ❏ Mail order (Name of catalog/mail order house _____)
- ❏ Other: _____

How did you hear about this book?
- ❏ Book review in: _____
- ❏ Advertisement in: _____
- ❏ Catalog
- ❏ Found in store
- ❏ Other: _____

How would you rate the overall content of this book?
- ❏ Very good   ❏ Satisfactory
- ❏ Good   ❏ Poor
- Why? _____

What chapters did you find most valuable? _____

What chapters did you find least valuable? _____

What kind of chapter or topic would you add to future editions of this book? _____

_____

Please give us any additional comments. _____

_____

How many computer books do you purchase a year?
- ❏ 1   ❏ 6-10
- ❏ 2-5   ❏ More than 10

What are your primary software applications?
- _____
- _____
- _____

Thank you for your help!

❏ I liked this book! By checking this box, I give you permission to use my name and quote me in future IDG Books Worldwide promotional materials. Daytime phone number_____ .

❏ FREE! Send me a copy of your computer book and book/disk catalog.

- -

Fold Here

IDG Books Worldwide, Inc.
155 Bovet Road
Suite 610
San Mateo, CA 94402

Attn: Reader Response / Excel For Dummies

Order Form

Order Center: (800) 762-2974 (7 a.m.–5 p.m., PST, weekdays)

or **(415) 312-0650**

Order Center FAX: (415) 358-1260

Quantity	Title & ISBN	Price	Total

Shipping & Handling Charges

Subtotal	U.S.	Canada & International	International Air Mail
Up to $20.00	Add $3.00	Add $4.00	Add $10.00
$20.01–40.00	$4.00	$5.00	$20.00
$40.01–60.00	$5.00	$6.00	$25.00
$60.01–80.00	$6.00	$8.00	$35.00
Over $80.00	$7.00	$10.00	$50.00

In U.S. and Canada, shipping is UPS ground or equivalent. For Rush shipping call (800) 762-2974.

Subtotal	_____
CA residents add applicable sales tax	_____
IN residents add 5% sales tax	_____
Canadian residents add 7% GST tax	_____
Shipping	_____
TOTAL	_____

Ship to:

Name _____

Company _____

Address _____

City/State/Zip _____

Daytime phone _____

Payment: ☐ Check to IDG Books ☐ Visa ☐ MasterCard ☐ American Express

Card # _____ Expires _____

Please send this order form to: IDG Books, 155 Bovet Road, Suite 610, San Mateo, CA 94402.
Allow up to 3 weeks for delivery. Thank you!

- -

Fold Here

Place
stamp
here

IDG Books Worldwide, Inc.
155 Bovet Road
Suite 610
San Mateo, CA 94402

Attn: Order Center / Excel For Dummies

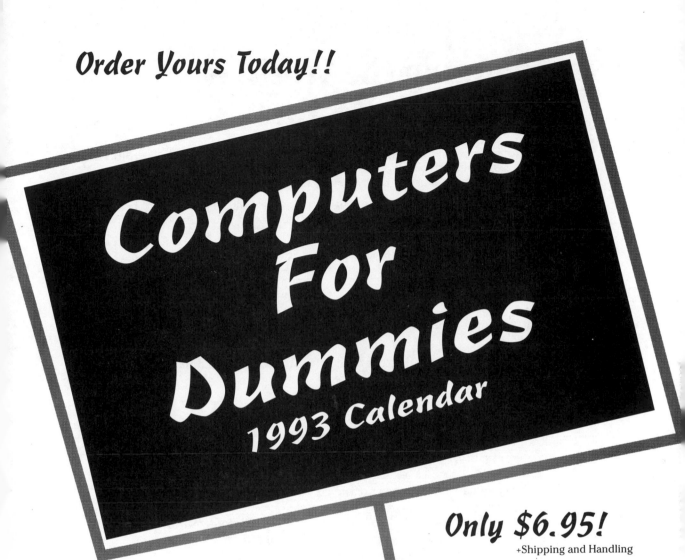

IDG BOOKS

Bringing the World of Computers to You!

Whether you're new to computers or looking for in-depth advice on sophisticated subjects, IDG Books has the right computer book for you. Carefully written by recognized experts, IDG Books are consistently praised for their high-quality content, innovative design, and superior value.

IDG Books organizes its books into series designed to meet the needs of a specific group of readers. When looking for the best in computer books, ask for the following series by name:

If you are a...	Ask for...
Reluctant, intimidated, and computer-phobic beginner looking for a friendly helping hand	**"...For Dummies" Computer Books from IDG™**
Confident beginner or new to a specific application or operating environment looking for a no-nonsense tutorial and concise reference	**You Can Do It Books from IDG**
Reader looking for an authoritative reference manual that includes timesaving tips, learning hints, and value-added extras that help you learn and master an application	**PC World Handbooks**
Intermediate to advanced user looking for a hands-on consultant's guide to performance-tuning and customizing applications, hardware systems, and operating environments	**SECRETS Book/Software Series from IDG™**

IDG Books. Available in book, computer, and specialty stores everywhere.

Or call 1-800-762-2974.